GLENN
THE
ASTRONAUT
WHO
WOULD
BE
PRESIDENT

Frank Van Riper

EMPIRE BOOKS
NEW YORK

To Judy—
For all of her faith
and all of her laughter

Acknowledgments

◆————————

Chronicling the career of John Glenn—war hero, astronaut, U.S. senator and presidential candidate—required the cooperation and patience of scores of people, including former astronauts, politicians, journalists, military men, historians and one octogenarian correspondent from Ohio who volunteered his written recollections of John Glenn's formidable mother, Clara.

In addition, both the Library of Congress in Washington and the John F. Kennedy Memorial Library in Boston provided invaluable assistance in the form of access to Glenn's personal papers and to oral histories on John and Robert Kennedy.

So, too, did the files of the *Cambridge Daily Jeffersonian, Zanesville Times Recorder,* the *Cleveland Plain Dealer,* and the *New York Daily News* help re-create an era, two decades past, when John Glenn burst into the world's consciousness as the commander of Friendship 7.

My best source, happily, was Glenn himself. Though pressured by the demands of his campaign for the Democratic presidential nomination, he submitted to hours of taped interviews over the past six months with unfailing grace and humor. Annie Glenn also took my repeated badgering in stride. Likewise, the Glenn children, Lyn and Dave, both of whom are now married and living in the West.

The people of New Concord and Cambridge, Ohio, proud of their famous son, were especially kind as I traced Glenn's childhood and college years. The archives of Muskingum College, Glenn's alma mater, provided ample material about the town of New Concord and its colorful past.

Small and large kindnesses multiplied. The warm cooperation I received from editor Jerry Wolfrom and his staff at the Cambridge "Daily Jeff" at the start of my research made the ensuing months that much easier.

Besides the Glenns, I thank the following people for all their help, counsel and time:

Robert Amos, Carl Anker, Steve Avakian, Warren Baltimore, Len Bickwit, Tom Brazaitis, Jim Bryen, Art Buchwald, Dale Butland, Jerome Cahill, M. Scott Carpenter, Rene Carpenter, Walter Chess, Tom Cronin, Alina Czech, Jake Dill, Eugene Eidenberg, George Embrey, Robert Farmer, Dennis Fitzgibbons, Carl Ford, Senator Wendell Ford, Wilbur Frame, Ed Furtek, Senator Jake Garn, John Giraudo, Wayne Hays, William Hines, Burt Hoffman, Maxine Isaacs, Frank Jackman, Ed Karas, Steve Kovacik, Henri Landwirth, Kay Lewis, Laura Logan, Susan Matthews, Father Richard McSorley, Roy Meyers, Ed Miller, Lt. Gen. Thomas H. Miller, Ralph Morse, Nolan Murrah, Lars-Erik Nelson, Bob Neuman, Monica Nolan, Don Oberdorfer, Peter O'Grady, Jody Powell, Catherine Prendergast, Harrison Rainie, Barbara Rehm, Abraham Ribicoff, Joe Rice, Richard Sachs, Martin Sammon, Prof. Arthur M. Schlesinger, Jr., Greg Schneiders, Bob Shrum, Peggy Simpson, Vann Snyder, Mary Steele, Harold Stern, Rep. Louis Stokes, Robert Strauss, Paul Tipps, Rep. Morris K. Udall, Mary Jane Veno, Robert Voas, Loudon Wainwright, Bill White, James Wieghart, John A. Wiethe, Woody Woodbury and Rick Zimmerman.

A special thanks to my editor and publisher, Martin L. Gross, who gave birth to this project and helped me develop it into a book.

Finally, a word about Jerry Greene. As I finished the last chapters of this book, I learned that my friend, mentor and former Washington Bureau Chief had died. Jerry, like John Glenn, was an ex-Marine colonel. He was also a good, gentle man and one of the finest journalists I ever worked under. He helped turn me into a reporter. I can never thank him enough.

Frank Van Riper
Washington, D.C.
August, 1983

Contents

1

◆

HELMET IN THE RING

Robert Strauss, then the chairman of the Democratic party, kept
an appointment on Capitol Hill. For months he had been jug-
gling "a hundred names" of politicians who were anxious to be
the keynote speaker at the Democrats' first post-Watergate national convention, to be held July 12-15, 1976 in New York
City.

"Governors, senators—everyone wanted it," recalls Strauss,
a brash Texas millionaire and Lyndon Johnson protégé. Aside
from the nominations for president and vice-president, the keynote slot was one of the party's richest prizes. The assignment
offered more than exposure on primetime television. It was a
traditional opportunity for a politician to shine sufficiently before his colleagues to be considered for the second place on the
national ticket. This year, Strauss decided, there would be two
keynoters, a chance to better project the image of a united party
untainted by the scandal that had forced Richard Nixon from
office two years before.

"I spent many months playing around with combinations
and individuals," Strauss remembers, "and I finally concluded

that this was the perfect one.'' The party chairman had located a political natural for one of the keynote assignments in his own home state: 40-year-old Congresswoman Barbara Jordan of Houston, an impressive, stentorian—and black—member of the House Judiciary Committee's 1974 impeachment inquiry. In the Watergate climate, she had accomplished her anti-Nixon chores with a dedication and solemnity that had impressed even the Republicans.

Strauss had chosen Jordan first, in October of 1975. For the other keynote position, he waited longer, patiently trying one name, then another, hoping to select someone who would complement the imposing black lawmaker. "It was in January or February, 1976," Bob Strauss recalls, that he walked into the office of John Herschel Glenn, Jr., the innocent-looking first-term senator from Ohio who also happened to be the first American to orbit the earth. "I just thought he had a hero's image and he paired off well against Barbara," Strauss says today. Glenn, who like Jordan had not lobbied Strauss for the keynote assignment, said that he would be honored.

One of the first things Glenn did was have the Library of Congress collect every keynote address for the last century. Reading them was one of the worst moves of his political career.

On July 12, 1976, in a well-guarded waiting room behind the podium in the convention hall at New York's Madison Square Garden, Bob Strauss took the first of his two keynote speakers by the arm. Strauss, his squat form dapper in a $300 suit, his small eyes riveting, looked up at John Glenn that muggy summer night and in his gravelly drawl warned him that the unruly crowd was not going to quiet down. "But don't worry about this hall," the chairman counseled as he firmly gripped Glenn's arm. "You worry about that television tube." Glenn managed a tight smile.

Ten minutes later Strauss walked upstairs into the klieg lights of Madison Square Garden. Banging his gavel at the blue plywood podium, he brought the raucous crowd of 3,353 delegates and alternates down to a more moderate roar. Glenn watched on the waiting room television monitor as Strauss began his introduction. The former astronaut smoothed over the remnants of his once carrot-red hair, and, at the words,

"Senator John Glenn of Ohio!" strode to the podium to deliver one of the worst speeches in contemporary political history.

The speech, actually a sermon-cum-civics lesson, was a boring, pious recitation. When CBS broke for a commercial immediately afterward, it was, appropriately, for a headache remedy. With its imprecise phrasing about "mature patriotism," and "bold and responsive government," the speech marked John Glenn—who had once held a joint session of Congress spellbound—as a dull speaker. It is a reputation that he labors to dispel, even to this day.

The disaster was not the result of a lazy mind. Glenn had worked over the speech for months. Several other people had contributed to it as well, though Glenn was careful never to divert from his original plan: to produce an uplifting, intentionally nonpartisan address. "I was at the McDowell Colony, which is a writers' and artists' colony in New Hampshire," recalls *Life* magazine's Loudon Wainwright, who had chronicled Glenn's astronaut exploits in that magazine in the early 1960s. "John asked me to come to New York and look at his speech. He had sent me an early draft so that when I came to New York, I could go over it with him.

"I told John that it was very earnest but dull, and that he wasn't going to attract any attention," Wainwright explains. "I told him that they were going to talk right through it. Among all his other gifts and characteristics, John is an extremely stubborn man. He didn't want to make any changes."

His speech, Glenn insisted, was to be inspirational, addressing the question: How do you get confidence back in the people around the country? "That's what I'm trying to do," Glenn told Wainwright. "It's hard to put it over. I guess it's a risk, but I've never played it safe." But Glenn had miscalculated the mood of the convention. It was a crowd of frustrated partisan Democrats, many of them veterans of political battles going back decades. The party had lost badly under George McGovern in 1972 and was determined to return to power through a post-Watergate victory. The convention was eager for a keynote speech that would echo that need, one that would deliver up raw partisan meat.

Glenn did not oblige. "We must select new leaders," he

naively admonished the crowd, "leaders with vision, leaders who will set a different tone for this nation, a tone of opportunities sought and seized, a tone of national purpose." He spoke of "ideals, beliefs and confidence." It was exactly what he wanted to say, but within minutes, Glenn looked up from the teleprompter to see Loudon Wainwright's dire prediction coming true.

"Inside Madison Square Garden, the place was like a beach," wrote Jimmy Breslin. "Half the place was walking out for hot dogs, the other half was sitting and talking. Here was Jimmy Mahoney of Pennsylvania talking about a septic tank at his father's old house in Breezy Point in Queens. Here was Bill Egan, the former governor of Alaska, talking about an FBI arrest, two prostitutes and the Alaska pipeline town of Valdez."

While Glenn was speaking, as if on cue, Hubert Humphrey, 1968 presidential candidate and grand old man of the party, entered the convention hall. He was followed by a newer party legend, Newark Representative Peter Rodino, the Watergate investigator who had chaired the House Judiciary Committee impeachment hearings on Nixon. Reporters soon swarmed around the two leading Democrats, each of whom held an impromptu news conference just below the podium where Glenn was sweating vainly to hold the delegates' attention. Even Chairman Bob Strauss was not listening to Glenn. He was angrily pacing in the waiting room, telling Barbara Jordan she would have to undo the damage being wrought by the amateur at the microphone.

"I worked four goddam years for this," Strauss growled to the Texas congresswoman, "and the Democratic party needs it. I got every chip I have bet on you, Barbara. Go up there and turn it on."

"If you can get these legs of mine up those stairs, I'll deliver," replied Jordan, referring to the calcium deposits in her knees that force her to use a cane.

"I had to almost lift her up those goddam steps," Strauss remembers, "but I got her up there and she turned it on."

In the brilliantly lit hall, Barbara Jordan began: "There is something different and special about this opening night. I, Barbara Jordan, am keynote speaker." The imposing black con-

Waterloo High School

1464 Industry Rd

Michael Marcello

Patron Number: 413

Date: 10/19/00   Time: 8:56

Materials being checked out:

11047 Glenn

    Date due: 11/02/00

Materials currently checked out:

    NONE

Materials with fines:

gresswoman, sounding all the right emotional chords, stilled the convention, then brought it to its feet. When she was done, Strauss turned to his friend and assistant, Gordon Wynne. "Gordon, we just knocked one out of the goddamned ballpark."

"Aw, no excuses," Glenn now says about his failed keynote speech. But at the time he seethed.

As Glenn was straining to be heard over the buzzing of the indifferent crowd, Jimmy Carter was watching the proceedings on television in his $750-a-day suite in the Americana Hotel, soberly taking in Glenn's performance. The former Georgia governor, who was now assured of the presidential nomination, was weighing several possibilities as his vice-presidential running mate. Among them were John Glenn, and Senators Walter F. Mondale of Minnesota, Edmund S. Muskie of Maine, and Frank Church of Idaho. But of the four, Glenn was the only one granted this precious television exposure. Conventional wisdom indicated that a sterling performance could earn him the vice-presidential spot.

Carter had turned his choice of running mate into high political drama. His campaign organization commissioned a nationwide poll on 14 potential candidates that included not only the obvious choices but such comparative unknowns as Governor Wendell Anderson of Minnesota, Mayor Tom Bradley of Los Angeles and Governor Michael Dukakis of Massachusetts. But as Carter himself later admits, these names were merely political window dressing.

"I made only one early decision about the vice-president," Carter insists, "that it was important for me to choose a member of Congress as my running mate in order to provide some balance of experience to our ticket." The former president notes that he was already leaning toward two favorites: Senator Frank Church and Senator Henry M. Jackson of Washington. Both had fought the once-obscure governor for the nomination, and Carter felt he knew them well enough to run with them. Jackson, however, would have given the ticket too conservative a slant, Carter's advisors felt; Church, Carter was told, had a priggish, schoolboy personality and was something of a wind-bag. Others considered Church too liberal.

The search continued up until the week before the convention, when Carter summoned a handful of hopefuls to his home in Plains, the tiny, sweltering, bug-ridden town off the main highway leading into Americus, Georgia. "Eventually, Senators Edmund Muskie, John Glenn and Walter Mondale in turn came down to Plains to discuss in depth the advisability of our joining together," Carter later wrote.

The three hopefuls dutifully trouped south and on July 8, the unexpected happened: Jimmy Carter found himself engrossed in enjoyable conversation with Fritz Mondale, a liberal Minnesotan and Hubert Humphrey protégé whom Carter had expected to find too liberal for his southern Democrat tastes. Months later, Mondale would describe the meeting as surprising to him as well. With the right chemistry working between them, the meeting lasted three hours.

Afterwards, Mondale joked that Muskie had ruined his chances by coming to Plains and telling Carter "he wanted to see all the peanut trees. Then John Glenn went down to Plains and whispered to Rosalynn that his favorite food was blue-eyed peas. Frank Church told Jimmy that he'd never been to Georgia himself, but a relative, William Sherman, had been there before. By the time I got there Jimmy said, 'Keep your mouth shut and the job is yours.'"

In fact, there was a touch of truth in Mondale's jests. Glenn followed Mondale to Plains several hours later. What happened after their private meeting was telling. The conversation lasted barely two hours, and when the two emerged for a press conference Carter's mood was almost surly. Recalls reporter Martin Schram: "Carter responded angrily when a television reporter asked if the questions could be delayed 'a few seconds' until his cameraman was ready. 'Do you want to come up here and run this press conference?' Carter snapped. 'Do you want to take over?'" Glenn left immediately thereafter; there was no tour of Plains.

"When John was going down there," recalls Stephen J. Kovacik, a Glenn backer and political advisor of long standing, "I said, 'John, you know I think you ought to read Carter's book, *Why Not the Best*. It's probably no good, but at least you can tell the guy: 'I liked what you said on page 52.' You know, it's just an old bullshit technique. John said, 'Yeah, that's a good idea,' but I guess he didn't."

Glenn himself was still expectant, but to no one else's surprise he was not chosen as Jimmy Carter's running mate. Contrary to widely held opinion, Glenn's convention speech had had nothing to do with Carter's decision; the job had been filled at least a week before the convention. Glenn might have been a national hero, but Mondale provided what Jody Powell, who had been Carter's press secretary, today describes as "our need for more of a bridge to traditional Democratic constituencies, which Mondale would bring to us more than Glenn or anybody else."

Speaking seven years after the fact, Powell all but admits that the vice-presidential search was a ploy to increase the drama at a convention whose main event—Carter's nomination—was already assured. "In fact," Powell says, "my impression—and this might conflict with what was said at the time, is that by the time we got to New York, Carter was strongly leaning toward Mondale."

"Oh, I would say it was 80-90% in the bag," echoes Greg Schneiders, now Glenn's press secretary, but one of Carter's top aides at the time. "The night before we all sat around with Carter in his suite at the Americana talking about it one last time. Different people had different candidates, but my impression was that Carter's mind had been made up for several days."

But to those outside the Carter suite, including a surprisingly innocent John Glenn, it was still a horse race that might be won with an excellent keynote speech. Glenn desperately hoped to duplicate the feat of Alben W. Barkley, whose stem-winder to the 1948 Democratic convention had thrust him onto the national ticket with Harry Truman.

Believing he was in contention up to the end, Glenn kept rewriting his speech until the day of the convention, stopping only when he was told the text had to be transcribed onto the teleprompters. But as he spoke it was obvious to all, including a frustrated Glenn, that few were listening.

Some believe that the noise and interruptions were not

spontaneous, but part of a plan developed by liberal and labor delegates who favored Mondale and hoped to deny the number-two spot to Glenn. Glenn's wife, Annie, is one of those who believe the disruption was purposeful. She grew concerned, then angry, as her husband struggled to be heard above the noise of the crowd. "There were people around me who had no idea that I was John's wife," she recalls, "and I could see that they had been told to talk while John was speaking. They had been very quiet and only began to talk just as John was introduced. There were several rows of people involved, and they all looked at each other and they sort of smiled and that's when they all began talking."

Was this a Carter ploy? "I don't think it was the Carter people," Annie says, without implicating anyone in particular.

"Yes," says Greg Schneiders, "I've heard the theory before. It was that the labor delegates, working on behalf of Mondale, planned the disruptions in the hall and arranged for Humphrey to arrive in the middle of the speech. But I have no independent knowledge of it."

Tom Miller, a retired Marine lieutenant general and close friend of Glenn's since they flew together in World War II, was at the convention that evening. He believes the evidence of a plot against Glenn is strong. "I tell you I saw politics at its worst," Miller recalls. "First you got to know that Hubert Humphrey wanted Mondale to be vice-president—there wasn't any doubt about it. John starts speaking, he's about five or ten minutes into the meat of what he was trying to say, and Humphrey comes on the floor, enters the door almost directly under the podium.

"The press forgot all about Glenn and went roaring over to him. There must have been 50 people rushing to him. Now how much more can you disrupt a speaker? Then he holds that little press conference. Then just as that's beginning to break up, who enters the floor but the congressman from New Jersey, Peter Rodino. It was just so carefully orchestrated."

Robert Strauss refutes the charge. "Ridiculous," he says. "I knew every goddam thing that was going on in that hall. If there had been any plot against Glenn, I would have known about it. I had people all over there doing nothing but watching just for that sort of thing. There was no point in being paranoid about it. Glenn simply gave a speech that was not well written."

Dejected, but still hoping the vice-presidential nomination was in reach, Glenn paid $229.49 for a special phone so that nominee Carter could call him directly. Carter used the phone, but only to give Glenn the bad news that he had chosen "someone else."

For John Glenn, the 1976 convention debacle was another defeat in a career of exquisite highs and painful lows. For anyone other than John Glenn, the speech would have been a one-way ticket to obscurity. Four years later, Michigan Rep. Guy Vander Jagt was both the Republican keynoter and a vice-presidential contender on the Reagan ticket. Vander Jagt considered himself an orator in the silver-tongued tradition of William Jennings Bryan; he practiced in the woods, speaking extemporaneously to the birds and the animals. They may have loved his homey metaphors, but the Republican convention found him a bore. George Bush won the vice-presidential nomination, and Vander Jagt later lost a bid to become House Republican leader.

But for John Glenn the humiliating experience was different, just as it always has been different for this unique national hero. Everywhere he went in New York City, he was besieged for autographs by people indifferent to his convention failure. As he entered the Pan Am Building to go to the Sky Club for dinner with Annie, there were calls of "Hey John!" from cabbies and smiles of recognition from everyone else.

"America liked him in spite of the speech," Strauss says. "We polled after it, and the ones who saw it on television liked him. The press just decided to paste him like hell and they did."

Once more, John Glenn would confidently start his recovery from defeat. Just as he had in 1964, when he was forced out of his first Ohio Senate race by a bathroom fall. Just as he had in 1970 when he lost his second try for the Senate after an inept and underfinanced primary. He was, and seemingly still is, sustained by a reservoir of good will toward John Glenn the invincible national hero, who is always there, stalwartly working to save John Glenn, the sometimes inept politician. Such public adulation is a potent weapon. When combined with political sophistication, anything, even the presidency, could result.

By 1980, Glenn had seriously begun to consider the possibility of becoming the 41st president of the United States. In the late evening of November 4, 1980, as the depth of Jimmy Carter's loss to Ronald Reagan was becoming apparent, the former astronaut sat in a crowded hotel suite in Columbus, Ohio, and watched his political fortunes soar. He was not unlike Carter in background and temperament: a single-minded, former military man who combined a righteous self-confidence and aloofness from his peers with a sometimes somnambulent speaking style. Only this time Glenn watched the television with a critical eye toward Carter, not the other way around as in 1976. The reversal felt good.

By evening's end, Jimmy Carter had lost 44 states to Reagan. As the president sat grimly before the TV in the White House and surveyed the dimensions of his loss, an exultant group of Glenn supporters, staff members and politicians crowded the ballroom of the Sheraton Hotel in Columbus, Ohio, and cheered a different bulletin. John Herschel Glenn, Jr., had been reelected to the Senate by the biggest plurality in Ohio history. He had won by a mammoth 1.6 million-vote victory margin that dwarfed even Lyndon Johnson's defeat of Barry Goldwater in the state in 1964. Glenn had put together a political coalition that included the blacks, Jews, labor, cities, and the more conservative farm and rural vote, capturing all but one of 88 of Ohio's politically diverse counties.

A victory such as Glenn's would have been impressive at any time. But coming on the same night that his fellow Ohioans were handing the state to Ronald Reagan by a convincing 52%-41% margin, it was phenomenal. It was a demonstration of political strength that elevates a politician to national status overnight. No one at the Sheraton Columbus that November evening knew this better than John Glenn.

The projections of Glenn's victory over a sacrificial Republican challenger, State Rep. James E. Betts, came immediately after the polls closed. A cheer went up among the shirtsleeved crowd in Glenn's hotel room as he kissed Annie. Glenn put on his jacket and was in the ballroom by nine o'clock, striding briskly to the podium and acknowledging the cheers of a crowd that included not only campaign workers and a busload of Washington staffers, but almost every Democratic state official who could crowd onto the platform to share the magic of a winner on that otherwise dismal night. Even the defeat of a Democratic president could not dampen the crowd. Ohio Democratic Chairman Paul Tipps used the occasion to introduce Glenn as "the next president of the United States."

"I'm Annie Glenn's husband," Glenn said in his best hometown style. He searched out across the happy crowd, his buoyant face reflecting the TV lights, his particularly small hands gripping the podium. "Tonight we celebrate a great victory. Six years ago, when the people of Ohio first sent me to Washington, I promised to serve them with courage and dedication and with integrity. I believe that I have fulfilled that promise."

Glenn coupled praise for Ohio's political and ethnic diversity with criticism of the "naysayers, the negativists—those for whom nothing is right in this country." Glenn never mentioned Jimmy Carter. Finally, to continued cheers, he made his way out of the ballroom and back up to his suite, where he greeted still more Ohio politicians and supporters.

"It's funny," remembers Steve Avakian, the Ohio political consultant who managed Glenn's Senate victory, "but I can't remember him ever saying, even privately, 'isn't this awful' about Carter's loss. Of course, he had been busting his ass the whole month of October, and there wasn't a whole lot of focusing on Carter."

But Jimmy Carter was now politically dead and Glenn's own fortunes were spectacularly on the rise. The next day, after a few hours' extra sleep, Glenn and Avakian sat behind desks in the Democratic headquarters at 88 East Broad Street in Columbus and spent the day writing hundreds of thank-you notes by hand to people who had supported Glenn in the race and who could support him in the future.

A few days later a friend visited Glenn for a brief chat that turned into a three-hour luncheon discussion during which Glenn laid bare his hopes and ambitions. "I'm just as smart as those guys," he said confidently, referring to Ronald Reagan and his fellow Republicans, "and just as electable. I think I'm going to run for president." The friend, who had witnessed Glenn's humiliation at the convention four years before, knew that, for all his outward indifference at the time, he had felt used by the Carter camp.

Glenn had endorsed Carter's failed reelection in the 1980 campaign, but without great enthusiasm. It was mainly because he felt Teddy Kennedy, whom Glenn dislikes even more than Carter, was shattering the party with his hapless challenge for the nomination. If Glenn disdained the talent available in the GOP, his view of the leaders of his own party was little better. Even before his reelection victory that year, Glenn had thought of '84. Now, he knew, it was time to act.

Few men have ever sought public office, be it in the Senate or the presidency, with so great an advantage as John Glenn. In a country that worships its stars and achievers, he is, literally, the last American hero. Glenn is the NASA astronaut who, as the first American to orbit the earth more than 20 years ago, recaptured America's honor in space at a time his countrymen desperately feared that the Soviet Union had overtaken America in discovery and innovation.

One of "the last of the single combat warriors," as Tom Wolfe dubbed the astronauts in his book, *The Right Stuff*, Glenn was the only one of the original Mercury 7 to capitalize on his fame by going into politics. "John was already thinking a generation beyond six other gung-ho pilots," says Rene Carpenter, former wife of astronaut Scott Carpenter, Glenn's back-up pilot and closest friend among the Mercury team. Even today, more than two decades after his five-hour space flight, Glenn's name and face are familiar to virtually everyone, a celebrity of stellar, sometimes incomprehensible, proportions.

Equally important to a politician, nearly everyone outside of politics who knows Glenn likes him and instinctively trusts him, even, as is often the case, if they have little idea what he stands for politically. It is as if Glenn the politician is somehow—inexplicably—apolitical. Even as he ran for reelection to the Senate in 1980, his pollster, Peter D. Hart, discovered among Ohio voters a curious "lack of ability to relate to Glenn's record as a senator."

That is the paradox of John Glenn. It is as if there are two John Glenns, each struggling against the other in the public perception. One is the obvious John Glenn, the righteous-living man of unimpeachable morality, a military hero in two wars, an astronaut, patriot and ostensibly a conservative or middle-of-the-roader, in whose hands the government would be secure against all enemies, domestic or foreign. As one political observer portrayed this Glenn, "He's Ike in a spacesuit."

But there is another, less advertised but just as real John Glenn. It is the liberal Democratic senator from Ohio whose support of ERA, organized labor, civil rights and abortion seems somehow out of character.

In this paradox, Glenn's personality seems to have facets that conflict with the popular image. One might expect the stubbornness that Glenn often displays in public and private life. But equally powerful within Glenn's make-up is a personal sensitivity that can bring him to tears and a tenderness to friends. As a husband, Glenn has spent 41 years married to a woman whose 85% disability stutter—until she was cured five years ago—never caused him embarrassment and often found him on the phone ordering groceries in her place. But, as others have learned, being an enemy of John Glenn is not an enviable position.

As a retired Marine colonel, one would expect Glenn to have a strong "military" view of world affairs. Glenn does fulfill that image with his support of the B-1 bomber and nerve gas, both of which he believes essential to the nation's safety. But as someone who says "I know the horrible side of war," Glenn has confounded his conservative supporters by his backing of the nuclear freeze and opposition to much of Reagan's foreign policy in Central America, which he regards as potentially dangerous.

Many in public life, including his colleagues in the Senate, see Glenn as an enigma, a loner who has remained private in a public business. Glenn is available to autograph seekers, but aloof from power seekers anxious to use his name, something he views almost as a national property. Glenn is among the last senators anyone will approach to co-sponsor legislation, part of the Capitol Hill ritual of mutual backscratching. One lawmaker, hoping to get Glenn to speak at his state party fund-raising dinner, recalls being shunted back and forth through Glenn's staff. He was never able to talk to Glenn himself and was finally told: "We don't do that kind of thing." The lawmaker doesn't talk about the incident in public. He is too busy savaging Glenn over it in private.

"Around here," says a veteran Democrat on Capitol Hill, "when you ask who his close friends are nobody seems to know. Glenn's all business. I've never seen him relax and bullshit and tell stories like all of the guys do. Maybe he does, but it's a side of him I've never seen." Still, many others are witnesses to his humanity. Comedian Woody Woodbury, who flew with Glenn as a fighter pilot in Korea, recalls Glenn's overwhelming concern for the safety of his men, as well as his "warmth, geniality and above all, ability to raise a little hell now and again."

Rene Carpenter, who was devastated when her marriage to Scott broke up, says: "It's an automatic response for John to be there when there is trouble. He picks up the pieces." Martin Sammon, an Ohio attorney and Glenn fund-raiser whose son was recently killed in an auto accident, recalls Glenn's canceling a day of campaign appearances to fly back home to attend the funeral mass. "If John asked me to crawl on my knees from here to Cleveland, I would," says Sammon matter-of-factly.

Glenn's national political appeal became a reality the first day he came to the U.S. Senate in 1974, and by 1976 had grown so rapidly that he was seriously considered as Jimmy Carter's running mate. In fact, advisor Steve Kovacik tried to convince Glenn to run for president even before the '76 election. Although Kovacik knew that Glenn was not then a matured national politician, he felt he had the enduring star quality that most politicians could only envy. But the inherently cautious nature of John Glenn—the part of him some find plodding, even dull—made him put aside presidential ambitions during his maiden years as a senator. All that changed after 1980.

Even today, Glenn's appeal is grounded not so much in his political ability as in the public's view of him as a potent mixture of John Wayne heroism, Buck Rogers fantasy and Huck Finn Americana. In Glenn's case, many of the elements are genuine, along with an extraordinary dose of ambition and calculation for leavening. He had distinguished himself as a wartime pilot, flying 59 fighter bomber missions in World War II and 90 in Korea. In Korea, he was dubbed the "MiG-mad Marine" by his fellow fliers, including Ted Williams, fighter pilot and baseball legend. Glenn chafed over not encountering any hostile aircraft during his initial stint as a fighter pilot, then downed three of the Communist fighters in the last nine days of the war.

If Lyndon Johnson could squeeze maximum political mileage out of a dubiously won Silver Star, what might John Glenn do with six Distinguished Flying Crosses, 18 Air Medals and worldwide fame as the first American to orbit the earth? By 1980 he had what he lacked when Kovacik first broached the subject of the White House four years before: the prestige and legitimacy of six years as a U.S. senator, reinforced by a huge mandate to another term.

In his personal life, Glenn seems firmly grounded in simple, rocklike virtue. At his home in the Potomac, Maryland, hunt country, a wealthy enclave whose one main intersection features a store selling riding tack, he never fails to say grace before meals in the centuries-old formulas of his Presbyterian faith. The two-acre ranch house, the Glenns' home since he came to the Senate in 1974, includes a book-lined family room, a big fireplace, a huge color TV and videotape recorder and plants everywhere. When they entertain—almost always small dinner parties with close friends, rarely colleagues from the Senate— Annie places candles in sconces all along the dinner table because, she says, "they seem to force you to slow down." The walls of the expensive, though unpretentious, home are hung with uplifting quotations worked in embroidery, placed near signed photographs of princes and presidents.

"I've had the ticker tape parades," Glenn says, adding that

he is running for president "for cause," not merely to feed his ego. "He really does have a sense of duty," says one of his closest aides, citing Glenn's 23 years in the Marine Corps. "But," this aide notes, "it sometimes is difficult for a person like Glenn to see where the sense of mission ends and the self-aggrandizement begins." It is not inconceivable that Glenn himself is not fully aware of the complexities of his motivation.

Still, there is a genuineness about him that is impossible to ignore, an all-embracing averageness that is at once comforting and disquieting. Earnest to a fault, he reflects the values and virtues of old-time America, much like Dwight D. Eisenhower, say his supporters; much like Ronald Reagan, say his detractors.

His casual, unhurried manner is a seeming contradiction in a man so driven to excel. He can arrive at the last moment for a flight or a TV appearance and seem as unruffled as if he had an hour to spare. ("Aw, we still got five minutes," he says to worried press secretary Schneiders, as he saunters into the studio for an early morning appearance on the *Today* show.) His idea of a great vacation is a camping trip. He can be waylaid by almost anyone asking for an autograph or a little conversation. While all politicians do this to an extent when it suits them, Glenn seems to do it naturally, out of good-mannered habit.

Except on the rare occasions when he loses his temper—such as the time he furiously confronted a political foe in Ohio whom he believed was spreading false divorce rumors about him and Annie—this outward demeanor effectively covers a hunger to succeed that is at times obsessive. It also disguises a streak of stubbornness that has hurt as much as helped him during his long tenure in the public eye. It is a stubbornness that has caused Glenn to persist despite failures and bad luck in both the space program and politics that might have disheartened a less resilient, less ambitious man. But it is a stubbornness that has also shown him to be bullheaded and insensitive to people and groups he must court as a public man.

He looks you in the eye when he speaks and seems to exude not so much confidence as sincerity. He tends not to gladhand or work a room like most public figures, but rather, blend in and mingle, nursing a beer or a soft drink while listening to the people clustered around him. "I respect people's privacy," he once said. "Maybe it's because I've had so little privacy all my life."

His appearance is average, even unprepossessing—save for his arclight smile and green eyes, one of which is noticeably smaller than the other. The carrot-red hair of his youth has turned to wispy gray, and the freckles have faded. While such politicians as Ted Kennedy or Ronald Reagan can fill a room with their resonant voices or movie star presence, Glenn, with an undistinguished middle-range voice and standing 5'11", cannot. (Had he been any taller, he would not have been eligible for the space program.)

Until he seriously entered politics, he favored loud bow ties, a taste he picked up from his father and which helped earn him a reputation as a sharp dresser during his boyhood in New Concord, Ohio. Today, his dress is appropriately subdued except for the heavy gold chronometer he sometimes wears facing inward on his wrist, a reminder of his days as a flier.

Glenn is at ease in the limelight; he has been in the public eye for more than a quarter century. In 1957, when Ted Kennedy was just out of college, Alan Cranston in California real estate, Fritz Mondale barely out of law school and Gary Hart still an undergraduate in Oklahoma, Glenn was the subject of his first "Man in the News" profile in the the *New York Times*. The story followed his record-breaking cross-country flight in a U.S. Navy supersonic jet, a project that was in many ways Glenn's idea. It was only one of several times during his career that he would involve himself in events from which he could profit.

An unflattering *New York* magazine article called this trait "sniveling" and quoted Glenn as saying: "It means going around and getting what you want to get even if you're not slated to get it. There's nothing wrong with it—and I was superb at it." After he saw the piece, Glenn quarreled with the context, but not the quotation. "Sniveling indicates you took unfair advantage of somebody and aced them out of something you both wanted, and I never did that in my life."

For most politicians, voter recognition of face or name— even unflattering recognition—is mother's milk. For Glenn, it is a given, something he will never have to seek but which he adroitly uses. "He is very sensitive to his public image in a positive way," says a friend of Glenn's. "And he doesn't want any tampering with that image." It goes back to his astronaut days, a simpler time when John Glenn's story was told in broad, red-white-and-blue strokes with no embarrassing detail or political criticism to clutter the narrative. Glenn has managed to go through public life dealing with the press and the public much on his own terms. He would hope to run for president the same way.

Glenn would not formally announce for the presidency until April 21, 1983, but as the press relayed semi-official word that he was in fact running, he started to show strength in the national polls. In August 1982, while Ted Kennedy was a possible candidate, a Gallup poll showed Glenn the first choice of only 7% of the Democrats. By December that number had risen to 14%, as against 24% for the front-runner, former Vice-President Mondale. By January of 1983, Gallup noted that in a general election Glenn would vanquish Reagan by 54% to 39%, a larger margin than Mondale. It was an indication that Glenn had more strength among Republicans and independents who see him as a national hero and military man rather than as a two-term liberal Democratic senator.

By April 1983, Mondale had consolidated his power, and both Gallup and the *Los Angeles Times* poll showed Mondale ahead (32-13 in Gallup; 34-17 in the L.A. *Times*) but with Glenn clearly the number-two candidate among Democrats and the leading Democratic candidate among all voters. Then in May, in a startling rise, Glenn passed Mondale among Democrats in the L.A. *Times* poll.

It was quite enough to sustain Glenn's confidence. He was to be the sixth major Democrat to announce for president, following Mondale, former Florida Governor Reuben Askew, and Senators Alan Cranston (Calif.), Gary Hart (Colo.) and Ernest F. Hollings (S.C.). All of them except Glenn and Mondale faced the problem of increasing their nationwide name recognition and had announced early in 1983. Mondale waited until February 21 when the Minnesotan announced his candidacy in St.

Paul, boasting that his campaign organization was active throughout the country and had raised more money than any other. Some, like Mondale and Cranston, had also staged their announcements against formidable backdrops—Mondale in the state assembly chamber, Cranston in the Senate Caucus Room in Washington.

"I'm going to leave the courthouse steps to the other guys," Glenn said the day before he announced in April 1983. "I'm going back home." But unlike Jimmy Carter, who loved Plains, or Lyndon Johnson, who longingly anticipated his weekend on the banks of the Pedernales, Glenn never seemed driven to return to New Concord, Ohio. There were the usual family holiday get-togethers, especially while his parents were still living, but those who knew Glenn best as a boy suspected he had not been unhappy leaving New Concord in 1942 to enter the service. The times he did return, said Don McKendry, principal of the new John H. Glenn High School named in his honor, he was more the long-lost cousin dropping in to say hello than the prodigal son come home to stay.

The announcement speech was labored over for weeks. It was cast and recast by a five-man team, including Glenn, to sound the "old values, new horizons" theme that would be the standard of his primary campaign, a theme that would unite the two Glenns of voter perception, the traditional small-town hero and the liberal Democratic senator. Glenn insisted on participating in all the planning, even down to the placement of the traveling press corps. Fearful of anything that might perpetuate his image as a "dull, brown and boring" speaker, Glenn repeatedly ordered his writers to throw in more and more rhetoric as announcement day neared.

"I want it more 'Sorensonian,'" he stipulated at one point, invoking the name of John F. Kennedy's former chief speechwriter, Ted Sorensen, a man whose talents for graceful imagery and contrapuntal phrasing had turned Kennedy into one of the best stump performers of his day. And so they labored: expert speechwriter Patrick Anderson, a veteran of the Kennedy and Carter administrations; Greg Schneiders; the junior man, Dennis Fitzgibbons, 27, five years out of Harvard and a former staffer on the Democratic Congressional Campaign

Committee; and Dale Butland, 35.

Butland was the closest of the group to Glenn, having written speeches for him during his 1980 Senate reelection campaign. A lanky, sonorous-voiced doctoral candidate in international economics, Butland had once played semipro baseball, but he stopped dreaming of the majors and turned to politics when he found he could not hit a curveball.

The staffers sat with Glenn around a wooden conference table in Glenn's new office on the fifth floor of the Hart Building on Capitol Hill, moving paragraphs, deleting, adding and changing phrases on long, white, legal-size sheets. Eventually, they produced a five-page document that did not once mention the word "Democrat" or "Republican." It sounded some of the same patriotic themes Ronald Reagan had used in 1980 when he sought the GOP presidential nomination. "Reagan does not have proprietary rights on can-do or patriotic rhetoric," says Greg Schneiders. "It's a very natural thing for Glenn, something he has been saying all his adult life."

To improve the flow of his words, Glenn practiced with his tape recorder. He listened intently as the small machine threw back at him, in tinny register, his flat Ohio delivery. He marched staffers into his private office and recited parts of the speech to them, gauging their reactions as carefully as he had once judged the actions of experimental jets. Two days before the Ohio announcement, he posed for his official family portrait and only briefly glanced up at the sound of the buzzer summoning senators to the floor. "They don't need you," said Kathy Belle, his cautious, protective executive secretary.

"This is one of the most important days of my life," Glenn declared, standing at the podium in the gymnasium of the John Glenn High School. It was April 21, 1983, the day of his presidential announcement. Glenn and his staff had decided not to concentrate on issues, but to emphasize Glenn's middle-American concern for old-fashioned values and his anger at Reagan for the nation's recession.

"Being back home here with all of you brings with it a flood of memories...places like the old home we still have down the road...the swimming hole...the old grade school...and the values, the striving toward excellence," Glenn told the audience of press and townspeople.

"We were taught honesty and fairness and compassion for those who had less, and a confidence and faith in the future that in this land a young person from this small town could aspire to anything.

"Two years ago, we elected an administration which likes to talk about values. Unfortunately, its deeds have fallen far short of its words. The policies of this administration aren't expanding opportunity, they're diminishing it. They aren't promoting excellence, they're discouraging it. They aren't fostering compassion, they're reducing it.

"All across this great country, we've seen millions thrown out of work—and millions more thrown into despair. We've seen factories close, small business bankrupted and farms sold at auction. We've seen bread lines and cheese lines, soup lines and shantytowns. We've seen people sleeping on grates and families living in cars. It's a national tragedy and a national disgrace—and I say we're going to put an end to it in November of 1984!"

For all the preparation and exalted rhetoric, Glenn's delivery was flat. Glenn stood stiff at the podium in his charcoal gray suit and red silk tie and blew applause lines right and left. He rushed through words and phrases that had been painstakingly placed to bring down the house, but which instead generated only polite murmurs from the crowd and a slow emotional death for the listening speechwriters, who feared it was another 1976 debacle.

Even Governor Richard Celeste, a canny politician with a sometimes shameless bent for self-promotion, seemed strangely listless. When he rose, he introduced Glenn as "our candidate for governor" before the surprised hoots of the audience reminded him of the error.

Later that day, during an open air rally on the quadrangle of Glenn's alma mater, Muskingum College, which finally awarded him a degree after his earth orbital flight, Glenn loosened up. But his words were so muffled by a mediocre sound system that they barely carried. A handful of anti-abortion demonstrators, critical of Glenn's pro-choice stance, probably could have shouted him down from their vantage point 50 yards away. But they were content just to wave their signs under the balmy skies, the first good weather the town had seen after weeks of continual rain.

It was as if the entire town were taking the air on its day off. Continuing long tradition, New Concord's shops and businesses close down Thursday afternoons. Glenn had scheduled the announcement to coincide with the half-holiday. Editor Jerry Wolfrom of the *Cambridge Jeffersonian*, the afternoon paper in the nearby town where Glenn was born, had platooned most of his small staff to cover the story, the first time that had happened since a fire at a nearby Holiday Inn claimed ten lives in 1979. Clapper's restaurant on Main Street in New Concord featured Glennburgers for 98 cents, with all the trimmings and a little hot sauce.

Only those close to Glenn that day knew he was exhausted. He had had little sleep in three days. Early that week, Glenn had stayed up till 4:00 A.M. working on his speech after returning from an appearance in Chicago. The day before Ohio, he had gotten up at 5:00 A.M. to be on the *Today* show, badly slicing his lip as he shaved. He did not get to bed until late that night after attending a Democratic fund-raiser. He was at National Airport early the next morning to make his charter flight, where all of Glenn's staff down to his two receptionists turned out to wish him "Godspeed to Ohio" over coffee, doughnuts and a few lonely bottles of champagne.

To all but a handful, Glenn masked his fatigue well. But his eyes, now surrounded by wrinkles, lose their sparkle when he is tired. And the difference in size between his eyes becomes more noticeable. After the speech, anxious staffers, having heard him do better just days before, warily asked each other about the announcement. Each looked to his colleague for a wink or a smile of reassurance. In their hearts they feared the boss had blown it—again.

But they were wrong. The Glenn luck, actually the Glenn legend, had worked again. The press was looking not at Glenn the politician, but at Glenn the last American hero, who transcends partisanship in the view of many Americans. In that legend, Glenn is a symbol of the nation itself. "The kind of hero's send-off most candidates only dream of," said the *Washington Post.* "Considerably more zip than that performance seven years ago," said the AP. Gushed *Newsweek* in a color spread that spanned two pages: "It was the right speech and the right setting for a candidate who seems sure he has the right stuff to win it all."

It was as if the Washington press establishment were apologizing for having rudely dismissed him as a dullard seven years before. It seemed Glenn's delivery that day had not only been adequate, but moving. In contrast, the local reporter from the *Zanesville Times Recorder,* immune to the musings of national commentators, called Glenn's appearance a "relatively subdued event" that generated only "modest applause." This minority view did not trouble Glenn's staff, suddenly euphoric over the unexpectedly upbeat national print and television coverage.

The network news shows that evening, on a slow day for which Glenn offered the only major political copy, gave him long and favorable exposure. On the cool medium of television, Glenn appeared forceful, able—even eloquent—as he reminisced to his audience about his small-town origins, his epic spaceride, then pronounced himself ready to lead the nation.

"Today, as I stand at the threshhold of an even greater journey," Glenn said, "my feelings are the same. I seek your support and God's guidance as once more I ask to serve.

"With confidence that my life has prepared me, with dedication to the promise of opportunity and the pursuit of peace, and with a firm belief that guided by the light of old values we can again reach new horizons, I declare my candidacy for president ofthe United States."

It had taken 21 years since his historic flight in space to convince millions that an astronaut could be seriously considered as a national politician. But now the press and public seemed willing to accept John Glenn not only as a great American hero, but as a true candidate for the presidency.

2

THE MAKING OF A POLITICIAN: THE LEGACY OF JFK

Two major events have shaped the public life of John Herschel Glenn, Jr. The first, of course, was his epochal 1962 ride in outer space. The second was Glenn's announcement in January 1964 that he would run for the U.S. Senate from Ohio. The close timing of the two events was not accidental: the orbital flight gave Glenn the recognition he needed to pursue his dream of public office, nurtured since childhood in the little southeastern Ohio village of New Concord.

But, in the end, it was another man, President John F. Kennedy, who first sensed the enormous political capital Glenn had set in motion some 150 miles above the earth. Kennedy sometimes acted publicly, other times behind Glenn's back, to start the boyish, green-eyed Marine on the tortuous political path that Glenn now hopes will lead him to the White House.

The afternoon of February 23, 1962, just 72 hours after Glenn had completed his space flight and became the first American in orbit, John Kennedy's presidential jet circled the airfield at Cape Canaveral. The Florida sun beat down on the tarmac as Air Force One, engines still roaring, taxied to a stop.

In the distance, a crowd of thousands—mostly Cape personnel and their families—strained for a better view of the sleek 707, one of the most luxurious passenger planes in the world. Blocking their ears against the noise, they squinted at the huge aircraft as its polished wings reflected the afternoon sun. The fuselage was arrayed in tasteful—and unmilitary—tones of white, silver and blue. The words, "United States of America" stood out in bold capital letters along each side. The plane's signature numbers and a small American flag graced the sweeping tail section.

Sitting on the tarmac that brilliant afternoon, the presidential jet looked like what it was: a great emissary from Washington that had arrived to pay homage to the freckled Marine astronaut standing on the ramp waiting patiently for President Kennedy to emerge and officially anoint him a national hero. John Glenn had captured the American imagination with his grown-up, small-town newsboy looks, and he was suddenly cast as the most popular idol since Dwight David Eisenhower, another military man who had gained the trust of the American voter long before he had made his first political utterance.

Kennedy and Glenn had met the first time just a few weeks before, on February 5, 1962, in a private session at the White House. "I had come home from Cape Canaveral over a weekend to be with Annie and the children in Arlington," Glenn now recalls. "We weren't getting much family time in those days, and the president sent word that he would like for me to stop by the White House." Even after the passage of more than 20 years, Glenn happily remembers his friendship with John Kennedy. Sitting in his Senate office, he recounts the meeting at the White House as though it took place yesterday. "It was a very cordial get-together," Glenn says. "He just wanted to talk about what was planned on the flight, and I went into some of the details of what we expected to experience."

The two men—the aristocratically handsome president, then 44, and the fresh-faced astronaut, then 40—took to each other immediately. Kennedy liked Glenn "immensely," recalled Ted

Sorensen. Not only was the pilot of Friendship 7 a man with whom Kennedy could identify, but by his success Glenn had stilled growing congressional criticism over the space program's lack of progress.

Kennedy saw in Glenn much of what the American public had already sensed in the young president: the intensity of youth and the need for challenge. Ben Bradlee, then Washington bureau chief of *Newsweek* and John Kennedy's Georgetown neighbor before the 1960 election, wrote in his diary: "Kennedy identifies enthusiastically with the astronauts, the glamor surrounding them and the courage and skill it takes to do their jobs. He knows them quite well." The president, Bradlee said, called John Glenn and Commander Alan B. Shepard "the personality boys."

But of them all, Glenn was unmistakably Kennedy's favorite. Within months after his flight, Glenn and Annie were regular guests at the Kennedy compound at Hyannisport. If Kennedy, who hid a bad back and Addison's disease behind his politically useful front of macho "vigor," had any doubts that Glenn belonged in his masculine hyperactive circle, they vanished after the first weekend at the compound. John and Annie Glenn eagerly went through the initiation of early morning swimming followed by sailing, touch football and tennis into the afternoon, often with the boisterous assistance of Bob and Ethel Kennedy and their large brood.

But it was the way the Glenns spent the afternoon quiet time—when others subjected to this regimen collapsed on their beds for two hours—that impressed the Kennedys. Instead of napping, John and Annie took a hike. It was as if the outgoing, competitive astronaut was saying to his hosts: "I'll see your bet, Mr. President. Yours too, Bob. And raise you."

The formality of the presidency seemed to fall away during the vigorous weekends on the Cape. Glenn recalls that he and his family were once invited up to the Kennedy compound for a weekend of sailing with Bob and Ethel. "We weren't aware that the president and Mrs. Kennedy were going to be there. I remember the way we learned," Glenn recounts. "Ethel Kennedy had suggested we go sailing. Well, I knew that they had a fairly large sailboat, the *Victura*. I had never been out in one like that, so I didn't feel qualified to take it out in the 25- or 30-knot wind blowing this particular day. Ethel said, 'No, no, that's all right. We'll go sailing; we can take care of it all right.' "

Walking down to the boat Glenn remembers that they spied two people in old clothes who might have been hired hands, rigging the sails. It was the president and Jacqueline, there to surprise the Glenns. As the trip began, Glenn's doubts about taking a boat out that day vanished. However, the heavy weather forced the president to make a rare public concession to his bad back. Kennedy turned the tiller over to Glenn's son, Dave, and shouted steering instructions to the delighted teenager as they sailed back and forth across the harbor.

At their initial meeting at the White House, Glenn says, he and the president talked "as one guy to another" about the upcoming orbital flight. Kennedy, barely masking his admiration for the superachiever sitting before him, peppered the deferential Marine with technical questions. "He was interested in real detail," Glenn relates. " 'What's the expected G-level during launch?' 'What kind of sensations do you expect during launch?' 'Are you actually going to drive your capsule like an airplane or are you pretty much at the mercy of the guidance systems?' "

Glenn was in his element talking about technology. Taken by Kennedy's casual charm, he lost his reserve before the commander-in-chief and began gesturing with his hands, his green eyes alight as they are only when he is talking about making things work or fly. Glenn went through his earnest lecture on how it was all supposed to feel, and how he and his fellow-astronauts had veto control over any aspect of the flight they thought was unsafe or liable to mishap.

The magic that had worked on the NASA selection team captivated the usually cynical JFK. A politician who trusted his instincts and was rarely guided by the conventional judgments of press or public, Kennedy, in Theodore H. White's view, often bestowed an "intense concern and flattering cultivation" upon men with talents or qualities he thought might one day be useful to him. Sitting with Glenn that day in the White House, the president realized that this affable Marine not only was going to be a hero but a valuable political ally in his upcoming drive for reelection. An idea began to germinate, but Kennedy kept silent as Glenn continued his wide-eyed dissertation on space travel. It would be better not to burden the pilot until after he came back from space alive and a hero.

Kennedy viewed the space race with Russia as a kind of contest, a supreme test of American will that carried with it enormous political implications. "Kennedy saw it originally as a competitive thing with the Russians," Glenn says. "We couldn't let them best us in this scientific field." It galled JFK to have to deal with the Russians from weakness. When forced to do so in the early part of his term, Kennedy tried to sound like a statesman but instead came across as listless and insincere.

"All of us salute the brave cosmonauts of the Soviet Union," Kennedy told the UN General Assembly on September 25, 1961. It was soon after the Russians had orbited the earth and the U.S. had made only two suborbital flights. Standing in the well of the huge assembly hall, Kennedy called for U.S.-Soviet cooperation in space as the best way to prevent tensions on earth from being played out in the heavens. "The new horizons of outer space must not be driven by the old bitter concepts of imperialism and sovereign claims," Kennedy said. "The cold reaches of the universe must not become the arena of an even colder war."

Kennedy was applauded, but only perfunctorily, by a grim-faced Soviet delegation. The Soviets had no reason to share their knowledge with the United States, which seemed doomed to play perpetual catch-up. The previous April, after cosmonaut Yuri Gagarin's orbital flight, NASA administrator James Webb paid Kennedy a buck-up call, bringing with him a plastic mock-up of a U.S. space capsule. After he left, Kennedy testily observed that, from the look of the contraption, Webb might have bought it at a toy store on his way to work. Within weeks, Kennedy ordered his vice-president, Lyndon B. Johnson, then chairman of the National Aeronautics and Space Council, to find out "where we stand in space."

"Do we have a chance of beating the Soviets by putting a laboratory in space?" Kennedy asked Johnson in a confidential memorandum. "Or by a trip around the moon, or by a rocket to land on the moon, or by a rocket to go to the moon and back with a man. Is there any other space program which promises dramatic results in which we could win?"

Within a month Johnson's panel concluded that the country's one chance to best the Russians—and only a 50-50 probability at that—was to beat them to the moon. Kennedy, gambling that the odds might improve, went before a special session of Congress on May 25, 1961, and declared: "I believe that this nation should commit itself to achieving the goal, before the decade is out, of landing a man on the moon and returning him safely to earth."

Kennedy's words remained little more than rhetoric for nine months, until John Glenn's flight proved the sophistication of American space technology. That morning, February 20, 1962, Kennedy and Johnson, like millions of others, watched the TV and waited as the countdown proceeded. Savoring the publicity bonanza to come, Johnson turned suddenly to the president and added an additional wish: "If John Glenn were only a Negro."

Now with the orbital flight completed, the door to Air Force One swung open, revealing the presidential seal. The steps were hurriedly rolled into place, and a throaty cheer went up as the president stepped into the ovenlike heat at Cape Canaveral. Vice-President Johnson, with Glenn's family in tow, had arrived earlier to greet the astronaut on his return to Florida from Grand Turk Island in the Bahamas near the spashdown point some 70 miles southeast of the Cape. The group was waiting for the president, who this time had come to see Glenn, rather than the other way around.

"As President Kennedy came down the ramp from Air Force One," Glenn recalls, "the honor guard was there. We went through the guard with him. Then he started off across to another area a couple of hundred feet away. The security wasn't very good on the Cape that day as far as crowd control was concerned. It sort of got out of hand."

In those less apprehensive times, the president found himself casually engulfed by a crowd of people. Glenn was still at Kennedy's side and the two walked about, smiling, shaking hands,

Kennedy in his custom-tailored Brooks Brothers suit, Glenn in his off-the-rack three-button with the too-long sleeves. A military band was playing "Hail to the Chief." Then, in the midst of the happy turmoil, the band broke into the "Marine Hymn."

"Isn't that the 'Marine Hymn' they're playing?" Kennedy asked Glenn.

"Yes, it is," Glenn replied.

"What do you normally do when they play the 'Marine Hymn'?" Kennedy inquired.

"Well," Glenn answered, "as a loyal Marine, I normally stand at attention."

"That's what I thought," said the former Navy officer. With that, Kennedy stopped and stood at attention as Glenn snapped to as well, to the puzzlement of the sweating crowd. On the baking tarmac, the two men stood almost as one: Kennedy the PT-boat skipper who had saved his crew in the Pacific during World War II and was now America's youngest president; Glenn the true-to-life Buck Rogers who had made the country proud again after an international humiliation.

Kennedy would not leave the Cape until he had seen it all. The president went to pad 14, where Glenn had been launched, as well as to the control center, where Kennedy was briefed by Christopher Kraft, the flight director. At the formal ceremonies, Glenn presented Kennedy with a Cape Canaveral hardhat, which Kennedy accepted but would not wear. JFK's aversion to hats was already legendary; he was always mindful of how ridiculous Calvin Coolidge had looked staring inanely at the camera in an Indian war bonnet. While in office, Kennedy eschewed even somber fedoras.

On Glenn's lapel, the president pinned the space agency's Distinguished Service Medal, a circular gold disk with a stylized moon orbiting the earth. For the first time the Marine's stalwart composure collapsed. Standing at attention with the flags whipping lazily in the thick hot air, as the commander-in-chief paid him honor, tears streamed down his face.

Glenn and his family spent the weekend after the ceremonies at a hideaway in Key West, their first quiet moments since the launch. The following Monday, the Glenns rejoined the president and the first family in Palm Beach and flew on to Washington in Air Force One. Annie Glenn remembers that hectic day. Jackie Kennedy, she recalls, was dressed not in a designer outfit but "just a very casual, comfortable dress," the better to tolerate the hot Florida sun. "I was struck by her friendliness and as a woman I was interested in her clothes," says Annie. She insists that she will always remember her first impression of the president that day: "His smile was so wide and his eyes—when he talked he talked directly to me. He just seemed as if I'd always known him."

During the flight back to Washington, Annie recalls that the president was considerate of both her and John's parents. "He watched over them to make sure they were comfortable on the plane. He came back several times and talked to all of us, and he seemed just especially pleased to include us in everything."

To Glenn's daughter, Lyn, then only 14, the presidential attention proved to be mortifying. "I used to get very airsick. I remember President Kennedy had his physician come and help me," Lyn, who is now Mrs. Lyn Glenn Freedman, recalls. "I don't know if most presidents would have noticed someone on board their plane turning green." The doctor helped Lyn through her nausea with deep breathing exercises. After a while, the president came to her seat. "He asked me what the doctor had said to do because he wanted to know what to do if he ever got airsick."

The plane arrived at Andrews Air Force Base in a driving rain, forcing cancellation of plans to have the Glenns land on the White House lawn by helicopter. Instead, they went to the executive mansion by limousine, where the president hosted a brief reception. Though she had been to the White House several times before, escorting visiting friends on the public tour, Annie Glenn had never been in the Oval Office. But there was no chance to admire the decor, she recalls. "It was just a great big mass of people wanting to get close to all of us."

Following the White House reception, Glenn and his family paraded triumphantly up Pennsylvania Avenue in an open convertible. A crowd of a quarter million welcomed the astronaut who, emulating his president at Cape Canaveral, sat bareheaded in the open Lincoln, rain dripping down his smiling face, as the multitudes bellowed their welcome. It was a day of pure exultation.

"There were jumpers too," one reporter said about the Glenn reception, "young girls who leaped for joy—the first jumpers political reporters had seen since John F. Kennedy was campaigning for the presidency in 1960." Onlookers, most of them teenagers, broke through police lines to shake Glenn's outstretched gloved hand. On Pennsylvania Avenue outside the District Building, the seat of local government, a triumphal arch was decked in a bright banner reading "Welcome to Astronaut John H. Glenn, Jr." Other signs along the way were much less formal: "Hi John!" they read, or "Welcome back to earth again."

Only one musical unit, the Marine Band, was willing to risk its instruments in the downpour to pay tribute to one of its own. They played through repeated choruses of the "Marine Hymn" and other martial airs as the motorcade went slowly down the "presidential mile" from the White House to the Capitol Building. Large plastic buttons sprouted on the raincoats of many in the crowd, the effort of one Manny Ress, a quick-thinking entrepreneur from New York. Beneath a smiling picture of the astronaut was the legend: "New Frontier Man of the Year," a designation no one could dispute that day.

When the welcome was repeated a few days later in New York, the traditional ticker tape parade was the largest in the city's history. Few even tried to estimate the size of the crowd that sunny, windy March 1. The pageant included not only the hundreds of thousands who were jammed sidewalk to storefront along the entire 18-mile parade route, but also the throngs that cheered from numberless office building windows in the city's canyons.

Unfortunately, the triumph was marred an hour before Glenn arrived when a airliner crashed at JFK Airport (then Idlewild), killing 95. This, combined with a major New York transit dispute, presented headline writers with a dilemma. The *New York Daily News* solved the problem with a classic response. Atop a front page photo of the Glenn parade was the headline:

DEATH, TRIUMPH & A BUS STRIKE.

The orgy of adulation that engulfed the handsome Marine would wash over every American. Its intensity would last, almost unabated, for more than a year and confirm Kennedy's hunch that John Glenn's future was no longer in outer space.

"Members of Congress," rasped the aging Speaker of the House, John McCormack of Massachusetts, "it is a privilege and I deem it a high honor to present to you a brave, a courageous American. A hero in World War II and in the Korean conflict who recently in a most notable manner added glory and prestige to our country—the first U.S. astronaut to have achieved orbital flight: Lieutenant Colonel John H. Glenn, Jr., U.S. Marine Corps."

The cavernous chamber erupted at the name and Glenn, smiling confidently, strode to the podium. He shook McCormack's hand and then Lyndon Johnson's before laying his typewritten speech on the same lectern John Kennedy had used just six weeks earlier when he delivered the State of the Union address. It was as if Glenn himself were president, and a hugely popular one at that. Before him in the white marble hall dating back to the time of George Washington were all the nation's senators and representatives. In the back of the chamber congressional staff members were crowded into the standing room just beyond the members' desks in front of the swinging mahogany doors leading to the cloakrooms. To Glenn's left as he faced the expectant crowd sat the diplomatic corps. Directly in front of him, in nine highbacked leather chairs, positioned just in front of the lawmakers, were the nine men of the Supreme Court, each wearing his black robes.

And as if to emphasize how special John Glenn suddenly had become, the rest of the astronauts (save Gordon Cooper, who had not yet returned from the Australian tracking station) sat mutely in the House chamber, listening to Glenn, now first among equals, describe how "I still get a hard-to-define feeling inside when the flag goes by." It was the perfect speech to cement Glenn's image as a small-town hero, good son and husband. "If my parents would stand up please. My dad and mother" (loud applause). "My son and daughter, Dave and Lyn" (louder applause). "And the real rock in our family, my wife, Annie. I'm real proud of her."

Footstomping and clapping filled the Chamber. Unashamed tears were on almost every face in the House. Commentators would later remark how often Glenn referred to "our efforts" and what "we" accomplished. Looking out into an audience that included millions who were watching on television, Glenn told the nation that "our efforts today and what we've done so far are but small building blocks on a very huge pyramid to come."

Then, in a reference to the criticism Kennedy had been receiving for committing the country to the expensive moon landing goal, Glenn declared: "Questions are sometimes raised regarding the immediate payoffs from our efforts. What benefits we cannot even detail; they're probably not even known to man today. But the exploration and the pursuit of knowledge have always paid dividends in the long run, usually far greater than anything expected at the outset."

Glenn had done comparatively little public speaking before, but he displayed surprising ease before a microphone. He had labored arduously on the address during his hideaway weekend in Key West and had had considerable professional help, including NASA public relations men who made sure that the references to continuation of the space program were prominent. Glenn himself inserted the one touch of humor. After Caroline Kennedy had greeted him on the flight back to Washington, she asked, "Where's the monkey?" Glenn, ever the deferential Marine, recalls he asked the president to look at the speech beforehand. "I asked him if he would have any objection to my using this little incident about Caroline. He laughed and laughed and said no; he would be glad for us to go ahead and use it."

Years later, as he fought the reputation of being a dull speaker, Glenn would look back on that speech for confirmation that his critics in the press were wrong. "I used to get medals for it before you guys started writing about what a dull speaker I am," he says. But of course that day in 1962, after his epochal spaceride, the U.S. Congress would have applauded Glenn if he had recited the sizes of his hat and shoes.

NASA itself did not anticipate the public response that the Mercury program would call forth. "When I first got the assignment of designing the selection program," says Dr. Robert Voas, the Navy psychologist who would ultimately choose the first astronauts, "I wrote a memo asking what were the prerequisites for the astronauts in terms of items outside the specific requirements of operating the vehicle. Did we, for example, want to have women? Did we have minorities involved in light of the fact thatI thought these individuals were going to be very much in the public eye? But the project management sort of laughed at that. NASA had never really had very many pilots or had run that many 'in the limelight' type of flight operations, and so I think they rather expected that the focus of attention would remain on the total project and on the engineering side."

Instead, the astronauts themselves came to personify the space program. No one else in NASA, not the director, not the chief engineers, would receive the recognition that was being lavished on the seven men the public took to be their saviors from Russian domination of outer space. And Glenn, far from avoiding the recognition, was eager for it. "While most of the other astronauts would shun that sort of thing," says Voas, "John would accept it and seek it out in some cases. Al Shepard used to go around in dark glasses and incognito and try to actually avoid being recognized."

More than shyness drew Shepard and the others away from the limelight. They felt that acting like Glenn—signing autographs and stopping every time a Boy Scout asked for the time of day—was simply showboating. It was not, they felt, proper behavior for a fighter pilot who hoped to impress his superiors and his peers. "They felt this could hurt them in subsequent peer votes for future flights," Voas says.

It was a peer vote—in which the seven astronauts were asked to nominate someone other than themselves as pilot for the first flight—that cost Glenn his chance to be the first American in space, an honor that went to Alan Shepard. Although the peer vote had been used in previous aspects of astronaut selection and training, it usually involved larger groups, giving scientists a reasonably accurate picture of the men they were testing.

But to use a peer vote among only seven astronauts smacked

to some in the program—particularly Glenn—as being unscientific, even unfair. Having lost to Shepard, Glenn felt that the space agency was ill-advised in being influenced by such a vote. He was almost in a rage over being rejected by colleagues whom he felt were jealous and less capable than he, a feeling that broke through his good-guy facade. "John was sure he would be selected to fly first," says Bob Voas. "Most of the others hoped they would be, but they didn't have the same feeling of assurance that John did."

"My father was very withdrawn for quite a while after he failed to get the first flight," Lyn recalls. "I remember him talking about why he felt a mistake had been made. He really felt that the people who were going to be chosen for the first flight were going to be heroes and should be examples to the country. But he felt that the people chosen were not the appropriate ones."

Voas, who was later to become one of Glenn's closest friends and political advisors, now notes: "In terms of what he saw as the requirements set by the officials at NASA, Glenn had worked harder and done more and was in a sense ahead of everybody else. So the failure to get that first flight hit him very hard. Purely by chance it worked out that he really got the best of the early flights—the orbital one—a year later."

Glenn had once more been rewarded by luck, the good fortune some believe that Glenn feels is part of his natural destiny. It is an inherent part of his Calvinist ethic that one makes his own luck through hard work and dogged pursuit of a goal. From the time he splashed down in the Atlantic, Glenn felt that the old rules, those that had "cheated" him out of the chance to be first in space, no longer applied to him. He sensed correctly that in piloting Friendship 7 through three orbits, not merely being a passenger in a glorified slingshot, he had changed the future of the American space program.

Although somewhat immodest in his evaluation of his own role, Glenn was basically correct. He had, in fact, been elevated to the god-man status enjoyed only by Charles Lindbergh before him. Even the rigid military strictures of rank no longer seemed to apply. Admirals, generals—even presidents—now saluted Glenn. It was he, not Shepard and not Gus Grissom (whose

capsule sank when the explosive bolts on the hatch unaccount-
ably exploded), who had put the United States firmly back into
the space race.

It was he, John Glenn, who personally brought the country
back from what even wizened old John McCormack had called
the brink of "national extinction." At least that is what many
Americans came to believe, frightened as they were by the
Russian monolith and guided by adulatory and selectively focused coverage of the astronauts and their families. The fawn-
ing newspaper and magazine articles suited Glenn, portraying
him in the uncritical light he thought fitting for America's first
team of space explorers.

There was simply no escaping the clamorous public, determined to demonstrate their approval of Glenn and his orbital
flight. That summer the Glenns borrowed a van to move from
Arlington to Houston, where Glenn was to begin work at the
Manned Spaceflight Center. They hoped that their little expe-
dition, through desolate stretches and near-deserted towns,
might provide a breather from all the publicity. But as soon as
they pulled into a campground, the tourists would swarm about
Glenn, waving pieces of paper and Kodak Brownies.

"I think that's when it really hit me that our life was going to
change," Lyn remembers, "that it was going to be normal to
have people come up to Dad all the time. When we stopped in a
gas station out in the middle of nowhere at night, even the gas
station attendant recognized him." The Glenns finally arrived
in Jackson Hole, Wyoming, where a friend had promised to put
them up for a brief rest and keep them out of the public eye. But
to accomplish that they had to go to the very edge of civilization.

"We went on horseback up into the mountains and just
camped there alone as a family," remembers Lyn. "And that
was probably one of the most special times we had. We didn't
take much food with us: Dad wanted to survive on the land. We
picked wild strawberries and fished; shot some birds and
plucked them. It was the first time I had ever plucked a warm
body. We built a latrine and tables and chairs and set up our
little camp out in the middle of nowhere. Dad wanted to go to
the end of where they normally go on horseback trips and then
go another five miles so that we could be completely alone and

out of touch for about four or five days.''

Glenn's mail began to double, then increased exponentially. It came in sacks from all over the world, much of it now stored in brown cardboard "bankers boxes" in the Library of Congress, juxtaposed with Glenn's handwritten, doodle-scrawled memos from his astronaut training. It sits alongside multiple copies of the *Congressional Record* sent to him by adoring lawmakers who had praised Glenn in speeches and who wanted him to have a copy of their plaudits.

During the year after the orbital flight, it was as if Glenn were never off the national stage. He had even taken it upon himself to carry the flag wherever he went, as if he had become the personal custodian of national pride and righteousness. Three weeks after his flight Glenn found himself standing on the lawn outside an Arlington, Virginia, home, arguing with a belligerent teenager who had attempted to crash a party attended by his daughter. Before it was over the cops had been called, and one youth had taken a swing at America's newest hero.

The teenagers had been drinking. When Glenn arrived at the home to pick up Lyn, one of the youngsters threw a beer can on the lawn. "Pick it up!" Glenn barked, then walked into the house. When he came out with Lyn, he was greeted by a chorus of "beer can in the ocean, beer can in the ocean," a reference to his space capsule. A newspaper account related: "Col. Glenn forcefully told the youth in effect that the orbital flight was not a personal but a national accomplishment undertaken for the benefit of all Americans and that no American should depreciate [sic] it."

Ignoring Glenn's lecture, the youths headed to the teen center of a nearby church. Anticipating trouble, Glenn followed them. At the church he encountered still another crowd of young beer-drinkers, who ignored Glenn's order to leave. One threw a punch when Glenn tried to get the license number of their car, but the youngster quickly found himself pinned against the vehicle by the now glowering, muscular Marine. Glenn called the cops and the gang fled. The incident, which mortified local officials because of the boorishness displayed to a national hero, was notable only in contrast to the ongoing adulation of Glenn displayed by the country as a whole.

More than a year of this kind of attention was having its effect on Glenn's never-banked ambitions. Public idolatry was helping to revive his desire for public office, an ambition extending back to high school days in New Concord and to a sympathetic teacher, Harford Steele, who instilled in a restless young man an awareness of the world beyond Ohio. But there was another factor pushing him into politics. That factor was the political acumen of John Fitzgerald Kennedy.

Project Mercury formally ended in the summer of 1963. With it disappeared any chance that John Glenn would ever again ride in space. The public expected that its hero of Friendship 7 would make at least one more trip, a hope Glenn himself nurtured until he learned that it already was too late. The White House had decided that Glenn's career as an astronaut was over. John Kennedy had other plans for the astronaut.

"President Kennedy questioned me about whether I would be used on more than one flight," Glenn remembers, "and I told him that I assumed that I would. No one was assigned to specific flights at that time, but we thought that everyone would be used again on other flights. But the president never went into it any further." Unknown to Glenn or anyone else outside the space agency and the White House, the president had already instructed NASA that he wanted Glenn grounded. The astronaut had become too valuable a political vehicle to risk in space flight.

A new set of eager, younger men were being named to the astronaut ranks for the Gemini and later Apollo programs, which would send astronauts to the moon: men like Frank Borman, who with Tom Stafford and Jim McDivitt had been test flight instructors at Edwards Air Force Base. Or Neil Armstrong, another Ohio boy, who looked nearly a decade younger than his 33 years and who had been a test pilot on the X-15.

Still there was no technical reason why Glenn could not suit up for one of the early Gemini flights, the way Gus Grissom or Wally Schirra had done after their Mercury missions. But the president was adamant. Even if Glenn had been ten years younger, his career as an astronaut was over. Walter D. Sohier, then general counsel to the space agency, recalled that "one thing that [President Kennedy] said to me...was that he thought it would be a great mistake if [Glenn] were used on any future flights, because [he was] such an important asset to this country....He said that to me two or three times."

Rene Carpenter notes that there was a "gang-up on John" to keep him on ground. "Oh, God yes," she exclaims, "John's schedule was now directed by the White House, the House and Senate space committee and the State Department."

Alhough Glenn professes ignorance of Kennedy's wish that he be grounded, he concedes the president had told him about his future plans. "He hoped that sometime when I was out of the space program, I would consider politics," Glenn recalls. In fact, Glenn and his confidant, Bob Voas, were already considering that possibility just as the president and his brother Bobby were privately discussing their own political plans for the popular astronaut.

"John and I had talked about his getting into politics for some time," says Voas, one of the few men whose relationship with Glenn spans both his career as an astronaut and politician. The two talked about politics for months after the flight, planned for it and fantasized about it by the big stone fireplace in the living room of Glenn's Houston home, just a few steps away from the memento-lined corridor hung with photos, charts and other icons of his glory days as an astronaut.

"I had thought about politics from the very first days he came aboard the space program because of the nature of the person he was and the way he affected people," admits Voas. "I expected to select—and be involved with—people who would get into politics because I expected them to be national heroes." Voas would ultimately quit NASA and join Glenn as soon as he announced for the Senate in 1964.

Glenn's interest in government and politics had been evident as early as high school when he wrote a civics paper on the workings of the Senate, at a time of life when most students were penning theses on their favorite sports heroes. Even in the 1950s, as a student test pilot at Maryland's Patuxent Naval Air

Station, Glenn would take time out during leave in Washington to sit in the cramped seats of the Senate visitors' gallery and watch men such as Everett Dirksen and Mike Mansfield debate the issues of the day. As a Marine he had voted, either by absentee ballot or in person, in every general election since 1950.

One report has noted that Glenn once described himself as "either a liberal Republican or a conservative Democrat," quoting him as stating that "in 1960, in a conservative mood, he had voted for Richard Nixon against John F. Kennedy." Glenn denies it today. "No, nope. I never told anybody that, but it got published anyway," Glenn now says. Had he ever voted for Nixon any other time, or for any other Republican for president? "No, I don't think so. I don't think I have. It's a long time ago."

During the spring and summer of 1963 Glenn began to sense that his star was in eclipse at the space agency. His new work at the Manned Spaceflight Center in Houston, helping to design future spacecraft, was just so much desk jockeying. He was 42, young, ambitious and receptive when the Kennedys finally made their move.

It was first broached to Glenn over dinner at Bobby Kennedy's Hickory Hill estate in McLean, Virginia, in the early fall of '63. Bobby Kennedy's proposal was simple enough. His brother John, facing a potentially strong Republican challenge in 1964, needed to ensure that the blocs of electoral votes that had elected him in 1960 stayed intact. For insurance, he needed to gain a few swing states. Ohio, a major industrial state with a strong Democratic constituency, had surprisingly gone for Richard Nixon rather than Kennedy in 1960. It was one of the great upsets of an election so close that only last-minute, controversial victories in Texas and Illinois granted Kennedy the victory over Nixon.

This time, with a vulnerable 74-year-old Democratic incumbent, Senator Stephen Young, at the top of the Ohio state ticket, the Kennedys were worried that history might repeat itself. Certain that Glenn's heroic image could be translated into Democratic votes, Bobby Kennedy, acting as his brother's surrogate, tried to prime the astronaut into running for the Senate. He found ready interest in the ambitious Glenn.

It was a time when Glenn and Bob Voas were shaping their own plans to leave NASA for a political career. That confluence of events, combined with later promises to Glenn from the Kennedys, finally thrust Glenn into the Democratic party. "I've been a Republican," Glenn later admitted, "but I think now I'm on the other—I know I'm on the other side." Long a middle-of-the-road-minded individual, Glenn had cast his lot with the Democratic party, a decision that over the next 20 years would inexorably move him politically leftward.

Of all the people he has met in his varied career—as war hero, astronaut, businessman and senator—few have had as much influence on John Glenn as the late Bobby Kennedy. Each shared a profound belief in the American system, each was devoutly religious, and each was consumed not only by an overwhelming need to succeed but to push themselves to the absolute limit. It is no surprise that both, in their time, would run for president. Their mutual tie was John Kennedy, a man whose friendship both cherished.

As a young boy of privilege, Robert Kennedy possessed only modest athletic talent and a slight build, but he drove himself at sports. At Harvard, he should never have made the football squad, but he did and he lettered. John Glenn, son of a small-town Ohio plumber, also lacked a natural athlete's grace. He was a slow, plodding runner in high school, but by the time he entered college, he was the only one in his class to have won three letters in sports. Decades later, the two driven men would ski and shoot rapids together.

More than any of his brothers, Bobby Kennedy read deeply in philosophy and religion. In Glenn, he found someone whose religious beliefs were equally unwavering and strong, a sympathetic listener who shared his wonder about the unknown. The same John Glenn who would later stand in the operating theater in Houston with Dr. Michael DeBakey to watch the famed heart surgeon perform, spent hours in conversation with Bobby talking about space, religion or the brilliance of a sunset viewed from earth orbit.

The Glenns, John and Annie, were favorites of the Kennedy children. In 1962, shortly after his flight, Glenn held an impromptu seminar on Bobby's lawn. "Now who can answer this question?" Glenn asked the youngsters gathered at his feet. "Suppose you had a ball tied onto a rope and you were swinging it around in circles over your head. How would you get the ball to go higher up off the ground?" It went on for a half hour, the kids occasionally giving nonsensical answers, but Glenn patiently laughing with them.

The easy friendship that had developed between John Glenn and Bobby Kennedy made it possible for them to talk frankly about the '64 campaign. Glenn had his eye on Young's Senate seat, but he was exhibiting his usual caution. The same John Glenn who calculated every risk he took as a test pilot knew the political danger implicit in challenging an incumbent senator. Overcoming those risks required more than Bobby Kennedy's broad assurances of support. "I'll run," Glenn told Bobby, "but only if I can get a clear shot at the nomination." The message was obvious: Senator Young had to go.

The matter rested for several weeks while Republicans, falsely convinced that Glenn was wavering about running as a Democrat, tried to woo him with offers of support for a House seat. But Glenn was not wavering; he wanted the Senate. He was biding his time until the White House acted to exert pressure on Young to vacate the Ohio seat.

Finally, in the late fall of 1963, Glenn received the signal he had been waiting for. "We were at a party in Houston and John and Annie had been up in Washington," recalls Bob Voas. "This was about October or November 1963. John came back from the trip and seemed quite happy and excited. He took me aside and said that Bobby Kennedy had talked to him about running for the Senate in Ohio and that they—Bobby and the president—were going to arrange for the incumbent to be given a position so as to open up the Democratic nomination."

There was, of course, no guarantee that Stephen Young or his campaign manager, a millionaire Cleveland attorney named Howard Metzenbaum who would loom large in Glenn's later career, would be receptive to the idea of Young giving up a reelection race for an ambassadorship or other sinecure in the Kennedy administration. But Bobby's offer was enough to convince Glenn.

At one point, the president personally took a hand to help Glenn gain the Senate seat. John (Socko) Wiethe, then Hamilton County Democratic chairman, recalls that JFK called him in 1963 to help ease Glenn's entry into the Senate race. "John F. Kennedy called me up on the phone and asked if I wouldn't introduce John Glenn to all the county chairmen and get him started," Wiethe recalls. Acting on orders from the Kennedy brothers, Wiethe personally asked Young, a onetime political ally whom Wiethe says"treated me properly," if he would consider stepping aside in return for an ambassadorship. Initially, Wiethe notes, Young was receptive. The political skids now appeared greased for Glenn's easy entry into politics.

Glenn's desire for a Senate seat was strong. Even before Glenn's conversation with Bobby that fall, Voas had quietly tried to raise some $200,000 for a Senate campaign by selling his own and Glenn's stories to the *Saturday Evening Post*, which was then in keen competition with *Life*. Voas said he came away with a gentlemen's agreement from the *Post* to pay $75,000 for his own story as the man who selected the astronauts, and more than $100,000 for exclusive rights to the inside story of John Glenn's first political campaign.

But the deal fell through when *Life*, unwilling to give up any aspect of the story to the competition, held Glenn to his exclusive astronaut contract. Glenn backed off, even though the *Post* already had sent to bed a magazine cover of Glenn standing in front of the U.S. Capitol. *Post* editors frantically tried to cobble together a story to go with the cover. The resulting piece, which originally had been planned as a major exclusive, was instead shaped almost entirely from clippings.

But the setback was not fatal. "The first concrete action I took," recalls Voas, "was to go to Ohio to meet with some of John's contacts and try to do the initial exploration, and set up a campaign committee and staff." The plan was for Voas to leave Houston for Washington on NASA business, then take a week's leave for some quiet politicking in Ohio—armed with the unofficial endorsement of the Kennedy White House.

Spirits high, Voas went to the Houston airport and there, in what then seemed a lucky harbinger, saw John Kennedy arrive on Air Force One for a round of fencemending among Texas

Democrats. Voas boarded his flight for Washington more confident than ever that the 42-year-old John Glenn would replace aging Stephen Young as the Democratic Senator from Ohio. It was November 21, 1963.

The next day, after rushing through his business at NASA, Voas hailed a cab for National Airport. An ashen-faced driver pulled to the curb and Voas stepped into the cab. The driver had just heard a car radio report: JFK has been assassinated in Dallas. Voas made it to Cleveland just as the great silver presidential jet brought the president's body home to Washington. Glenn's aide never consummated his political meetings in Ohio, and suddenly the sure Senate nomination that Glenn had counted on was no longer so certain.

In the painful days following the assassination, Glenn mourned the loss of president and friend. The brutal death, in the words of Kennedy biographer Herbert Parmet, was "the first of that decade of political murders" that shattered a more innocent world. Kennedy had been president for 1,037 days and, in the end, the machinery of the government meshed together for an orderly transition. In the late evening chill, bathed in the glare of television lights, Air Force One came to a silent stop at Andrews Air Force Base outside Washington. The pilot had landed downwind, cut the plane's engines and let the craft roll mournfully to its location on the tarmac.

Lyndon Johnson, now the president of the United States, emerged from the forward door as Kennedy's bronze coffin was brought from the rear. Almost immediately Johnson flew to the White House by helicopter. With him were Kennedy's national security advisor, McGeorge Bundy, Defense Secretary Robert S. McNamara and Under Secretary of State George Ball. Wrote Theodore H. White: "Johnson asked the little trio in the President's helicopter whether there was anything they felt he must decide that night. McNamara said no. Then Ball said no. Then Bundy said no." The transition was accomplished and the president flew home.

John Glenn, who had known Kennedy best, was chosen by

the astronauts to represent them at the funeral. Late the night before, Glenn, accompanied by Bob Voas, had made an unscheduled trip from his hotel through the hushed streets of the capital. At the Lincoln Memorial, he stood with Voas in the night air and silently read the words of another martyred president. The two men were not totally alone, but the few people at the memorial kept a respectful distance as Glenn, tears brimming, read the words of both Lincoln's second inaugural and the Gettysburg Address.

Glenn and Voas returned to their car and drove the short distance to the Capitol Building, where the crowds stretched for blocks waiting to file past the Kennedy coffin as it rested on a black catafalque surrounded by a military honor guard under the Capitol dome. Capitol police, recognizing Glenn, led him through a VIP entrance to the great rotunda, where he paid his respects under the gaze of hundreds in the hushed hall. Five years later, he would pay a similar farewell to Kennedy's brother Bobby.

It would become part of John Glenn's official history that Kennedy's murder galvanized him into running for public office. "I guess along with many other tens of millions of Americans we all sat back and took stock of ourselves and our country and what our responsibilities might be and reassessed things," Glenn now says. "And I did exactly that."

In reality, rather than galvanize Glenn to run, the assassination almost convinced Glenn to quit. Glenn's race had greatly depended on John Kennedy's persuading Senator Stephen Young to step aside to ease the way for the younger man. But the assassination had changed that careful equation. Glenn knew that he had a problem. "The problem, of course, was that there was a new president," Voas recalls. "Bobby Kennedy had lost his capability to make the arrangement of getting the incumbent out of the race. The whole thing was now very much up in the air. You have to remember that Bobby Kennedy was on the outs with Johnson; he was even seen as a possible challenger to Johnson. And Steve Young was a strong Johnson supporter.

"I attempted to make some inquiries at the White House and get some feel whether Johnson was going to take any action," Voas continues. "But I wasn't an insider. It became clear that Johnson was going to keep his hands off the Ohio race. That being the case, Young wasn't going to drop out."

Glenn returned to Houston uncertain and dismayed. He felt an obligation to stay with NASA until all of the information gathered from his flight had been plowed back into the space program. But the certainty that he would never fly again drained him of enthusiasm. Never a wealthy man, Glenn toyed briefly with choosing among the corporate offers that cluttered his mail. One offered him $1 million over ten years just to endorse a breakfast cereal. But he turned them all down; he could not stop thinking about a seat in the U.S. Senate.

Glenn's letters to friends that December and January took on a political cast, as if he were trying out his campaign rhetoric. There was a blandness in some of the phrasing, but eloquence as well. He wrote of extremists of the left and right "so blinded by their beliefs they find the smallest disagreement and any opposition an evidence of treason. These black spirits line the main road of our nation's progress as a funeral mob shouting profanities at each other and all those that march steadily toward the future."

To this day, Voas, a psychologist who knows Glenn's mind as well as anyone, has no idea what made Glenn finally decide to make the Senate race. In retrospect, he assumes that the answer is simple ambition, the fulfillment of a boyhood dream, one undoubtedly nurtured by his stirring appearance before a joint session of Congress less than two years before. "The thing that's true about John Glenn is that for something he wants he'll work harder than most people. The Senate was something that John wanted."

In January 1964, nearly six months after Bobby Kennedy had first broached the idea to him at Hickory Hill, Glenn decided to challenge Stephen Young in Ohio's Democratic senatorial primary that May. The transition from astronaut to politician had begun.

3

DAYS IN NEW CONCORD

On the day John Glenn was born in Cambridge, Ohio, July 18, 1921, with a thatch of red hair and weighing a robust nine pounds, the local newspaper reported on a "glorious meeting" held the previous evening in the town park. Two weeks before President Warren G. Harding, a former Ohio newspaper publisher, had signed the joint congressional resolution declaring peace with Germany, Austria and Hungary. The nation looked forward once again to prosperity and a return to what Harding had called "normalcy."

"More than a thousand people gathered in union worship—many direct descendants of the first settlers," the *Daily Jeffersonian* said that day. "The lake was as peaceful as Galilee after Christ stilled the storm. A hush came over the audience as Our Band swung into the oldtime hymns so dear to childhood. Then they all stood reverently and saluted America."

Born into this pious Scots-Irish community, where perseverance and patriotism were the prime virtues and indolence a sin, there was little chance that John Glenn, Jr., would grow into anything but a resolute, godfearing man with an unshakable belief not only in his God and his country but in his own ability to live, and prosper, by the demanding precepts of his Presbyterian faith.

In the early twenties, neighboring New Concord, Ohio, where Glenn grew up, was a hilly coal-rich interruption along the National Road where descendants of the Scots-Irish immigrants nurtured their religion and ferocious patriotism with a zeal that brooked little dissent. As a pioneer community in the 1800s it supported no fewer than seven churches. Its one institution of higher learning, Muskingum College, was founded in 1837 by a people just barely removed from frontier primitiveness, but who had a respect for study as old as the Scottish Reformation.

Muskingum students, who were later to include John Glenn, were bound by a rigid code of behavior that included mandatory chapel and strictly enforced curfews. With the coming of the automobile, those who lived on the tiny campus were forbidden to drive, lest they veer toward such places as Zanesville, where liquor was sold surreptitiously in the basements of near-beer saloons. Smoking a cigarette, even off campus, was grounds for suspension. Not surprisingly, when conductors on the old Baltimore & Ohio and Pennsylvania Railroads bellowed "New Concord!" as they approached the tiny hamlet, they derisively added its nickname: "Saint's Rest."

It was then, and remains today, an insular area, a collection of tiny towns in southeastern Ohio. In the words of a local historian, these Presbyterian communities are "content to look inward, content to let the outside world reach in." The people of New Concord kept largely to themselves during the turmoil of the twenties, the agony of the Great Depression, the World War II years and after. It was a place where generations stayed rooted, where ideas and attitudes calcified and where the comforting soporific of cultural sameness made one grow smug.

"A community like this has no shootings and no red-light district," says Dr. Walter Chess, a towering deep-voiced man who was a classmate of Glenn's at Muskingum College. Glenn's daughter, Lyn, who lived there with her mother and brother in the fifties while Glenn was overseas, remembers it as "probably one of the best places to be a kid." A visitor to this well-tended town today would be struck by New Concord's unhurried warm atmosphere, as well as its residents' pride in their famous son. They might point out the old B&O railroad bridge that young "Bud" Glenn used to "shoot" in his 1929 roadster, The Cruiser, revving the battered convertible to maximum speed, then taking the bridge on the fly, blind to oncoming traffic.

Doubtless, too, the visitor would be shown the cemetery off Bloomfield Road—since renamed Friendship Drive after Glenn's space flight—where John Glenn, Sr., an old World War I bugler, played taps on Decoration Day as his son bugled the echo from over the ridge. The first-time visitor might be offered only a cursory tour of Muskingum College and thus miss the bronze plaques in Cambridge Hall commemorating the college's past benefactors, including the local branch of the Ku Klux Klan.

Few in town want to talk about the cross burnings—either the ones that children of John Glenn's age would gawk at in innocent wonder on summer nights in the late twenties on the hills outside of New Concord and Zanesville, or the burning on the lawns of white high school girls from Cambridge who were friendly with black boys. Anyone looking for news of the incidents in "The Jeff" would have been disappointed. While the paper knew about them, the editor decided there was no need to air the incidents since the victims had not come forward to complain.

"They're all good people around here," declares Walter Chess, contentedly lighting his pipe in his woodpaneled living room just a few blocks from the white-shingled house where John Sr. and Clara Glenn moved after leaving Cambridge in 1923, when John Jr. was two. But Carl Anker, owner of Anker's Appliances and another of Glenn's boyhood friends, describes the idyllic childhood in New Concord differently. "We were never aware of any problems," he says, "because we didn't look for any."

At first, New Concord was only a foot trail, hacked out of the lush forests of southern Ohio in 1797 by Ebenezer Zane. Hardly a road, it was more a path, or trace. "Zane's Trace," as it came to be called, helped resume the westward migration that had been thwarted during colonial times by the British Proclamation Act, which had sealed the borders of the 13 colonies to consolidate England's holdings in North America.

But by 1812, dozens of families had used Zane's Trace and other trails to open up the eastern part of Muskingum county. A cluster of cabins rose across the Trace at Locust Grove as scores of pioneers, mostly Scots-Irish Presbyterians transplanted from Western Pennsylvania, fanned out for miles, clearing the rolling land of dense stands of timber that would soon be converted into still more homes.

These rugged people, the cultural and racial antecedents of John Glenn, carried the blood of the Scottish Lowlanders who had emigrated to Ireland in the early seventeenth century before coming to America. "In their native land of Scotland they had already become a mixed race," explains Professor William L. Fisk of Muskingum College. "In their veins ran the blood of the savage Picts of Galloway, the most barbarous of the Scottish people, and of the Roman and Saxon soldiers who fought against them. Viking plunderers left their legacy of red hair and ruddy complexion among them, and Norman baron and Flemish artisan added to their genetic heritage. By the time they left Scotland, they had already become a kind of prototype of the product of the American melting pot."

Just as Zane's Trace helped open Ohio to settlement, so did the opening of the National Road become "the great event of the third decade of the nineteenth century." Slowly, the road moved west toward the now-settled prairie, reaching the rolling lands of Guernsey and Muskingum counties by 1827. There, surveyors for the road laid their stakes across the land of an enterprising Irishman, David Findley, who had prudently purchased 193 acres at the site, just north of Zane's Trace, for $2,500 in 1820.

No sooner had the surveyors left than Findley began laying out a village he called "Concord," after his home in Pennsylvania, and named the part of the National Road going through his property "Main Street." By 1830, the road was complete. The United States Post Office added the word "New" to "Concord" to distinguish it from another, already established, post office, and within two years New Concord's population had risen to 32. By 1833, it had grown to 75. By 1837 there were 200, and by the middle of the century still more settlers had come to south-eastern Ohio, among them the ancestors of John and Annie Glenn.

The town became staunchly Republican, and the 1860 election of President Lincoln prompted a wild celebration in New Concord's streets featuring pyramid-shaped tar barrels set ablaze and fireballs of waxen rope flung into the air. The firing on Fort Sumter the following year produced a remarkable call to the colors among the patriotic settlers. Muskingum County filled its first draft levy within 12 hours, a third of the enlistees coming from New Concord.

Throughout its growth the influence of the Presbyterian Church was pervasive among New Concord's Scots-Irish flock. Just as it had guided the life of the Lowlander in Scotland, and later in Ulster, the church was a strong factor in the life of its descendants in Ohio. The ministers in the tiny frontier churches, the spiritual heirs of John Calvin, instituted a system of discipline by the elders of the congregation. Even charges of "occasional hearing," meaning attending the services of another Presbyterian denomination, brought a reprimand from the elders. The churches eventually abandoned this strict discipline, but its aftereffects lingered well into the twentieth century and into the New Concord of John Glenn's childhood.

John Glenn's parents greeted each day with spoken prayer and Bible reading. His father, a large man whose hearing was damaged in World War I during the heavy shelling at Verdun and St. Mihiel, opened a plumbing and heating business in New Concord shortly after he and his wife moved there from Cambridge in 1923 with their infant son. It was a bustling town that attracted Herschel Glenn, a congenial atmosphere in which business and religion easily comingled.

Glenn Sr. was a devout, round-faced Presbyterian with a barrel chest and a fleshy nose who was proud of the fact that the

East Union United Presbyterian Church had been founded in 1841 on his great-grandfather's Ohio farm. He was proud, too, that both his grandfathers had fought for the Union during the Civil War. Though hard drink never passed his lips, he delighted in hot food, the hotter the better. He would pick and eat wild horseradishes whenever he could. Those who knew him recalled his humor, though he was hardly a gregarious man.

"My grandpa Glenn was quiet," recalls Glenn's daughter. "The kind of person who would watch and listen and then would come out with one of those sentences that kind of finalizes everything. He was also a very strict disciplinarian. When my brother and I would go down to the plumbing store, we would play hide-and-seek in the display cabinets. Though he didn't get angry often, that was one thing that made him angry."

"My father was a plumber," John Glenn often tells a crowd, "and he taught me the value of hard work. But after a few summers of swinging a pick and helping him put in water lines, I came to agree with Abe Lincoln. Lincoln said that while his father taught him to work, he never taught him to like it."

But like it or not, hard work was necessary. Glenn's mother, Clara, taught him that. Clara Sproat Glenn, two years younger than her husband, was an outgoing woman—a striking blonde in her early years—who taught elementary school and Sunday school and who instilled in her son a drive to excel. "John's mother was a Sproat and a small town near Lore City was named for her family. It still stands," recalls Wilbur Frame, a contemporary of Clara's who gives his age as past 80. "The town had a dead-end railroad to Old Washington which Clara and I rode to the county fairs."

Frame, a chipper, loquacious man, speaks well of Glenn's parents. "You found them teaching in the schools and helping in entertainments," he says. "There was a Frame family reunion every summer, and John's mom gave speeches and sang with the others. She also helped serve the food at the reunion, usually held in a shaded grove. She passed me the first yellow sliced tomatoes I ever saw. I thought they were cheese, as there was a county cheese factory in the neighborhood."

Unlike her husband, who had only gone through high school, Clara Glenn had attended Muskingum College for two years and was proud of her education. She repeatedly told her son that each person is placed on earth for a mission that he or she is obliged to fulfill for the glory of God. Later, when her son left New Concord and his father's business to enter the military, she accepted it as God's will. Still later, when Glenn entered politics, according to a friend, Clara said, "maybe he was born for a time such as this."

Her son never forgot this sense of righteous mission, nor tired of repeating it in public. In 1959, when he was introduced to the press as a NASA astronaut, Glenn told reporters in no uncertain terms: "I am a Presbyterian, a Protestant Presbyterian, and I take my religion very seriously. We are placed here with certain talents and capabilities. It is up to each of us to use those talents and capabilities as best we can. If we do that, I think there is a power greater than any of us that will place the opportunities in our way, and if we use those talents properly, we will be living the kind of life we should live." It was the perfect juxtaposition of religion with ambition, a life-style encouraged by the Presbyterian faith. In seeking to become an astronaut, John Glenn was merely reaffirming his place as an "elect" of the Lord.

In 1921, the year of Glenn's birth, New Concord was a simpler town than it is today. There were barely more than a thousand people, and no need for traffic lights. The streets— only wooden boardwalks ten years earlier—were finally paved by the time Glenn was born and illuminated by "modern" gas lights fed from fields in Bloomfield several miles away. The town's sober inhabitants were proud of how much had been achieved between 1900 and the War to End War.

New Concord had begun the century with a busy business area for so small a community. It had two phone companies—the "New Concord-Adamsville-Bird's Run Company" and Ohio Bell, offering party-line service on crank-activated wall phones. It also had its own fire engine and a local bank, two hardware stores, three dry goods stores, six groceries, a drugstore, two restaurants, two ice cream parlors, two jewelry shops, a millinery, two furniture stores and two undertakers. There were also two tin shops, three dealers in agricultural implements, a cooperative creamery as well as a produce and poultry store that each week shipped thousands of chicks from the railroad depot.

The community and its godfearing inhabitants supported four blacksmiths and four doctors, a dentist—who by 1910 had an X-ray machine—two insurance agents, two real estate offices and a cigar factory. Only electricity and running water were lacking. (The Wilson and Atchison tonsorial parlor sought to capitalize on the lack of running water by offering customers a bath with each haircut.) Electricity, meanwhile, came to the hamlet in 1910, paradoxically on the wages of sin, from the fines on illegal whiskey produced in nearby Zanesville.

"New Concord is still dry and I'm sure the sale of liquor would be voted down today," declares New Concord resident Mary Steele, a spry woman of 78 and wife of former New Concord High School principal Harford Steele. "That's how we got our first electric light plant, you know. We had oil lamps up until about 1910, but in 1909, the county passed a 'Rose' law—I think a man named Rose introduced it—making selling liquor illegal in the whole county."

The force behind the temperance movement was John Knox Montgomery, a stentorian Presbyterian minister who had been named president of Muskingum College several years before and who viewed his mission in life as "the building of men." Godfearing men, Montgomery believed, did not touch liquor. He had worked for the Prohibition party, at one time standing as its candidate for lieutenant governor, and was head of New Concord's Anti-Saloon League.

Although thirsty Zanesville had resisted the initial efforts of dry forces, the Rose Law empowered any township officer to enforce laws throughout his county. This legal anachronism created a weekly ritual in which New Concord marshals continually arrested Zanesville saloon keepers for violating New Concord's blue laws. The showdown came in 1910 when the entire county became dry. Zanesville saloon keepers kept offering the "real stuff" under the table to patrons tired of near-beer, the weak brew that was legal during Prohibition.

"So the constables from New Concord went down and

bought the liquor," Mrs. Steele recalls, "and with the proof they arrested the men and confiscated all the rest of it." Later, the teetotaling constables posed proudly with their booty before pouring all of it out onto a New Concord cornfield. The fines that day totaled roughly $1,000, Mrs. Steele recalls, and the money helped finance the town's first electric light plant.

In the decade of the twenties, life in New Concord entered a pattern of complacent harmony. On crisp fall days, one would see young "Bud" Glenn, his books under his arm, walking down Bloomfield Road to the two-story elementary school a few blocks away on Main Street. His mother dressed him in white shirt, bow tie and knickers, and as he walked along the road his most visible characteristic was his carrot-red hair. Oftentimes, he would have to make sure he was not followed by Ike and Mike, his two beagles. The dogs would scamper after their freckle-faced master, who loved to hunt with them in the nearby woods just beyond the Glenn house on the edge of New Concord.

John got into the type of mischief one might expect of a high-spirited kid, who even then had an inordinate interest in exploring and trying to figure out what made things work. A scarlet fever epidemic kept John housebound for several weeks one winter. As a result, his room in the house on Bloomfield Road was soon cluttered with models of biplanes that he and his cousin, Bob Thompson, would painstakingly fashion out of balsa wood and glue.

His mother, who died in 1971, remembered John's fascination with airplanes and his delight at seeing them close up whenever they traveled to Columbus. His father, who died in 1967, once recalled John and his friends racing about the backyard, pretending they were flying. "They'd spread their arms out like wings and go 'zzzoooomm' as they ran around, dipping their arms as they banked for a turn."

Later, when Glenn was a teenager, his love for airplanes persuaded his father to take him to the famed Cleveland air races, to watch the gaily colored biplanes speed around the towers in quest of prize money. The elder Glenn didn't require much persuasion; it became a yearly outing young John looked forward to, until a series of crashes forced cancellation of the event.

His friends recall young Bud as an outgoing boy who seldom needed discipline. But he did once feel the switch when his parents were entertaining in the backyard and a ball he was playing with somehow landed in the food. "He was just a normal youngster," Mary Steele recalls. But in one respect, John was unusual, although no one was aware of it at the time. He was unusual because, almost from the time he could walk, he knew the girl he was to marry.

Little Anna Castor—called Annie by everyone—was the eldest of two daughters of Dr. and Mrs. Homer Castor of New Concord. Shortly after the Glenns moved to the town, they joined the Castors in the "twice five club," an informal dinner group in which, as Annie now recalls, "five couples got together each month for a potluck supper." In addition, she says, with a grin, the twice-fivers brought their children "because nobody had babysitters back then."

On one such occasion, Annie, four, literally bumped into Johnnie, three, and the two became inseparable. They played together as children. They started going steady in the eighth grade, when, Glenn remembers, Annie towered over him. As teenagers neither dated anyone else, with the possible exception of one occasion in high school when Annie invited a mutual friend, Lloyd White, to a Girl Scout picnic in order to make John jealous. John obliged; he wouldn't talk to White for a week.

Annie's mother, the only parent of the couple who is still living, had complete faith in John as a suitor. "They didn't sit in the dark or things like that. You could trust John," she says. When 10:00 P.M. came—and if John and Annie were still sitting in the parlor talking—Mrs. Castor would simply call out: "John, it's time to go home." And he did.

Today, both John and Annie try to explain what made them so close so early. John, displaying the certainty he feels once he has made up his mind, argues that his infatuation with Annie, a lovely girl with huge brown eyes and an incandescent smile, was immediate. It grew rapidly into affection, then blossomed into love. Once that happened, he says, he saw no need to date anyone else. Annie puts it this way: "Well, both of us had so much in common. We enjoyed the same things and had a lot to talk about." They seemed to complement one another. Annie was as outgoing as John could be quiet at times. Her friends recall Annie's wry sense of humor and fun-loving nature, qualities that have helped her occasionally to bring her much-revered husband down a peg.

Glenn likes to tell the story of Annie's realistic appraisal of him. At a banquet Glenn was introduced as "one of the few truly great men in the world who are still living." Glenn relates the rest of the story: "On the way home in the car I was musing aloud to Annie that there were indeed very few great men in the world still living. Then Annie shot right back: 'That's right. And I'll tell you one thing—there's sure as heck one less than you think!'" Even today, when someone asks her about the mannequin in Washington's Air and Space Museum that wears her husband's spacesuit, she can, with a mischievous gleam in her eye, call it "the other dummy."

Annie's extroverted nature (a friend has said, "You are never a stranger to her for more than five minutes") is the more unusual because of her serious speech impediment. It was clinically diagnosed as an 85% stutter, and until 1978, when she received successful speech therapy, Annie Glenn could not even order a meal in a restaurant without help. Annie seems to have inherited her stutter from her father, the town dentist, though her younger sister, Jane, does not have it.

Fortunately for Annie, she inherited her father's outgoing personality as well as his disability. "When I was growing up, I had all kinds of friends. I was a happy girl," Mrs. Glenn recalls. "But I can remember once in the sixth grade, each of us had to go up in class and recite a poem. I was trying to recite my favorite poem, which was 'The Highwayman.' It was very noticeable that I had a speech impediment and I remember there was snickering from some of my classmates."

But Annie never let her halting delivery keep her out of activities, and her friends quickly became used to her faltering speech. During their life together, John Glenn has been Annie's "voice" on many occasions.

"I can reeeeeemember my———dad was a———stutterer. I was nnn——nnever really mmmmmmmmmade to speak out in school." This tape recording of Annie Glenn's words before she underwent successful therapy five years ago stands out in near-miraculous contrast to the voice of Annie Glenn today, a soft and gentle one that only occasionally hesitates.

She credits the efforts of Dr. Ronald Webster of the Communications Research Institute at Hollins College in Roanoke, Virginia, with changing her life. Her contact with the school came accidentally when her husband happened to hear the institute mentioned on a morning news program. He called to inquire about it. "I described Annie and all she'd been through before," Glenn recalls. "Dr. Webster asked her to come down. He would make a place for her." What followed were three weeks of live-in treatment in which patterns of communication were reprogrammed in long, slow sessions.

"My mother doesn't even remember when I first began stuttering," Annie says. "And there have been a lot of my friends who have known me all these years who said that was just a part of me." It was no accident that Annie gravitated toward music at Muskingum College, learning to play several instruments, including the organ. Stutterers tend to take up pursuits in which speaking is not vital.

"When I went out into that cruel world," Annie recalls, "my stuttering was the thing that was the hardest." Often, salesclerks simply assumed she was backward when she summoned up enough courage to speak. When she was alone at an airport, Annie would write notes to the ticket agents, who, meaning well, would write notes back, thinking she was deaf.

There was thoughtlessness and lack of understanding at all levels. Lyn recalls one trying incident at a congressional reception after her father's address to the joint session. "Three senators that I had seen on TV and whom I recognized came up to Mother and one of them asked her a question," she relates. "When she started stuttering, trying to get her answer out, all three turned around and walked away."

There were other, more serious trials associated with her disability. "One summer when we were stationed at Quantico and the children were young," Annie recalls, "Lyn stepped on a nail while walking barefoot." Responding to her child's crying, she tried to pull the nail out, not realizing that it was actually long and bent. Lyn's screams and the gushing hole in her foot quickly turned the accident into an emergency. Unable to speak on the phone, Annie had to frantically search out a neighbor to call the hospital.

"The telephone to a stutterer is like an invention of the devil," Glenn notes. "Not using the telephone in the modern era is really something most people don't appreciate. The only way Annie would use the phone was if I or one of the kids got the other party on the phone—even close friends—and said, 'Annie wants to talk to you.'"

Even today, Annie concedes that she will "always have" some difficulty speaking, but she answers her own phone now and bears in mind the three rules she learned in therapy: 1) Full breath, relaxed throat; 2) finish final sounds; and 3) keep the sound moving.

Why would John Glenn, the popular redhead everyone called Bud, fall in love with and marry a girl more than a year his senior who stuttered? Neither of them can really answer the question beyond saying that they grew so close so early that such things never mattered. "I never knew Annie at a time she did not stutter," Glenn says. "We grew up together. We were babies together." It is, Annie adds, a "very special" relationship with a man who seems never to be impatient with her, never hurries and always listens. Throughout Glenn's career in the military and in politics, Annie has always been with him as a loving constant. He feels literally incomplete without her.

From his perspective today, Glenn looks back fondly on summers in New Concord, times when the swimming hole at Crooked Creek was filled with laughing children and when pickup games of softball and "shinny"—a type of street hockey played with a crushed tin can and broom sticks—were plentiful. The numberless cinder alleys were perfect for marbles, and Glenn and his friends spent hours at the game until their parents called them home to dinner.

"That was great sport," remembers Carl Anker. "We'd do it in the alley, draw a big circle, maybe ten feet around, and everybody'd put some of their marbles in the middle. Then, when it was your turn, you'd take your 'shooter' and try to pop 'em out of there.'' The standard arsenal included glassies, aggies, steelies and commies—the latter referring to glazed clay marbles, so named because they were "common."

Even then, as a freckle-faced boy in knee pants, Glenn showed initiative. Glenn was anxious to become a Boy Scout, but there was no troop in his tiny hometown. Glenn formed his own unofficial troop, with his friend Lloyd White, and called it the Ohio Rangers. "We used the Scout handbook and everything," Glenn recalls. "We even put out our own little paper once a month, and went camping."

A small town in the summertime offered limitless opportunities for a boy, the most spectacular being the fireworks on the Fourth of July. Since it was coal mining country, people would augment their firecrackers and Roman candles with blasting caps and black powder and vie with one another to create the loudest bang. One resident recalls his father making a "super-bomb" out of a piece of pipe filled with powder and detonated with a blasting cap. It nearly toppled the outhouse. Other times, Glenn would amuse himself watching the blacksmith sweat and pound in his shop off Main Street, or trail after the ice man as he made his rounds, hauling the huge frozen cake from door to door, cracking off great chunks at each stop. Ice cream from the man who hawked it for a nickel a cone from his pony-drawn cart was a treat, but free shards of ice from the ice man were even better.

It was an era of innocent conviviality, not unlike that glorified in American musical comedy. There were ice-cream socials in the summertime, kite flying in the spring. Teenagers organized hayrides and cookouts. Even the Muskingum College campus was turned into an arena for youthful play. "When John and I were growing up," Annie recalls, "all of us would take our roller skates and skate all over the college quadrangle." The now polluted college lake, where John and Annie learned to swim, also made for a perfect winter ice-skating rink, where John would impress his girl with his aggressive hockey playing. After the first snowfall, everyone would bring sleds to a nearby sloping hill, and John made his first attempt to ski.

Annie was included in virtually all of John's activities except his exploits of derring-do, particularly "shooting" the old B&O railroad bridge. An early indication of Glenn's fascination with speed was his handling of the dilapidated 1929 roadster that his father gave him when he was 16. It was a battered old car with a canvas top that John always kept lowered. He painted it bright red and affectionately dubbed it "The Cruiser." Glenn and friends would pile into The Cruiser for rides into the country-side or to the ice-cream parlor.

Though it was hardly a fast vehicle, John would hurtle it over the railroad bridge at top speed. It was a risky endeavor, for the bridge was only a car wide in width and quite steep, making it impossible for Glenn to see oncoming traffic until he was over the crest. Once, local legend has it, Glenn took the bridge on the fly just as another car was coming over from the other side. The driver had to slam on the brakes and swerve out of the way to avoid colliding with John. Glenn is supposed to have stopped the practice after that. "John never did that with me," Annie recalls. "But he loved that car. He's had a number of convertibles since."

The area of New Concord and Cambridge was never agri-cultural. Its lush rolling hills, though scenic, were difficult to farm. Instead, the population relied heavily on industry to sur-vive. "This was primarily a steel town, a steel and coal town," recalls Robert Amos, former publisher of the *Cambridge Jeffer-sonian*, whose family had run the paper for nearly a century before selling it to a chain in 1976. "Muskingum County was the third-largest coal producer in the state at one time, with its rich deposits of soft coal." There were also two mills—one for sheet metal, the other for tin—that provided employment for many in the area. In addition, the region produced ornamental Cam-bridge Glass, popular in home decoration for a time in the twenties. It was marked by heavy ornamentation and sentimen-tal design and is now a collectors' item.

In the days before federal environmental regulations, young boys of John's age would fish in places like Wills Creek, snagging carp and catfish, rarely throwing anything back. The only time it was impossible to fish was when the sheet metal plant re-charged its pickling vats every three years. The pickling vats were filled with acid used to galvanize sheet steel, and when the old acid was dumped into the creek it turned the water a dull red and killed fish by the hundreds.

The period of postwar "normalcy" carried with it a wariness of European entanglements and outsiders in general, an attitude that increased the traditional insularity of New Concord. "In the south and midwest," notes author Alistair Cooke, "the chauvinist fever took a virulent form all too common among Anglo-Saxons and Celts when they are touched by panic: it bred a bigot army, led by the Klu Klux Klan, dedicated to the harassment, beating and occasional lynching of any 'foreigner' who could not claim Anglo-Saxon Christian origins, that is to say the Jew, the Roman Catholic and the Negro."

There was a Klan in New Concord, and its influence seems to have been not as minimal as some local people claim. The public record and recollections of residents show the hate group active over a period of several years in the New Concord, Cambridge and Zanesville area while Glenn was a boy. In nearly all cases, the KKK's actions appear to have centered around cross burnings on the hills outside of New Concord and Zanesville.

Glenn's memory of the incidents is vague, except that he recalls his parents' outrage over them. "Oh, yes. I think it only happened once and it created quite a stir," Glenn says. "I never saw them; but I remember hearing about them. It was over by Zanesville someplace. It wasn't at New Concord, not that I recall."

Glenn remembers his parents' discussing "how awful it was," and how the minister denounced the incident at the white clapboard church that he and his parents attended. No, he says, he was unaware of the Klan's ever giving money to his college. Mary Steele, who was in her twenties at the time of the Klan activity, does recall a cross burning just outside of New Concord. "I was scared to death," she says.

But it is Carl Anker's memories that are most vivid. "Oh, yeah, I remember them," he recalls. "They weren't from the south; they were local people. I remember that Cambridge had a KKK. You know the road from Cambridge, the first hill you go over, going west on 40. That's Tunnel Hill, named for the tunnel where the railroad goes through. On a summer's evening, maybe once every summer, there would be a cross burning up on that hill. I didn't know who they were, but they had this huge fiery cross, and they would burn that thing which was a warning, an implied threat to this small percentage of blacks that they had better not get out of line. On the question of whether there was a Negro problem, there wasn't as long as they stayed in what the whites regarded as their place."

The influence of the Klan diminished over the years, but at least one reminder of its presence is in Cambridge Hall, one of the oldest buildings on the Muskingum College campus. Several bronze plaques hang in the entranceway, commemorating those who contributed to the school. On one of the plaques, sandwiched in between "W. D. Archer" and "Dr. and Mrs. F. M. Mitchell" is listed "Guernsey County Klan No. 16."

As the years after World War I passed and America entered the thirties, the nation drifted unwittingly toward the worst economic catastrophe it had ever experienced. In New Concord, the effects of the Great Depression were deep. "We were like a lot of people at that time," Glenn recalls, though, in fact, both his parents and Annie's were among the better off in New Concord. Glenn's father was one of the town's more prosperous businessmen and Annie's father was a dentist.

"My dad had built up his business and he had done very well," Glenn recalls. "They had enough." But, he quickly adds, "enough in New Concord is not a huge amount of money," especially when people can no longer afford to spend money on their plumbing. Still, it is one measure of the comparative prosperity of the Glenns and the Castors that both families had electricity and indoor plumbing as well as telephones. First, these were party-line crank phones, then individual lines (The Glenns' number was 3562; the Castors' 3134). By contrast, Carl Anker recalls he didn't enjoy indoor plumbing until he was in high school.

Nevertheless, both families did feel the threat of collapse, the worst time coming when young Glenn overheard his parents wondering aloud whether their mortgage would be foreclosed. "That struck mild terror into an 11-year-old heart," Glenn recalls. In the end, however, the Glenn home was saved.

Although Herschel Glenn and his wife were among the few Democrats in New Concord, they were not especially strong fans of President Roosevelt. The number of Democrats in New Concord at the time is open to question, but ex-publisher Robert Amos points out that Muskingum County was the only county in Ohio to support Herbert Hoover for a second term. Asked if his parents had "strong" ties to FDR, Glenn hesitates and says: "They were in favor of most of the programs," indicating that not all of Roosevelt's policies were to their liking. "But people were hungry then," Glenn says finally.

It is clear that Glenn's parents believed in self-reliance and practiced their principle by planting rows of vegetables near the house as well as by the plumbing shop during the Depression. "Behind my dad's plumbing shop, there was a garden that had been there a long time," Glenn recalls. "Down one whole side of this garden was very rich soil. And there was a rhubarb bed along the side of this. Well, let me tell you, it was the biggest, best, huskiest rhubarb you ever saw, far more than we ever needed. So in the spring when the rhubarb came up, I'd go cut the stuff, we'd wash it, clean it, tie it up in little bundles and I'd put it in my wagon and cart it all over town and sell it for a quarter a bundle."

Glenn entered New Concord High School in 1935, beginning the personal metamorphosis that would distinguish him from his peers. He quickly emerged as a class leader and star athlete, a kid whose cooperation stopped short of apple polishing, but who got on well with his teachers. Among them was a tall, bearlike man with a balding head, shining eyes and high expectations for anyone he taught. Harford Steele, husband of Mary Steele, became principal of New Concord High and had John as a pupil in American government and math.

John was never less than an outstanding student. He achieved A's in every subject during his final semester, aided by an excellent associative memory that even today helps him recall phone numbers from decades past. But Steele gave Glenn something more than a glimpse at history or numbers; he offered the bright, redheaded teenager a look at the world outside, beyond New Concord. "Oh, yes, I'm sure of that," declares Mary Steele. "My husband always had a deep interest in current affairs."

Harford Steele, who is now retired, had made his students work for their grades, requiring them to keep notecards to review their lessons during free moments. Something in Glenn responded to Steele's no-nonsense, even gruff, manner and triggered a fascination with government, especially the workings of the U.S. Senate. In later years, when Glenn fulfilled a fantasy by running for the Senate, Harford Steele's early influence on the candidate was accurately cited. Today, in the lobby of New Concord's new high school there are three large color portraits. The two immediately facing the visitor are of John and Annie Glenn. But on a wall immediately to the right is an equally large portrait of Harford Steele. In a corner of the portrait, in white ink, is the inscription: "To Harford Steele— Good friend and the best teacher I ever had—John Glenn."

Glenn's high school career was exemplary. He was an honor student, was elected president of the junior class, was active in Hi-Y, and had the lead in the senior play, *Fanny and the Servant Problem.* As junior class president, Glenn helped plan the junior-senior prom and, characteristically, he chose an aviation theme for the gala. On the cover of the program was a picture of a Ford Trimotor and the legend "NCHS [for New Concord High School] Senior Airways. Dependable, Safe Service. Port NCHS to Port Brown Chapel [the chapel on the Muskingum campus]."

Glenn even managed to earn an A in home economics, a class he took as a lark with several other members of the high school football team. Mrs. Winifred Conley, whose wire-frame glasses and hair pulled into a tight bun make her the model of a small-town teacher, sought to take some of the mystery out of Swiss steak and potato soup. Her text for the course was of her own design and titled, "Come into the kitchen, gentlemen."

"We all thought it would be a big deal because they taught you to cook," Glenn recalls, laughing. "I think half the class was made up of the football team." No, he says, responding to the inevitable question, he did not take the class to meet girls. "They went into a great many things: home repair, elementary cooking and sewing on buttons. It was fun. In fact, the teacher claimed that we made better cakes and biscuits than the girls because we beat the batter harder." At the conclusion, John Glenn had once again conquered, earning a 95 as his final grade. "Whatever he did," Mary Steele remembers, "he put his whole self into it."

On the playing field, Glenn demonstrated the doggedness that would serve him both as an astronaut and a politician. Glenn was not a natural athlete. He was a chunky kid who carried a lot of his weight in his thighs. Though the only one in his high school class to letter in three sports—football, basketball and tennis—he was actually a slow runner. Glenn made up for his slowness with hustle, and helped lead the basketball team to the Muskingum County Championship before losing the state championship by nine points. During his senior year, he collected 47 points in an era of low-scoring games, leading the team in scoring one night. Years later, when one of his high school teammates, Johnny Hadden, learned that Glenn had set a transcontinental speed record in a jet, he laughed. "It would take John longer to run three laps around the football field than it took him to fly coast to coast."

All through high school, Glenn continued to date Annie; by now the two were widely regarded as a fairly serious item. Once when Annie came down with the mumps and was under quarantine the day of a school dance, John skipped the festivities and went to her house. He moved toward her bedroom window with his radio and placed the electric cord through a hole in the screen. The two sat together, John on the outside, Annie inside, the radio playing in the background.

John and Annie paired off regularly after class and could often be found walking by themselves alongside the college lake or joining friends for a sundae at the Ohio Valley Dairy on Main Street. The 1938 high school yearbook, featuring a list of improbables, speculated: "just imagine—Annie Castor without Johnnie." She, too, was an active honor-roll student in high school, though her interests centered largely on music. Annie was a member of the choral club, where her stutter magically vanished when she sang; she also played the trombone and the organ in the school orchestra.

The storybook quality of Glenn's life in New Concord is not inaccurate except for one painful problem which clouded most of his early years, and about which he still says little. It involves his adopted sister, Jean, who was a source of worry to his parents. Jean is the sister of Glenn who is no longer listed in his official biography and is mentioned only reluctantly by the family. Clara Glenn, who longed for a larger family, had lost one child before John, a son who died in infancy. Then when a second baby born after John died, she finally decided to adopt her next child, a baby girl, Jean.

Within a few years, it was clear that Jean was different from the other Glenns. It was a trying period, for Jean, although not retarded, could never match her brother in skill or grow close to him or his friends. "John and Clara Glenn did the very best they could for Jean," recalls Mary Steele, "and they certainly gave her a home that was full of love." Jean, an unhappy child, could not reciprocate. There were blowups at the dinner table and other episodes that left Glenn's parents feeling desolate and guilty.

Recalls Jim Bryen, a college classmate of Glenn's and now a journalism teacher at the local high school: "Jean was very different from the Glenns. I knew John's mother and father well, and they were very intelligent people. But Jean was a very average kind of person. It was difficult for Jean to try to measure up to them, though I don't know of two people who would try to get along with others more than Mr. and Mrs. Glenn. Jean kept to herself, really. She didn't try to be a part of the family circle."

Mrs. Glenn obviously wanted great things for her only son, expected them, and drew solace from his achievements. He was, despite Jean, basically an only child and exhibited all of the self-possession associated with first-born or eldest males. The presence of Jean may have increased John's desire to succeed, to give comfort to the parents he loved.

Ultimately, Jean married, had a son, was divorced and is now living by herself in the South. In the years after her divorce, the Glenns took in Jean's son and raised him as their own. A group photograph, taken while John was in Korea, shows Glenn's parents and Annie smiling in the foreground with the two happy Glenn children, David and Lyn, in the rear. Only Jean's son,

Billy, standing next to the other children and directly behind
Annie, is unsmiling. He is grasping Annie's left shoulder with
both hands, as if to hold onto the woman he came to regard as a
surrogate mother. Today, married and on his own, he has little
contact with his natural mother but remains close to John,
Annie and his cousins.

Before they died, Glenn's parents asked their son to take
care of Jean, a responsibility he takes very seriously. Glenn sends
Jean monthly support checks and speaks to her regularly on the
phone. But his memories of their shared childhood will always
be painful.

As John and Annie began their studies at Muskingum College in the fall of '39 the conflict in Europe that would lead to
World War II had begun. But for two years their lives were
filled with the camaraderie of the campus. Here, too, Glenn
showed traits of personality that would carry over in later life: a
desire to position himself with the "right" crowd; an infectious
enthusiasm that won over everyone; a stubbornness that threatened anger if he was pushed too far.

There were no fraternities at Muskingum, but social clubs
such as Stag, Alban and Mace were reasonable substitutes.
Glenn was a "townie" who did not live on campus, but he was
anxious to join a prestigious club. The Alban Club, in which
Carl Anker was rush chairman, tended to attract the studious,
student government types. "It was the campus leader-type
club," Anker recalls, noting that two of Muskingum's Albans,
Phil Caldwell and Chuck Pilliod, went on to become the chief
executive officers at Ford and Firestone. It was natural that
Alban would attract "Bud" Glenn, the friendly junior class
president. Anker approached John and invited him to the rush
party that Wednesday.

"No. I can't come that night," Glenn told Anker bluntly.

"Well, I thought nothing is that immovable; he should be a
little more flexible." Anker asked Glenn again. "He told me he
was supposed to be at Annie's place," Anker recalls. "I think it
was a regular Wednesday night date. Of course, we couldn't

move our party around. The rest of the week was taken up by the other clubs." Anker tried another tack: maybe this one time John could skip Annie's place. But Glenn repeated his refusal, now obviously annoyed.

"When I pushed him on this, that's when I saw a bit of this stubbornness come through. He seemed to have that quality that he could, if pushed, go on to something else. But of course, you didn't push people back then."

What Glenn did not tell Anker was that he had his eye on another club, the Stags. The Stags were mostly athletic, and young John, for all his slowness, fancied himself a potential football hero. In addition, the Stags were the smoother and more gentlemanly of the campus jocks—Mace men tended to be more raucous—and were generally spoken of as "the lookers and the dressers."

"John was always a little too small for college football," Anker recalls, "but he always wanted to be around those guys." Glenn was welcomed into the Stags and pretty soon could be seen around campus in natty clothes of the period: wide-lapeled tweed sportcoats that set off striped shirts with starched high collars. "Glenn always was a neat dresser," Anker recalls. "In fact, John's overall image, at least the way I saw him, was of a Boy Scout working on his next merit badge. He was the bright-eyed, clean-cut kid that seemed to have a lot of energy and could do whatever was required of him to get to the next step."

But for all of Glenn's efforts, he never made it as a football star. He played on the freshman team and finally moved up to the varsity, under coach Stu Holcomb, who later won fame at Purdue. But in the end, Anker was right: Glenn was just too small. If Glenn was crushed by failure to win athletic fame, he did not show it. Most afternoons after class, he and Annie could be found at the Ohio Valley Dairy, where Annie would always order a dish of chocolate ice cream with marshmallows and John would exuberantly devour a hot fudge sundae. It was usually a loud, laughing group at the Dairy, a big place with large booths and a jukebox that ceaselessly played the big band hits of the day.

"One thing I'll always remember," says Jim Bryen, "was that one of John's best friends was Dane 'Pop' Handschy, a large fellow. John used to get a kick out of getting Dane excited or angry." For all Pop Handschy's imposing size, the most he would say when riled was 'heavens!' and John would say almost anything to get Handschy to that point. "Then John would say, 'Dane—go heavens!' and he would just collapse and laugh," Bryen recalls.

Someone would feed the jukebox. Each play was a nickel, the same price as the Cokes. The sundaes, big tubs of homemade ice cream, were a dime, unless they came with a topping, in which case they were fifteen cents. Banana splits, even today remembered as works of art, were a quarter. The "OVD" actually was a dairy, or at least the retail outlet for a cooperative of dairy farms around the area. If one walked out the front door and circled to the back, one could see cows grazing lazily in the afternoon sun, readying themselves for their next milking. Today, the dairy is gone, replaced by an industrial supply store.

For all the horseplay at the OVD, life in the college town, especially for the students, remained comparatively cloistered. Even in the late thirties, cigarette smoking was banned, a restriction that surprised Jim Bryen when a faculty member spied him smoking a cigarette off campus one day. Bryen was suspended. He switched to a pipe, which for some reason the faculty condoned. In addition, the evening curfew on female students was strictly enforced, and out-of-town students were forbidden to drive."Those of us who lived in the dorms were captives," remembers Bryen with a smile. "It was tougher on the girls. The girls had to be in by ten during the week, eleven on weekends and twelve if there was a big dance. It didn't matter for us. They figured that if the girls had to be in at a certain time, automatically we would be too."

The social event of the spring was the Sejuna, the Senior-Junior Annual Dance. Students participated in the planning of the formal affair, but they were blocked by the administration when they attempted to book a black band. "I was on the committee to get the band," Bryen recalls, "and I was a jazz nut. At that time, Cootie Williams had just left Duke Ellington—he was a trumpet player, one of the Ellington greats—and formed his own band." Bryen knew of a booking agent who handled Williams and learned he could get the band for only $400. "I went to the administration and said: 'This is the band I want and this is the promoter who will handle it and this is the cost.' They listened and said 'No.' We weren't allowed to because it was a colored band."

In fairness to Muskingum College, Bryen says it may have been the first time the administration had to confront the question of allowing a black band on the all-white campus. He notes that the next year, by the time both he and John had left for the service, the college did allow another well-known black jazz band, headed by King Kellogg, to play at the Sejuna.

Racial attitudes seemed to die hard in New Concord but no more so than elsewhere in the country. Ironically, in the twenties, Muskingum had admitted three black students, Ethiopian princes sent by crown prince Ras Tafari, later to rule as Emperor Haile Selassie. The prince had sent the members of his royal household to Muskingum because of what was described as "the good auspices of a friend of Muskingum in the United Presbyterian mission in Ethiopia."

In later years, Muskingum would remain an almost all-white, all-Protestant school. A brief attempt to "assist the cause of racial justice" in 1966 accounted for the admission of 25 black transfer students from outside the area. Disenchanted and isolated, the students demanded—and received—segregated housing and a small black studies program. But in five years' time, the number of blacks on campus had once again dropped to a handful.

By their second year at Muskingum, John and Annie knew they were going to be married. Both sets of parents happily embraced the idea. John's parents looked forward to John's graduation. They hoped he would join his father in the plumbing business and forget about flying. But world events and the love of flying had already captured their son.

In 1939, the Nazi-Soviet nonaggression pact freed Germany to attack Poland. Britain and France, which had guaranteed Polish independence, declared war on Germany, and within months, Russia seized East Poland and took the Baltic states.

The Nazi Blitzkrieg then engulfed Denmark, Norway and the low countries and by 1940 had toppled France. The rumblings of the conflict were felt even on the campus of Glenn's tiny college.

"Resolved: That the United States should follow a policy of strict military and economic neutrality toward all nations outside the Western Hemisphere engaged in armed international or civil conflict." This was the thesis the Muskingum College debating society addressed in 1940. One of the Greek letter clubs, Pi Gamma Mu, had chosen as its project a study of "fanatical Hitler, cautious Mussolini, crude Stalin, war-torn China and valiant little Finland."

For Glenn, the debating was superficial. Convinced that the United States would one day be drawn into war, he was among the first to volunteer for civilian pilot training at the airport in nearby New Philadelphia. As had happened in the past, Glenn had to overcome a serious obstacle to reach his goal. This time it was his father.

"We were sick when he took up aviation," Herschel Glenn recalled. Though the elder Glenn used to joke about his World War I experiences—saying his hearing aid was the only decoration he brought back from overseas—he had been sobered by the horrors of war. Both he and his wife were distraught over the prospect that their son's love of the sky would take him into dangerous aerial combat. "It was like taking him out and burying him," his father said.

Another obstacle for Glenn was less formidable, but equally real: He was kicked out of the program to make room for a girl. Carl Anker, another fledgling pilot, recalls the incident. "They could only take ten flyers at a time, and we had 11 people in the class. So they kicked John out because he was an underclassman and could take it the following year. We had one girl in the class, and I thought it was terribly unfair to John." They had only one plane to train in, Anker recalls, "a little taildragger, a Taylorcraft single-engine trainer that had almost no equipment."

Glenn waited a year, then went through the regimen, finding the exhilaration of flight all he had hoped it would be. After 65 hours of flying time, including 30 hours' solo, he received his private pilot's license on July 1, 1941. Five months and six days later, the Japanese attacked Pearl Harbor, devastating the U.S. fleet, leaving 2,300 dead and plunging the United States into World War II. Immediately, John Glenn dropped out of college and, with his parents tearful blessing and Annie's full support, enlisted in the Navy Air Corps and began pilot training at Corpus Christi, Texas.

He had left behind New Concord and was about to begin one of the most exciting decades of his life.

4

---◆---

THE WAR YEARS:
WORLD WAR II AND KOREA

He did not set out to be a hero, nor even plan to be a career Marine. But by the time World War II and Korea had ended, John Glenn was known as one of the best combat pilots the Marines ever produced, a holder of five Distinguished Flying Crosses "for heroism while participating in aerial fights," as well as a dozen-and-a-half Air Medals. He began World War II as an aviation cadet and was a captain at its conclusion. Glenn's heralded bravado during both wars was tempered by deliberateness; he was able to make the successful completion of the most hellish mission—whether dive bombing runs in the Marshall Islands or dogfights with MiGs along the Yalu River in Korea—seem inevitable.

Yet for all his boldness, Glenn's sensitive, even emotional, side was often close to the surface, his war colleagues remember. On Glenn's first combat mission overseas, a close friend was literally shot out from under him. When he returned to base, Glenn cried unashamedly, shaken by how personal the war had suddenly become. Even as a 21-year-old cadet, Glenn displayed maturity in a letter to the mother of a comrade killed during flight training. "I want to let you know," Glenn said to the mother of the 19-year-old cadet, Anderson Stock, "that there are those of us here who have not forgotten Andy and are waiting for the day when we can even up the score a little for those who started this war.

"I know I am very crude in trying to put into words what I feel," Glenn went on, "but Andy gave everything for his country just as though it had been on a battlefield, and we'll always remember him as a true friend and comrade."

As a politician and a presidential candidate, Glenn is regularly exposed to criticism. But those who served with him in war portray him as a genuine hero. Comedian Woody Woodbury, who flew with Glenn in Korea, puts it simply: "If there was ever combat again, I sure as hell would go with John, because he's a cool-headed son of a bitch who cares the world for his men—a smart, cool, calculating, thinking type of a guy you have to have respect for."

John Giraudo, a retired Air Force major general, remembers Glenn's prophetic warning to him in Korea about "flak traps"—trucks posing as enticing targets that were actually rolling anti-aircraft platforms. In 1953, Giraudo was shot down by a flak trap in Korea while flying alongside Glenn. Glenn stayed on the scene, hovering over Giraudo, trying futilely to summon rescue helicopters before his comrade was taken prisoner. Realizing that his fuel was now nearly gone, Glenn used his remaining gas to soar skyward for maximum altitude, then glided the hundred miles back to his base, making the only "dead stick" landing of his career.

Immediately, Glenn took off in another jet to rescue Giraudo, but he was too late. Giraudo had already been shot through the shoulder and taken prisoner by the Communists. Months later, Glenn flew to the site of the Korean War prisoner exchange to greet Giraudo when he was set free in Operation Big Switch.

The John Glenn of 1943 was an innocent about war and death, seeing some glamour in the act. In the last nine days of the Korean War, Glenn downed three MiGs, marveling at "how the bullets sparkle when they hit a plane." In a letter after the first confirmed kill, Glenn proudly told his wife: "Really spread that plane out thin. Nothing left." Today, 40 years later, he sees it somewhat differently but feels no remorse at having killed in battle. "In a war situation, you go ahead and do it, and I didn't have any qualms about that. Did I like it? Certainly not. War isn't very pleasant, no matter how you cut it. But it's kill or be killed. You go into combat with as much intensity as you can and try to do the job that has to be done."

In the beginning, Bud Glenn had no interest in a military career. Like millions of other young men in 1942, all he wanted to do was serve his wartime hitch and come home. Glenn began flight training that year at the Corpus Christi naval air station as a beefy 21-year-old whose patriotism was expressed in an ache for adventure and flying. But his dream was actually a postwar one: to become an airline pilot and steer the big Pan American Clippers to exotic places around the world. It was a dream the young Glenn would soon share with a rangy boy from Texas who mirrored Glenn's love of air and speed. Together, John Glenn of New Concord and Tom Miller, from the unlikely sounding town of George West, Texas, nurtured their hopes of becoming commercial pilots.

Eventually, both men surrendered these plans to the Marine Corps. In the process, Miller, now retired as a Marine lieutenant general and former head of Marine Aviation, came to be one of John Glenn's closest friends, one who can talk about him dispassionately and critically, but always with affection.

Miller and Glenn today seem worlds apart in political ideology: Glenn is a liberal Democrat, while Miller, a typical military career officer, tends to be conservative, defending a strong foreign policy and a traditional domestic stance. But despite the apparent differences, the two men are still inseparable. "I'm about the closest thing to a brother John has," Miller says in his soft Texas drawl.

In the paradox of John Glenn—the small-town superpatriotic American hero contrasted with the liberal Democrat running for president—Tom Miller figures uniquely. He either represents the "old Glenn," the traditionalist remembered by his friends in New Concord but whom they fear no longer exists; or he reflects the more conservative Glenn, hidden from the public through the necessities of liberal Democratic party fashion.

When Glenn and Miller arrived in Corpus Christi, Texas, in 1942, it was a sleepy town unprepared for the influx of sailors and would-be naval aviators. With the opening of the naval air station, some 25,000 high-spirited young men flooded into the area.

The two did not fit the conventional mold. "John and I kind of hit it off because we were raised pretty much the same," recalled Miller as he thumbed through a collection of nostalgic photographs. "He came from a small town and so did I. We went to church together, and our values in life were pretty much the same." Neither smoked or drank and both had little interest in wartime carousing. In any case, no overnight passes were extended to the fledgling aviators in the two dozen E-shaped barracks on base. "They let us out Saturday evenings," Miller recalls, "but we had to be back by midnight. Then on Sunday afternoon, if we didn't have a flight scheduled, we had liberty in the afternoon until 10:00 P.M. John and I would go into town, more or less to sightsee. We'd watch high school basketball and football."

Neither Miller nor Glenn womanized in Corpus Christi, but few shared their restraint. "I remember seeing it in the paper that in the first year that the Navy was in Corpus Christi, some 400 Corpus Christi high school girls turned up pregnant," Miller declares.

"Of course, after that, the people of Corpus Christi just slammed the doors shut to all of us, and it was very difficult to get dates with a real nice girl. But the churches set up some places, and that's where John and I went a couple of times. Places like the Union Community Center. Parents brought nice girls there, and there were numerous chaperones all over and a dance floor and a nickelodeon. I remember at the end of the evening the mothers and the fathers were there in their cars to pick up those dollies. They weren't going to let them out of sight."

Miller recalls that John had little interest in meeting girls in Corpus Christi. "It was obvious to me John was already committed to Annie, and he really didn't have much interest in any females. Not that he didn't go out and enjoy some social relaxation." Still, Miller cannot recall his wartime comrade even dancing with any of the "nice girls" at the community center during those warm summer nights.

The flight training absorbed most of their time. Glenn's first taste of military flying was in the old PBY "flying boats"—ponderous multi-engine seaplanes. "I went through advanced training in the PBYs," Glenn recalls. "I was out making landings and doing gunnery and navigation, bouncing around Corpus Christi bay. Then, of course, when there was a sub alert, they'd haul us out in the middle of the night to look for them."

The training suited both Glenn and Miller because of the similarity of the PBYs to civilian planes they hoped to fly after the war. "Everybody was interested in their future," Miller maintains. "And even though nobody knew how long the war was going to last, and even though I was only twenty and John twenty-one-and-a-half, we wanted to prepare ourselves for the time the war would be over."

It was obvious that the two young cadets—the carrot top from Ohio and the 6'2" Texan—loved to fly. Both young men, caught up in the fervor of war, thought their greatest contribution would be as fighter pilots, but they realized that experience flying fighters would be less valuable in civilian life. "John and I talked about this considerably," Miller says, "trying to figure out which was the best way to go." Finally, practicality prevailed. "We decided that since the most expensive training, if you had to buy it as a civilian, was in multi-engine aircraft, the best thing to select was the flying boats. And that's what we did."

The P-boats, as they were called, were ideal for submarine spotting because they could fly so close to the water. Consequently, over-water navigational flights in the Gulf of Mexico doubled as submarine patrols against Nazi U-boats. "I chased one all night long," remembers Miller, "and dropped a couple of depth charges. But we never saw any results." Glenn says that he never even saw a sub, much less attacked one.

The first months of training confronted eager young Glenn with the inevitable drudgery of military routine. It also gave him the first chance to use a skill that he later developed into an advanced art: getting around military bureaucracy to make things happen for him. In his 23-year military career, Glenn admits that he often pulled the right strings to get what he wanted. "It was called sniveling," Miller recalls, "but it was a good thing. To 'scrounge' or 'snivel' meant making your own opportunity. That's a quality that we consider in the Marine Corps to be top notch: knowing whose string to pull and who to get to help you. If you want something bad enough, you work like hell to ease your foot in the door. It's pretty much the way John got in the space program."

Today, Glenn is noticeably ambivalent about "sniveling." The problem is the difference between the military and civilian definitions of the usually pejorative term. Tom Miller uses the word to describe a legitimate but calculated attempt to get interesting assignments and duty stations. But having developed a politician's sensitivity, Glenn now shies away from the word.

The dictionary defines "sniveling" as the actions of a weak, whining individual. This is clearly not what Miller means when he explains how he and Glenn used their brains not to goof off, but to get more duty, particularly situations where they could show off their skill and bravado to their superiors. Just as clearly, Glenn the politician realizes that most people will negatively react to boasts that he is a "sniveler."

Twenty years before the space program, Glenn was new at the game of making his own luck. Occasionally, he even found himself in trouble with his superiors because of his restless ambition. But most times, Glenn and Miller found it easy to move ahead of their peers, discovering that most people did not share their intensity.

"For example," Miller recalls, "during our P-boat training, we made friends with the yeoman, the administrator who worked with the flight officers who scheduled the P-boat instructors." Normally, an instructor would take up three students for six hours at a time, giving each student two hours at the controls. The remainder of the day would be spent in ground school. But an instructor would sometimes be unable to take his class up and the cadets were forced, as Miller puts it, to "just sit on the deck."

"Well, when this happened to us, we went to the yeoman

and found there was always some cadet who had a cold who couldn't fly that day. Well, after a while, we had this yeoman pretty well trained that whenever he had an extra slot, to let us know. We'd take our books and sit on the floor outside the yeoman's office. He'd come out and say 'Okay, I got a spot for one of you,' and we'd grab it. We wound up getting through the P-boat training a hell of a lot faster that way.

"Why did we do it?" Miller goes on. "We did it because we liked to fly. Who wants to sit on his butt? It was purely the individual pleasure of flying and of course getting on with the war. There was no fear of going to war back then. It was more like 'just gimme that Jap' or 'gimme that German.' It was a kind of attitude that's hard for people to recognize today."

For all their eagerness, neither man initially intended to make the service a career. John Glenn's life in the military, and then in space, began inadvertently one day after lunch when Glenn and Miller returned to their barracks to find a notice posted on the bulletin board. "The following personnel," the notice read, "have a sufficiently high grade in ground training and in flight school to be accepted for a commission in the Marine Corps. All those interested report down to the cadet rec center at 1900 hours." Near the top of the list were the names John H. Glenn, Jr., and Thomas H. Miller.

Glenn and Miller dismissed the idea of a Marine career but went along to the meeting as a lark. "We finally decided to go down to the rec center and hear what kind of story they'd tell, with no thought that we'd go into the Marine Corps," Miller says. At the rec center, a young Marine captain with light blond hair, looking almost as youthful as the fliers in the audience, yet already a veteran of heavy action in the South Pacific, was delivering the service sales pitch. "It was the usual Marine stuff," recalls Miller with an avuncular laugh. "Always pattin' himself on the back, saying 'we're the best and if you wanna be the best you ought to come to the Marines.'"

Then suddenly the captain challenged the young men. "'We don't think you're good enough to be one of us.'"

"Well with John, that was just like waving a red flag in front of a bull," Miller says. "If there's anything you want to get John to do, you wave a red flag in front of him and challenge him, because John just lives on individual challenge and then perfection. They passed out the blanks and we signed up.''

"Miss Anna Margaret Castor,'' the yellowing newspaper clipping begins, "daughter of Dr. and Mrs. Homer Castor of New Concord, and Lieut. John H. Glenn Jr., son of Mr. and Mrs. John H. Glenn, also of New Concord, were married this afternoon.'' Following regulations to the letter, Glenn had waited until the end of his flight training to marry his childhood sweetheart on April 6, 1943.

The Glenns' nuptials were comparatively informal. Their wedding portrait shows Annie in a frilly white dress with a rose hat sitting high on her head in the fashion of the forties. She is gazing to the right, smiling in three-quarter profile, with her beaming husband hovering over her from behind. He is in Marine uniform, a Sam Browne belt across his chest, his new aviator's wings proudly displayed on the left breast of his blue tunic. Annie's younger sister, Jane, was her only attendant during the wedding; Glenn's boyhood friend Lloyd White was best man. "A small reception was held at the bride's home following the wedding,'' the newsclip continues, "and there the decorations were all of yellow and white, the flowers being attractively arranged.A wedding cake occupied a prominent place in the decorations.''

It was the beginning of an uncommonly strong marriage, one that has survived the prolonged separations of two wars, seemingly endless public scrutiny and the several defeats of a second career in politics. They had grown up together in the friendly confines of New Concord, which became a second home for Annie whenever John had to move on, as he did shortly after their marriage.

After graduation as lieutenants, Glenn and Miller were ordered to Cherry Point, North Carolina. "We had heard that they had the new Havoc bomber down there,'' Miller recalls, "a low-altitude, two-engine plane that attacked ground targets.'' But when they got there, all Glenn and Miller found were a lot of other second lieutenants itching for a chance to fly. And no

Havocs. "We were pretty upset and frustrated," say Miller.

But it was only the first of several disappointments the two anxious fliers would endure before seeing action. Over the next year, Glenn and Miller traveled cross-country in search of fighter planes, thwarted each time by the seeming perversity of the military bureaucracy. At Cherry Point, Miller recalls, "there were something like 150 second lieutenants reporting in, and there was no way anybody was going to get any flight time. They'd have us do higher math then for want of anything better to do, they'd have us run just to see how long it'd take us to run 15 miles. John and I called it a labor camp."

Finally, Marine headquarters, seeing the bottleneck at Cherry Point, passed the word that the new crop of pilots could put in for any duty they wanted. By now Glenn had forgotten about the awkward PBYs, and was caught up in the youthful interest of one-on-one combat. Glenn and Miller immediately requested fighter pilot training, hoping for a chance to fly the F4U Corsair, which was the Navy's most advanced and fastest fighter plane.

The prospect of flying fighters was made more tantalizing by the fact that a new squadron of Corsairs had just been stationed at Cherry Point. "We thought we'd just walk across the field to that squadron," Miller recounts. But again they were disappointed. No sooner had they signed up for their new assignment than they were transferred 3,000 miles away to Camp Kearney, California. They were to fly lumbering transport planes.

Once again, the two young Marines found more pilots than airplanes, a situation that threatened to pinch them financially. "We had to fly four hours a month to get flight pay," Miller remembers, "but even with that our pay was only about $270 a month and it was pretty hard to keep eating regularly on that kind of money, especially with a wife to support." By this time, Miller too had gotten married.

The answer to their prayers was just a few hundred yards away on the same airfield. There sat a fighter squadron of F4F Wildcats. The two fliers literally drooled over the sleek airplanes; although no match for the Corsairs, they were fighters.

This time Glenn had a plan. "John's plan was for us to get to know the skipper of this fighter squadron and see what we could do to get transferred to his outfit," Miller recalls. Miller and Glenn finally decided to waylay the skipper in the mess hall, hoping to win him over with their youthful enthusiasm. "The C.O. was a major," Miller remembers, "and he looked so young himself, kind of a rosy-cheeked guy with a fabulous personality." The skipper was Major J.P. (Pete) Haines. Their first meeting would mark the beginning of a friendship that lasted for decades until Haines's death in the early sixties from Hodgkin's disease.

Haines was friendly, but he told the two young pilots that the rules had to be observed. Despite the admonition, Glenn persisted—and at first failed—providing a lesson in how best to snivel that he never forgot. Glenn successfully got Major Haines to say yes, but only on the condition that Glenn could get through the Marine red tape and get the transfer approved. The plan was to get the approval of the major who headed the transport squadron, then take the matter up with the group commander, a lieutenant colonel responsible for all the squadrons on the base.

"I was rather ignorant of the ways of the military back then," Glenn confesses, "even though I had gotten my bars on my shoulder by that time." "Now you've got to remember," Miller adds, "that anytime John gets his sights set on something, it's Katy-bar-the-door. But there was a certain bit of military protocol that had to be observed. I knew this but I'm not sure John ever did get it, or really cared about it."

Miller obediently went to Major Zoney, the C.O. of the transport squadron, who gave him approval to transfer to Haines's unit. Then he dutifully marched over to the lieutenant colonel to tell him about it. Arriving at the group commander's office, Miller encountered Glenn. Miller assumed Glenn had been through the same routine, and both he and Glenn convinced the colonel to approve the switch.

Everything seemed in order except for one thing. "John had never been to see Major Zoney as I had," Miller explains ruefully. "They were all set to cut our new orders, but then it came to the attention of Zoney that Glenn had gone over his head. Zoney simply called up the colonel and got the whole damn thing squashed." It took a demonstration of uncharacteristic humility from Glenn to get Zoney to relent.

Finally, after months of effort, Miller and Glenn were transferred to the fighter squadron. One week later they were transferred again. This time, the trip—90 miles west to El Centro, California—would be the jumping-off point for Glenn's first overseas combat assignment, in the Marshall Islands of the South Pacific.

El Centro Air Station was like walking into an inferno. "It was so hot that when we stepped off the plane we thought the heat had to be coming from one of the plane's engines," Miller relates. "But it wasn't. It was just 115 in the shade." The summer heat was so intense that training flights were extended round the clock, to prevent blowouts of airplane tires when the planes came in to land on the baking runway. It was at El Centro that Miller and Glenn finally got their first experience in fighter planes, on F4F Wildcats.

Later, in September 1943, on what Glenn considers one of the greatest days of his life, they graduated to the storied Corsairs that Glenn would pilot with devastating effect during diving bombing missions against Japanese supply bases in the Marshalls. The Corsairs that Glenn first flew at El Centro were the so-called birdcage kind. These earliest versions of the propeller-driven fighter, the F4U/1, had a domed canopy with so many structural members that, in the words of one pilot at the time, "it made you feel like you were in jail."

The Corsair was difficult to fly. A huge plane with massive engines, it taxed a young pilot like Glenn because of its peculiar, even hazardous, characteristics. "If you stalled it on landing," Miller recalls, "and the wheels weren't already on the ground, the left wing would always go hard down." This forced pilots to land the Corsair wheels first, which was out of character for naval aviators. Glenn had been taught to hit the ground tail first, the routine way for aircraft carrier landing, in which the plane's tail hook latches onto a cable strung across the deck.

At El Centro, Glenn would have a glimpse of his future in the person of Charles Lindbergh, to whom he would be compared after his orbital flight in space. In 1943, Glenn, an anonymous young pilot, actually met the world-famous aviator when he made a brief stop at the air station. The "Lone Eagle," who had conquered the Atlantic in the *Spirit of St. Louis* some 16 years earlier, was serving the military as an advisor and had also accompanied American pilots on combat missions in the Pacific.

One afternoon in the fall of '43, Lindbergh flew into El Centro in one of the new versions of the Corsair, without the "birdcage" dome. Glenn stood gape-mouthed as he stared at the plane and its legendary pilot. Glenn and Miller walked out to meet the plane. As they approached Lindbergh, the Marine major he was talking to introduced the brash young fliers. Glenn immediately told Lindbergh how much he had admired him from the time he could first read. Glenn's boyhood bedroom at New Concord, filled with balsa wood airplane models, contained numerous books about Lindbergh's solo flight across the Atlantic in 1927. For all the deferential admiration, however, Glenn was not content to shake hands and gawk.

"Colonel Lindbergh," Glenn asked, "is there any chance of us getting to fly that plane?"

To their surprise, Lindbergh grinned his agreement. "Sure, I'd be glad to let you fly her," he said. Today, Glenn remembers Lindbergh as a "quiet individual who gave us a lot of information about the new specifications of the Corsair." He adds that Lindbergh, who lived to see Glenn's space flight in 1962, wired his congratulations, repaying over a span of 35 years the admiration Glenn felt for the first man to fly solo across the Atlantic.

Glenn's orders to report overseas finally came in February 1944, barely ten months after his marriage to Annie. Glenn, Miller and the rest of Marine Fighter Squadron 155—as well as 4,000 other Marines from Camp Pendleton—set sail for Hawaii on a jammed cargo ship, the *Santa Monica*. It was a rough crossing for Glenn, who was very susceptible to nausea, a fact his fellow Marines were soon apprised of.

"It was literally an old banana boat," Glenn recalls. "It had plied someplace between San Francisco and South America. Only now instead of big holds they had put in decks with bunks. We went to Hawaii on that thing, bouncing around with everybody seasick. At least I was seasick. I spent most the trip up on deck. I'd get a blanket and just slept there because down below it was steamy, hot and sweaty. The bunks were about 18 inches apart."

"It took about five days to Hawaii," Miller remembers, "and John was looking pretty white. The rolling and pitching of this old mud scow didn't sit too well with hardly anybody, but it obviously had John right on the verge." One day during the crossing, while standing in a long chowline, a fellow Marine told the wretched-looking Glenn he would be fine as soon as he wolfed down some "nice greasy spam." Glenn was able to make it up to the deck and to the ship's rail just in time.

Soon after Glenn was dispatched on a three-month tour to the island of Midway to help protect the submarine base, which was crucial to Allied efforts in the Pacific. Planes were airborne at dawn and dusk, the prime times for attack by the Japanese. Four fighters were always on "strip alert" halfway down the runway so they could take off in either direction. Crews of these planes waited in the ready room, wearing flight gear and set to scramble as soon as the alert siren sounded. A buzzer phone signaled whether two or four planes were to be airborne. If only two planes were to scramble, the pilots had an informal rule that the first two airplanes in the air were given the mission.

"We all devised certain techniques to be first," Miller recalls. "We would bound into the cockpit and hit the starters. The skipper had to clamp down on us because there were one or two times—and I'm sure John did it too—where we took off without even our safety belt hooked." The enthusiasm of the group was reflected in its nickname—Ready Teddy—and in the emblem painted on each of the Corsairs, a teddy bear in flight gear scrambling toward his plane. The name, as well as the prototype sketch of the scrambling teddy bear, came from Glenn.

The war in the Pacific was being won at terrible cost in places like Tarawa and Kwajalein, and even years after the invasion the stench of death filled the air. "I can remember," Glenn says grimly, "walking around on the beach on Tarawa and seeing what looked like pieces of petrified flesh. Starting up my engines once, I saw the exhaust stir up skulls and bones out of the sand."

Such heavy American losses influenced the decision to bypass the other atolls in the Marshalls. Instead, it was decided to neutralize the Japanese-held islands by massive bombing. Glenn's squadron was catapulted off the deck of an aircraft carrier and landed at Majuro atoll, the storage area for a huge fleet of replacement aircraft and a prime target for enemy attack. It was at Majuro that Glenn completed his first combat mission and in the space of a few seconds suffered the most devastating personal loss of his combat career.

The fighting assignment drawn by Glenn was not as glamorous as the one-on-one combat he would engage in later in Korea. But precision dive bombing required a particular skill and, if done correctly, a matador's bravado. Skipper Pete Haines described what it took to be a dive bomber.

"With a Corsair, you drop the wheels and they act as dive brakes so that you hit terminal velocity at around 400 miles per hour in a vertical position, and you can trim your plane so that it flies practically hands-off. Then your flight path is the gunbarrel and you can get pinpoint accuracy. John would truly disdain outfits that would try to bomb wheels-up in fighter swoops with increased speeds that diminished their accuracy."

On July 10, 1944, Glenn was ordered to make a bombing run on the Japanese island of Maloelap. The four man group consisted of Glenn and Miller, the two leaders, Miller's wingman, Edward "Tyrone" Powers and Glenn's wingman, a young lieutenant from Harrisburg, Pennsylvania, Monte Goodman.

"We trained together for a year or so, and Monte Goodman was one of our closest friends," Glenn relates. "We had flown together all the time." Glenn remembers Goodman as an outgoing kid who loved Frank Sinatra, and as the high-spirited accomplice who joined him one night for a joyride on a huge grader the Seabees were using to build a new runway at Midway. The episode prompted a chewing out from Pete Haines.

"Monte was a terrific kid," Miller says, "a Jewish boy who was full of life. His family had a big furniture store in Harrisburg. He was a pretty good singer too, and he'd take a broomstick and emulate Sinatra, running his hand up and down the thing."

The bombing mission went off seemingly without a hitch. "We were all making our dives," Miller says, "and I was just off to the left. Neither John nor I saw anything happen to Monte because at a time like that you're concentrating on diving at your target. You generally dived together and as rapidly as possible so that the Japanese couldn't concentrate on one guy; they'd have to split up as to who they were shooting at. I remember we were diving to the east. We had come over and had rolled in and we were really going like hell, about 400 to 450 miles an hour. The old Corsair really begins to sing when the speed gets that high."

Says Glenn about that day in 1944, his voice growing softer: "We made our run and there was some anti-aircraft fire, and when we joined up off the island at the rendezvous point Monte wasn't there."

"Who was that went in the water?" someone called over the radio. "We immediately looked for our own wingman," Miller recalls, "and John looked like he couldn't find Monte so he finally opened up on the radio and called him.

"'Red 2, are you aboard? Red 2—where are you?'"

There was no answer.

"We went back in toward the island," Glenn recalls, "and all we could see was an oil slick. That's all we ever found."

Suddenly over the blue Pacific on the early morning of July 10, 1944, John Glenn found, as he says, that "warmaking got very personal very fast."

"That was really a jolt to John," says Miller. "I don't know if I've ever seen anything that touched him more. I guess John felt a certain amount of responsibility for his own wingman. Of course, there wasn't anything John could have done about it, but it really hit John hard."

Later, as word of the popular pilot's death spread, a pall seemed to fall over Marine Squadron 155. "It lasted two or three days," Miller recalls. "You'd sit around and not talk much and kind of draw into your own inner shell and fight the problem of sorrow within yourself. Because in a squadron like that, it's very important not to get the whole squadron any more upset than necessary; otherwise, it can affect the whole unit." He recalled an earlier incident, in which two men were killed during a fiery runway mishap. "You go through that kind of trauma. I don't say you get hardened to it, but you kind of learn how to swallow and take it. You can't change fate."

The Pacific war ended on August 14, 1945, with Glenn facing a major decision. From his first days in the Marine Corps he had hoped his flying experience would equip him to become an airline pilot. In New Concord, Glenn's father hoped his son would return to take over the plumbing business. Now a third option loomed: to make the Marine Corps a career. There was really little contest.

Pete Haines paid Glenn the ultimate accolade. In a do or die situation, when there was but one chance to succeed, Haines insisted he would always choose John Glenn. "When you have something to do where you can't miss," Haines declared, "John is the one you select. If John were digging a ditch or if he were president, he would do the job."

In 1945, Glenn accepted the Marine Corps' offer to make the service his career. The years between World War II and Korea were formative ones for the young Marine captain. Glenn was involved in intensive flying, first at Maryland's Patuxent Naval Air Station, later at El Toro, California, where he served as operations officer. But his most interesting duty came the following year, when he was dispatched to Nationalist China to serve on patrol duty in the northern provinces. His unit, Marine Squadron 218, was originally based in Peking and later in Tsingtao.

In 1947, as the civil war in China raged between Mao Tse-tung and Chiang Kai-shek, Glenn's unit was tranferred to Okinawa, awaiting reshipment to a permanent base in Guam. He was only there a few weeks when his second child, Carolyn (Lyn), was born. The Glenn's first child, David, had been born in 1945. The first birth was easy, but this time Annie did not fare as well and nearly died.

At first, the birth went without incident. Lyn was born a healthy child in an uncomplicated delivery on March 15, 1947, in the hospital at Zanesville, near New Concord. "I was in the hospital a week," Annie recalls. "Back then they always kept all mothers in bed that long. Not like today."

Annie was discharged from the hospital a well and happy mother and returned to the New Concord home of her parents, where she and her children lived while John was overseas. But within a few weeks, Annie began feeling feverish and weak, the classic symptons of puerperal, or "childbed," fever. At one time this infection of the uterus had been fairly common in women after childbirth, particularly before antibiotics were in widespread use.

"It was an emergency," Annie says about the incident, her voice growing strained. "The complications developed after I had gone home. My parents rushed me back to the hospital." At the hospital, Annie's fever quickly rose to 106 degrees, a life-threatening temperature at which the body is unable to regulate itself; irreparable brain damage can occur if the fever persists for any length of time. As her family looked on and prayed, the hospital staff frantically covered the weakening mother with icepacks, stuffing them under her armpits, at her groin, and especially around her head.

The physicians administered penicillin, hoping they had acted in time. But the fever persisted. Meanwhile, a top priority message was relayed to Glenn in Okinawa telling him his wife was in serious condition back home. A message like that, to a Marine accustomed to long separations from his family, could only mean one thing: Annie was near death. Glenn was immediately granted emergency medical leave and flew home, first on lumbering military transports, then on commercial aircraft at his own expense from California. The three-day trip seemed maddeningly slow to Glenn, who feared that the woman he loved was dying after having given birth to their only daughter. He prayed he would arrive in time.

When Glenn arrived at Annie's hospital room, the young Marine flier's heart sank at the stricken form he saw. "My temperature was so high I really don't remember much about the very first days of my illness," Annie says. She was so delirious that at first she did not even recognize John when he approached the bedside.

But finally the ice and the medication began their cooling magic and her temperature began to drop. "I slowly came out of it," Annie says. She was again able to enjoy the sight of her little girl, now nearly a month old.

Once Annie was safely over her crisis, Glenn returned to Okinawa, then to Guam, where the distance from his growing family weighed heavily on him. But for the first time in his overseas tour, he was allowed to send for his family. The move was not smooth. In New Concord, Annie, with three-year-old David and infant Lyn, found she had three days' notice to pack up and be on the West Coast to make her military flight across the Pacific. She made it, but only after a full-scale mobilization of friends and neighbors, some of whom washed clothes, others of whom packed, while still others made hurried shopping trips for last-minute items.

The three-month tour in Guam would have been considered hardship duty by almost any standard, but to Glenn, now rejoined with his family, it was one of the most congenial times of his military career. Life was far from plush. Quarters were provided for the families, but they were little more than shelter. All four Glenns lived in a Quonset hut, reclaimed from the jungle by the Seabees and set up on concrete blocks. The Quonsets at least had electricity and rudimentary plumbing, but it was up to each resident to finish the interior. Donald L. May, a fellow Marine, recalled that Glenn enthusiastically wielded hammer and paintbrush after his daily duties and that, in a while, as he says, "a thriving community of wives and children gradually blossomed."

It was a remarkably self-sufficient group, which lacked only certain niceties of American life. Once, Glenn's parents recalled, they received an odd request from their son and daughter-in-law.

"Onions!" the letter implored. "Send us some onions."

Glenn's father promptly picked out eight of the best and airmailed them to Guam for the then-staggering sum of $2.95. "Bud told us later he and Annie were the most popular couple in Guam as a result of those onions," Glenn's father recalled.

The Korean War, the United Nations "police action," gave Captain Glenn the chance for aerial combat. In the course of it, he shot down three MiGs and was nearly killed several times by enemy fighters and anti-aircraft fire. To his colleagues, he came to be known as the "MiG Mad Marine" and "Old Magnet Ass."

The war experience also laid the groundwork for much of Glenn's future career. The friendships formed during his Korean tour helped advance him up the military ladder and garner some of the choicest assignments. Each of these friendships helped weave a khaki old-boy network, granting Glenn chits to call in as needed. The time would come in the late fifties, when Glenn, convinced his military career would be stymied by his lack of formal education, used every favor at his disposal to accomplish the ultimate snivel of his military life by crashing his way into the space program.

When he arrived in the southeast corner of Korea near Pohang Dong Ni on February 3, 1953, for duty as operations officer with Marine Fighter Squadron 311, hardly anyone had heard of John Glenn. "He was just a nonentity; just another Marine pilot," recalls Woody Woodbury. Glenn seemed all the more obscure in the company not only of Woodbury, but of Boston Red Sox star Ted Williams and New York Yankee second baseman Jerry Coleman, both of whom had to leave baseball temporarily after being called up in the Korean War. Williams, who became Glenn's wingman, once commented on Glenn's daredevil flying style: "The man is crazy."

The 311th was a fighter bomber squadron. Its pilots flew F9F Pantherjets, airborne arsenals laden with one- and two-thousand-pound bombs and armed with 50mm machine guns and 20mm cannon. "The fighter bomber flying really carried the punch to the enemy," Glenn wrote at the time. "Those were missions involving bombing, strafing, rocket firing and napalm drops on enemy targets."

Morale in the unit was high, reflected in the sky blue scarves, dotted with half-dollar size red hearts, that each of the pilots wore. The amorous connotation came from the unit's nickname, "Willing Lovers," prompted by the tail designation on their planes: WL. Glenn did not suggest the group's name, but he notes that the scarves were more than just the ostentatious trademark of a "hot" pilot.

"Your eyes are the best thing you've got when you're flying

fighters, and you can just chafe the devil out of your neck during your 'scan pattern,'" Glenn says. "They always joke that pilots wearing scarves are supposed to be super hot. But I tell you if you're on an honest-to-goodness fighter mission, you're like this all the time [he swivels his head in an almost complete turn]. I used to be able to turn my head an abnormal distance simply because you develop the muscles so much just by doing it. You could turn back and darn near look back over your own tail. So you really needed those scarves for protection against chafing."

"A typical day during the war," recalls Woody Woodbury, "was contingent on the night before. The word would come down from headquarters on what kind of missions were to be flown and who going to fly them." A normal day would see the men of 311 and their counterparts in Squadron 115, approximately 60 in all, rising at 6:00 A.M. for their assigned missions. "We'd usually fly two missions a day, sometimes three, depending on the information from the front. We'd often work with the Air Force, who would fly high cover for us to keep the MiGs away."

Glenn found his assignment interesting, but as in World War II, it was not the one-on-one fighter interceptor flying that he wanted. It may not have been as competitive, but it was dangerous work; his time as a fighter bomber pilot brought Glenn the closest to death he has ever been.

The Marine fighter bombers were vulnerable both from above, where the MiG interceptors prowled the skies above the 38th parallel, and from below, from anti-aircraft batteries that dotted the rugged hillsides, hidden from all but the most perceptive scrutiny. One day Ted Williams was almost killed by enemy ground fire. "We were over the 38th parallel," Woodbury recalls, "and Ted was flying his jet maybe 75 feet off the ground. When he finally made it back they counted over 150 bullet holes from small-arms fire alone! But his big problem was that he was on fire. Nothing worked except the engine. He had no radio, no hydraulics, nothing. He couldn't get his speed brakes down, couldn't get his flaps down, couldn't get his landing gear down. It was all shot.

"When he did get up to altitude the fire would go out because of the thin air, but as soon as he'd go into heavier air and try to land, it'd burst into flames again. It was an incredible thing to watch. I had landed ahead of him at a front-line Air Force base and had a ringside view of the entire thing. Finally, he landed on the runway with no wheels and the plane skidded right up to the fire truck. You should have seen Williams scramble from that airplane. He got out a hell of a lot faster than he ever ran around the bases. It was the first time I'd ever seen the scene of the fire come to the firetruck."

Tom Miller, who was doing fighter bomber duty in Korea before Glenn, visited his friend and tried to instill in him "a few of the golden rules." "I told John that the Koreans were a hell of a lot more serious than the Japanese were in the Marshalls," Miller recalls. Looking intently at Glenn, Miller admonished his friend: "I know your enthusiasm. Just be careful. Don't make two runs if you don't have to, because you can be sure the guys on the ground are watching you and will be able to shoot more accurately at you the second time.

"I told him to be careful how he jinxed [flew in a zig-zag pattern to avoid anti-aircraft hits]. I said 'even if you can't see any rounds being shot, if you're below 7,000 feet, you jinx, because there may be somebody shooting at you who you don't see and can't hear." Miller left, hoping his lesson had sunk in. As he would find out barely a week later, his note of caution had little effect on Glenn.

Glenn's commanding officer in Korea, Colonel F. K. Coss, had adopted a formal combat policy and written it down for his pilots so there would be no misunderstanding. Basically it stated: "No North Korean target in itself is worth the life of an American pilot or an aircraft, both of whom can return again and again on repeated strikes. When the 'calculated risk' position is reached, the pilot is to take appropriate action to save his life and preserve his plane."

Glenn did not always obey Coss's stricture. In early 1953, he was on a four-plane bombing mission when he saw an anti-aircraft gun to his right firing at him. "There was a captain leading this particular flight," Miller remembers. "By that time John had been promoted to major. The flight leader always had full authority, regardless of rank, but there are damn few captains who are going to object when a major says he's going to do something.''

"I see that son of a bitch and I'm going after him," Glenn barked into his radio to the flight leader, who said nothing. Glenn's strafing attack destroyed the gun position, but at the instant of passing, as he prepared to climb from a bare 15 feet off the ground, Glenn took a 90mm shell in his plane's tail section.

It blew a huge hole, forcing the aluminum in the tail to flare out from the other side and snare his elevators. Plummeting to his seeming death, Glenn pulled back on his elevator control— but it refused to move. Finally, by sheer desperate strength, he was able to get enough "flipper" to take the plane out of the dive. When he finally brought the plane home, it had 250 holes in it. Glenn told his fellow pilots that it was as close as he ever had come to "buying the farm."

Two weeks later, on another mission, Glenn forgot to jinx. Another 90mm shell exploded just below him, and "sieved" his plane. Fortunately, it did not damage either Glenn or his controls. On his return to base Glenn was promptly dubbed "Old Magnet Ass," an allusion to his habit of drawing enemy shells.

Glenn gradually honed his skills and curbed his enthusiasm enough to become an outstanding bomber fighter pilot. Completing 63 missions with the 311th, he set his sights on his next goal: to get into fighter combat with the MiGs and become an ace.

The Air Force finally provided Glenn with his opportunity. He transferred to a front-line Air Force fighter squadron as part of an interservice exchange program and promptly began flying the hottest plane of the war, the F86 Sabrejet. He flew every flight he could get, just as he had during training at Corpus Christi. Glenn was not shy. He boasted to everyone that he was going to be the second Marine ace of the Korean War, after Captain Jack Bolt. His fellow pilots kidded him good-naturedly; then, one morning, Glenn awoke to find his Sabrejet decked with the legend "MiG Mad Marine" alongside the names of his wife and children.

Glenn got an immediate start on his boast. He downed his first MiG the very first day he encountered enemy fighters. It was July 12, 1953. "Today, I finally got a MiG as cold as can be," he exulted in a letter to his family. "Of course, I'm not excited at this point. Not much!" In the letter, Glenn related the entire mission. He began by cruising his Sabrejet at 43,000 feet, then dropped down to 23,000 near the Yalu River. He spotted one enemy plane, but lost it in the clouds at 2,000 feet. A few seconds later, though, he spotted another and the fight began.

Glenn and his fellow pilots began a wide sweeping turn to make a run on the MiG and his comrade, who had now reappeared at six o'clock. "Closed to short range, with a high closing speed and opened fire," Glenn wrote. "Fired continually until I had to pull up to keep from ramming his tail. Flame started out of the right wing fuselage just before he hit the ground and disintegrated. Pattern on the ground was very similar in appearance to a napalm drop. Confirmed Kill."

Glenn, who is not always at ease with descriptive phrasing, became nearly poetic over his accomplishment: "Funny how the bullets sparkle when they hit a plane like that. Just light up like little lights every time a bullet hits."

Only a week later, Glenn made his second MiG kill, in a dramatic dogfight of eight American jets outnumbered by twice as many MiGs. Just three days after that, Glenn bagged his third MiG, in an attack in which two other members of his four-man flight also recorded kills. "The three MiGs we got on that flight were the last three shot down before the truce," Glenn recalls, adding that it may have been the only time in the entire conflict that a single four-member fighter team had been so successful.

Glenn had shot down three MiGs in only nine days of combat, and appeared destined to become a prime ace of the Korean War. But he soon ran out of war. On July 27, 1953, only five days after his third victory, the United Nations and the North Korean Communist government declared a truce that ended hostilities.

More than a decade had passed since 21-year-old John Glenn had begun flight training at Corpus Christi, Texas. Now he was a veteran of not one, but two, wars and had conducted himself with honor in both. The freckle-faced youth who had once dreamed of flying Pan American Clippers had now flown 149 missions in combat and was a career Marine and a hero.

Glenn had begun a route that seemed as far removed from political success as one could take him. But his insatiable drive to excel, whether in war or peace, was moving Glenn inexorably toward national recognition.

5

———— ◆ ————

THE YEARS BETWEEN:
A TASTE OF GLORY

In military shorthand it is called Pax River, short for the Naval
Air Test Center at Maryland's Patuxent River Naval Air Station. Physically, it is an unassuming place in rural southern
Maryland, sitting among the scrub pines on a fingerlike penin-
sula in Chesapeake Bay. But in the years immediately after the
Korean War, it was the one place an ambitious naval or Marine
aviator wanted to be. For medal-bedecked John Glenn, it was
the only assignment he wanted.

"I had decided I wanted to get into test work," Glenn says.
"But test pilot training involves a lot of math and calculus, which
I didn't have." Most of the other pilots accepted for the prestigious program were Annapolis graduates who had studied far
more higher mathematics than Glenn, whose only college education was two-and-a-half years at tiny Muskingum. Though he
would later argue that he did have enough background in mathematics to meet the minimum requirements, Glenn only made it
into the test pilot ranks with deft maneuvering. Afterwards, he
confessed to friends that he almost washed out because the math
training was so difficult.

F. K. Coss, Glenn's commanding officer in Korea, is aware of how deceiving Glenn's eager grin and casual manner can be to those who first meet him. Speaking of Glenn's efforts to get into the test program, Coss says: "John has a grim determination and is fully capable of exerting tremendous pressure on both his superiors and subordinates in a quiet but effective manner."

Tom Miller, a decorated flyer himself, was asked if it were normal for someone with Glenn's meager academic credentials to be accepted at Pax River. "Well, it was considered a prize billet for any pilot who loved flying the way John did," he replies. "The problem that John faced was an educational one. John may have had geometry in college or high school, but he certainly didn't have analytics and trigonometry. Still, his superiors in Korea had a very high regard for his ability to overcome these obstacles by sheer work, so they got him the billet. I couldn't say exactly how much string pulling John did, but he was always very good at it."

Glenn describes his efforts to get into the test pilot training program for new Navy and Marine jets as simple routine. "You put in a request for the duty you wanted when you got back to the States from Korea," Glenn recalls. "The requests were all forwarded to personnel at Marine headquarters in Washington —and sometimes you even got what you wanted."

In reality, Glenn desperately wanted Pax River and was determined to make sure that his application would not be lost in a welter of others. To red flag his request to the Marine hierarchy, Glenn solicited endorsements from important senior officers and enclosed them with his application. "Colonel John L. Smith had been a World War II ace," Glenn recalls, "and he had been my C.O. at Pohang when I went up to fly with the Air Force. I asked for his endorsement." Armed not only with Smith's backing, but that of the C.O. who replaced him and his own combat record, Glenn was accepted at Pax River. "They wanted a lot of combat time from people going into test work to know whether a plane was good enough for combat," Glenn recalls.

It was a difficult time for Glenn, whose poor academic training was now his major handicap. "They gave us an extremely short little brush-up course in calculus," Glenn says. "Only I was starting calculus from scratch. I must have had every primary book in calculus you ever saw. I was burning the midnight oil until about three every morning—sort of 'Calculus Self-Taught.'"

Tom Miller recalls Glenn's misery during the first months at Pax. "John said that he damn near busted out of it a couple of times because they were throwing math at him that he just didn't have any background in. Boy, did he study. He left Annie back in Ohio during those early days and just kept his nose in his books."

Glenn's heavy academic load did not excuse him from flying duties. "I was keeping up, but it was only with a tremendous effort," Glenn says. "We were running a flight schedule every day and also writing flight reports at night." But with the doggedness that justified his former C.O.'s faith in him, Glenn completed the course. In August 1954 he was graduated as a Marine test pilot, the crucial step that would lead him to international fame and the political arena.

Glenn stayed at Patuxent for two years as project officer on several new airplanes, including the F8U Chance-Vought Crusader, a formidable plane whose potential for sustained supersonic speed intrigued Glenn. Hal W. Vincent, a Marine aviator who attended test pilot school with Glenn, recalls that Glenn was a "terrific competitor" who "scrambled for everything and never wanted to be topped."

Pax River selected their best men to put the high-performance Crusader through its armament and flight tests. Glenn was chosen and found himself in the company of Vincent and a coolly professional naval officer named Alan Shepard, later to be a fellow astronaut. Glenn and the seemingly standoffish Shepard never established a close relationship at Pax. In fact, years later it would become a widely held view in the Mercury program that no one knew "the real Al."

There was no astronaut program at the time. Glenn's concentration was on the superfast plane: on what it could do for the image of the Marine Corps, and not incidentally, for his own military career.

❁

By 1956, at age 35, Glenn was transferred to Washington, D.C., and assigned to the fighter design branch of the Bureau of Naval Aeronautics ("Bew-Air"). Glenn's office was in the World War II-era "temporary" buildings that for decades sat on a long grassy strip in the heart of Washington near the Reflecting Pool. It was too much desk work and not enough flying for Glenn, who grew restless. Fortunately, the Crusader became his ticket out of bureaucracy.

The mid-fifties after the Korean War were a time of keen competition with the Soviet Union in aviation. It was a competition that would soon grow frenzied over the Russians' perceived advantage in the exploration of outer space. One measure of the competition was the performance of military airplanes—which nation could fly higher and faster. "John knew the military was going to shoot for some records," Tom Miller recalls. "So in his usual fashion, he was able to snivel himself into a first-class position. Because he had flown the Crusader down at Pax River, he was able to get himself named as one of the pilots for the speed run."

The "speed run" was a transcontinental race that would take the Crusader to its limits. It soon became Glenn's own project, an example of his talent for taking an idea that is not original and capitalizing on it by acting while others are talking. Glenn notes that the idea of breaking the transcontinental speed record had been discussed for months, but only in joking terms, at the Bureau of Aeronautics. "But after joking about it, I thought perhaps we could really do this thing," Glenn recalls. "So I sat at home and doodled out the figures and drew up some graphs and charts. Then I refined my data, got some engineering figures from Chance Vought and worked out some 'pro formas' on it—what could and could not be done—and finally it looked pretty good. I went to the admiral on it and that's how the whole thing started."

In fact, a determined Glenn had to propose the flight four times before the Navy Department and the Pentagon took him seriously. When they finally approved the flight and scheduled it for July 16, 1957, Glenn was chagrined to find that the project, for insurance, now called for a Navy pilot to fly another Crusader in tandem.

Major Glenn personally dubbed the speed trial "Operation Bullet," reflecting an amateur flair for the dramatic that Rene Carpenter contends would have made Glenn a good actor or talk show host. The route was west to east, beginning at Los Alamitos Naval Air Station in California and ending at Floyd Bennett Field in Brooklyn. When it was over, Glenn said it was more like sitting inside an IBM calculator than in a fighter cockpit, an understatement considering the number of obstacles he faced en route.

Acting as his own navigator, Glenn marked check points every three-and-a-half minutes. Shortly after takeoff he took the sleek jet up to 30,000 feet and accelerated to speeds of more than 1,000 miles an hour. Once at altitude he began a "slow cruise climb." "As fuel goes down you let the plane ease up on and hold the same speed," he notes. He was flying at 50,000 feet, nearly ten miles high. The trip required airborne refueling three times: at Albuquerque, New Mexico; Olathe, Kansas; and Indianapolis, Indiana. Over Albuquerque, the Navy flier on the same transcontinental mission, Lieutenant Commander Charles F. Demmler, was forced to return to base because of mechanical problems. Glenn's plane, the only one now in the race, continued to function smoothly.

Glenn knew that to achieve the speed record his refueling stops would have to be made quickly, like airborne pit stops. The maneuver required flawless flying. For that critical procedure, Glenn reduced speed and dropped from 50,000 to 25,000 feet at the moment of rendezvous. He approached the tanker— "an old prop plane," Glenn recalls—at an exact 205 knots. The maneuver had to be accomplished gently. With a mistimed approach the drogue trailing from the tanker might wrap itself around the Crusader's wing. A poor withdrawal could jerk the hose from the tanker and leave it stuck in the jet.

Over Albuquerque, Glenn eased the plane to the airborne tanker, filled up, and was out of the "pits" only 20 seconds behind schedule. The second fueling was perfect. But the third, over Indianapolis, could have ruined Glenn's chances for the record had he not planned so carefully in advance. With foresight, Glenn had arranged to have not one, but two, tankers in the air at each rendezvous. On this third crucial refueling, the primary tanker was six miles off course. Glenn had to rely on the back-up tanker, even though it could pump fuel at only half the usual rate. This meant Glenn had 1,000 pounds less fuel than planned for on the home stretch.

Praying for no mishaps, Glenn hit his afterburner and gunned the plane to speeds approaching more than one-and-a-half times the speed of sound. When he finally reached Floyd Bennett Field, three hours, 23 minutes and 8.4 seconds after leaving California, he had broken the transcontinental speed record. But he had arrived in New York with only enough fuel to make one circle of the field before landing.

For most of the trip there were no complaints about sonic booms from communities below. At the beginning, Glenn notes, a number of atmospheric conditions helped to dampen the booms. These included cloud layers and temperature inversions, as well as alternating hot and cold layers of air. But for the final leg of the trip, from Indianapolis to New York, the conditions for sonic booms were perfect, "almost textbook," as he says. The boom path now trailed behind his plane like a huge cone, producing two explosive noises, the first at the leading edge, the second at the trailing edge of the cone.

Glenn explains what happened when his speed plane crossed over his hometown of New Concord, Ohio. "The course was not intentionally planned to go over New Concord," Glenn says. "It just happened to be right on course. My mother had told some of the other people about it. They couldn't see me, of course, but they knew roughly the time I'd be coming by there.

"Well, apparently," Glenn says, "when I went supersonic, even though I was at about 40,000 feet and heading up, I was dragging enough of a shock wave cone behind me that when I went over the town there was a big double boom—whomp-whomp!! One of the old women up the street, Mrs. Gillogly, I think, called mother and said: 'Oh, Mrs. Glenn, Johnny dropped a bomb! Johnny dropped a bomb!'

"In fact," Glenn notes with a wry grin, "the shock wave was strong enough so that as I came east, there actually were broken windows along the route, though none in New Concord. The Navy and Marine Corps had to pay damages for some of them."

At Floyd Bennett Field, Glenn was greeted by Annie and the

children, as well as an enthusiastic press corps and a military band produced by a confident officialdom. "It's a real kick," he said as he stepped out of the cockpit. "Anybody like to try something like this?" No one volunteered. On the flight, Glenn carried with him a letter from the mayor of San Francisco to the mayor of New York, as well as souvenirs for his children. "Here's your supersonic knife, Dave," Glenn said, returning his son's Boy Scout knife, "and here's your supersonic cat, Lyn." Glenn had carried her Siamese cat brooch cross-country as a good luck charm.

Glenn was self-effacing as he began a publicity tour designed by the military but eagerly accepted by the 36-year-old Marine major who chafed at the obscurity under which he labored at "Bew-Air" in Washington. Glenn explained to his audiences that "flying at 1,000 miles an hour, you don't feel speed as much as you do driving 70 miles an hour down the highway. You don't have much spare time for thinking. Your speed varies 12 to 15 miles a minute. Every three-and-a-half minutes another check point comes up. By the time you check against your chart, it's time to do it all over again."

"The flight was real fine," Glenn declared. ("Real fine" was rapidly becoming his favorite phrase.) "No strain at all. But now I've got to go back to work. I flew coast to coast, but I didn't even make my flight time for the month," an allusion to the fact that he needed four hours a month in the air to make the extra flight pay so important to pilots. Glenn also paid tribute to his teammates on the project, in the Navy and Air Force as well as the Marines. He said they did a "real, real fine job."

But there was no mention of Charlie Demmler, the Navy pilot who had to turn back. "Well, Charlie and I worked together on it, but I put the thing together," Glenn now says. "He was low on fuel and went into Albuquerque."

"There was a little animosity among the Navy guys that Glenn was the only one to make it all the way through," Tom Miller says. "The Navy knows that the Marines are the guys that are always sniveling and getting the good deals because they work hard at it. The same thing happened to me when I set the speed record in the Phantom. There was quite a bit of animosity. At the time we were stationed in Washington and we got to fly for the records, and the guys down at Pax River were just madder then hell because the admirals up there approved us being the pilots."

The successful completion of the flight earned Glenn his sixth Distinguished Flying Cross, awarded by Secretary of the Navy Thomas S. Gates. It was presented to Glenn by Brigadier General C. A. Roberts during a Labor Day weekend welcome home ceremony in New Concord, an occasion that coincided with the town's annual potato and flower show.

Immediately after the historic flight, Glenn appeared on TV and radio shows in New York, mainly interview programs in which he repeated his appealing low-key message that he could not have done the job without the help and support of his teammates. The *New York Times* made Glenn its "Man in the News," misspelling his middle name as "Hershall" instead of "Herschel." The profile maintained that "at 36, Major Glenn is reaching the practical age limit for piloting complicated pieces of machinery through the air." *The Times* would correct itself five years later in its second "Man in the News" profile on Glenn, following his epochal space flight.

An unanticipated benefit of the flight arrived as Glenn and his family were shopping in midtown Manhattan. As Glenn recalls: "I literally was walking down the street. We were in Saks and I had Annie and the kids with me and this gal kept looking at me. Finally, she came up and spoke to me. It turned out she was one of the people charged with recruiting people for *Name That Tune*." *Name That Tune*, one of the more popular of the 1950s television game shows, awarded sizable cash prizes to two-person teams who could guess names of popular songs played on the show.

The talent scout claimed she did not know who Glenn was, but Glenn was skeptical. He notes that he was in uniform at the time and had been the object of tremendous press coverage, including the *Times* profile, which had been accompanied by a photograph of Glenn and his family. Glenn agreed to talk to the producers of the program, then got permission from his Marine superiors to appear on it. (He also appeared on *I've Got a Secret*. His secret, naturally, was that he had just set a transcontinental speed record.)

Glenn's teammate on *Name That Tune* was a gregarious young boy named Eddie Hodges, who would later star in the Broadway play *The Music Man.* Together, they made an engaging pair. A publicity photo of the two shows Hodges in his Cub Scout uniform looking up wide-eyed at Glenn, in his own Marine dress uniform with a chestful of medals.

Glenn had a knack for remembering song titles and tunes, and after several weeks running, he and his young colleague retired undefeated with the grand prize of $25,000, which they split. "After taxes," Glenn recalls, I wound up with $8,000." Part of the money went to buy a home electric organ for Annie, which they still have; the remainder was put aside for Lyn and Dave's education.

Ironically, the year after Glenn's appearance the quiz show scandal broke, resulting in perjury convictions and ruined careers for contestants and producers of several programs. Glenn laughingly says that *Name That Tune* may have been the only quiz show of the era that was not rigged.

The transcontinental flight was a turning point in John Glenn's life. He had long been a military hero, known to his peers and superiors as a promising individual. But now, having set a transcontinental speed record, Glenn's face and name were receiving public recognition for the first time. John Glenn found that he loved basking in the public eye.

As he set his supersonic speed record Glenn remarked that he did not expect it to last long. "It can be done in two hours," he said, "and later on even in one hour." In fact, within five years he would travel in another vehicle that crossed the nation in ten minutes. But within only three months of his transcontinental jet flight the luster of his triumph was virtually gone. On October 4, 1957, the Soviet Union placed into earth orbit a 184-pound satellite called Sputnik. The competition between the United States and Russia, earthbound till then, suddenly moved into the heavens. A small metal ball had struck competitive terror into the hearts of America's public and its policymakers.

In successfully launching Sputnik I in 1957, the Russians demonstrated more than a capacity to put a tiny ball into orbit around the earth. It also meant that the Russians now had the capacity to hurl their recently developed atomic bomb at the U.S. on an intercontinental ballistic missile in much the same way. Sputnik I and the other Soviet satellites that followed also played on the fears of Americans grown suspicious of the Soviets in the rancor of the cold war and the aftermath of Korea. It was essential that America retake the high ground.

"The Roman Empire controlled the world because it could build roads," declared Senator Lyndon Johnson of Texas, then the Senate Majority Leader. "Later, when it moved to sea, the British Empire was dominant because it had ships. In the air age, we were powerful because we had airplanes. Now the Communists have established a foothold in outer space." Echoed House Speaker John McCormack of Massachusetts: "It cannot be over-emphasized that the survival of the Free World—indeed all the world—is caught up in these stakes."

The competition for space soon proved embarrassing to America. Every time the United States announced—in full view of everyone—its plans for a satellite launch, it was one-upped by the secretive Russians. A U.S. earth satellite by 1958? The Russians did it in late '57 with Sputnik. A satellite around the sun in March '59? The Russians accomplished it in January. The most embarrassing episode took place when the United States tried to launch its first satellite two months after Sputnik I. The big Vanguard rocket exploded on the launch pad, then fell languidly to the ground, all on national television.

"There had been some talk about an astronaut program when I was in Bew-Air," Glenn recalls. "Of course, the Sputnik had occurred and we were all watching and wondering how we were going to get into the space program. There had been some talk of not only orbiting an object but of putting man in space. The Air Force had been advocating a program called MISS, for 'Man in Space Soonest,' but it never got very far."

The fact that the United States had not orbited its first satellite increased public anxiety, as well as pressure on the military and the scientists. When the first U.S. satellite, Explorer I, finally was fired into orbit on January 31, 1958, few knew that the announcement that orbit had been achieved was not based on hard facts, but only on the blind faith of a 33-year-old physicist, Dr. Albert R. Hibbs, who had once spent hours watching a roulette wheel in Reno and then managed to parlay $125 into $7,000.

After the Explorer was launched, two out of the three systems designed to confirm orbit of the Explorer had failed. Hibbs was forced to gamble once again and base his calculations of orbit solely on when the satellite's signal disappeared over the horizon. "We waited to see when we lost the signal," Hibbs recalled. "If it were going too high, we'd lose the signal later than our standard trajectory figured; if it were going too low, we'd lose the signal earlier. On the basis of this single bit of data, we took a flier and started figuring out a perigee/apogee, period of time around the earth—even a lifetime in orbit."

Finally, 45 minutes after the signal disappeared, Hibbs raced into the office of the general waiting to make the news public. He began spouting his numbers. "All right," the general interrupted impatiently, "just tell me: is it in orbit or not?" Crossing his fingers, Hibbs replied: "General, it will be in orbit for four years."

The general picked up a phone and called the Secretary of the Army. Then he and Hibbs rushed to a press conference at Patrick Air Force Base. While the general assumed a confident manner with the press, Hibbs kept looking at his watch. He knew that if Explorer really had achieved orbit it would soon be coming up on its first revolution of the earth. As casually as he could, Hibbs reached for a phone and called his office for word. There was none. The minutes seemed endless before he finally heard that not only had Explorer achieved orbit, but it was in a higher orbit than anticipated. It would stay aloft not four years, but ten.

The launch had been successful, but Explorer was, in the words of NASA's Robert Voas, just "another grapefruit-sized satellite." Nothing would long assuage American fears of the Soviet space hegemony except a successful manned U.S. space mission.

The decision to proceed with the manned space program originally came during the Eisenhower administration. As first planned, the selection of astronauts was to be similar to other government recruitment: a notice would be posted throughout the federal civil service for individuals with specified qualifications, such as advanced degrees in math or physics, and a demonstrated ability to perform under stress. The civil service announcement would not even use the word "pilot" in describing the job function. The announcement would mention test pilots as fitting the description, but so too did submariners, arctic explorers, mountain climbers, deep sea divers, combat veterans and those who had volunteered for the Navy and Air Force acceleration and atmospheric tests.

Ultimately, President Eisenhower rejected the idea of a national competition for astronauts on two compelling grounds. Says Bob Voas: "For one thing, he felt that we would be embarrassed by having a highly publicized program to select astronauts when at that time the only thing we had launched was a small satellite." For another thing, a public call for astronaut candidates was bound to include an army of crazies and other unqualified people. The government could not afford the time to weed them out.

Eisenhower's counterproposal instead called for absolute secrecy. The space effort itself would be civilian controlled, but the astronaut candidates would be culled solely from the existing pool of 540 active duty military test pilots. The entire program would be kept quiet until it could be unveiled in a controlled atmosphere to the press and public.

Rene Carpenter recalls the extent to which the president wanted to maintain secrecy. "The first inclination of Eisenhower was that the astronauts should live in a star village, much like the Russian cosmonauts," she notes. "It was Arthur Godfrey who talked him out of that." Carpenter explains that Ike was dissuaded from having the American space fliers and their families live in isolation only through the combined efforts of Godfrey and a close mutual friend, attorney Leo DeOrsey. DeOrsey, a wealthy Washington tax lawyer who was once considered by President Truman to head the IRS, had represented a number of show business figures, including Godfrey, and also

had represented Eisenhower in negotiating the deal for publication of his memoirs. DeOrsey maintained that an arrangement
such as a "space village" would smack of totalitarianism. Eisenhower was influenced by the argument and dropped the idea.

The fact that Eisenhower had considered placing the astronauts in such strict isolation illustrates his view that the men to
be selected for the mission were simply military volunteers,
subject to whatever strictures the commander-in-chief deemed
necessary. Eisenhower's successor, John F. Kennedy, the product of a far different generation, realized the enormous political
potential of the astronauts and all but made them unofficial
members of his administration.

Despite the official secrecy surrounding the manned space
program in 1958, test pilot John Glenn soon learned about it
from leaks from his superiors at the Bureau of Aeronautics. He
hungered for the assignment the moment he heard of it but, as
Glenn recalls, he anxiously wondered whether he could meet
the program's criteria. There were four obstacles to surmount,
any one of which could have disqualified him. One, in fact,
almost did.

By the standards set by the new National Aeronautics and
Space Administration, he was considerably overweight at 208
pounds, as evidenced by his round face and thick thighs. He was
also 37 years old, two years under the cutoff age of 39, but still
considerably older than most of the candidates likely to apply.
He also lacked a college degree. The criteria were clear on this
point. And lastly, he was too tall. A 5'11" cutoff had been set in
order to ensure sufficient legroom in a cramped space capsule.

Today, in an era of roomy space shuttles with five-member
crews, it is hard to believe how critical were the tolerances in
inches of the fledgling American space program. "The height
maximum was 5'11"," Bob Voas recalls. "We had to put the
capsule on top of the rocket we had, and that meant that the
capsule itself was of a specific size. Maybe we could have taken a
short-trunked, long-legged guy who was over the maximums,
but we didn't want to go to that extreme."

In his official NASA biography, John Glenn's height is listed
at 5' 10 1/2", but Tom Miller tells another story. "John was six
foot," he says flatly. In order to meet the requirements for the

astronaut program, Glenn literally tried to shrink himself down to size. At the time, Miller and Glenn lived next door to each other in houses they had built Arlington, Virginia, and both worked in the Bureau of Aeronautics. "Every evening for at least two hours," Miller recalls with a smile, "John would sit and walk around the house with about twelve inches of books strapped to his head, trying to get himself smaller."

"He had a mark on the wall over there," Miller adds, gesturing to a doorway in his own den, "where he'd stand up every night and measure himself." It was seemingly in the manner of a little boy hoping to see if he had grown, but Glenn's hopes were in the reverse direction. Miller says that Glenn ultimately met the height requirement. "I don't know whether it was the books or the fact that he was close enough to 5'11", but he was able to stand slightly slouched in such a way that he finally did measure the right height."

Glenn tackled the weight problem with equal zeal. "I'm going down to 167," Glenn declared to Miller one day. "John," Miller replied, "you're out of your mind. You'll look like a warmed-over deathtrap if you get down to that."

"Nope. I'm going down."

"We started every evening," Miller remembers. "We'd leave the office and go by the Pentagon Officer's Club and work out. Trampoline, swimming, barbells—everything to sweat it off. And that son of a gun did it. I could only get down to about 192, but John just kept going lower and lower. He really looked like death warmed over. His goddam eyeballs went clear back into his head."

There was nothing Glenn could do to alter his birthdate, but at least he was not overage. His lack of a college degree was his most difficult problem. The rule for astronaut selection was quite specific: college graduates only. There are differing accounts about how Glenn managed to have the rules changed in his favor, but that he did is not contested.

Glenn's assault on the astronaut selection process was taking place on a number of fronts. One tactic was to get his face known to anyone who might have a say in selecting America's future spacemen. Another was to participate in collateral programs that would give him an edge when selection was finally made. To experience the high G-forces of rocket flight, Glenn volunteered to ride the Navy's human centrifuge machine at Johnsville, Pennsylvania.

Another opportunity came at Langley Field. "They had some computer studies hooked up to simulate space flight, orbital flight and the different types of re-entry characteristics," Glenn recalls. "They were having people come down two or three days at a time and fly this thing, using different kind of control handles. So I went down and did that and talked to the people, with the idea of following their progress for the Bureau of Aeronautics." Later, Glenn admits, "when NASA finally put out a request for people, why, obviously I was in a pretty good position because of all the work I'd done."

Despite his herculean efforts, Glenn was almost overlooked for the astronaut program. While he was gaining experience and impressing space scientists, Dr. Robert Voas at NASA was putting together the final selection criteria for the first of the American manned space missions, dubbed Mercury, after the messenger of the gods. "I was the Navy representative on this selection group," psychologist Voas recalls, "and I made the error of assuming that the records of the Marine Corps pilots would be in the same files as the Navy pilots', since they went to the same Patuxent training center." One retired Marine colonel, told of Voas's oversight, laughs at the psychologist's naivete. "With the kind of rivalry between the services, do you really think the Navy was going to bend over backwards to include the Marines when they don't have to?" the colonel asks rhetorically.

"It wasn't until we had selected almost all the 110 candidates that it was called to my attention that we didn't have any Marines," Voas relates. "So we had to make a quick contact with the Marine Corps and they found two pilots who fit the requirements. One was John Glenn."

Glenn was now a potential candidate, but his lack of a college degree still blocked his chances. He was rescued by Colonel Jake Dill, the man Glenn credits with getting him into the space program. Jake Dill, a career Marine, had been Glenn's commanding officer at Pax River and had grown to admire his junior officer. Carrying with him the fury of a Marine scorned, Dill confronted NASA officials in 1959 and demanded that Glenn and another Marine flyer be considered for selection in the program.

"I recall personally going over to NASA headquarters, located then near Lafayette Park by the White House, and talking to whoever was making the selection," Dill says. "I pointed out the characteristics that I knew John Glenn had, and recommended very strongly that he be the guy."

Both Glenn and Dill deny they pressured NASA to include him in the original selection. Tom Miller, however, maintains that Glenn and Dill "worked out a deal to ask NASA if they would let the Marine Corps provide an observer to oversee the selection process so that the Marine Corps would better know how to select people as astronauts in the future."

Regardless of exactly what took place more than 20 years ago, Glenn's troubles now centered mainly about his lack of a college degree. It is a sore point with him as well as with his alma mater, Muskingum College. "Frankly," says Glenn with some feeling, "I had more than enough credits for a college degree. In fact, I probably had enough for a masters, based on all the academic work I'd done at Patuxent, as well as college-level course work I had done right after World War II through the Armed Forces Institute. Around that time, I had also gone to the University of Maryland extension division two or three nights a week at the Pentagon.

"I had transferred all this back to Muskingum, but they still wouldn't give me a degree. They held it up on a residency requirement, of all things! I'd only spent the first 20 years of my life there, and they still stymied it on that."

Glenn again petitioned the college for the sheepskin in 1961, after his selection in the Mercury program. But it was turned down even then. Finally, after he orbited the earth, the college relented. "It was good for him and good for us," recalls Dr. William McClelland, a Muskingum professor, in retrospect. Meanwhile, the University of Maryland, anxious to claim a famous figure for its alumni roster, let it be known that on the basis of the extension service credits Glenn had earned, it was more than willing to grant him a college degree.

Bob Voas downplays the controversy over Glenn's degree, though it was obviously real enough to Glenn at the time. "From the beginning," Voas maintains, "it was felt that while John didn't have a formal degree, he had the outside course work, and that was the equivalent. We didn't take these requirements that rigidly. What was most important was the nature of the flight record, and John's was outstanding." Whether true or not, no one had bothered to inform Glenn, who flatly maintains: "If it hadn't been for Jake Dill, I wouldn't have gotten into the program."

Within days after the initial screening, sealed top secret orders were cut for the 110 test pilots selected, ordering them to report to the Pentagon in groups of 35, wearing civilian clothes. The groups were divided in order of priority based on their military records, the most desirable of the candidates being called first.

At the briefing, two of NASA's highest ranking engineers, Abe Silverstein and George Low, began by telling the pilots that the space agency needed volunteers for suborbital and orbital flights. They likened the space program to wartime mobilization, telling the men that the mission could be dangerous. It would not be held against them if they did not volunteer. But many in the group, including Alan Shepard, Wally Schirra and others whose names would soon be household words, were disappointed. They were not concerned about the danger; what troubled them was that there was no real flying involved—flying as they knew it, anyway. Equally important to the ambitious young men was the fact that the program was run by civilians. Obviously, the space program was not part of the regular military ladder of advancement that led to general or flag rank. In short, they feared that volunteering for such a program might actually hurt their careers.

Voas notes that this attitude troubled the NASA scientists as they searched for the men to fly America's first space vehicles. At Edwards Air Force Base, where some of the country's finest test pilots worked, it was no accident that the commanding officer let it be known that he thought Project Mercury was an egregious waste of time and talent. Anyone taking part, he said, would simply become "Spam in a can."

Among the 110 military men brought to Washington, Voas explains, were some "with such a significant and important service position that, in the Navy, for example, they were on a fairly set path to flag rank." Many of them did not want to upset that goal with something as unpredictable as the space program. Even the nature of the proposed flights had an air of hurried haphazardness. Might not these "hot" pilots better spend their time on the X-15, unveiled the previous year and considered by many in the military to be the closest thing America had to a real spaceship? One that would "land with dignity," not drop helplessly into the ocean to be plucked out by a hovering helicopter?

One pilot called to the secret Pentagon briefing was an Air Force officer who had just been selected to spend three years at M.I.T. to earn a Ph.D. in astronautics. He had to choose whether to study about space or fly in it. After listening to Silverstein and Low, he chose to study.

But to the space agency's ultimate surprise, when the time came to call for volunteers, more than 80 of the 110 signed on. In speaking to the men in terms of "highest national priority" and "hazardous undertaking," NASA had pressed the right emotional buttons. The pilots, many of whom had found the war years the most exhilarating time of their lives, were in the mood for an exciting assignment.

For John Glenn, the space call was irresistible. At 37, and stuck in a desk job, he had no qualms about upsetting his career. Months earlier, he had told a friend he felt he did not have the education to reach the top in the service. As much as he loved research and development work, he knew it was not the route to promotion in the Marines.

A few weeks after Glenn had signed on in Washington and then taken a series of written tests, he received a letter at his home on North Harrison Street in Arlington. "Dear Major Glenn," it opened, "You and your record made a very favorable impression on our selection committee. As a result, you are invited to continue on to the second and third phases of this competitive selection program."

He was ordered to report—again in civilian clothes to preserve secrecy—to the Lovelace Clinic in Albuquerque, New

Mexico. "During this period of temporary duty, only key personnel at the Lovelace Foundation and in Washington will know the reason you are being tested. Please do not discuss Project Mercury unless authorized to do so."

John Glenn had no desire to break official secrecy. There would be plenty of opportunity for the world to hear of him later on.

6

PROJECT MERCURY: SELECTION AND REJECTION

His colleagues in the Bureau of Aeronautics wondered about the absences. One day Glenn would be in the office, poring over reports and specifications for new aircraft. The next day he would be gone, often for days at a time. When he returned, he would say nothing about where he had been. The cycle would then repeat all over again.

"During the first months of '59, the secrecy in the astronaut program was real tight," recalls Tom Miller. "One night, though, John told me about it in the car going home." On that night Glenn spoke about the space program with a mixture of secretiveness and excitement. "He said I couldn't breathe a word about it to anybody," Miller recalls. "He said, 'Jake Dill has worked out a deal so that I can go over and be an observer on the thing.'" Of course, Glenn was more than an observer: he was in the thick of the American competition with the Russians to put the first man into outer space.

"They winnowed the group down to 32," Glenn recalls, "and I was part of it. That's when they put us through all the tests known on how to assess a human being." Security was so tight during the testing that each of the 32 was known only by a number, which he was to use in all correspondence ("Number 12 will arrive TWA flight 138 arriving Dayton at 23:30 Saturday, February 28"), and even in phone conversations ("This is Number 4. I will require a car at 1400 hours").

Astronaut candidates traveled separately on commercial airlines, trying to assume the protective coloring of a businessman on the road or a soldier on leave. Though some of the pilots knew one another, the deliberate staggering of test and travel schedules left each candidate on his own as he went from one test site to the other.

But the elaborate subterfuge fooled few of Glenn's Washington colleagues. They surmised that his absences had something to do with the much-rumored space effort. It did succeed, though, in fooling much of the press, which failed to note an unusual number of new arrivals at the diagnostic clinic at Albuquerque, New Mexico. Lovelace Clinic, named after the space scientist W. Randolph Lovelace II, was a private hospital specializing in aerospace medicine. Its ties to the military were obvious to anyone looking at its chain of command. It was run by a retired general in the Air Force medical corps, Dr. A. H. Schwichtenberg, whose mission was to oversee the physical testing of the prospective NASA spacemen.

Schwichtenberg subjected the group to so rigorous, painful and at times humiliating a regimen that a number dropped out in anger. But it was part of the plan to see who among the 32 were "highly motivated" enough to endure almost anything to make the team. John Glenn relished the program, quickly surmising what was happening and how he should respond. In the end, recalls Bob Voas, Glenn's "cooperative attitude" at Lovelace, and later during psychological and stress testing at Wright-Patterson Air Force Base in Dayton, Ohio, earned him high grades from all the scientists. Higher grades, in fact, than he possibly deserved.

"The interesting thing about John is that he overwhelmed everybody," says Voas. "He has a charismatic personality, and just about everybody who dealt with him was highly impressed and rated John right up at the top. I always smile a bit about that because, in some of the physical and mental tests, for example, his scores weren't all that much better than those of some of the other candidates. But the physicians gave him top evaluations due largely, I believe, to his strength of personality and dedication."

Such an attitude was unusual because the relationship between pilot and doctor tends to be adversarial. Each time a pilot undergoes a physical exam, he risks being grounded, risks being summarily excluded from what he loves and does best. A physical was something to be endured and gotten over with, generally by telling the M.D. as little as possible.

It was natural for the 32 men at Lovelace during those weeks in 1959 to be apprehensive. They were treated as little more than specimens, to be prodded and probed with maddening frequency. The doctors at Lovelace seemed to have an anal fixation. The prostate exams, for example, were administered with such force that some of the men actually passed blood. After that they were forced to ride the "Silver Stallion," in which a metal probe was inserted up the rectum and cranked open to permit close inspection of the bowel.

Talking with the detachment of 25 years, Voas concedes that the tests were designed to establish a high "motivational barrier" that only the most determined would pass. In addition, he notes, they served to protect NASA's investment: "The medical tests were required not just to see who could withstand the rigors of it all, but also to ensure that, after we had put something like a million dollars into each one of these guys, that we had a good long-term investment."

The astronaut candidates were told little. When anyone asked why something was necessary, they were icily ignored. Why, the test pilots wondered, should they have to undergo a sperm count? But there, sitting on a table near the bathroom, was the little glass beaker for that purpose. No one told the pilots there was a long-range reason for the test: to gauge what effect, if any, radiation in space might have on the reproductive organs. The result was humorless jokes about having to masturbate for Uncle Sam and needing an attractive nurse to assist. And beneath it all was a feeling that the whole exercise was unnecessary.

The tests seemed endless: X rays, serology, electrolyte determinations, tests of blood sugar, cholesterol, liver function, urea clearance, as well as gastric analysis, urinalysis and tests of stool samples and throat cultures. One especially nasty and seemingly pointless test involved insertion of a long needle attached to an electrical wire into the large muscle at the base of the thumb. Current which passed through the needle forced a strapped-down hand to make and release a fist at astonishing speed, completely apart from the subject's control. Queries about the test were answered with frigid indifference: It did not concern them.

An original astronaut candidate, a Navy officer named Charles "Pete" Conrad, was so incensed at the seemingly intentional humiliation that he marched into General Schwichtenberg's office and plopped an enema bag onto his desk. He bluntly told the general he had given himself his last enema. It was not really the enema that he minded. It was the hellish embarrassment of first having to undergo a lower G.I. series—with barium pumped into his bowels—and then being forced, hunched over and exploding, to follow an orderly to what was purported to be the nearest bathroom, two floors below the examination room, through public corridors and elevators.

What Conrad had done, of course, was trip over his motivational barrier. He was scrubbed from consideration for the original Mercury team as being "not suitable for long duration flight." Ten years later he walked on the moon.

John Glenn permitted himself no such indiscretions. He followed directions, smiled, and earned the daily points toward selection.

Wright-Patterson Air Force Base, or "Wright-Pat," presented similar obstacles, but the stress testing of simulated flight was more like the military pilot's normal routine. Glenn once more impressed the doctors and other scientists with both his easygoing manner and outstanding responses to questions. Another of the candidates responded in much the same cooperative way: a handsome, crewcut Navy commander named Scott Carpenter. The testing at Wright-Pat would reveal both men to be willing to pack more experiments into flights than the others, many of whom regarded experiments as bothersome distractions from the real business of jockeying the capsule up and back. Unlike some others, Glenn and Carpenter viewed the testing at Lovelace and Wright-Pat as a challenge to be met rather than an ordeal to be overcome.

"I had known, or had known of, John at Patuxent," Carpenter recalls. "I was glad to see him and took an immediate liking to him. We managed to squeak through the selection and became the closest of friends during the Mercury time." The two men even seemed to like the psychiatric exams. "It might well be that we had more of a sense of wonder about the program," Carpenter says. "It's probably why we were so close."

The two fliers shared a common view of the space program, but they differed in significant ways. Carpenter, though the seeming model of a career naval officer, never hungered for the challenge of combat as did Glenn. Nor was he as driven to excel. When Russia beat the United States in launching a man in space, sending Yuri Gagarin on an orbital flight in April 1961, Carpenter cheered. "I was happy to see the Russians do it," he recalls. "I was never able to understand the public's preoccupation with who was going to fly first."

During the Korean War, while Glenn was flying combat runs and angling to be transferred to fighter combat, Carpenter was flying P2V patrol planes in the Pacific. Rather than "squeak" through the space program as Carpenter says, both men did outstandingly well. Unlike Glenn, who was confident of being chosen, Carpenter seemed surprised, both when he made the initial cut to 32 and when he made the final team. Also unlike Glenn, Carpenter today betrays ambivalence about his time in the military, believing it pushed some fliers to excess, both professionally and personally. The toll was sometimes extracted in marriages ruined by alcohol, as happened with Carpenter, who views himself as one more victim of a problem common to military fliers. But he remembers with gratitude that when he needed help, Glenn was there to provide it.

The two-part testing at Wright-Patterson, carried out under strict security, was designed to find the candidate "for whom space flight will impose no stress at all," declared Air Force

Captain George E. Ruff, a medical officer on the selection team. "Since such men are probably nonexistent, our objective is to learn which potential candidates will adapt most effectively."

The physical tests presented a special challenge to the candidates, nearly all of whom excelled at some competitive sport. Carpenter, a former University of Colorado gymnast and accomplished underwater diver, broke the 91-second record in measuring lung capacity by going without air an astonishing 171 seconds. He was able to show how large a reserve of oxygen the body can retain after every neural signal is calling for more air. Few others were able to match the 91-second record, much less beat it. One who also shattered it, at 150 seconds, was John Glenn.

There were esoteric tests as well. In the heat test, the subject had to endure two hours in a 130-degree chamber. In another, candidates were strapped into a device that shook them violently while subjecting them to high energy sound that became progressively, even excruciatingly, loud. In the cold pressor test, the men plunged their bare feet into ice water to let technicians monitor changes in their blood pressure. Finally, there were the "complex behavior" stress test and one of the most painful of the set: the flack test.

In the former, each subject sat before a console decked with buttons and switches. He was told that he had to respond to 14 different signals by quickly activating varied combinations of switches and buttons. But shortly after the test began, the signal lights began flashing too fast for any human being to respond. The "stress" involved was coping with being unable to pass the test.

In the flack test, the men were dressed in partial-pressure suits and forced to breathe pure oxygen for two hours. After that their baseline blood pressure and heart rates were measured. They were then placed in a pressure chamber to simulate an altitude of 65,000 feet. The ugly result was tremendous pain, coupled with near panic for some. As breathing became almost impossible, the men had to force old breath out in order to bring new oxygen in. This test, like many of the ones at Lovelace, also gauged a subject's motivation. Said a NASA physician: "Mild hypoxia [an oxygen deficiency of the tissues] coupled with subjective discomfort and pooling of blood produced by uneven pressure of the suit, make the experiment a severe test of motivation, as well as of cardiovascular and pulmonary efficiency."

Today, Glenn looks back on the tests with mixed feelings. But he concedes: "We didn't know what was going to happen in space back then. It's hard to believe, but it really was primitive. We really didn't know what changes a human body might undergo."

Or, for that matter, a human mind. The psychological stress testing at Wright-Pat sought to screen out those who might be unable to adjust mentally to the black unknown of outer space. To eliminate those who might be claustrophic or uncomfortable without the presence of known external stimuli, candidates were strapped in a chair in a dark, soundproof room and told they would be there for an indefinite period. They were left there for three hours of darkness and silence.

The psychological testing, including a lengthy psychiatric examination, covered the existing universe of methods of probing the mind. The Rorschach, or "inkblot," tests showed most of the successful candidates to be well organized thinkers, but not overly rigid. However, the results "did not suggest much imagination or creativity," according to one NASA scientist. "The candidates did not seemed concerned with amassing data for its own sake." For example, 39% of this select pilot population did not know the distance from New York to Paris, but 95% knew the height of the average American woman.

Besides interpreting inkblots, the candidates underwent "thematic apperception" tests in which they were asked to tell stories suggested by a series of pictures. There were "Draw-a-Person" tests in which they were asked to create male and female figures, in order to assess the subject's "body image and feelings about his place in the universe." Sentence completion tests, including ones in which candidates were asked to complete twenty statements, each beginning with the words, "I am..." helped scientists discover their subjects' "social roles and awareness."

The psychiatric interviews were the most nettlesome to the pilots, who were wary of doctors in general and of psychiatrists in particular. It was a time to tell the doctors what they wanted to hear and never to reveal much about oneself. The fact that a gushing NASA would later remark on how "comfortable, mature and well-integrated" all its astronauts were seems, in retrospect, a function of the astronauts' ability to stick to non-revealing, non-threatening accounts of themselves in interviews with the naive psychiatrists.

The seven who made the Mercury team avoided talking flippantly of the risks and dangers inherent in test piloting or in the space program. To the psychiatrists, they sounded like prudent men. Even if he fancied himself the greatest throttle jockey in the service, even if he felt the most alive when daring death in a supersonic plane going to the limits of "the envelope" in the sky, the pilot held this back from the white-jacketed men and women at Wright-Pat.

Anyone who has flown fighter airplanes will talk in private about the hellraising: the "rat-racing" in high-speed, high-performance jets; the "hassling"—mock dogfighting—in planes costing millions of dollars. The same yeasty motivation that made Glenn take off during World War II in search of enemy fighters without seatbelts or parachute in place was the same odd mix of courage and recklessness that made a man a potential war ace. They were possibly the very same traits that made a good astronaut. But the men knew enough not to tell that to the psychiatrists.

No, they said, they did not regard Project Mercury as being especially hazardous. Rather, they were certain that such a high priority project would observe, as would any sane pilot, all the correct procedures and safety considerations. In fact, they added, the safety precautions would probably be even greater than those undertaken for all their previous flight tests on planes like... They would then reel off letters and numbers in casual succession: F-100F, F-4B, F-102.

The dissembling worked like a charm with the psychiatrists. They had gone into the tests looking for men "with no evidence of impulsivity, who will refrain from action when inactivity is appropriate" and who, in their tortured jargon, would not "require motor activity to dissipate anxiety in stress situations." They got what they were looking for.

"These men are comfortable, mature, well-integrated individuals," the NASA psychiatrists concluded in their reports on the men recommended for the program. "Ratings in all categories of the system used consistently fell in the top third of the scale. Most are direct, action-oriented individuals who spend little time introspecting. They do not become overly involved with others, although relationships in their families are warm and stable."

"Danger is admitted, but de-emphasized," the doctors reported. "Most feel nothing will happen to them, but this seems less a wishful fantasy than a conviction that accidents can be avoided by knowledge and caution. They believe that risks are minimized through planning and conservatism. Very few fit the popular concept of the daredevil test pilot."

The psychiatrists were especially concerned about one thing: the sexual symbolism of flying. "Because of the possibility that extreme interest in high-performance aircraft might be related to feelings of inadequacy in sexual and other areas," they wrote, "particular emphasis was placed on a review of each candidate's adolescence." But they finally discarded the theory. "Little information could be uncovered to justify the conclusion that unconscious problems of this kind were either more or less common than in other occupational groups."

Four of the seven selected were eldest or only children. Glenn, in a way, fit both categories since he was the eldest and his younger sister Jean had been adopted. "The psychiatrists really went into that," Glenn recalls. "There's a pattern of first-born males being the big achievers in families, and I don't think they really know why. Maybe it's because they get more tender loving care as the first kid. It's the same with the only child."

In the words of Bob Voas, Glenn "sailed through" the tests, both at Lovelace and at Wright-Pat. In April 1959 he was named one of the nation's first seven astronauts. Glenn received the word while stationed at his desk in Washington, but Carpenter's notification reflected the secrecy surrounding the new space program. He received a telegram the day before he was to ship out on the USS *Hornet* for a seven-month tour of duty of the South Pacific. The telegram said his orders were on the way. "I said to myself they better get here in a hurry because the ship leaves tomorrow," Carpenter recalls.

Carpenter had to tell the *Hornet*'s captain that he would have to find a replacement on a day's notice. "I was the intelligence officer, and that was going to leave him with a hole in his crew of some importance," Carpenter recalls.

"You'll leave this ship over my dead body," the captain responded. "What's this all about?"

"Well," Carpenter replied, "we're all gonna ride in the nosecone of a rocket and go around the world three times."

"Bullshit!" the captain retorted.

Bob Voas, assessing Glenn among the field of others trying out for the space program, declares: "You had to be pretty highly motivated to put up with all of this, and people got ticked off. One or two even left early. But John went through all of it not complaining, fussing, challenging or giving anybody a hard time. That, plus the fact of his charismatic personality, resulted in his having top ratings just about everywhere."

How much of Glenn's attitude was genuine and how much was calculated? "I'm not quite sure how you distinguish that," Voas says. "The thing that's true about John Glenn is that for something he wants, he will work harder than most people will. Throughout the entire program, not only during the candidate screening but later, when the stakes were who was going to fly in space first, Glenn took the challenge right on, putting in the extra hours, working very hard and very disciplined. Others might have argued about whether something really needed to be done, or tried to do as little as they could get away with.

"If you ask whether it was put on," Voas says finally, "I guess it was all put on. Because he wouldn't do it if he wasn't motivated to be an astronaut."

One-thirty P.M., April 9, 1959. In a crowded conference room of the Dolley Madison House, fronting on Lafayette Park alongside the White House, Ralph Morse checked his cameras one more time and waited. The squat, hyperactive Morse, a legendary *Life* magazine photographer, was there to cover the first public appearance of the seven Mercury astronauts. Reporters and photographers representing publications and news agencies around the world were crammed into every part of the small briefing room, some hanging from ladders, others, like Morse, squatting on the floor near the curtained stage. Banks of hot, glaring television lights bathed the crowd in brightness. Morse was sweating.

He had become a legend for his ability to make the impossible shot. In later years, the remote control contraptions he would rig at missile launch sites—sometimes inside the launch towers themselves—would provide unequaled pictures. On that frenzied day in 1959, Morse's assignment was simple: grab an astronaut and stick to him like a second skin.

"We didn't have any of the names beforehand," Morse recalls. "But we did have the hometowns—somebody had leaked those to us. I got assigned to the guy who lived in Arlington. I was supposed to go home with him."

At 2:00 P.M., the curtain pulled back and seven men in nondescript suits walked onto the stage and sat at a long table covered in felt. Seven microphones lined the table in front of which stood a four-foot-high model of an Atlas rocket, topped with a tiny cone-shaped object: a Mercury capsule. The tension in the room was palpable, especially among the wire service correspondents and reporters for afternoon newspapers, whose deadlines were fast approaching. They would have to bolt to telephones as soon as they got the press kits listing the astronauts' names—before they even uttered their first public words. Crowded in with the other photographers, Morse scanned the seven, wondering which was the one who lived in Arlington. Finally, as the noise level lowered to a tense hum, a NASA public relations man named Walter T. Bonney walked out from behind the curtain and addressed the crowd.

"Ladies and gentlemen," Bonney began, "may I have your attention, please. The rules of this briefing are very simple. In about sixty seconds we will give you the announcement you have all been waiting for: the names of the seven volunteers who will become the Mercury astronaut team. Following the distribution of the kit—and this will be done as speedily as possible—those of you who have P.M. deadline problems had better dash for your phone. We will have a ten- or twelve-minute break during which the gentlemen will be available for picture-taking.

"There will be no talk, however," Bonney added. "Then we will reconvene, hoping that the P.M. boys have done their filing and come back and start the presentation and the Q and A."

Several functionaries, laden with half-inch-thick press kits, began handing them out to reporters. The men on deadline bolted out of the room, the luckier ones leaving their back-up people behind to take notes. Along the bank of phones, it was all shouting. "We got the names! Gimme dictation... New Lead astro... No, not Shep-HERD; ShepARD!: S, H, E... Schirra's got a 'C'... —of New Concord, Ohio. No, I don't know where it is. And it's Glenn, with two 'Ns'..."

In the ballroom, meanwhile, Bonney, gesturing to the silent panel of seven behind him, declared: "These are the astronaut volunteers! Take your pictures as you will, gentlemen."

The photographers surged forward. They squatted in front of the astronauts, the photographers with shorter lenses in front, crouched down at table-top level, the ones with the tele- photos behind. The air was filled with the noise of releasing shutters and the whirr-click-whirr of motor drives. After a short while, Bonney and others began shooing the photographers away and the director of NASA, T. Keith Glennan, an Eisen- hower appointee, took the stage for the formal introductions.

"Ladies and gentlemen," Glennan began, "today we are introducing to you and to the world these seven men who have been selected to begin training for orbital space flight. These men, the nation's Project Mercury astronauts, are here after a long and perhaps unprecedented series of evaluations which told our medical consultants and scientists of their superb adapt- ability to their upcoming flight.

"It is my pleasure," continued Glennan, "to introduce to you—and I consider it a very real honor, gentlemen—Malcolm S. Carpenter, Leroy G. Cooper, John H. Glenn, Jr., Virgil I. Grissom, Walter M. Schirra, Jr., Alan B. Shepard, Jr., and Donald K. Slayton.

"The nation's Mercury astronauts!"

The pilots themselves had not formally met as selectees until the night before, at Langley Field, near Newport News, Vir- ginia. They were a curious mix. Three from the Air Force, three from the Navy and one Marine. The service symmetry was laughable, though at the press conference, Bonney would insist, "They did it by the numbers, not by the service. It just happened that way."

There was Carpenter, the laconic Navy lieutenant who had never flown in combat. Neither for that matter had Gordon Cooper, the seemingly confident Air Force flier with a toothy grin that looked somehow cold. Even though the Navy's Alan Shepard was regarded as one of the best during his time at Pax River, he too had never seen combat. Three had seen some action: Grissom and Schirra in Korea, where each had won a Distinguished Flying Cross; Slayton in World War II, on bombing runs. Only Glenn, the oldest of the group at 37, was an acknowledged hero of two wars, with six DFCs, eighteen Air Medals and three confirmed MiG kills.

Glennan finally hushed the crowd as the seven astronauts nervously looked at each other. It was the first time they had ever experienced anything like this. The military was, almost by definition, a place where one labored in anonymity, where the press was an annoyance, even a danger. If ever a career officer found himself in contact with a journalist, the safest route was to fob him off on the public information officer. Reporters were trouble.

But on that April day in 1959, it was bizarre. The press were no longer inquisitors, but idolaters. Or so they seemed. Even Glenn, the best known of the group, had never seen the press behave this way. It was a signal of what was to come, though he had no way of knowing it at the time.

One reporter asked Glennan who among the seven would be the "first to orbit the earth?" "I cannot tell you," the NASA director replied. "He won't know himself until the day of the flight." There had been comparatively little discussion of any flight order. At the time there was little consensus on the flights themselves: how many suborbital flights it would take before NASA and the White House gave the go ahead for the first earth orbit.

It was clear that NASA was peddling personalities, not flight plans because, in fact, it had none. To the assembled press, preparing to make heroes of the seven men sitting at the felt-covered table, it mattered little. The questions quickly turned trite, sentimental, and to some astronauts, just plain silly. Only Glenn seemed at ease with the type of questioning that is common when reporters confront an issue they can barely understand.

"I'd like to ask Lieutenant Carpenter," said a voice from the crowd, "if his wife has anything to say about this, or his four children."

"They all are as enthusiastic about the program as I am," Carpenter replied tersely.

Walter Bonney began orchestrating things. "Suppose we go down the line, one, two, three, on that," he said unctuously. "The question is 'Has your good lady and your children had anything to say about this?'"

The astronauts were arranged alphabetically, with Carpenter on the left, Slayton on the right. Glenn sat near the middle. Most of them mouthed the same answer as Carpenter, in one form or another. Shepard, who was to develop a deep disdain for reporters, scowled. "I have no problems at home. My family is in complete agreement," he replied tersely.

Slayton publicly revealed the private attitude of most of them when he bluntly said: "What I do is pretty much my business, professionwise. My wife goes along with it." Later in the press conference, he elaborated with an answer typifying the times. "My wife isn't too concerned about what I do professionally," Slayton maintained. "She's more concerned with whether I can find a babysitter and whether there's a commissary nearby to buy groceries and that sort of thing." He added: "Whether I'm in this program or a filling station, it doesn't make any difference."

Glenn's answer was more like Carpenter's, but with one important addition. He too said his family was enthusiastic about the program. But unlike Carpenter—and not at all like Slayton—Glenn indicated Annie and the children had a say in it. What's more, Glenn presumed to speak for all seven when he said:

"I don't think any of us could really go on with something like this if we didn't have pretty good backing at home, really." Most of the others stared out grimly into the crowd. "My wife's attitude toward this has been the same as it has been all along through all my flying," Glenn continued enthusiastically. "If it is what I want to do, she is behind it. The kids are too, a hundred percent."

As the press conference progressed, the pattern rarely changed. On almost every question, Glenn had a quotable answer. One could see the pens and pencils racing faster across the paper every time Glenn leaned his crewcut and bow tie into the microphone.

When asked about their religious affiliations, all mumbled something vague and noncommittal, since there were few regular churchgoers. All but Glenn. He proudly described his staunch Presbyterianism, which he took "very seriously, as a matter of fact," and his belief that each person is placed on earth with a specific set of talents to be used to the best of his ability. He had an answer—a small speech, actually—ready for almost everything. After his comments about his backing at home, for example, Glenn lightened things up with a joke.

"I got on this program because it probably would be the nearest to heaven I would ever get and I wanted to make the most of it," he said, to appreciative laughter from the audience and pained looks from his colleagues. He followed with a homily about the Wright brothers. "This whole project," Glenn declared, "sort of stands with us now...like the way the Wright brothers stood at Kitty Hawk fifty years ago, with Orville and Wilbur pitching a coin to see who was going to shove the other one off the hill down there...

"I think we are very fortunate that we have, should we say, been blessed with the talents that have been picked for something like this." Then once again he presumed to speak for the others. "Every one of us would feel guilty, I think, if we didn't make the fullest use of our talents in volunteering for something like this, that is as important as this is to our country and the world in general right now."

Yes, he answered, he had thought of space travel before, in his test pilot work, when he made "zoom flights" to bring a plane to maximum altitude, to the edge of the atmosphere, on a climb. "I don't think I ever made a zoom climb," Glenn said, "where I didn't have the feeling, 'if I just had the power to loop this thing on out a little bit.'"

Despite Walter Bonney's efforts to steer questions to "brother Grissom" or "brother Shepard," Glenn was becoming the spokesman of the group. Even on the question of which of the screening tests they liked least, Glenn had the obvious reference to the Silver Stallion that made the papers. "It is rather difficult to pick one," he said with a wide grin, "because if you figure how many openings there are on a human body and how far you can go into any one of them, you answer which one would be the toughest for you."

At which point Schirra piped in: "I think that goes for all of us."

"That was the toughest one for me," Glenn declared.

"I don't know which it is yet," the reporter persisted.

"I think he answered it very well," Gordon Cooper said, ending the discussion.

The clock showed that the press conference had been going on nearly one-and-a-half hours, long by Washington standards. Suddenly, May Craig, a sharp-tongued Texas newspaperwoman who had become a fixture on the early *Meet the Press* broadcasts, said: "Could I ask for a show of hands of how many are confident that they will come back from outer space?" The seven squirmed uncomfortably, knowing they would have to raise their hands like schoolboys, being thoroughly embarrassed by the theatrics. Once again, Glenn set himself apart, raising both hands up in the air.

Finally at 3:25, someone asked the last question: "How did you eliminate men who had unsympathetic wives?" Bonney responded: "The answer to that is that they didn't volunteer."

The competition to become an astronaut had tested Glenn's ability to excel physically, mentally and bureaucratically. Now one of the chosen seven, he faced another challenge: to become the first human being to fly in space. As he has throughout life, Glenn met the challenge with his eyes, in the words of friend Rene Carpenter, fixed on an imaginary horizon line. But by the time the first Mercury flight was set, Glenn had alienated almost all of his fellow astronauts. It was not only because of his single-minded zeal to be first, but because of what some felt was an ostentatious way of showing it.

It was Glenn who was always "on," anxious to go into his patriotic act whenever he was stopped in public or asked to speak. It was Glenn who moved into the bachelor officers' quarters at Langley during his training, as if to show a monklike devotion to the cause. It was Glenn who always seemed to be jogging around the BOQ grounds or on the beach in Florida, in what some colleagues took as an effort to curry favor with NASA superiors. There was something else about Glenn they didn't like: his unbending Calvinist view of personal morality, something he later tried with little success to impose on the others.

Still, Glenn's hidebound morality as well has his open ambition could not mask a certain guilelessness that captivated the press, if not his fellow astronauts. Ralph Morse recalls what happened after the press conference. "Glenn turned out to be the guy from Arlington and I was supposed to go home with him for some pictures but wound up staying three days." He remembers showing up at the Glenn's well-kept ranch house on Arlington's North Harrison Street shortly after the press conference, expecting to find an army of reporters and photographers. There were none. "I was all set to muscle my way in, to get there and put my foot in the door," Morse recalls with surprise, "but it was a wide open reception."

"They couldn't have been nicer," Morse remembers, "John, Annie, the kids, all of them." Glenn would hardly be rude to a *Life* magazine photographer looking for exclusive photographs of Glenn with his family. But that simple courtesy could have extended merely to a half-hour photo session. Instead, Morse was invited to say for dinner and waterski. He did, and prudently laid the groundwork for a professional relationship that ultimately turned into a genuine quarter-century friendship. It also has produced some wonderful photographs of John Glenn.

After the press conference, the media were caught up in an ecstatic love affair with their first spacemen. James Reston in the *New York Times* was typical: "They spoke of 'duty' and 'faith' and 'country' like Walt Whitman's pioneers," he wrote in his column. "This is a pretty cynical town, but nobody went away from these young men scoffing at their courage and idealism."

The men were patriotic career military officers, but the press was reading into them what the nation seemed to need at the time. To most of the astronauts the Mercury program was a job. An important job. A potentially dangerous job. A job that had worldwide implications. But still, a job.

"It was," says someone who watched the astronauts train over the ensuing two years, "a feeling of 'OK, we're the hot pilots who are gonna do this job. Let's get it done, don't fuck up. For Chrissakes, get it finished and let's go to the Paris Air Show.'" Until the space program, in fact, no one outside the aviation fraternity cared who was inside such early prototype space vehicles as the X-15 rocket or the X-20 "Dyna-Soar." Only other pilots knew the name of Chuck Yeager, the weatherbeaten World War II ace from West Virginia who had broken the sound barrier in the X-1 while secretly nursing the two ribs he fractured after falling off a horse two nights before the flight. Or Iven C. Kincheloe, the movie star handsome and supremely able test pilot who, like one in four of his colleagues, died in flames.

Other "hot" pilots in the aviation community, like those who dismissed Project Mercury as "Spam in a can," were less than pleased with the sudden prominence given the astronauts. To them they were seven men whom they saw as very good—but by no means the best—test pilots. Chuck Yeager, for example, stunned reporters with his attitude. Expecting Yeager to glorify his colleagues, he instead made the blunt observation that the Mercury project did not require much skill from its pilots. It was to be a totally automated flight. Besides, Yeager said, a monkey was going to make the first journey.

Yeager and his colleagues at Edwards, of course, had their own bureaucratic wars to fight over NASA and the Mercury program. Money spent on Mercury was money not spent on the X-program. But Yeager's views were unexpectedly negative. It was not what the press, and by extension, the public, wanted to hear. His remarks received almost no coverage in a sustained publicity blitz that transformed seven obscure pilots overnight into public icons. They were suddenly seven brave souls who would go forth to do battle against the Russian monolith.

The pacesetter for the flattery was *Life* magazine, but the instigator was NASA itself. Fearful not only that "the boys," as they often were called, would be "duck-nibbled to death" by intrusive reporters, NASA was equally concerned that each of the astronauts might want to make his own publicity deal on the side, dangling in front of the highest bidder lurid stories about death-defying exploits in outer space.

Bob Voas recalls: "The idea was one hundred percent NASA's. They sold it to the astronauts within 30 minutes after they arrived. They hadn't yet had their news conference, and the plane was waiting outside to take us all to Washington. It was suggested to them that they had a valuable property in their personal stories, and that the best way to handle it would be to have all their stories contracted for at one time."

The prospect of additional income to fliers making little more than $12,000 a year, including all allowances and flight pay, was welcome. Leo DeOrsey had already proposed a plan to sell book and magazine rights on their personal stories to the highest bidder. Once he received the go-ahead from all parties —the White House, NASA and, finally, the astronauts themselves—he began soliciting bids with a floor of $500,000.

Life, which was one of the few magazines that could afford that sum, bid the minimum and won. In return for exclusive rights to the astronauts' personal stories, *Life* would equally divide the half-million dollars among the seven, and spread the payments out over the three years the Mercury program was expected to run. It amounted to an extra yearly income of $23,809 for each astronaut, a tripling of family income while he was in the program. In addition, it meant that the astronauts had every right to ignore—in fact, were prohibited by the contract from speaking to—any reporter seeking information about their home or personal lives. They had only to deal with the polite men and women from *Life*, who, operating under unusually tight constraints, had to clear everything they wrote not only with the astronauts but with NASA.

The arrangement produced a uniform picture, bereft of controversy or excitement save for a few breathless retellings of war exploits or flight test emergencies. Anything that was not standard Apple Pie America simply did not see print. No one, for example, read that Deke Slayton's wife, Marge, had previously been divorced, or that Gordon Cooper and his wife, Trudy, had been separated, or that Annie Glenn had such a severe stutter that she could barely complete sentences.

No one read about the after-hours activity with the willing female "groupies" at Cocoa Beach and elsewhere. Instead, *Life*'s readers were treated to the astronauts as devoted family men, devout Christians, and above all, heroes. Even the wives got their own *Life* cover, featuring a heavily retouched and studio lit portrait of them all, similar to one made of their husbands just a few weeks before. It ran with the legend: "Seven Brave Women Behind the Astronauts."

Loudon Wainwright, now assistant managing editor of the resurrected monthly, concedes that, as a journalist, he "squirmed" under such censorship. "There were times when I wished we didn't have the contract," he maintains. But he adds: "I found out alot of stuff that I never would have been able to get under any other circumstances. Still, it's boring not to be able to say what you want on your own."

Wainwright, a graceful writer, did much of the ghostwriting of the early astronaut-signed articles on their training, both at Langley Field in Virginia, the established headquarters, and at Cape Canaveral. "The astronauts worked on the articles too," Wainwright notes, "and had very much to do with the content of the pieces, as well as their tone. In fact, we reporters always felt uncomfortable with that arrangement."

The "*Life* deal" had other reporters crying foul from the start, claiming that they had been cut out of one of the biggest stories of the century by checkbook journalism. And *Life*, through DeOrsey, kept tight rein on the astronauts. A November 27, 1959, letter from DeOrsey to Glenn warned him and the others about any contact with reporters that could be turned into an exclusive, or exclusive-appearing, story. The letter, on heavy bond stationery of the law firm of DeOrsey and Thompson, noted a magazine reference to a book on the astronauts called *The Star-Struck Seven*, to be published by Popular Mechanics Press. "Dear John," DeOrsey's letter began, "I enclose herewith an excerpt from a local magazine. You see how dangerous it is to give anyone any length of time to discuss matters with you. I think it is only fair to *Life* magazine that we do not permit such things as this to happen. Will you convey this thought to the rest of the boys, and remember me to them and their better half. Kindest regards, Leo."

"I can't get excited about whether it was the wrong thing to do, whether it was immoral or whether people were cheated," declares Wainwright. "There was a lot of criticism at the time from the rest of the press. I would have been making the same noise too if I had been on the outside since everybody was getting screwed because we had the inside deal.

"But President Kennedy connived in the deal, and so did the astronauts and so did NASA. That was the way they wanted to handle it. In effect, they got a paid life-insurance policy since they could control what the closest sources to the astronauts said about them."

It is important to remember that the vast majority of reporters did not think *Life*'s coverage wanting at the time. They were upset only at being deprived of the chance to write the same type of story. The American press during that pre-Vietnam, pre-Watergate period of the late fifties and early sixties took it upon itself to see that the niceties were observed, determined that the astronauts were to be portrayed only in the most glowing terms, any contrary facts notwithstanding. It was an attitude, Wainwright contends, that played to John Glenn's strengths. "I think Glenn felt he articulated a real responsibility about the image the astronauts would convey to the public. I think he always felt that very strongly. Was any of it forced or strained? I think not. I don't think it was forced. I think John believes what he says."

Besides working smoothly with Wainwright, Glenn was simultaneously trying to keep unfavorable references to the astronauts out of print elsewhere. In 1963, for example, long after his own space flight, Glenn managed to persuade the *Houston Chronicle* to kill an article by syndicated columnist Arthur Hoppe that was critical of the astronauts for peddling their personal stories. The article portrayed a fictional moonlanding in which every response to a reporter is quashed because all the astronaut's answers, including ones about his blood pressure and pulse, have already been contracted for by someone else.

"Kill this," wrote the editor in the margin of the column. "Funny, but false premise, sez Glenn." The false premise, maintained Glenn, was that scientific information was being withheld from the press because of financial arrangements. In fact, Glenn maintains, only personal stories were covered by *Life*. It was a fine distinction, but it was one that ultimately persuaded President Kennedy to let the arrangement continue after he took office.

Today Glenn sees the adulatory *Life* coverage—which, for all its shortcomings, was deftly written, crammed with information and well laid out—as a function of the time. He understands that it was an approach that could not be taken today, but he does not say it was wrong.

"At that time, I don't know how else you could have done it," Glenn maintains. "I won't say we were figments of the imagination of the press, but, putting yourself back 21 or 22 years ago, we were so new and so different that it was very difficult for anyone to 'Walter Mitty' himself into our position." Certainly, Glenn says, almost anyone can relate to a racing car driver hurtling around a track because at one time or another one has spun out or skidded. "But in the space program, we were into something so new that I think we took on a dimension bigger than ourselves. There was no base point from which to relate to it that the press could use as a common ground."

Lacking such a base point, the press fell back on an old standby: hero worship.

Shortly after their first exposure to the public, the seven began what one person close to them calls a "year-long dog and pony show." It included visits to several sites where Mercury project components were being built or where communications and tracking equipment was based. The wife of one of the astronauts says that during these visits there was "a lot of screwing around" by some of the men. "There was a lot of drinking and all of that stuff." Admits Scott Carpenter, "It was more fun than I can tell you."

In the early phase of their preflight training, astronaut

headquarters was at Langley. But as the months went by, more and more time was spent in Florida, at Cape Canaveral, and in the evenings, at nearby Cocoa Beach. There were few amenities in the little community of Cocoa Beach. It was there they first encountered Henri Landwirth, an immigrant Belgian Jew who came to the United States with $20 in his pocket after escaping the Nazis in World War II. Twenty years later, he was running a hotel. A gregarious Hans Conreid look-alike with a showman's zest and a promoter's eye, Landwirth cultivated the astronauts and became their friend. Later, when he took over the Holiday Inn nearby, they moved in there.

Cocoa Beach was a sparse, bug-ridden stretch of land, featuring rock-hard beaches and faded stucco cottages. The astronauts loved it. The work days at the Cape were long and tedious. Often the work stretched on for ten or 12 hours, many in the cramped flight simulator, a cone-shaped object made to resemble a Mercury capsule in which each astronaut would go through the flight routine over and over.

There was precious little flying, and many of the frustrated team let off steam in other ways. One was by driving fast cars, leased through a friendly Cocoa Beach GM dealer and former Indy 500 champion, Jim Rathmann. They were soon tooling around south Florida at night in Corvettes, Maseratis and, in Carpenter's case, a Shelby Cobra. Glenn stuck to his own car, a pathetically underpowered Prinz that was forever giving him trouble. (His letters to the dealer complaining about the car would one day fetch several hundred dollars at auction.)

Both Glenn and Scott Carpenter confirm that another way some of the Mercury team relaxed was through sex. It was easy, available, fleeting sex, with the willing young women who appeared in Cocoa Beach as the boom town grew. "There was a lot of socializing," recalls one of the seven, not referring to cocktails. How prevalent was it? he is asked. "The best answer is that it is endemic among military aviators," he replies. Asked about one of his colleagues, widely known as "the greatest swordsman in the Navy," the astronaut replies: "Oh, I think everyone saw that it was part of his personality."

One might make a case that events naturally conspired to place members of the Mercury team in bed with women who were not their wives. The long, tedious workdays, followed by the steamy Florida evenings around the motel pools, with the setting sun casting a scarlet wash over a succession of lovely women, might lead a lonely man astray. It was especially tempting if wives were deemed off limits at the Cape, which they were.

Glenn was a conspicuous exception to the promiscuity. Not only did he ignore the groupies, but he worked to keep the astronauts' behavior from becoming a national scandal. The rampant carousing in late 1960 and '61, as the new administration took office and reviewed its options about the space program, was making Glenn nervous. He was afraid the press would abandon its self-imposed Victorian blinders in favor of a damn good story. Finally, the potential for a true scandal, complete with a late-night effort by Glenn to quash a news story and incriminating photographs, led to an angry showdown between John Glenn and Alan Shepard. The effort may have cost Glenn his chance to be the first American in space.

"Jerry Weisner, who was to be President Kennedy's science advisor, and some of the other people advising the incoming president were very concerned that if there was an early failure in one of the flights, it would be a tremendous setback for the country and also for President Kennedy," Glenn now says with a deep breath, as he begins a story that was not easy for him to finally tell.

"At the time, they were suggesting that it might be wise to go to a greatly increased number of chimp flights before we tried one with a man. They were serious enough about this to actually propose to Kennedy that the manned flights be held up for an indefinite period. We had to put together a big briefing to counter it. A whole team from NASA headquarters came down to talk about the status of the program. I was afraid that any bad publicity might have an impact on whether we really had a manned program for a while.

"I talked about this at some of our meetings," Glenn says firmly. "I said I thought that everybody should be more careful about their outside activities. Bad publicity could have an impact and cancel the program. Everybody said, 'Well, you're probably right,' but there still was more activity than I thought there should be. We talked about this a number of times.''

Glenn's prophecy finally came true at two o'clock one morning, while the astronauts were in San Diego for a tour of a rocket plant. The phone woke Glenn in his hotel room. On the other end was an agitated John "Shorty" Powers, the NASA spokesman.

"What you've been talking about has happened," Powers said in a tight, nervous voice.

"What do you mean?" Glenn asked, waking abruptly.

Powers said he had just received a phone call from a newspaper saying it had "compromising" photographs of one of the astronauts with a woman. They were planning to run them in the next day's editions. Not only that, a reporter as well as a photographer had been following the astronaut all evening in San Diego and in Tijuana across the border. They had put together a chronicle of what was bound to look like an international debauch by one of America's presumptive space heroes.

Glenn told Powers to come to his room. In the predawn, as Glenn dourly entertained visions of the Mercury project being killed, they decided the only course was to try to suppress the story. It would take more than some NASA flack to kill it. Glenn decided to pick up the phone and call the paper himself.

"I talked to both the reporter and to the photographer and later the publisher or the night editor," Glenn recalls. "I talked about the Russians, 'godless Communists,' how you gotta let us get back in the race.' I pulled out all the stops."

It worked. "The story did not appear in the papers. But it well could have if I hadn't talked to them," says Glenn, who prefers not to name the offending astronaut.

The next morning, when the astronauts assembled, Glenn announced that he had something important to say. Both Glenn and Scott Carpenter reconstruct what happened at that meeting.

John Glenn angry offers a different picture from the benign face in press photographs. His fair skin flushes, his green eyes flash and the mouth that easily relaxes in a bright, wide smile tightens ominously. Dammit, he thundered, he was not going to see this project jeopardized by a group of hyperthyroid pilots who couldn't keep their pants zipped. He had told them before and he was telling them for the last time: There was just so much that the press was going to wink at it before it printed a story that could kill it for all of them.

The faces of his fellow pilots were sullen. Across the room, Shepard rose to accuse Glenn of stepping way out of line. He told Glenn to mind his own business; that the company of women was no one's business but their own as long as it did not affect their work or the image of the project.

"Everyone resented John's intrusion on their private behavior," recalls Scott Carpenter, the only one of the group to fully side with Glenn. But Glenn wasn't buying any of it. He retorted sharply that the image of the project would have been fatally compromised had it not been for his own efforts earlier that morning. Anyone who could not see that was simply putting his private life ahead of his public responsibilities. The old rules no longer applied, Glenn told them. They were public figures, whether they liked it or not.

Schirra and Cooper tended to back Shepard, arguing that what a pilot did on his off hours was his own concern, as long as he did his job correctly. Grissom and Slayton said they could see Glenn's point, but had no real enthusiasm for it. It was basically five against two: Glenn and Carpenter against five test pilots who were accustomed to getting their own way. When it was over, Glenn knew he had not made any friends, but he had made his point.

There are differing views about peer votes, particularly the one that Mercury project director Bob Gilruth asked the seven astronauts to cast among themselves in the waning months of 1960. Tension was rife in the agency: Embarrassing technical failures and possible budget cuts could sharply curtail, if not actually dismantle, the manned space program.

Scott Carpenter calls peer votes "a valuable input" in decision-making. Bob Voas believes it may have been "something Bob Gilruth decided to do on his own" to lessen the onus of having to make the difficult choice himself. Glenn dismisses peer votes as unreliable "popularity contests."

The proposal was simple: Though Gilruth and his deputies in the Space Task Group were going to make the final selection, Gilruth wanted each of the seven to vote for the man they would choose to make the first flight if he himself could not go.

The seven made their choices in confidence. Glenn voted for Scott Carpenter. Over the next three months they plunged back to work with renewed vigor. With the future of the program at risk, there was little time to worry about who would make the first flight. The agency had had two damaging fiascos in the preceding six months: the fiery blowup of a Mercury-Atlas Rocket on July 29, 1960, and the less dramatic, but even more embarrassing, failure of a Mercury-Redstone rocket shortly thereafter. The former lifted off the pad at Cape Canaveral before an audience of VIPs, only to explode. The latter simply belched flame for a while, stopped, and then popped its capsule escape tower into the air like a champagne cork.

Now, on January 19, 1961, the day before John Kennedy was to be inaugurated, Gilruth once again called the seven men into his office. He had originally planned to keep the identity of the first pilot secret until the eve of the flight itself. But, Gilruth said, that would not be practical. The pilot selected should have maximum access to the training equipment before launch. Thus, he told them, he had decided who would fly the first mission.

Glenn stared intently at Gilruth. He had worked, planned, even saved the program from scandal in pursuit of a prize he felt he deserved.

Gilruth began to speak. The first pilot would not be John Glenn. NASA had chosen Alan Shepard.

7

THE VOYAGE INTO SPACE

The anger John Glenn felt in losing out to Alan B. Shepard to be America's—and possibly the world's—first spaceman was deeper than any he had felt in his life. Never before in his military career had he suffered such a blow to his self-esteem. The most highly decorated of all the astronauts, the record-breaking test pilot, the candidate who breezed through the testing at Lovelace and Wright-Pat, was being passed over for Alan Shepard. The fact that Shepard's test scores also had been superb, in fact higher than Glenn's in the critically important procedures trainer, would, as Glenn later reflected, assuage his grievously wounded ego. But for now, Glenn had only his rage.

It was an impotent rage: there was nothing Glenn could do to reverse what he felt was a humiliating wrong. Instead, he had to smile graciously at Shepard, shake his hand and, worst of all, begin a maddening charade with the media who assumed that Glenn, the senior man and de facto leader of the seven, was still the most likely candidate for the history-making voyage.

Even if he had wanted to, Glenn could not totally mask his feelings. The day after the announcement, on January 20, 1961,

John F. Kennedy was being inaugurated 35th president of the United States as Glenn drove from Norfolk, Virginia, to Washington with Loudon Wainwright. Glenn was giving the writer a lift to National Airport before heading home to Arlington.

It was a brilliant, icy cold day, following an unexpectedly severe overnight snow that had blanketed the city and forced a hurried street-clearing in the predawn. Some streets remained treacherous, and Wainwright marveled at how well Glenn, whom he now regarded as a friend, negotiated the slippery roads. "As John and I drove," Wainwright recalls, "I remember remarking to myself how terrific a driver he was. But he was very upset."

Every time Wainwright tried to make conversation, Glenn would stare fixedly at the road. He was uncharacteristically somber. "We were trying to listen to Kennedy's inauguration speech on the radio," Wainwright remembers, "and we couldn't get him—his voice kept going in and out—and John kind of hammered the wheel. He seemed really very upset, and I thought at the time that he was moved by the president's speech. But I think that really, in retrospect, he was just pissed off."

When Wainwright arrived home, he immediately told his wife about Glenn's dark mood. Her reaction was perceptive: "Oh, I bet they selected somebody else," she declared.

Two months later, as the time neared for America's first space mission, and after NASA disingenuously announced that Glenn, Grissom and Shepard had been chosen as the "prime" candidates, the press still ballyhooed Glenn as the probable first astronaut. "Marine Stands Out as Astronaut Choice," headlined *Space-Aviation* magazine on March 21, 1961. Wrote the editor: "We say this because Glenn, at 39 the eldest of the group, has always been the father of the seven-man team, a leader without appointment, an officer particularly respected among the astronauts—and apparently all others in the Mercury Program—for his personality, his dedication, his skill and experience."

As the three "prime" pilots went through their training in early 1961—with Shepard secretly being allowed maximum use of the facilities—it was apparent the Soviet Union was nearing the end of its initial manned flight testing. They had successfully launched and retrieved two dogs in spacecraft containing dummy astronauts. Although time was precious to officials at NASA, Gilruth and Dr. Werner von Braun recommended one final test of the Redstone rocket that was to take Shepard in space. The test went perfectly.

Shortly after, on April 12, 1961, the Russians beat the United States into space with a man by launching a huge, five-ton rocket and placing a 27-year-old test pilot named Yuri Gagarin into space. The cosmonaut made one revolution of the earth and landed near the Soviet village of Smelovka. "Well, they just beat the pants off us, that's all," Glenn declared. "There's no use kidding ourselves about that. But now that the space age has begun, there's going to plenty of work for everybody."

Shepard made his 15-minute suborbital flight a few weeks after the Russians on May 5, 1961. It went off near-perfectly. Glenn served as a mere spectator when President Kennedy pinned a medal on Shepard the next day in the White House Rose Garden. "Then the second flight came up and John thought, 'I'll make that one,'" recalls Tom Miller. "His spirits were still low, but when they announced that Grissom was going to be number two, it really hit him hard."

Glenn was so discouraged by being overlooked that it began to affect his homelife. "He was very withdrawn," says Lyn. "I absolutely recall that. You see, Dad lived down at the bachelor officers' quarters at Langley and he would commute back and forth. We would see him on weekends a lot during that time. I remember all of us talking about it."

"When he came home weekends," Tom Miller recalls, "he wouldn't go anywhere. He didn't want to see any of his friends. He actually felt that he had failed personally. We used to love going waterskiing together with our families, but once John failed to get selected for the space flight, he started to withdraw into a shell. He wouldn't do anything; Annie would come, but John'd always have some damn excuse. Well, finally, I got good and mad. We were out in the yard together and I called him everything I could think of, the nicest thing being selfish. 'You may hate me for this,' I told him, 'but I think you're wrecking your family and yourself. You don't know when you're well off! Now get off it, dammit!'"

Chastened, but still miserable, Glenn realized that his friend was right. Later, Miller tried to persuade Glenn that missing out on the first two suborbital flights was no tragedy. It might even be a blessing.

"Hell, John," Miller said, "you don't want those goddam suborbital pump-up flights. Get the orbital flight if there's one you have a chance to select." To this day, Miller believes that NASA had always planned to hold Glenn until the first orbital mission, convinced it would be the program's most significant achievement. On the surface, his logic is compelling:

"The Grissom flight was certainly not the most exploratory," Miller contends. "And it did not require the greatest skill because Al Shepard already had done it with little or no hitch. Al had a hell of a lot of flight test experience; on the other hand, Grissom did not. So figure: Here's a flight where you have a few things to wrap up before the orbital one. Let's not spend our top dog in case something goes wrong."

Though several people would speculate that Glenn was somehow "saved" for the first orbital mission, the facts strongly indicate otherwise. "I think under many circumstances, John would have been chosen for the first flight," maintains Bob Voas, who insists it was "pure chance" that Glenn "got the best of the early flights." The "chance" Voas refers to had nothing to do with NASA; the space agency originally hoped to send up as many as five suborbital flights before attempting earth orbit.

Glenn's chance to make history must be credited to the Russians. Until August 6, 1961, the third mission was scheduled to be still another up-and-back suborbital flight atop a Redstone rocket. Another such suborbital seemed essential since Grissom's flight had ended with the loss of the capsule.

The spacecraft had been fitted with explosive bolts designed to open the spacecraft's hatch quickly once the capsule was secure on the deck of an aircraft carrier. As Grissom waited to be plucked from the Atlantic by a recovery helicopter, the bolts mysteriously blew. The capsule flooded and disappeared forever in water three miles deep. Six years later, on January 27,

1967, at Cape Canaveral, Grissom was killed along with astronauts Edward H. White and Roger B. Chaffee when fire raced through their three-man Apollo capsule during a launchpad test. To date they are the only U.S. space fatalities.

August 6, 1961, was the day that changed the course of the Mercury project, and with it, John Glenn's future. On that day, just two weeks after Grissom's ill-starred ride, the Soviet Union proved that its one-orbit adventure with Yuri Gagarin was not an isolated success. The Soviets hurled another mammoth rocket skyward; this time they kept their man aloft for sixteen orbits, spanning more than an entire day—25 hours and 18 minutes. The mission, called Vostok 2, was commanded by cosmonaut Gherman Titov.

It had an unnerving impact on the United States, which had yet to make even one orbital flight. Especially galling was the fact that the Soviet capsule passed over the United States three times, kindling fears about enemy killer satellites in the sky. Still, the Russian flight had one salutary effect. It forced NASA to conclude the Mercury-Redstone program and attempt an orbital flight using the Atlas, even though the more powerful rocket had done poorly in early trials.

The man chosen for the historic flight was the next in line, John H. Glenn, Jr. His back-up pilot, appropriately enough, was Glenn's friend Carpenter. In the waning months of 1961, the two men trained together intently, repeatedly going over flight procedures not only at Langley Field and the Cape, but at the naval air station at Johnsville, Pennsylvania, where they rode the huge centrifuge to familiarize themselves with the G-forces of liftoff and re-entry.

The lengths to which NASA went to simulate Glenn's actual flight were impressive. Grissom had reported that during his flight, when he viewed the huge missile gantry moving away from him in the moments before launch, he had had the odd sensation that the gantry was falling over. A little thing, perhaps, but one that could raise Glenn's anxiety level before takeoff. Glenn was strapped into his capsule atop an Atlas rocket and instructed to watch the gantry as it moved away.

Such thoroughness also extended to the postflight period. Fearful that the space capsule might land in an uncharted or unfriendly area, the astronauts underwent survival training at Stead Air Force Base in Reno. Glenn's handwritten notes from that period show that the astronauts were warned to "take it easy" and not to be "overfriendly" with natives they might encounter. "Observe natives and do as they do," Glenn wrote. In addition, each astronaut was given a phrasebook of expressions in such exotic languages as Swahili. "Interestingly," Glenn noted at the time, "in all of the languages, the word for stranger was 'enemy.'" They also learned to develop a taste for wild pig.

During survival training, the astronauts were told that the conventional wisdom about preserving water in desert climates was wrong. It was better to take healthy swigs of the water they had than to dole it out "Captain Bligh" style, a spoonful at a time. All that would do, the instructors said, was guarantee death by dehydration.

The astronauts were taken out to the Nevada desert and placed a half mile apart. They were expected to survive with the materials they would have on the flight, including parachute cloth, the space capsule itself, and a survival kit that included a large knife and shark repellant.

After survival training, physicians at the U.S. Naval School of Aviation Medicine in Pensacola insisted on still more medical tests. They were concerned about the eyes; many scientists feared the effects of prolonged weightlessness on all the senses, but especially on sight. "Some of the doctors thought that your eyes might change shape in weightlessness over a period of time," Glenn recalls. The doctors had no cure if this happened, but they wanted to know from Glenn immediately if it did. "If you were to look over at the instrument panel of the spacecraft," Glenn explains, "you'd see miniaturized versions of the Snellin chart, the eye charts you'd use in school or a doctor's office. If my eyes were to start to change shape and I started getting astigmatic and couldn't focus, or if I perceived any change in colors, I was to tell them.

"One of the basic purposes of that first flight," Glenn declares, "was for me to literally be a sponge of information: sensations, any impression I could possibly make. They wanted a record of it all. It's one of the things that made the space program so exciting—this experimenting on yourself. They had a little onboard recording tape and I was supposed to talk into it all the time." But for all of Glenn's current enthusiasm about being a "human sponge," his handwritten debriefing notes immediately after the flight make a mild complaint about "too much communicating."

The flight was scheduled for December 20, 1961, but the weather would not cooperate. As clouds loomed dark over the launch site, the flight was postponed. It was postponed several times well into the new year, because of both weather and mechanical problems. Dr. Constantine Generales, Jr., a space medical researcher who had no connection with NASA, suggested that Glenn should have been removed from the mission after so many postponements. "Anxiety had undoubtedly built up in Glenn's subconscious from all the stops he has encountered," he said.

Actually, Glenn's emotions were well in check. He helped keep them that way by sober thoughts on his possible death in space, a concern he shared with his wife and children on a quiet weekend shortly before he blasted off. It was important for him to involve his family in what he was facing, including the possibility that the luck that had sustained him through two wars might run out on launchpad 14.

"Maybe I was fortunate in that I was the oldest of that first astronaut group," Glenn says, looking back. "My kids were a little bit older too, and better able to understand what was going on. Whenever we could, we'd have the whole family sit around and I'd describe everything I could to them. I wanted all of them, Annie, Dave and Lyn, to feel the same confidence that I had. I even made some tape recordings for them, reflecting on the observations I had made during training."

Annie recalls watching her husband go through underwater escape drills from his Mercury capsule. Dave looks back fondly on the two weeks he spent one summer with his father in the bachelor officers' quarters at Langley, when he shadowed Glenn the entire time. He jogged with his father on the beach in the morning, then watched him train on simulators and other formidable equipment that awed the 15-year-old. The period Glenn spent with his son served two purposes. It offered Dave a better appreciation of his father's mission and gave Glenn, who still feels guilty for having been an absent parent during many of the years when his children were growing up, a rare chance to experience the communion he had missed with his son.

As Dave remembers it how: "I really think my understanding of the mission was an enormous help to me when it came time for him to perch on this explosive vehicle going off into the unknown. We all were really scared, but at least it wasn't something I knew nothing about."

To his family, Glenn did not gloss over the dangers of the mission. Privately, he was convinced that one of the original Mercury seven would die in America's first space program. In the final weeks before his much-delayed liftoff, on a crisp winter day, Glenn took his family for a picnic to Great Falls, Virginia. "Up until that time, we had talked mostly about technology," Lyn remembers. "Dad had brought home mockups of the capsule and we had gone over his flight plan. We understood a lot of that side of it. But sitting out on those rocks that day at Great Falls was the first time Dad—or any of us—had discussed the possibility of his dying."

Gone was the beaming hero who would captivate a nation with his self-effacing manner. Glenn was now a father struggling with the thought that this might be the last time he would see his family. "Dad did all the talking," Lyn recalls. "He said we'd gone through his training together. He wanted to be sure that if anything happened to him, that we didn't blame anyone for it. He said that all of us had made the decision for him to make this flight, and he didn't want us to be bitter if he should die. He didn't want us to blame him. He didn't want us to blame NASA. He didn't want us to blame God or lose any of our religious feeling if—he said again—he might die.

"I was just so stunned that I couldn't even respond," Lyn continues. "We had a brief discussion about it, but it was really overwhelming at that point. That was the first time—and the only time—that we discussed the possibility of his death."

The solid foundation that John and Annie had built on in their relationship with their children sustained them—not only through the excitement and dread of the space flight, but later, when the overwhelming media attention would disrupt their lives. Still later, when both Lyn and Dave needed support during their own personal trials, their parents were there to provide it.

Like most parents, the Glenns had their measure of self-doubt and anxiety over their children. The first occasion was when Dave went through a long period of alienation and rebellion while a student at Harvard; then later when Lyn suffered through, and finally ended, an unhappy marriage. "Do I like them?" Dave, now 37, declares. "Oh, my God, yes. I can't imagine better parents." Lyn, now 36, says the same.

"I give Annie the biggest credit for that," Glenn says about the closeness of their family. He adds that because he felt guilty about often being away while a Marine flier, he tried all the harder to be a parent when at home. "When we were together, we tried to do everything possible as a family," he says. Glenn stresses that he did not forget about the children while he was overseas. Both Dave and Lyn recall that the many letters their father wrote to their mother always included a long handwritten section for them.

Annie notes that when her husband did come home, he was careful not to overwhelm the children with sudden displays of affection. "John just gradually would make up to them," Annie explains. "At the age Dave and Lyn were, to see someone you had only seen in pictures as this great big person, why it took a little time. But after a while it just seemed very natural for them to be together."

Dave recalls these early separations from his father. "As far back as we can remember, at important times like holidays when you feel the separation even more than usual, Dad would often call from Japan, or wherever he was," says Dave. "Back then, a phone call from overseas was an incredible thing. And later on, when he was with NASA in Florida or wherever, he'd be on the phone quite a bit."

The phone calls remind Dave of what he considers the worst aspect of military life: its rootlessness. "My sister and I probably feel the same way," he says. "After we'd been somewhere for three years, we would develop a lot of pals. Then those friendships would be broken—most often forever—and that was really hard to swallow. As a reaction to that, I want to find one place now and stay there."

In later years, when Glenn had settled into a comparatively stable routine as a test pilot, the dinner table served as the center for family communication. "We made it a standard practice every night after dinner," Glenn recalls. "You didn't just leave the dinner table; you had to spend about 15 minutes as family time, reviewing what each one had done during the day."

"And," Glenn adds, "we'd try to stress the idea of family, that each one of us had a responsibility to the group. I had a certain job to do. I was flying. And Annie was doing her job in the house, and the kids each had their job to do in school." After the brief review of the day, Glenn notes, "There always would be questions about something or other, and the encyclopedia was right there. Likely as not, we'd get wound up looking something up and talking about it."

Both the Glenn children remember their home life as congenial but comparatively strict. Glenn does not deny this, but says that usually the discipline took the form of "restrictions on what the children could do and could not do, rather than physically pounding on them.

"But if discipline was to be administered," Glenn adds, "it was done on the spot, as close to the scene of the crime as possible." Both parents shared disciplinary duties, neither believing in the "wait-till-your-father-comes-home" theory.

The Glenns tried to instill in their children the same strong religious beliefs that guided their own lives. Their efforts have produced mixed results. While both children describe themselves as religious, neither is a devout churchgoer. Dave recalls chafing every Sunday at having to stay close to home with the family, unable to play with his friends. Later, in college, as part of his rebellion, Dave fell away from the strict precepts of his parents' Presbyterianism in favor of a far more relaxed personal code.

But Dave does not deny all religious feeling. "Probably because of my religious upbringing, I somehow have a very large capacity for religious sensitivity, a sense that the world is a mysterious and holy place. I don't know how I'd label myself except to say that I feel quite religious. I don't belong to any cults, but I have dropped away from my belief in the typical Presbyterian Christianity I was brought up with."

In marked contrast to his father, Dave no longer accepts much of the Christian doctrine. "My problem is taking Jesus to be a person who was raised from the dead and went up into heaven and walked around the face of the earth. At some point in college, I guess I realized I just didn't believe that anymore.

"It's a question Karen and I are dealing with right now," Dave adds, referring to his wife, a young woman he met while she was doing advance work for Glenn's 1974 Senate campaign. "We have a brand-new baby boy [Glenn's first grandchild, Daniel Erik] and we have to give some thought as to how to raise him. What place will the traditional American religions have in his upbringing? I certainly couldn't tell him I believe things I don't believe."

Dave, who is both articulate and candid, concedes that he drifted far apart from his parents—much farther than his sister —during a trying time at Harvard in the sixties when drugs, casual sex and rampant opposition to the Vietnam War prompted conservatives to label the school the "Kremlin on the Charles River." Later, after a stint in the Navy, Dave let his hair grow shoulder-length and wore a leather thong around his head. Though, as he says, not "a total weirdo," Dave Glenn bore no outward resemblance to his father at Muskingum College in the late thirties.

"It was during the middle of my college years that I made my emotional separation from my parents," Dave says. "At the time I felt I had an awful lot of trouble talking to them. I was getting so smart up at Harvard that I felt: 'What did they know, my old parents?' But they didn't make any threats. They didn't say that if I didn't behave they would withdraw their emotional closeness.

"Drugs? I'd just say no comment to that. I was never into LSD at college, but beyond that, I'll just leave it at that. I was never an acid head. I never really flipped out. It was just a difficult period of time to decide what the limits were."

Today, speaking about his son's period of rebellion, Glenn says: "Was I apprehensive? Sure, but I didn't despair. I was anxious about it, because a lot of kids were going off the deep end and doing things that would affect them the rest of their lives. I certainly didn't want Lyn and Dave to be part of that. But Annie and I always had reasonable faith that they had been brought up with certain values in school and in church and at home. We knew that at the very least they knew what we thought was the right thing. The big question was how far they'd go to kick over the traces and throw it down the tube."

Glenn, the mild disciplinarian, says it would have been foolish to forbid his children to ever take drugs or engage in premarital sex. "I did, however, talk to them about how ridiculous it would be," Glenn says. "They were old enough to make their own judgments. Just to come out and say, 'I forbid you' with kids of that age would probably be the best way to force them into trying it."

The Glenns remain a close family. Lyn, now happily remarried, lives in Vail, Colorado, with her husband, Phillip Freedman, a doctor, whom Dave regards as a brother. Always active in Democratic politics, Lyn is a key part of her father's presidential campaign. Dave and Karen live with their baby son near San Francisco, where Dave is an anaesthesiologist at Marshall Hale Hospital. With a certain sadness Glenn notes that his family has been scattered all over the country. Annie, who longs to see her grandson far more often than she does, is frustrated by the 2,000 miles between them. It is far different from the time more than 20 years ago when her world was centered on Harrison Street in Arlington, Virginia, and for a time on a single launchpad at Cape Canaveral.

That launchpad was the focus of an emotionally wrenching day for the family when Glenn's flight was delayed again on January 27, 1962. Glenn had already endured more than five hours in the Friendship 7 capsule when the mission was postponed with only 20 minutes to go because of heavy cloud cover. Back in Arlington, Annie, the children, a few friends and Loudon Wainwright of *Life* were watching the scheduled launch on television when word came that the vice-president of the United

States, Lyndon B. Johnson, was parked in his limousine waiting to see Mrs. Glenn and the Glenn children.

Named by Kennedy to be his liaison with the space program, Johnson had brought along a horde of reporters and photographers. They soon joined those on the front lawn of the Glenn house, newsmen who were being kept at bay by the terms of the exclusive *Life* contract. When Johnson's aides asked when the vice-president could pay his call on the Glenns, they were bluntly told he could not enter the house. Thus started the confrontation that has grown to legendary proportions.

In Tom Wolfe's book *The Right Stuff*, Glenn is portrayed as fiercely backing up his stuttering wife by telephone when she forbids the vice-president from entering their home following the crushing news of the mission's cancellation. As Wolfe tells it, Johnson was salivating to "pour ten minutes of hideous Texas soul all over her on nationwide TV."

Once Glenn, then in a NASA hangar, was told about Annie's plight over the phone, he stood, according to Wolfe, "with half his wire mesh underlinings hanging off his body and biosensor wires sprouting from out of his thoracic cage" and told her: 'Look, if you don't want the vice-president or the TV networks or anybody else to come into the house, then that's it as far as I'm concerned. They are not coming in—and I will back you up all the way, one hundred percent, and you tell them that. I don't want Johnson or any of the rest of them to put so much as one toe inside our house!"

It is very dramatic, and true as far as it goes. But Glenn's chivalrous support of Annie had little to do with her stuttering and nothing to do with Johnson's "hideous Texas soul." It had a great deal to do, however, with *Life* magazine and its lucrative exclusive contract.

"Wolfe has got it kind of right and kind of wrong," says Loudon Wainwright, who witnessed the confrontation. "I was in the house with the photographer and we didn't want Johnson to come into the house because, if he came into the house, all of the other Washington press would come in with him. Annie didn't want him to come in, either. She felt it was a real invasion of her privacy to have about 50 people in the house. She really didn't need the vice-president, but she didn't want to be rude to him. As I remember it, she held him off. It was with my complete agreement, because I didn't want him in there either."

As Annie Glenn now recalls the incident, "It had come to the point where John was almost going to be launched and it had to be scrubbed. I was really tired and I was getting a migraine. I was just plain going to bed, and then there was all of that commotion and everything."

Lyn Glenn also remembers that day: "We kept watching what was going on, peeking out the window. I could feel the tension. I knew that Mother didn't want the visit to occur. She just didn't want to have Vice-President Johnson in the house. That really was it. During that period of time, mother's speech was so bad. Among us, if she was more relaxed, she could express herself better. But I remember her just being as tense and angry as I've ever seen her. She just didn't want this intrusion."

The core of the controversy, however, was not Johnson himself, but the terms of the *Life* contract. "For reasons that I never quite understood, the vice-president said he was not going to come into the house unless Loudon Wainwright was out," Glenn says. "Apparently, this was because of the vice-president's relations with other press people."

It was obvious that the frustrated reporters camped on the lawn would finally have a chance to get inside the Glenn fortress on the coattails of the vice-president. Johnson, in turn, was happy to provide them that access in return for their coverage of his meeting with the Glenn family on what had been planned as an historic event. If Johnson had gone in by himself, with Wainwright still in the house, it would have been yet another coup for *Life*. Wainwright would once again have been the only reporter present. But if Glenn's recollection is correct—that Johnson, acting on the advice of his press contingent, wanted Wainwright out of the house while he was inside—it would obviously have been an attempt by Wainwright's fellow reporters to give him a taste of what they had been experiencing for a year.

"That was the big question: was Loudon going to be kicked out of the house?" Glenn now says. "That was the day of the big scrub. I had been on top of the booster for five and half or six hours, flat on my back. When I got out, I was sweaty. I was tired. And I got out of the spacesuit and was in a terry cloth robe on the way to the showers when someone in NASA said they wanted to see me. Instead of saying: 'Buck up, we've just scrubbed the Free World's first effort at manned orbital flight,' the question was whether I was going to let the vice-president into my house. I just told them to do whatever Annie wanted, and that whatever agreement we had made before still stood. I went off to the showers and that was that."

If Wainwright had not been there, did Glenn think there would have been that much of a problem?

"Oh no," Glenn replies matter-of-factly. "No. Did I object to the vice-president calling on Annie? No, not at all. It was the insistence that somehow we were supposed to abrogate the agreement we had made with *Life* and get Loudon out of the house. I just thought that wasn't the agreement we had made. And Annie was up there under the gun. I went off to the showers, and when I came back the vice-president was gone."

The next attempt to send the first American into space orbit came some three weeks later, on February 20, 1962. "I woke up at about 1:30 in the morning, half an hour before I was sched-uled to get up," Glenn recalled. "I'd slept fine, and I just lay there for a while running mission procedures over in my mind." There had already been a maddening total of ten scrubs, and Glenn was pessimistic, concerned that he was going to witness the eleventh abort. "When 'NASA flight surgeon' Bill Douglas came in to wake me he verified that the weather was still 50-50. I was lying in the top bunk of a double decker. Bill rested his arms on the bunk and we talked quietly. The count was moving right along on schedule, he told me. My back-up, Scott Carpenter, who'd got up at midnight to check out the capsule for me, had called back to say that the capsule was ready."

The next several hours were spent in final checks and prepa-ration. Glenn's low residue breakfast, which he later said left him feeling hungry and full of gas, was steak, scrambled eggs, jellied toast, Postum and orange juice. Later, after Glenn had suited up and as Douglas administered a final check of the integrity of the pressure suit, Glenn casually asked him if he realized that two of his tropical fish were floating belly-up in their tank. Douglas blanched. He had run a hose from Glenn's main air supply tube into the tank as an informal gauge of the purity of the air reaching Glenn. It was only after Douglas raced over to the tank and saw that the fish were fine that he realized that he had been taken in by Glenn's effort to ease the tension.

As dawn approached, Glenn was driven by van to the launching pad. He peered through the van's windows at the mammoth Atlas rocket. "It was a great sight," Glenn recalls. "It was still dark but the big arclights shone white on the Atlas booster and on the gantry around it. We stayed in the van during a couple of holds, and finally, at one minute before six, we all walked to the elevator."

Despite all of the delays, the ground crew seemed to sense that this would finally be it. They worked with grim earnestness as Glenn was finally bolted into his titanium-skinned "garbage can." Shortly before liftoff, he made one final phone call. Talking over a special line, Glenn repeated to his wife the flippant phrase he used whenever he was sent overseas, a private signal that made the goodbyes somewhat easier.

"Well, I think I'll go down to the store and buy some gum," Glenn said. Annie told him not to be long. With tears in her eyes she put down the phone and sat before the television. Annie and the children began their wait while the crowds outside the Glenn house grew larger as the time for launch neared. There were books, maps, a large globe and three television sets in the living room. It was 9:30 and the final countdown was minutes away.

"The Mercury space capsule umbilical is out," came the voice at Mission Control at 9:46. "We are at T-minus 19 seconds." Glenn began to feel the bellow of the Atlas engine beneath him. "T-minus ten seconds." His blood pressure rose only slightly to 110. Like a supplicant before his priest, he mouthed the final numbers of the countdown in unison with the disembodied voice in the blockhouse.

"Ignition!" the voice cried at 9:47.

With an unholy roar, flame suddenly poured from the base of the mammoth booster and for a few seconds the rocket lingered on pad 14. Then, slowly, majestically, it began to move.

"Liftoff!" came the hoarse cry from the loudspeaker at Mission Control as thousands at Cape Canaveral and millions around the world caught their breath.

"Liftoff!" echoed Glenn, exultant. "The clock is operating; we're underway."

Within minutes of the launch, Alan Shepard, serving as "capcom," or capsule communicator, radioed to Glenn the words he was waiting to hear: "You have a Go—at least seven orbits."

"Roger," Glenn replied in a firm, proud-sounding voice. "Understand Go for at least seven orbits."

His voice over the loudspeakers from more than one hundred miles up was calm, even chatty during the early stages of the flight. Glenn was like the youngster in New Concord, "shooting" the old bridge in The Cruiser. He experienced three sunsets in the space of five hours and marveled at the brilliant colors. "The sunsets always occurred slightly to my left," Glenn reported, "and I turned the spacecraft to get a better view. The sunlight coming in the window was very brilliant, with an intense clear white light that reminded me of the arclights while the spacecraft was on the launching pad."

He commented that the sun was completely round as it approached the horizon. As it finally reached the horizon line, it seemed to "spread out to each side of the point where it is setting.

"This band is extremely bright just as the sun sets," Glenn noted, "but as time passes, the bottom layer becomes a bright orange and fades into reds, then on into the darker colors, and finally, off into the blues and blacks as you get farther toward space."

After nearly an hour, Glenn reported seeing a huge pattern of lights along the Australian coast. They were a greeting from the people of Perth and Rockingham. Glenn told the ground control: "The lights show up very well. Thank everybody for turning them on, will you?"

The strangest sight he encountered in space was thousands of tiny "needles" that seemed to be floating, flickering brilliantly on and off like fireflies. "I felt certain they were not caused by anything emanating from the capsule," Glenn said. "I thought perhaps I'd stumbled into the lost batch of needles the Air Force had tried to set up in orbit for communications purposes. But I could think of no reason why needles should glow like fireflies." On Glenn's return, a puzzled NASA simply labeled the phenomenon "The Glenn Effect."

Until trouble with his automatic control systems forced him to take over partial, then full, manual control of the capsule's position, Glenn kept up with his scientific checklist. One of the key unknowns was whether Glenn's prolonged weightlessness would make him nauseous and unable to function. The Russians had reported that Gherman Titov had felt that way during phases of his much longer flight. Glenn tried to make himself feel dizzy, but he could not. "I was shaking my head and rolling it and nodding it as fast as I could, with no more sensation than one would expect doing this on the ground," he reported.

Today, Glenn reveals the extent of NASA's concern, one that persists because of spacesickness suffered by crew members on the space shuttle. "They were so concerned about this," Glenn says, "that they not only gave me the anti-nausea tablets to take if I was feeling nauseous, but they put some of it in solution. They designed a special hypodermic needle that was springloaded and placed in my flightsuit in a little pouch. If I was getting so sick that I had to make an emergency re-entry, I could take the needle out, take off the safety catch, hit my leg and drive the needle through the suit. By injecting the fluid, I would get an immediate effect and be able to bring myself back down."

Glenn did not make his seven orbits. The problems with his guidance systems, though not critical, dictated prudence. But controllers on the ground wished that was the only problem they faced. For a few tense hours it appeared as if Glenn, the first American to orbit the earth, might be burned alive as he hurtled back into the atmosphere after his triumph.

As NASA officials cautiously tracked Glenn's progress during his second orbit, they suddenly became aware that a small meter—"segment 5-1" in the space jargon of the time—was registering that Friendship 7's landing bag had been prematurely deployed. This could jeopardize the most important piece of equipment on his craft: the huge dish-shaped ceramiclike heat shield attached to the spacecraft's wide bottom. The rubberized landing bag, which was to be deployed and inflated with air just before impact with the ocean, was located between the titanium skin and the heat shield of the capsule. Its purpose was to absorb the shock of landing. And several ground monitors were indicating that the landing bag had indeed deployed prematurely while Glenn was still in orbit. If this were true, it had loosened the shield, rendering it potentially useless.

There was no way Glenn could survive without the shield. Its function was simple: to protect the pilot from the tremendous heat generated by the friction of the space capsule with the atmosphere as it re-entered earth orbit. "The part of the flight that you had most apprehension about was re-entry," Glenn recalls. "On re-entry you had the greatest number of different forces working on the spacecraft. If anything is going to go wrong, there is a good chance of it happening then. There's the problem of deceleration, followed by the highest heat that any man has ever worked through in any vehicle, not to mention falling straight down at supersonic speeds heading toward the earth." Glenn estimates that the heat of re-entry less than three feet from the space capsule was nearly 10,000 degrees.

At first, Mission Control decided not to tell Glenn about the problem. Instead, they tried to elicit as much information from Glenn as possible. "We have a message from MCC [Mercury Control Center] for you," said the Indian Ocean capcom, "to keep your landing bag switch in the off position." Glenn affirmed that it was. Six minutes later, as he again flew over Australia, capcom Gordon Cooper came in with a similar instruction. "Will you confirm the landing bag switch is in the off position?" Cooper asked. He added: "You haven't had any banging noises or anything of this type at higher rates?"

"Negative," Glenn responded.

Meanwhile, on the ground, feeling that Glenn's fate was in their hands, the people at the Cape worked the telephones, calling the manufacturers of the capsule and the NASA space center in Virginia. They tried to figure out what to do if the heat shield was indeed detached. For nearly three hours, they agonized, then finally told Glenn about the problem.

"Friendship 7," said the capcom. "We have been reading an

indication on the ground of segment 5-1, which is landing bag deploy. We suspect this is an erroneous signal. However, Cape would like to check this by putting the landing bag switch in auto position, and seeing if you get a light. Do you concur with this? Over."

Glenn concurred, but reluctantly. If there were some malfunction in the switch or the electrical system, his fooling with it might actually deploy the bag if it were not already deployed. This could be an irreversible, fatal mistake. Glenn was angry. For three hours, the news of the danger had been kept from him. When Glenn found out about it he felt it was a serious breach of correct procedure by ground control. "The questions they were asking me from the ground could only mean one thing: that the heat shield was loose," Glenn says today. "I wanted them to say it." Later, in his formal mission report he would recommend that pilots be kept fully informed of developments like this, lest communications fail totally and the pilot be forced to make "all decisions from onboard information."

Glenn had taken no religious object with him on the flight. "I have no use for the kind of religion that's just an ace in the hole when you're in a tight spot," he said. But as a devout Presbyterian, he prayed for his own safety and the success of the mission.

The risks in the flight were viewed as so great that no insurance company would underwrite Glenn. Leo DeOrsey, the astronauts' garrulous, rotund guardian angel, had even approached Lloyds of London to write a $100,000 policy on Glenn covering the flight. They replied they would, but that the premium would be $16,000. "Leo called me up one day during my training and told me about it," Glenn recalls. "I said, 'Leo, look, I'm in the middle of all this training. You're handling all my affairs. I'll leave it up to you.' He said he'd call me back. A couple of days later Leo called me back and said, 'I've made a decision. We're not going to get the policy. But if something happens to you, I will see to it that Annie gets the money.' Leo was wealthy, but not that wealthy. But he had the check all drawn out before the flight, to be given to Annie immediately if something were to happen."

Behind the closed curtains on Harrison Street, 15-year-old

David Glenn nervously watched the television with his family and studied the globe. Like the rest of them, he was acutely worried about his father's safety, but he tried not to show it. "The whole thing went on for more than four hours, and I think we were all about as keyed up as we'd ever been in our lives," Dave recalls. The potential disaster of the heat shield, he admits, "made you worry if he was going to be your father or a cinder when he arrived back on earth."

Dave adds: "I knew of course that I might be the only male left in the family and there I was, my little 15-year-old self, thinking, 'Gee, I guess I better be pretty manly about this time and act tough.' By then, we were all clearly aware that Dad was really risking his life and that he might not come back."

In his capsule, as the hour approached for re-entry, Glenn prepared to throw the landing bag switch to the automatic control position as NASA had requested. In fact if the landing bag had prematurely been deployed, the light would show "On" when Glenn threw the switch.

"Okay," he said, "if that's what they recommend, we'll go ahead and try it. Are you ready for it now?"

"Yes, when you're ready."

"Roger." Glenn reached out and flicked the toggle switch in front of him. There was no light. He quickly flicked it off.

"Negative," he reported. "In automatic position, did not get a light and I'm back in off position now. Over."

"Roger, that's fine," the capcom replied. "In this case, we'll go ahead and the re-entry sequence will be normal."

But it was not entirely normal. With the landing bag indicator still sending its ominous message, the scientists could not be sure the heat shield was secure as Glenn prepared to fire the retro rockets that would slow him down sufficiently for re-entry.

Veteran science reporter William Hines, who covered the space program for the *Washington Star*, recalls the dilemma. "With only minutes left, the final decision was made. Glenn would fire the rockets as planned, but then—deviating from normal procedure—he would leave the package containing the spent rocket bodies in place in front of the heat shield. Flight officials reasoned that if the shield were really loose, the tight metal straps holding the package in place would keep the vital shield snug against the capsule, preventing, or at least minimizing, leakage of re-entry heat into the area where Glenn sat.''

Glenn turned the capsule into re-entry position and began the descent to earth. "From where I sat, it was probably the most spectacular re-entry that anyone will ever have," Glenn now says. "And I don't say that lightly. It was because we left the retropack on. They had run some aerodynamic experiments about what would happen if you had to re-enter like that, and they found that while it would reduce the stability of the spacecraft, you could nevertheless make a safe re-entry.''

Since no one had ever experienced such a return to the earth's atmosphere, Glenn was unsure what it was supposed to look or feel like. As a result, he had one final scare before hitting the blue skies over the Atlantic. "During the heat of re-entry," Glenn recalls, "I felt sort of a thump and I thought it may have been the retropack going because it was springloaded and designed to go off rather forcefully.

"So sitting there in the capsule, I saw these burning pieces start coming by the window. I couldn't be sure whether it was the retropack breaking up or the heat shield. Obviously there'd be a big difference as to my longevity depending on which it was. As it turned out, it was the retropack. It made a very spectacular re-entry; all I could see for a while were flaming chunks this big around coming off and going past the window.''

Glenn splashed down in the Atlantic at 2:43 P.M. in a cloud of hissing steam. It was four hours, 56 minutes—and 81,000 miles—after he had hit what NASA called "that keyhole in the sky" and achieved earth orbit. A small flotilla of Navy vessels and helicopters raced toward him, hoping for the honor of retrieving the now-famous space pilot. The destroyer *Noa* won, hoisting the Friendship 7 capsule—with Glenn still inside—onto the deck at 3:04 P.M., just 21 minutes after splashdown.

When Glenn emerged to the cheers of the crew, his footprints on the carrier deck were traced in white paint for later exhibition at the Smithsonian Institution. The moment he stepped on deck, the Post Office Department in Washington ordered postmasters around the country to unseal the tightly wrapped bundles they had been sent weeks earlier. They were to begin selling the Project Mercury four-cent commemorative stamps that had been secretly printed before Glenn's flight.

At the White House, President Kennedy, who had spoken to Glenn by phone and told him he would be there to greet him on his return to Cape Canaveral, issued a statement of praise. "We have a long way to go in this space race," Kennedy said. "We started late. But this is the new ocean, and I believe the United States must sail on it and be second to none."

"Some months ago I said that I hoped every American would serve his country," the president went on. "Today Colonel Glenn served his, and we all express our thanks to him."

When Glenn finally reached home, one of the first people he saw was Leo DeOrsey, who was grinning broadly. "You old son of a bitch, I'm glad you made it!" DeOrsey exclaimed as he tore up his check for $100,000.

John Glenn's history-making trip to the heavens was to be followed by an outpouring of affection and adulation unmatched since the days of Charles Lindbergh. Over the succeeding two years, it would fan political ambitions that had burned within Glenn for years. He had mastered the heavens in a five-hour space flight. Mastering politics, however, was to take him considerably longer.

8

THE FIRST FALL: THE CAMPAIGN OF 1964

The orbital flight had transformed John Glenn into a public figure of extraordinary proportions. The attention lavished on him by the nation after his space mission could not be explained solely by the glamour of his flight, for Shepard was actually America's first man in space and Grissom second. There seemed to be a quality in Glenn himself that attracted the public; an appearance, background and attitude which conjured up a view of the country that was equal parts fantasy and nostalgia.

The nation and Glenn simultaneously became aware of this phenomenon shortly after the orbital flight as an orgy of praise engulfed the space hero in the form of ticker tape parades and even a personal address before both houses of Congress.

By the end of 1962, Glenn and his family had moved to Houston, where he worked on spacecraft design at the Manned Spaceflight Center. But Glenn chafed at the desk work and passed his off hours talking politics with his confidant, Dr. Bob Voas. Three orbits around the earth was hardly sufficient fulfillment for Glenn, now in his prime at 41.

JFK and RFK had by this time become Glenn's political

mentors. They seemed to be guiding him toward an effortless campaign for the Ohio Senate seat, then held by the 74-year-old Stephen Young. But the death of John F. Kennedy in November 1963 removed the only person with the power to make the 1964 election risk-free by persuading Young to step aside. In pragmatic political terms, Kennedy's death meant the deal was off. But Glenn was not convinced that the race was impossible.

"I talked to Bobby again about it, but he felt it was too late, that there was not enough time to really put the whole thing together," Glenn now says. Though still numbed by the murder of his brother, Robert Kennedy realized that the landscape had changed markedly now that John Kennedy was dead. In fact, the whole Kennedy rationale for Glenn's candidacy was gone.

No longer was there any special need to make the Ohio ticket stronger with a glamorous, if untried, new face. What had once seemed likely to be a hard-fought reelection race between Jack Kennedy and whomever the GOP nominated, now seemed likely to turn into an outpouring of support for the new Democratic incumbent, Lyndon Johnson. Sensing this, Young quickly pledged his support to Johnson, his old Senate ally, and positioned himself for the campaign ahead.

It seemed hardly the time for amateur John Glenn to break into politics by challenging an incumbent senator of his own party. Although Young was not a dynamic vote getter, he seemed likely to ride in on the Texan's coattails; he also had the support of the Ohio Democratic organization. But Glenn was unmoved by conventional political logic. As he characteristically does, Glenn relied instead on his instincts: "I decided to go ahead and run anyway," he recalls. Glenn correctly sensed that his announcement would dramatically change the political balance among Ohio Democrats. What he did not foresee was how suddenly and how easy it was to lose his hero's immunity from criticism.

Forty-eight hours before his formal announcement, rumors about it were already surfacing in Ohio, Washington and Houston. In a statement that made no mention of politics but whose intent was obvious, Dr. Robert Gilruth, director of the Houston center, said that Colonel Glenn had "requested to be relieved of his assignment" and that "the request had been granted."

On January 17, 1964, before an audience of a hundred at the Neil House, a venerable hotel in Columbus, Glenn formally announced his candidacy for the U.S. Senate. He did not mention JFK, but said that politics was "a high challenge and a great calling." The astronaut conceded that he had never registered with any political party until then. Fielding questions about his previous voting record, Glenn answered that he had split his votes in the past between Republican and Democratic candidates, but added that both his parents were Democrats. "The party affiliation I have chosen is a natural one," Glenn assured the audience.

"I believe President Johnson has presented a program for our country which a majority of Americans will support," Glenn stated in the closest he would then come to a partisan position. "In the Senate I would hope to be able to help him reach the objectives of that program." He noted that he had entered politics partially because he was "too old to shoot the moon" as an astronaut.

Glenn openly admitted that he had no experience as a politician, but he did not see that lack as a handicap. "I can get the political experience," he insisted. No, he insisted, he did not think he was trading on his name and fame for political advantage. "My father has been in the plumbing business in New Concord...that's where I got my good name," Glenn said ingenuously as he flashed his broad Ike-like smile to a roomful of reporters.

Standing to the side of the microphones was the core of his small political organization: Bob Voas, nervously wondering whether he had pushed his friend into making a big mistake; Donald R. Gosney, an obscure Democratic county chairman; Clarence Graham, an old friend of Glenn's father; Robert (Mic) McDaniel, an Ohio soft drink bottler; and Wayne Hays, an eight-term congressman little known outside of eastern Ohio.

First elected to Congress in 1948, Wayne Hays was an acerbic, savvy politician who saw an opportunity to use Glenn to take over the regular Democratic organization in Ohio. Hays's emergence as chairman of the House Administration Committee and one of Congress's most feared members was in the future. So too, was the scandal that would lead to his defeat in

1978, after it was revealed that he had included his buxom mistress, Elizabeth Ray, in his congressional payroll in return for her sexual services.

In 1964, Hays was one of the few political professionals to rush to Glenn's aid. The senior congressman helped convince Glenn that he should challenge Young despite the odds. He told Glenn what he was predisposed to hear: that his public appeal would transcend any limitations he might have as a politician. "Ohio needs new blood, and Glenn will provide it," Hays told his constituents. Significantly, the Ohio congressman was on friendly terms with both John and Bobby Kennedy. He had let it be known that he had been "authorized" to discuss an "ambassadorship" or some other assignment for Young if he would step aside.

Many politicians dismissed it at the time as the hollow posturing of a self-important congressman, but Hays's claim was accurate. "The Kennedys wanted Young out of the way," Hays now recalls. "And they told me: 'Tell him he'll be taken care of.' If he wanted an ambassadorship, they'd give him one." Hays was already making plans to replace Ohio state chairman William Coleman, a Young backer, with his own man, John (Socko) Wiethe, a gregarious bull-necked Cincinnati attorney and Hamilton County Democratic chairman.

The Glenn scenario suited Hays, a humorless man with thin lips and a bullet-shaped head whose acid tongue on the House floor had intimidated many of his colleagues. Once Glenn wrested the nomination from Young, Hays calculated, he would gain control not only of the state party but of its national patronage. Hays assumed that the politically inexperienced Glenn would look to him for guidance. Gambling that Glenn could win the Senate seat, Hays risked his position with the state party organization to back Glenn. But Young, an equally experienced gut fighter, had no intention of surrendering his seat. And the aging senator was angry.

Today, Wiethe recalls the 1963 phone call from President Kennedy asking him to sound out the incumbent about stepping aside. "I talked to Senator Young about it," Wiethe recounts. "At first he wanted not to run. He wanted the post Kennedy was offering. It was an ambassadorship." But after talking it over with his advisors, Wiethe says, Young changed his mind. It was the beginning of his grudge against Glenn that has lasted ever since. Now 94, Young has been confined to a Washington nursing home since 1982.

The timing of the announcement for the Senate would have been fatal for anyone except Glenn. He seemed to have waited too long; many in the state party, though partial to the astronaut, had already endorsed Young. Even former President Truman had endorsed the incumbent. And Glenn's first political plunge came just three days before state party leaders were to convene to make their endorsement for the May 5 primary.

"It was a terribly traumatic time for me," recalls Bob Voas, "because I felt very responsible. It just seemed foreordained that the convention would endorse Young. When we arrived in Columbus for the news conference, I had arranged with one of the reporters I knew to close the press conference off when I gave him the signal. But it was a real problem since John was very reticent about taking any political positions while still in uniform. So we had this news conference to launch a political campaign, and Glenn couldn't make any political statements. At the same time the battery of reporters were obviously pressing to get some real information."

Glenn's reluctance to divulge his political leanings reflected more than just his fear of violating federal law against political activity by government employees. As far as he was concerned, it was no one's business how he felt on issues. Nor would he listen to anyone who tried to tell the hero-turned-politician otherwise. Glenn's view of politics was unique, and underscored the gulf between his desire for office and the reality of attaining it.

"He was very upset that people were asking for a commitment as to what his position would be on certain issues, especially organized labor," recalls *Washington Post* national reporter Don Oberdorfer. At the time, Oberdorfer worked for the *Saturday Evening Post* and, at an editor's suggestion, was briefly serving as an unpaid advisor to Glenn. He spent several weeks showing the untried Marine the political ropes and discussing national and international issues with him. Though *Life*'s caveat had cost the *Post* its chance for an exclusive on Glenn's first political campaign, the editors felt that sending Oberdorfer to Ohio at their expense to conduct what amounted to on-the-job training would buy goodwill from the astronaut-politician later on.

Meeting Glenn for the first time, Oberdorfer says he was struck by the former astronaut's unwillingness to be drawn into even the most rudimentary give-and-take of a political campaign. "He felt very strongly that the electorate and interest groups should elect him as a U.S. Senator and then trust him to use his good judgment," Oberdorfer recalls. "I tried to explain to him that under the democratic system people felt they had a right to know where the person stood when they decided whether or not to give him support." But Glenn refused to accept that commonsense premise. He kept repeating that people should trust him to know what was best and to do what was right for the country.

Talking with Glenn, Oberdorfer got the unmistakeable impression that he was uncomfortable with his new role as candidate. He sensed that Glenn was not at ease with the idea of staking out positions on issues that did not easily lend themselves to careful breakdown and analysis, like the inside of a space capsule or the properties of a rocket. Oberdorfer even wondered if Glenn knew what he was getting into; whether he had what it took to stay in the race.

At the time, Glenn projected the image of an innocent in the tainted world of politics. "I'll never forget the first time that Voas and he came in and we had our first meeting with the top five or six county chairman," Socko Wiethe recalls. "It was in Columbus and it was John's first political meeting. He wasn't smoking or drinking at the time and as soon as he arrived he had to leave the room because there was so goddam much smoke. I went out to talk to him. He just said he couldn't stand the smoke. I told him to forget about the smoke, those guys are looking to see you and you better come back in the room."

Did he go back in?

"Sure he did," Wiethe recalls, laughing.

Predictably, Glenn's eleventh-hour decision to take on Young did not sit well with the irascible senator or with members of the party establishment who had already endorsed

Young. (Glenn cannot remember, but he "assumes" that he telephoned Young in advance to tell him he would be opposing him in the upcoming primary.) Young quickly attacked the novice, even on his accomplishment as an astronaut. "John Glenn never walked on the moon," Young reminded his constituents. "John Glenn never went near the moon. All John Glenn ever did was go around the world in a semi-crouch position." During one campaign stop in February, Young sarcastically paid tribute to "America's first space heroes," then ticked off the names of the space apes, "Able, Baker, Ham, and Enos," in an obvious dig at his opponent.

In a harbinger of trouble Glenn would later have with the regular Ohio party organization, Cleveland Representative Charles Vanik warned that Glenn's move would only divide the party. "The high office of United States senator should not be made a hero's pawn," Vanik said. The criticism stung Glenn. It was the first time he had ever experienced anything other than adulation in public. The candidate grew more uncomfortable as the primary progressed, to the irritation of Wayne Hays, who kept telling Glenn that if he wanted to survive in politics he had better develop a thick skin and also stop referring to himself in private as "a national hero." "That monkey's as much of a hero as you are," Hays said during one particularly heated exchange.

The Republicans had tried hard to woo Glenn to their side, but after he spurned them, they too became critical. Said Ohio Secretary of State Ted Brown, himself a candidate against Robert Taft, Jr., for the GOP Senate nomination: "I notice Glenn had a little difficulty in finding a landing space in either of our great parties. I don't exactly know what he means when he says his political beliefs lie somewhere between a liberal Republican and a conservative Democrat." And besides, Brown asked, "What does Glenn know about the day-to-day problems of politics?"

Lyndon Johnson was equally unenthusiastic about the Glenn candidacy. Young had quickly allied himself with the new president and former Senate Majority Leader. Johnson had no love for Glenn's friend Bobby Kennedy, or for any of the Kennedys, and he was notoriously protective of his political turf. From this evolved a noticeable coolness between Johnson and Glenn. One measure of the distance between them is the fact that, despite Johnson's role as chairman of the National Aeronautics and Space Committee and his purported friendship with Glenn, he neglected to mention Glenn's name in his memoir, *The Vantage Point*.

Looking back, Glenn dismisses the criticism that he was an inexperienced outsider in politics. "Some people worked their way up the political ladder, inch by inch all their lives, from precinct person, to ward leader to whatever," he says. "I happened to have had my name well enough known that I could even hope to run, from another source: the space program. I know that people who come up through the political ranks and gain high office from that route sometimes look askance at other routes to the same position, but that doesn't make them any less viable. We've had some people become president who have never been in politics at all."

Glenn's allusion to nonpolitical presidents clearly refers to Dwight D. Eisenhower, a former president and military man whom many believe he resembles in style and background. While Eisenhower, the Supreme Allied Commander in World War II, was never involved in politics before he ran for president in 1952, he did serve in key public policy posts between the war and his election: as Army chief of staff, president of Columbia University and NATO commander. But while the '64 Glenn did not have the credentials of the '52 Ike, he shared one aspect of Ike's political strength: He was a popular hero in the most contemporary sense.

Glenn had little else to sell to the voting public. Because he had announced for the Senate while still in the U.S. Marine Corps, he had to observe—or hide behind—the provisions of the Hatch Act, which forbids political activity by government employees. The act seemed made to order for Glenn. In public, Glenn said he looked forward to talking issues once his retirement from the Marines came through. "But for now," Glenn told audiences, "I'd certainly like to hear what you think." The tactic was brilliant, and it worked.

Glenn was forced to shed his amateur standing within days after he announced, at the Ohio Democratic convention. It was the first time John Glenn had ever faced a test of his political appeal, but the ensuing melee left him wondering whether the whole thing was worth the process. "I think he thought that he was going to come back home to Ohio and be elected by acclamation," says Don Oberdorfer. He adds that the roughness of party politics "was a whole world that was foreign to Glenn."

Glenn had deliberated so long over the decision to run that many top Ohio Democrats had already committed themselves to Young. When he finally announced, Glenn had little organization, other than Voas and a handful of others, and no money. "He was terribly unsophisticated when it came to politics," recalls one observer. But if he was unsophisticated about the intricacies of political barter, Glenn knew instinctively what the public wanted. He has an intuitive sense of good political sell that hides behind his guileless smile and disarming "aw shucks" rural demeanor.

Glenn is also armed with the firm belief that political rules do not apply to him. A close Glenn associate points to the 1964 Senate race as the first of several manifestations of a trait Glenn tries—generally successfully—to hide. It is the conviction that because of his heroism in war and in space, and his decent life as a family man and a citizen, the nation owes him the chance to lead. During the 1984 presidential nomination race, Glenn's campaign director, Bill White, had to warn him not to give the impression he "deserves" to be nominated for president because of his purported "electability."

When the 672 Ohio Democratic delegates convened on January 20, 1964, at the Neil House, just three days after Glenn's announcement at the same hotel, it looked like Young's territory. In his eighth-floor suite, where he had deliberately removed himself from the delegates, Glenn looked glumly at Annie and then at Bob Voas. "I wonder if we ever should have got into this thing," he said. He had refused even to go down to the hotel lobby to buy a newspaper, lest it appear he was politicking and violating the Hatch Act. Instead Glenn had his staff usher delegate after delegate up to his room to shake hands, where the politicking, though just as real, seemed less obvious.

"His friends just kept bringing delegates from the floor," Voas recalls. "John is just terribly impressive with people, particularly in small groups."

The awed delegates crowded his suite, pumping his hand, asking him to autograph their badges, or failing that, their crumpled Kleenexes or handkerchiefs. Serving nothing harder than soft drinks, John and Annie Glenn learned the political ceremonies that would serve them well in later years. In the overwhelmingly friendly confines of their hotel suite, Annie's stutter became muted as she cheerfully pumped hands along with her husband. Once, during the impromptu reception, a young woman removed a gold pin in the shape of the Democratic donkey and began to pin it on Annie's dress. "Oh no," Annie protested, "that's yours." "Then I can give it to you if I want to," the woman replied in a matter-of-fact tone. "It looks nice on you." Annie beamed and acquiesced.

Not everyone, however, was looking for as little as a smile and a handshake from the astronaut candidate. "I represent 15,000 industrial workers," a labor boss whispered in Glenn's ear after drawing him aside. "What will you do for us?" Black leaders, too, wanted specifics on Glenn's plans for the minorities. But the candidate refused to say anything of substance. "Good to see you," he murmured over and over. "Thanks for coming." "Oh yes, I remember you," he would say, occasionally stretching the truth like a true professional.

In the jammed hotel suite it was a case all over again of the swarming tourists at the campgrounds, the bug-eyed kid at the gas pump in Wyoming. But when the last delegate had left the room to go down to vote, neither Glenn nor Voas was sure what impact the candidate had made. In fact, Voas thought the campaign was all over before it began. "I had no real feel for the situation," he recalls. "I thought for sure we were losing."

But Voas, and perhaps Glenn himself, had underestimated the power of heroism in the American political experience. Shortly afterward, there was a knock on the door. When Voas answered, he found it was a small delegation of Young supporters bearing a peace offering. While Glenn stayed closeted in another room of his suite, the Young delegates made their offer: Have Glenn abandon his challenge to Young and they would support him for an at-large House seat. It was as close as Glenn would come to the free uncontested ticket to Congress he had discussed with Bobby Kennedy.

Voas told the delegation to wait outside; he would talk to his man. But Glenn would have none of it. "John wasn't interested," Voas recalls. "He wanted to be in the Senate." Rebuffed, the Young delegation glumly went back downstairs. Equally glumly, Voas returned to the suite where John and Annie sat, nervously wondering whether they had just lost their only chance to go to Washington. "Don't worry, honey," Annie Glenn said, her large brown eyes warming, reassuring her husband. "We can beat 'em all alone." But neither Glenn nor Voas was as certain.

Minutes later the door burst open. Someone shouted to Glenn that the convention had bolted the party leadership. They had refused to endorse Young or Glenn, but Glenn had won the majority of the votes. Glenn sat mutely in his chair. Recovering quickly from the welcome shock, the candidate asked, "How many votes did they say we won by?" "Fourteen," Voas replied. "This was the crisis, John. Young wanted the endorsement and he didn't get it. Now things will start to move our way."

Glenn recalls that the workers on the floor had told him that if they had pressed for it, they could have gotten him the endorsement. But Glenn chose not to try because there were already hard feelings in the party. "We felt it was going to split the party and might wreck any chance we would have of going all the way," Glenn says. "I chose not to push it through the convention even though we felt we could do it at the time."

How hard these feelings were would become obvious within just a few days. But for the time being, Glenn and the relieved Bob Voas exulted in the victory. "The whole place was beginning to swing to you," Voas told Glenn, beaming. "You're going to the U.S. Senate."

During the next two months, Glenn was introduced to politics at its roughest. He was the victim of Young's wrath, as the incumbent blasted his opponent in what Young now realized would be an uphill fight to retain his Senate seat. Young had reason to be concerned. Almost immediately after Glenn announced, polls showed the astronaut to be the clear favorite over the aging incumbent. It was clear confirmation of Glenn's intuition that his national fame could be translated into political support. "I never doubted Glenn could win it," recalls Wayne Hays. "Too many people thought that Young couldn't win against a Republican in November. It was as simple as that. The party wanted to hold onto that Senate seat."

But despite the polls and the divided convention, Young's supporters were not surrendering. In February, a flier distributed by "Ohio Democratic Office Holders for Young" tried to link Glenn to conservative Arizona Republican Barry Goldwater, who would soon become the Republican presidential nominee. The attempt was crude but it demonstrated that the Young camp was determined to tarnish Glenn's immaculate image. The flier, printed on bright red stationery, was a montage of newspaper clippings critical of Glenn for challenging Young. It included a detached headline: "Goldwater Convinced Glenn."

"This is a dreadful attempt to make people think that Goldwater somehow put Glenn into the race against Steve Young," fumed Kenneth Weinberg, an attorney who was then a Glenn campaign staffer. "I got the whole newspaper column of the original story. What it actually said was that Glenn got angry when he heard Barry Goldwater was advocating that American field commanders be allowed to decide whether to use nuclear weapons. It shows that Glenn decided right then he could not run for office on a ticket with such a man as Goldwater. It says just the opposite of what Steve Young's handbill was insinuating. I knew that Steve Young was running scared, but I didn't realize he was panic-stricken."

Young's argument was that Glenn was not a true Democrat. He cited Glenn's admission that he had voted for Republicans in the past, and claimed that Glenn had voted for Richard Nixon over John Kennedy in 1960. His authority was the *Saturday Evening Post* profile of Glenn. Glenn denied that he had voted for Nixon.

Young attacked Glenn on the racial issue as well. He accused Glenn of having a financial interest in a Cocoa Beach, Florida, hotel that discriminated against blacks. It was the Cape Colony Inn, in which Glenn and his fellow Mercury astronauts had invested money from their *Life* magazine contract in the early sixties. When Glenn angrily denied the accusations, Young said his remarks had been misinterpreted.

Meanwhile, Glenn continued his own low-key campaigning, looking forward, he told voters, to March 1, 1964. His retirement from the Marines would then take effect and he would be free to speak his mind on the issues of the day. But one of Glenn's backers, Congressman Wayne Hays, was having doubts about Glenn's willingness to campaign in earnest. He had begun to wonder whether he had backed the wrong horse.

Once before in his life John Glenn had confronted what he considered true failure—when his astronaut rival Alan B. Shepard was chosen over him to be the first American in space. But as he prepared for the May 5 Ohio primary, Glenn had no way of knowing that his first try for elective office was about to fail far more dramatically.

On the morning of February 26, 1964, Glenn was sitting in his pajamas and robe on the living room sofa in the Columbus apartment that had been donated by a backer, Trent Sickles. Glenn was listening intently to Don Oberdorfer's briefing when an aide came in to remind him of a meeting he was to have in 40 minutes. "I better get dressed," Glenn told Oberdorfer, then walked down a long corridor and into the bathroom to shower and shave.

Meanwhile, the three men who were to see Glenn that morning, Warren Baltimore, an Ohio insurance executive with a lifelong love of politics, and attorneys Bob Kosydar and Jack Dilenschneider, arrived in the lobby of the apartment complex and started up to Glenn's flat near the top floor. It was a measure of Glenn's naivete as a politician, Baltimore now recalls with a laugh, that he would rely on the untried trio. "I don't remember what we were supposed to brief him on, but it demonstrated how unprofessional the campaign was," he says in retrospect. "We were up at the university library the night before trying to look up what we were going to brief him on the next day. We didn't have any resources at all. All we had was a long line of bullshit."

The three men went up the elevator and headed down the hall to Glenn's apartment. Inside, Oberdorfer sat on the couch, waiting for Glenn to emerge from the bathroom. "All of a sudden," Oberdorfer recalls, "I heard this loud crash. At first I thought, 'no, it must be outside, down the hall someplace.' But then I had a feeling that maybe it might not be since the bathroom was also some way away, down an internal corridor." The sound Oberdorfer had just heard was to signal the end of Glenn's 1964 Senate campaign.

"We had one of those big cabinet mirrors and it wouldn't slide on its tracks," John Glenn remembers. As he finished shaving, he removed the mirror and cleaned out the tracks. "I started to put the mirror back, but it slipped in my hands." Ducking instinctively to avoid being hit by the falling mirror, Glenn tripped on a throw rug and fell to the floor. His head crashed against the porcelain edge of the bathtub. Had Glenn not been holding the mirror he probably would have survived the fall with hardly a bruise. His former pastor, the Reverend Frank Erwin of Arlington, recalls Glenn slipping on a patch of ice outside his home during one of the long waits after his mission had been postponed. "Most people would have tried to break the fall with outstretched arms," Erwin remembers, "but John doubled knees-to-chest and took the tumble harmlessly."

But Glenn's skilled reflexes were of no value that morning. Approaching the closed bathroom door, Oberdorfer called softly: "John?" When he heard no answer, Oberdorfer opened the door. In the steamy room, all he could make out at first was the broken glass on the tile floor. Then he saw Glenn, in a dazed heap on the floor, bleeding from the temple. Meanwhile, Baltimore, Kosydar and Dilenschneider entered the apartment and realized that something was very wrong.

In minutes, all was pandemonium. Bob Voas, upstairs in another apartment, received a frantic phone call. "I'm not sure who called us," he recalls, "but they said John had fallen and that he was hurt. I rushed downstairs." In the bathroom, he found Oberdorfer trying to minister to the dazed and bleeding Glenn. Even semi-conscious, Glenn could tell that his injury was serious. Terrible pressure began building in his head, far worse than that which would accompany even a severe concussion. He tried to look up but was stopped by the pain.

"Call...for help," he whispered. "Call an ambulance."

"There was a fair amount of blood coming down his cheek," Voas relates. But to his relief, Voas saw at once that it was not coming from Glenn's ear, the likely sign of an injury even more serious than the one Glenn had sustained. Baltimore, a large beefy man with a shock of white hair, ran to a phone and called his wife Judy. "We didn't know what to do. I called Judy and asked her for the name of a doctor. I think they ended up taking him to the emergency room at Grant Hospital." Baltimore recalls particularly that his early attempts included political damage control. "I remember asking Judy for the name of a doctor who might keep his mouth shut. I thought it was all high drama."

"The place was soon full of people," Baltimore explains. "There was a lawyer, who is now dead—a black guy. He was writing something. I remember him sitting at a table at a portable typewriter. He just kept writing.

"John had to be carried out of the bathroom. He couldn't do it on his own. Somebody had his feet and somebody had his shoulders." Slowly, they carried Glenn into an adjacent bedroom and placed an icepack on his head. Meanwhile, Trent Sickles, who was unaware of the drama below, had sent down his houseboy with sweetrolls and coffee for Glenn and his party. "In the midst of all this commotion, this guy comes in with his white jacket and he's gonna serve! Somebody was on the phone to the hospital while somebody else was trying to get the houseboy to leave," says Baltimore.

Looking back on the incident, Baltimore insists that, for all the alarm, he was not unduly worried. "I thought that the guy whacked his head, the next week we'd be on the campaign trail. Pretty soon I'd be in Washington as an assistant to a U.S. Senator."

But at the hospital, X rays revealed the seriousness of

A snapshot of Glenn at age four in New Concord.

John and Annie as teenagers in his 1929 roadster, which he dubbed "The Cruiser." Glenn enjoyed "shooting" the B & O railroad bridge at top speed.

Glenn as a 20-year-old naval air cadet. He received his private pilot's license in July 1941 and enlisted soon after Pearl Harbor, which worried his parents "sick."

Lt. Glenn and the former Miss Anna Margaret Castor on their wedding day, April 6, 1943. The two had been going together ever since grade school.

A bemedaled Major Glenn, with his parents, John H. Glenn, Sr., and Clara Sproat Glenn. They instilled in him a Calvinist drive to excel.

The "MiG Mad Marine" fighter pilot next to his F-86, in which Glenn downed three MiGs in the last nine days of the Korean War.

Glenn demonstrates flying tactics to his children Carolyn (Lyn) and Dave in 1953, shortly after he returned home from the Korean War.

Glenn at Floyd Bennett Field in New York after setting a transcontinental speed record in July 1957. In an F8U Crusader he crossed the country in 3 hours, 23 minutes, and 8.4 seconds as part of "Project Bullet."

The seven Project Mercury astronauts at their first press conference in April 1959. Those who believed they would return from space alive were asked to raise their hands. Glenn raised both. Left to right: Donald K. Slayton, Alan B. Shepard, Jr., Walter M. Schirra, Jr. (also with both hands raised), Virgil I. Grissom, Glenn, Leroy G. Cooper and Malcolm S. Carpenter.

The seven astronauts in their space suits. Front row, left to right: Schirra, Slayton, Glenn and Carpenter. Back row: Shepard, Grissom and Cooper. Glenn was angry that Shepard and Grissom were chosen over him for the first flight in space.

Glenn undergoes respiratory training. Although demanding, it was far less rigorous than the physical tests used to select the astronauts at Lovelace Clinic.

Astronaut John Glenn is lowered into the Mercury spacecraft Friendship 7 before launch. Glenn's flight was scrubbed ten times before he became the first American to orbit the earth.

Looking like a true spaceman, Glenn gives the "thumbs up" sign to his friend and back-up, Scott Carpenter, whose reflection is visible in Glenn's suit.

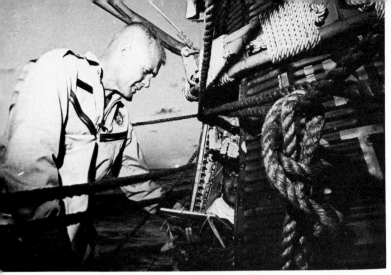

Back from space, Glenn happily checks the Friendship 7
capsule on the deck of the destroyer *Noa*.

With President John F. Kennedy at Cape Canaveral. JFK gave Glenn
the Distinguished Service Medal and a push into national politics.

This sign at the outskirts of New Concord, Ohio boasts of the town's most famous son.

Glenn, Annie and Vice-President Lyndon Johnson in a New York ticket tape parade. Glenn found that he loved the limelight.

Glenn shown addressing a joint session of Congress, a rare honor accorded the space hero. He was greeted with footstomping, applause and tears. Behind him are Vice-President Johnson (left) and House Speaker John W. McCormack. It was perhaps here that Glenn first felt the desire for the presidency.

Glenn poses with his family after receiving an honorary degree from his alma mater, Muskingum College. From left: John H. Glenn, Sr., Clara Glenn, Dave, Lyn, Glenn, Annie and her parents, Dr. and Mrs. Homer Castor.

Speaking from his hospital bed, a frustrated John Glenn bows out of the 1964 Ohio Democratic party senatorial primary. A freak fall in the bathtub forced him to abandon a race others thought he might have won anyway.

Glenn skiing with RFK. Despite some political differences, Bobby was a close friend for whom Glenn campaigned in 1968 and for whom he still grieves.

With Ohio Democrat Ralph Barrett (center) looking on, Glenn smiles at Howard Metzenbaum, whom he bitterly fought for the senatorial nomination in 1970 and 1974.

With Jimmy Carter in 1976. Glenn falsely thought he would share the ticket.

Right: Glenn at the 1976 Democratic convention. Below: Giving his poorly received keynote address. Glenn has since tried to dispel his image as a dull speaker.

As Annie looks on, Glenn takes the oath of office for his second Senate term from outgoing Vice-President Walter Mondale, whom he now contests for the presidential nomination.

The Glenn family gathers. Standing: Lyn Glenn Freedman, daughter-in-law Karen Glenn. Seated: son-in-law Philip Freedman, Glenn, Annie, grandson Daniel Erik, David.

In the gymnasium of John Glenn High School, where Glenn announced for the presidency, as Annie and Ohio Governor Richard Celeste looked on.

Annie and John Glenn photographed in their Potomac, Maryland home. Their relationship spans nearly sixty years.

Glenn's injury. The impact of his head against the bathtub had caused an immediate buildup of blood and fluid in the left inner ear. It was a "severe injury," says Dr. Richard H. Mattson, an Air Force neurologist who treated Glenn. "The shock of the blow was transmitted to the left temporal region of the head, just above the ear, and damaged the vestibular system, which is primarily located in the internal portion of the ear within the temporal bone."

The concussion and subsequent swelling and bleeding, Mattson explains, so disrupted Glenn's inner ear canals and nerve connections that he immediately began suffering from "disabling symptoms," including nausea and lack of balance, for which there was no immediate cure. "It was the toughest wallop I've ever taken," Glenn recalls. "They said it was a mild concussion. It didn't seem so mild to me." Even to breathe made him nauseous.

Annie Glenn, meanwhile, was a thousand miles away in Houston, oblivious of the accident. "I had gone back to our place by the space center, making lists of things that the apartment in Columbus needed to make it look like home, when I received a telephone call," she remembers. "I was told that I had better bring the children up on the first airplane that I could catch because I might not see John alive." She recalls that doctors were fearful that Glenn had developed a potentially fatal blood clot on the brain.

That her husband might be dying, or even dead, by the time she arrived was a terrifying prospect. To add to her apprehension there was no way, with her stutter aggravated by tension, that Annie could call the local high school to summon Lyn and Dave home. "I couldn't call, so my good friend, Jean Gilruth [whose husband, Robert, was head of the Manned Spaceflight Center] came right over. She was the one that called to get the kids out of school."

Lyn recalls that taxing day. "Dave and I both got called to the principal's office. There had been a phone call from Jean Gilruth, and all we knew was that Jean had asked the principal to get us home, that Dad had been hurt. Riding home in the car, we couldn't figure out why Jean would call. What was she doing at the house?"

"Maybe Dad is dead," Lyn remembers wondering.

Annie and the children arrived in Columbus on a commercial flight that evening. Bob Voas and a crowd of reporters were waiting at the airport. Rushing past the reporters, they raced to Grant Hospital, where in a darkened hospital room Annie saw her husband sedated and lying on his back.

"He recognized all of us," Annie recalls. "We all embraced him and he talked a little. He wasn't in pain, but they were keeping him quiet. They kept looking in his eyes to check the size of his pupils. I didn't ask him anything about the accident because the doctors had told me not to excite him." As evening wore on, the doctors continued their testing, still fearful of a blood clot. Annie spent the night at her husband's bedside.

She speaks about the incident now with some detachment. reflecting what friends and family members say is an inborn inner toughness strengthened during the years John spent as a combat pilot and astronaut. But Annie Glenn is not a physically strong woman. She nearly died giving birth to Lyn in 1947, and a painful gynecological condition forced her to undergo a hysterectomy in the sixties that was followed by several cancer scares, all of which proved negative. In addition, the passage of time has aggravated a bursitis condition she had had for several years, compounded by the pain she sometimes feels from calcium deposits in her right shoulder.

But despite her illnesses, Annie remains a vibrant personality. Annie's friend, Rene Carpenter, reminds outsiders: "We're all tough. Military wives in the service who have to pick up and move every couple of years can't let something like a pregnancy or cancer stop them."

During the tumultuous month after the fall Glenn's supporters, including Wayne Hays, Annie, and Rene Carpenter, tried to keep the campaign alive while the candidate himself withdrew farther and farther from it. After a brief stay in Grant Hospital in Columbus, Glenn transferred to Wilford Hall Air Force Hospital in San Antonio, where Glenn's "traumatic vertigo" was confirmed. But, fortunately, neurosurgeons discovered nothing wrong with Glenn that rest would not cure.

In the meantime, the best Glenn could manage was to walk with his head held perfectly still at a 45-degree angle facing downward, shuffling along hospital corridors with his feet spread wide apart. The slowness of his recovery forced the astronaut to delay his retirement from the Marines until at least April 1, 1964, if not later. Otherwise he would jeopardize receipt of disability payments if he decided to quit before fully cured. Glenn spent much of Easter Sunday that year sunning himself on the hospital's rooftop while Annie looked on quietly.

In Ohio, Glenn's supporters searched for ways that would allow him to renew the campaign if he should recover quickly. At the same time they instituted plans to have surrogates take his place on the hustings. At no time was serious thought given to Glenn's dropping out. Everyone assumed he intended to stay in the race.

Annie and Rene Carpenter made headlines with their stumping on Glenn's behalf. Annie would say a few words beforehand, then turn it over to Rene, whose presentations were compared to those of a down-home preacher. "Why would a good Christian man like John Glenn do a grubby thing like entering politics?" she asked. Then, after ticking off a laundry list of Glenn's virtues, she cried: "Why must politics be something dirty? Why can't you believe that there is such a man—almost too good to be true? I know that's his flaw. We've heard the 'Jack Armstrong' remarks, but you have to know this man to appreciate him!"

Part of the effort was intended to buck up John back in his hospital bed. "Annie was concerned that John would not recover if he worried," says Rene Carpenter. "So she'd call him every night from the road and they'd talk, and then she'd tell audiences the next day what John said."

It was not traditional politicking, but it was effective, and it was taking its toll on Young. "How do you campaign against a national hero who is at this moment flat on his back in a military hospital?" Young asked rhetorically. "I'm in a hide-and-seek campaign and I know it. I'm not even sure what I'm campaigning against."

Newspaper and private polls showed Glenn's lead over Young slipping because of the accident, but he was still the favorite. "John Glenn would have been a U.S. senator if he was never able to speak another word from his hospital bed," asserts

Warren Baltimore. Hays, too, believes Glenn could have won handily over Young. But Glenn, disillusioned and in pain, finally decided to end the effort, raising questions that linger to this day.

On March 30, Glenn called reporters to Wilford Hospital. Glenn spoke to them from a hospital bed that had been wheeled from his private room into a larger one to accommodate the news media. Looking gaunt from the loss of 17 pounds, he said: "Additional tests have been conducted by specialists. These tests have led to the conclusions that the conditions causing my difficulties will probably not be resolved for a least a number of months.... To make full recovery most probable, they strongly recommend that I discontinue any plans for activities for at least the next several months."

Then, sounding oddly like his critic, Representative Charles Vanik, just a few weeks earlier, Glenn declared: "I do not want to run just as a well-known name. No man has a right to ask for a seat in either branch of Congress merely because of a specific event such as orbiting the earth in a spacecraft, any more than he would have the right just by being a lawyer and having tried a few cases at the local courthouse. I regret that I must withdraw my name from consideration for nomination as a Democratic candidate for the United States Senate."

Young received the news of Glenn's withdrawal with a feisty harrumph. "I call on all Democrats to reaffirm their faith in the Democratic party, our president, Lyndon B. Johnson, and in me as their agent and public servant in Washington," Young said. Ohio Republicans meanwhile rejoiced at the prospect of running against Young, whom they considered one of the weakest Democrats in the Senate.

Glenn returned home to Houston to enter one of the most depressing periods of his life. Each day, under the solicitous care of Annie, Dave or Lyn, Glenn would slowly try to walk the long corridor of his Houston home, keeping both hands on the walls so he would not fall. For Lyn, then 16, the spectacle of her father in such a helpless state was painful. "That may have been the first time that I realized my father was human," she says.

During the months of his recovery, even the slightest head movement would make Glenn nauseous. Riding in a car could be torture. Recovery was a series of small victories over vertigo as Glenn's body slowly repaired itself. Annie recalls it as a series of "plateaus" reached after her husband mastered one mundane chore followed by another. "Just for him to walk out on the patio was very special," she remembers. "For him finally to walk out and eat with us was very exciting. That didn't happen until the summer."

Though the impression would persist that Glenn's fall and subsequent vertigo were somehow related to his space trip, it was not the case. Glenn chalked it up to his own clumsiness. "One hundred and fifty missions in two wars...test flying and the flight into orbit, and never been scratched," Glenn mused glumly. "Some re-entry, isn't it?"

In an attempt to stifle speculation, Glenn's doctors issued their own statement the day Glenn withdrew emphasizing that he had suffered no brain damage. There was "absolutely no relation between Colonel Glenn's orbital space flight and his present medical condition," they stressed. With his activities severely limited, Glenn found some solace in combing through the thousands of letters he received, both after his space flight and after his fall. He and his family culled the best from the post-spaceflight ones to make up a small volume entitled *P.S., I Listened to Your Heartbeat.*

Glenn describes the injury as having "the same effect as Ménière's Syndrome"—an inner ear disorder characterized by lack of balance and nausea—but notes that although Ménière's can result from an allergy, his injury was the product of "a straight physical injury" that permitted blood and fluid to collect in the area of damage.

"It was almost nine months before I really was back to normal again," Glenn states, adding that he did not realize he was going to be totally cured until it happened. "I would see no real improvement for a couple of weeks, and I thought, 'This is what I'm going to live with the rest of my life.' That was pretty discouraging. Then over a period of three or four days, I would suddenly notice a day-by-day improvement. Then I would go another ten days or two weeks with no change. It was a series of steps like that. But I just kept going. Finally, after I got full recovery, I went down to Pensacola and went through some of the old balance tests of my astronaut days just to see if I had full recovery."

Glenn's injury was severe, but it was not life-threatening. Wayne Hays guessed that Glenn might even have benefited from it in the May primary through a sympathy vote. This fact, combined with Glenn's consistently high showing in the polls, prompted some to doubt that the fall was the only reason the astronaut quit.

"The thought crossed my mind, then and after, that the fall might unconsciously have been a way out," says Don Oberdorfer. "My impression from the couple of days I spent with him was that he was very uncomfortable in the political role. He was not then mentally prepared for it, and he was not used to it."

Glenn contradicts Oberdorfer's view. "Politics wasn't genteel then or now," he says. "I could have bowed out the first few days in the hospital, but I stuck it out. I kept hoping that I'd recover. But in fact I didn't see that much recovery day by day. It was six weeks before I felt well enough to leave the hospital.

"The doctors weren't guaranteeing anything. They said that somewhere between two-thirds to three-quarters of the people who have had an injury like that get full recovery. Perhaps 25-to-30% of the people have some sort of residual difficulty the rest of their life—generally in getting around. I had no way of knowing at that time what percent I was going to be in. The odds were in my favor, but I just couldn't see staying in and being a 'hospital candidate.'"

Wayne Hays, who had dared go out on a political limb to support Glenn against Young, turned on the astronaut with vehemence after he quit. Hays does not even believe the bathroom accident story. "He claimed he fell in the bathtub," Hays now declares."Hardly anybody believed it. I didn't argue with him. I talked to him earlier and he talked about dropping out, and I just finally said to myself, 'to hell with him.'"

Pressed on whether Glenn actually ever told Hays he was going to drop out before he took the fall, Hays replies: "I'm not sure he told me that, but the word was out. I don't think he could take the criticism. I don't think he thought he could win.... He had that goddam psychiatrist [Voas] around him all the time, and he wouldn't do anything unless he consulted him. Everybody in the party was getting fed up. Nobody really sat down and wept about it when he dropped out."

Socko Wiethe disagrees with Wayne Hays that John Glenn somehow faked his illness. "Hell no," he says. "At first I thought it might be an excuse, but after we got the medical reports on how seriously damaged John was, we saw that everything he said was true."

Glenn now responds to Wayne Hays's skepticism with a tolerant chuckle. "Wayne wouldn't believe anything," Glenn says. "When I was hurt, he kept calling and sending messages almost every day. 'Stay in. You can be elected from the hospital if you have to,' he said. But I didn't want to do that. I was in the hospital almost six weeks. At that time they were predicting that whatever recovery I would have would take eight to 12 months —time for the stuff to reabsorb out of that bony structure around the ear. I couldn't see myself running as an absentee, hospital-ridden candidate. It wasn't the way to go about it. I didn't think it was right. I decided to get out, recover, and then see what I'd do next."

Despite his unqualified statement that he was out of the race, Glenn's name remained on the Democratic party ballot that May. He drew 206,956 votes to Young's 520,641. In the general election that November, Young squeezed out a reelection victory over Robert Taft, Jr., by a scant 16,000 votes, a margin so small that it seemed certain he would have lost without the outpouring of votes for Lyndon Johnson.

It was a desolate time for Glenn and his family. "After Dad's fall, the only political people who called were Bob and Ethel Kennedy," recalls Lyn Glenn. During the difficult ensuing months Annie Glenn would also go through a cancer scare that eventually proved unfounded. At the same time Glenn's father, the burly, devout former World War I bugler, would succumb to the disease after a long and wasting battle.

Money too was becoming a problem; the only income Glenn could count on was his Marine pension. "If our son David hadn't had a $1,000 scholarship to Harvard," Glenn says, "we could not have afforded his schooling." There was a real question whether the Glenns would be able to hold onto their home in Houston.

Suddenly, the American hero and fledgling politician who had been so grandly courted by both parties, felt lost, even forgotten.

9

THE MILLIONAIRE BUSINESSMAN

The accidental bathroom fall in 1964 left Glenn with one un-usual liability—the fear of financial ruin. Not even the Depres-sion of his childhood affected Glenn as much as did the accident. With it came the nightmarish prospect that he might be virtually immobile the rest of his life with only a meager Marine pension to provide for his family and put two children through college. "When I fell and was hurt I was out of everything," Glenn recalls. "We had saved a little money for the kids' college—largely from the proceeds of the *Life* magazine contract—but I had no way of raising money."

In addition to his personal financial crisis, Glenn's abortive primary campaign against incumbent Young produced a large deficit. Feeling personally responsible and rejecting the com-mon political device of staging a fund-raiser to erase the debt, Glenn paid the $16,000 campaign deficit out of his own pocket. "It was everything we had in the world," he notes. The prospect of going broke was particularly painful when Glenn considered the lucrative business deals and promotional schemes he had passed up just two years before because he felt they were not consistent with the dignity of the astronaut program.

Part of Leo DeOrsey's job as attorney and father-counselor for the astronauts was to make sure that they were not exploited. He was to advise them on who to do business with, guide their investments and make money for them. The half-million dollar deal with *Life*, which DeOrsey negotiated for the astronauts, was the most notable, and possibly the most controversial, of his efforts on their behalf. DeOrsey became the astronauts' unpaid, unreimbursed agent, who screened anyone wanting to cash in on the astronauts' fame. Most of the schemes were turned down out of hand. DeOrsey and the astronauts—and Glenn in particular—were insistent that the space program not be exploited by promoters. One such deal could have made Glenn a millionaire simply for endorsing what undoubtedly would have come to be called the "breakfast of astronauts."

Shortly after his orbital flight, Glenn was approached by a number of firms, including a breakfast food company. Glenn vaguely remembers that it was General Mills, but adds there was nothing vague about the money. "They were talking million-dollar figures and that was just the start.

"What they were after was the regular 'Jack Armstrong' picture on the box," Glenn says. "But I didn't want to trade on the space experience just to make a million bucks. That wasn't the purpose of it—it was for a higher purpose. I didn't want to go with any company that was just setting out to use me for advertising purposes."

Still, Glenn admits that the offer seemed attractive to a Marine lieutenant colonel who was trying to raise two children on a military salary of $16,700, including $1750 in flight pay. "We did have a steady income coming in every month," Glenn notes, "but at the end of the month, the money would sometimes just run out. We had a good life and we enjoyed it, but when you come out of that situation into one in which someone is dangling a million-dollar contract in front of you, it's pretty hard to turn down."

Another business deal, which Glenn and the others did not reject, turned into a public relations debacle that ultimately forced a polite showdown between a worried President Kennedy and a defensive John Glenn. DeOrsey's instincts usually were sound, but "the Houston Homes Deal" was his most notable failure. Shortly after NASA centered its operations in Houston's Manned Spaceflight Center, the astronauts prepared to move to that city. A group of Houston homebuilders joined together to provide homes for the seven astronauts, free and clear, in the wealthy enclave of Sharpstown in southwest Houston.

"At first we thought we should turn this down," Glenn recalled at the time. "We didn't want to get caught up in any scheme promoting a certain area of Houston. Then Leo looked into it. It turned out that this was from the whole Houston Homebuilders' Association. It appeared to him that there were enough people involved so that no one particular person was going to benefit by our being there." DeOrsey had no qualms about the astronauts' accepting the huge gift as long as no one builder was able to claim credit for it. "After having sweated over this for, I guess, several weeks," Glenn recalled, "Leo finally decided that it would probably be all right."

But it was not all right. DeOrsey had been caught in a classic bureaucratic trap. He had dutifully run the Houston proposal by several government agencies, never receiving a flat rejection. But, significantly, he had never received approval, either. No one wanted to deny the seven heroes their homes; at the same time no one wanted to be on record as having approved so large an outright gift to federal employees. Once news of the gift appeared in print, the same government agencies DeOrsey had solicited now proffered their objections. Finally, Glenn recalled, it was decided that the best course was to drop the project "and get out as best we could."

The bad publicity, as well as the constant harping in the press about the "unfairness" of the *Life* deal, reached President Kennedy, who began having second thoughts about the magazine's exclusive. During a relaxed weekend with Glenn and his family at Hyannis Port in the summer of '62, JFK even debated whether the *Life* contract should be allowed to continue.

The president, relaxing in swimming trunks on the fantail of his yacht, *Honey Fitz*, asked Glenn to justify the *Life* contract, particularly in light of the controversy surrounding former President Eisenhower's sale of his memoirs, a deal that had also been negotiated by DeOrsey. Glenn, smarting from the Houston fiasco, was prepared for the president's question. He replied that the *Life* contract did not cover experiences from the space flight; it merely gave *Life* reporters exclusive access to their family and homes—their personal stories.

"I told President Kennedy that I was as much as anyone against selling what we were actually doing on the flights themselves," Glenn recalls. "If anyone could show me anywhere we ever held back one iota of information that we gained on a flight, I'd like to know about it." Glenn maintains that Kennedy "hadn't understood it in this vein at all. I explained this very carefully, that the personal story was the only thing that was for sale."

Seemingly mollified, Kennedy asked Glenn if the astronauts incurred unusual expenses as a result of their public exposure. Glenn said they did. "They weren't tremendous," Glenn told the president, "but if you're in the public eye all the time and your family is being looked at, naturally you buy a few more clothes for the family. You take them along with you to some of the big events. Their way is not being paid by the government, so you pay it yourself.

"Following our conversation," Glenn noted, "I remember very clearly that the president turned—near the end of the conversation—to the attorney general, Bobby Kennedy, and said: 'Maybe we ought to reconsider this whole thing.'"

Kennedy's decision was in favor of retaining the *Life* contract; the deal had been saved by Glenn's lobbying. The *Life* contract was of some help financially, but when Glenn almost went broke paying off his campaign debts, he began to think seriously about accepting one of the lucrative commercial offers he had been receiving.

An automobile manufacturer wanted him to endorse cars. A sporting goods firm sought to use his name and likeness to promote its equipment. Only Royal Crown Cola, a comparatively unknown but long established soft drink firm in Atlanta, seemed interested in actually giving him a job. "I told them," Glenn recalls about his entry into American business, "that if they were talking about a real honest business association with the company, where I would be in the company hierarchy helping to make business decisions, then we could talk.

"There were several other companies involved at that time," Glenn says, "but nobody except Royal Crown would say they wouldn't expect me to do commercials." Nolan Murrah, general counsel to Royal Crown, who served with Glenn on the company's board of directors, recalls the excitement in January 1965 when Glenn was introduced to company executives at a Royal Crown convention in New Orleans. Glenn's election as a director of the firm had been announced the previous October at a New York news conference by company president W. H. Glenn, who is no relation.

"It was quite an occasion," Murrah remembers. "Glenn had been pretty highly sought after, and we thought it was a pretty rewarding thing for him to sign on with us." One inducement for Glenn to join Royal Crown was that a major portion of the firm's ownership was held in Columbus, Ohio. When Glenn's appointment was made public the previous year, it was announced that he had been elected to the board of directors and would be named vice-president for corporate development. At the time, the company emphasized that Glenn "would not serve in an advertising, promotion or public relations capacity."

But neither did anyone anticipate that Glenn, the world-famed astronaut, would become a full-time executive in return for a $50,000 annual salary and "inducement options" to purchase 90,000 shares of Royal Crown stock. In fact, Glenn's schedule shortly after he signed on with the firm included several public appearances, not only for Royal Crown but for the Boy Scouts of America as well as NASA.

"Glenn maintained his headquarters in Texas, which is where he had been with the space program," Murrah recalls. "He just kept the same office he had, with the same staff. Of course, there were enormous demands for public appearances by him, and he stayed pretty much free to make those appearances when he wanted."

Glenn seemed to enjoy the business world. He agreed to serve on several other corporate boards, collecting fees and other compensation in return. He was named to the board of Questor Corporation, an Ohio-based firm that began as an auto parts manufacturer and later diversified to include Spalding

Sporting Goods and a division that produces pollution control equipment. "I had gotten to know the president and chief executive officer," Glenn recalls, "and he asked me if I wanted to come on the board. I thought it was a good Ohio company and a good connection to have there and so I did.

"This was in the days before people started making careers out of being on boards of directors," Glenn says, "but for the time I had to spend there, it wasn't a bad $5,000 or $6,000 a year." Glenn also was able to take advantage of a deferred "phantom stock" compensation plan under which he was paid an amount equal to the dividends he would have received had he owned a set amount of Questor stock.

Besides Questor and Royal Crown, Glenn was also involved in the world of information. He was named to the editorial board of World Book in Chicago, publishers of an encyclopedia. Then in 1967, Glenn signed on with Wolper television productions for a project that appealed to his explorer's curiosity. Traveling with an entourage of 50, Glenn retraced the route that Henry M. Stanley took through Africa in search of Dr. David Livingstone, the elderly Scottish missionary who had disappeared and was living with the natives on the shores of Lake Tanganyika. Glenn's trek, complete with the former astronaut sweating in the safari suit and rumpled hat that he had bought from an outfitter in New York, was filmed for a television series on great explorations.

More than a decade later, Glenn made a similar journey when he represented the United States during independence ceremonies for the Solomon Islands. During a one-day layover, Glenn prevailed on officials to make a side trip to an aborigine village in New Guinea that had been discovered only 30 years before; its inhabitants had only recently been converted from cannibalism. The American missionary who translated for Glenn mistakenly told the chief that Glenn had been to the moon and back. This greatly impressed the chief, who told Glenn that the moon glowed because it contained the spirits of the dead. Glenn gave the chief an American bicentennial medal; the chief responded by giving Glenn his feathered and beaded body ornament. The intricate piece of native art now hangs in Glenn's Senate office next to a picture of Glenn and the wizened native elder standing together.

In 1965, Glenn began working for Royal Crown on a day-to-day basis as an executive. He found the work interesting and was surprised that the luster of the space program remained high among the corporate hierarchy and their wives. "We had a big blowout for him at the company headquarters in Columbus and had invited all the important people in town," recalls Nolan Murrah. "This was a very important event for us."

Murrah recounts that his wife met Glenn for the first time that night. "Of all the things she could think to say to this world figure and national hero, she asked him if he believed in flying saucers. I was absolutely mortified." Glenn, however, showed his small-town nature. According to Murrah, he passed up the chance to make small talk with the movers and shakers of Columbus in order to spend "most of the rest of the night taking every opportunity he could to talk to Barbara about flying saucers."

Glenn's relationship with Royal Crown flourished. He was promoted from his $50,000-a-year post as a corporate vice-president to a higher paying position as the president of Royal Crown International. The post moved Glenn to New York City, where he and Annie lived for nearly two years in Royal Crown's luxurious corporate apartment near the company's headquarters at 545 Madison Avenue. The job provided Glenn with his first true opportunity to function as an executive while keeping himself in the public eye. He traveled around the world, promoting Royal Crown Cola. He was instrumental in introducing the soft drink into Italy, even though Coca-Cola and Pepsi were already entrenched there. Glenn cemented the deal between Royal Crown and San Pellegrino to introduce Royal Crown into the country. San Pellegrino, a producer of bottled sparkling water now sold in the United States as a rival to Perrier, remains RC's franchisee in Italy.

"John had an entree to talk to people like that," Murrah remembers of Glenn's Italian negotiations. "He could demonstrate the virtues of our product. We were very small overseas in those days, and it didn't hurt that John's face was known all around the world." About this time, Murrah adds, another political figure, a former vice-president, was also traveling the world, doing for Pepsi Cola what Glenn was doing for RC. "It worked well for Pepsi and it worked well for him," Murrah says. That salesman-politician promoting Pepsi was, of course, Richard Nixon, soon to become president of the United States.

Glenn had established himself as a corporate executive, a point he often makes to counter the impression that his background includes only military service. It improved his finances, but he did not make his fortune at Royal Crown. That was accomplished at Holiday Inn, for which he has to thank his friend Henri Landwirth.

Landwirth, who pronounces his first name "Henry," is one of a handful of people truly close to Glenn. He came to the United States in 1949, after he survived Nazi concentration camps, including Auschwitz, when a Nazi guard hit him on the head with a rifle butt and left him for dead. "I don't know how long I lay there," Landwirth recalls. "When I woke up I was picked up by some Germans and put in jail. Then I escaped from the jail and wandered for about 30 days. This was near the end of the war. In fact, the war was over two days before I heard about it. And I still have a big hole in my head from where I was hit."

After the war, Landwirth returned to his native Belgium, where he was trained as a diamond cutter. On the promise of a job in New York, Landwirth came to the United States in 1949 with no knowledge of English. He worked in Manhattan's 47th Street Diamond Center before going into the Army during the Korean War. "I was at Fort Dix, and they were just about to send me to Korea," Landwirth recalls, "when they pulled me out because they thought from my background I could be a crystal cutter." Actually Landwirth had no experience in that field and lacked the necessary mathematical skills for it.

"After I came back from the Army," Landwirth continues, "my hands weren't steady enough for diamond cutting." Looking at the courses offered under the GI Bill by the State University of New York, he became intrigued by one entitled "hotel technology." That was in 1952. By 1954 he had married and moved to Florida, where he became involved in the running of several hotels and restaurants, including the Starlite, which Landwirth describes as the "first luxury hotel on Cocoa Beach."

It was there that Landwirth met Glenn. As public interest in the astronauts increased, so did the number of reporters and photographers covering their activities in Florida. Everybody wanted a room from Henri, first at the Starlite, then at the Holiday Inn, which he ran after that, and finally at the Cape Colony Inn, which Landwirth built during the height of public interest in the space effort. There were never enough rooms. "They used to call me 'Double up Henri,'" he recalls, "because I made everyone double up in the rooms. Everybody coming down there was a big shot who had to have a private room. I said to myself, this isn't worth getting sick over, so I just treated everybody the same way.

"One day Harry Reasoner came in and said, 'Henri, I need a room.' I told him, 'Harry, I don't have a room for you.' He said 'What do you expect me to do?' I said 'I don't know.'

"He slept on a couch in the lobby."

Even the astronauts had to double up on occasion, though Landwirth concedes this was rare. Less rare were run-ins with the astronauts over the hotel service. Glenn, Landwirth recalls, "was always complaining about not having enough towels." One day, he remembers, Glenn came storming down to the front desk in mock rage demanding his towels. "I told him to stop pounding on the desk, I'd give him his towels."

When Glenn came back to his room that evening after a day at the Cape, he could barely get through the door. The room was crammed with hundreds of towels that Landwirth had delivered in his absence. "You couldn't see the bed," Landwirth recalls, smiling. Another time, Landwirth asked Scott Carpenter to move into another room so that an incoming party could have adjoining suites. Carpenter refused and threatened to sue Landwirth if he touched one item of his clothing. "I didn't touch any of his clothes," Landwirth recalls, "but I did remove every stick of furniture in the room. He called me up when he got in that evening and said, 'I guess I better move, huh?'"

Glenn and Landwirth became close friends. Glenn was drawn to Landwirth not only because of his irrepressible spirit, but because he admired Landwirth's ability to overcome adversity. Landwirth also knew how to effectively turn a dollar, a quality Glenn was learning to admire. In the late sixties, while Glenn was still with Royal Crown, he and Landwirth decided to go into the hotel business together. Their goal was to build a group of Holiday Inns in Florida.

Both Glenn and Landwirth agree that it was Glenn's connection with Royal Crown that helped them secure the hugely successful Holiday Inn franchise near Disney World in Orlando. Glenn, Landwirth and a Florida broker named John Quinn sought to win the franchise over dozens of other applicants. "It didn't hurt," Landwirth concedes, that Glenn was a well-known figure. But of greater import was Glenn's connection with a Cleveland bank that was prepared to lend the partnership construction money for the hotel.

"It was strictly on financial stability and credit and reputation," declares Landwirth, noting his own 15 years of success with Holiday Inn. Today Glenn recalls the details of the venture that made him rich. "There was a very big competition for that one," Glenn says. "We worked very hard for it. When you apply, you have to show your financing, how you plan to develop the inn and what kind of management operation you're going to have. You also have to show your plans for the size of the hotel, since, obviously, Holiday Inn wants it to be as big as possible.

"We made a number of trips back and forth to Memphis, where Holiday is headquartered. I had the contacts to work out our financing through a Cleveland bank. The franchise is not the main expense. The actual cost was $15,000 at the time. But then you have to build the hotel."

"It has been a real moneymaker," declares Glenn, one of the wealthiest of the presidential contenders. "That's the reason for my financial security today." The mammoth, 513-room "Holiday Inn East of Disney World" has been expanded twice since Glenn and his partners built it. It is one of several Holiday Inns in which Glenn is part owner, including one ten miles away that sits across from another Florida tourist attraction, Circus World. Landwirth manages the Disney World Holiday Inn and stresses that he avoids trading on Glenn's fame to attract crowds. "We do not even advertise, or even tell anybody, about

John's owning this place," Landwirth insists. Few of the guests at the lavish hotel realize that the firm of "Friendship Management" that operates the inn is named after Glenn's space capsule, Friendship 7.

His real estate and investments in some 75 companies generate a yearly income of well over a half million dollars, and have given Glenn a net worth of more than six million. Glenn's financial disclosure form to the Senate Ethics Committee showed that he made $669,912 from the hotel just in 1982, a year in which his Marine retirement pay as a colonel came to $15,096.

Glenn's presidential campaign manager, Bill White, notes that all of Glenn's holdings are in a "discretionary account" handled by the Boston investment firm of Pell, Rudman & Co. "That means they can buy and sell without his approval," White says. But the arrangement differs from a blind trust in that Glenn can ask his investment counselors the composition and amount of his holdings. "But," White maintains, "he never asks. He never knows from day to day what's in there."

Glenn recalls that things were nothing like that for most of their lives. "Annie and I joke to this day that in 1957, when I was making the cross-country flight, all we wanted to do was get $1,000 in the bank for emergency purposes if something happened to us." Though Glenn is not a man of expensive tastes, he enjoys the comforts and most important, the security, of his wealth.

Having suffered political humiliation in 1964, spent all his saving to eradicate the campaign debt, and endured a difficult recovery from his bathroom fall, Glenn had bounced back once again. This time he did it by providing for himself and his family in a way, as he says, "an old rhubarb peddler from New Concord with no college degree" could never have imagined.

In the four years following 1964, Glenn had used his energies and capitalized on his fame to become a rich private citizen. To most, he seemed content, perhaps even to have forgotten the political arena. But beneath the bustling business life of soft-drink executive and hotel owner John Glenn was the soul of a frustrated politician. All it would take for it to surface again was a call from Bobby Kennedy in 1968.

10

JOHN GLENN AND RFK

John Glenn speaks quietly of Robert F. Kennedy and still grieves for him. "I went with him on the very first campaign swing that he ever made," Glenn recalls, "the first swing he made out of Washington, down to Vanderbilt and down to Alabama. And then Annie and I gave him as much time to his effort as we possibly could. We traveled all over with him—it probably averaged at least a couple of days a week—all during that period."

The Glenns were with Robert Kennedy at the beginning of the 1968 presidential campaign, and they were with him at the end in Los Angeles. It is a measure of their friendship that, on the morning after Bobby Kennedy died, it was Glenn who broke the news to Bobby's children. He still cannot talk of that time without tears.

In temperament, if not always in political ideology, John Glenn and Robert Kennedy were remarkably similar. Both were strivers and both needed to excel. Robert Kennedy's primary race for the presidency against Eugene McCarthy—after Lyndon Johnson had announced his retirement—also renewed in Glenn an ambition for public office that would compel him to run for the U.S. Senate for the second time in 1970. It is likely that John Glenn would not have run for president had it not been for Bobby's compelling example in 1968.

"John has always lived on a kind of an edge—as a test pilot, as an astronaut," says Glenn's boyhood friend and best man Lloyd White, now a retired Methodist minister. "It takes a certain kind of personality, one that is never quite satisfied. He needs that kind of an edge, that kind of stimulus, to keep himself going." Such a stimulus obviously was lacking for Glenn in corporate life.

For Bobby Kennedy, there was something more as well. "[He] was haunted by the omens of failure," wrote attorney and political advisor Richard Goodwin. "He wanted much from life, but tempted death, even dared it." His favorite admonition, both to himself as well as his children, was from Ralph Waldo Emerson's *Essays:* "Always do what you are afraid to do."

"Look at the kind of guys Bobby liked," recalled Pierre Salinger shortly after Kennedy's death, "the John Glenns, the Jim Whitakers, El Cordobes, Jose Torrés. They were all adventurers, all guys who took their lives in their hands, and who were willing to lay their lives on the line for something they believed in, whether it was flying in space, or climbing a mountain, or facing a bull. There was the element of challenge and danger to them."

Glenn and Kennedy enjoyed physical activity together, even reckless activity, although Glenn says, "I don't recall him taking what I would consider foolish risks." Kennedy, small of build, nonetheless possessed remarkable physical strength. Socko Wiethe, the Ohio Democratic leader whose nickname calls up his career as a professional football player for the Cincinnati Bengals in the late 1930s, remembers Byron R. White, himself a former professional halfback, telling him that "inch for inch, Bobby was the strongest person he'd ever met." Glenn, who sets great store on fitness born of discipline, respected this trait in Bobby.

"The middle fork of the Salmon River?" Annie Glenn asks with a smile. "Oh, that was the best place just to get away." There in tiny kayaks Glenn and Kennedy would take the rapids, the white water boiling around them, the sound of the cascade bouncing off the jagged canyon walls. "The Salmon was by Sun Valley, where the Kennedys and us always used to ski together," Annie adds. "In the summertime we would go into Sun Valley and stay all night and then in the morning catch a small plane to ferry us over to the river." They stayed in Averell Harriman's lodge and rarely had to fend off autograph seekers among a well-to-do population that, as Annie says, "was used to celebrities."

Tom Miller ascribes the closeness of the Glenn-Kennedy relationship to Bobby's huge family and to his outgoing wife Ethel. "Both John and Annie had a great affection for Ethel," Miller remembers. "I got the impression that, of all of the Kennedy wives, Ethel was the most likeable. Jackie Kennedy was not nearly the warm vivacious personality that Ethel was—and she wasn't nearly as active in sports. Of course, Ethel and Bobby also had a houseful of kids, and it was the kind of family life they lived that attracted the Glenns."

Every bit as ambitious as the hero-astronaut he befriended, Robert Kennedy was concerned, even obsessed, with the have-nots in this country, especially after his brother's death. It was a marked change, a transformation that brought to the fore sympathies and concerns not readily apparent during Kennedy's years as assistant counsel to Senator Joseph McCarthy's subversive-hunting committee and as chief counsel to the Senate Rackets Committee.

It was this concern, not Bobby's opposition to the Johnson administration's war policies, that appealed to Glenn. Glenn states that his feelings on social questions were markedly similar to Bobby's, but he differed on foreign policy. Glenn remained ambivalent on the wisdom of the Johnson administration's Vietnam policy long after Bobby had decided it was disastrous.

"I think a lot of the basic feelings about humanity were shared by John and Bobby," says Tom Miller. Much has been written about Glenn being mesmerized by the Kennedys and falling under the magic spell of Camelot. "It's true, the astronauts did become the Kennedys' pets," notes Rene Carpenter, adding that Glenn was their favorite. There is no question, too, that Glenn delighted in his friendship with John and Bobby Kennedy and realized as early as 1963 how helpful they could be to him politically. Conversely, in 1968, the prospect of Robert Kennedy in the Oval Office was obviously appealing to a still politically ambitious Glenn. His aid to the RFK campaign would not, judging from past Kennedy performance, go unrewarded.

The Kennedys were obviously of importance in his politically formative years, but to find the actual source of Glenn's "liberal" instincts—a feeling that government, like individuals, has a responsibility to the less fortunate—one must look to Glenn's formidable mother, Clara. It was Clara Glenn who instilled in her son a sense of mission and responsibility to others, but tempered always with the view that there is a limit to how much one can do for another.

"I don't know of two people who would try to get along with others more than John and Clara Glenn," recalls Glenn's Muskingum College classmate Jim Bryen. It took many forms: teaching Sunday School, shepherding softball teams to nearby towns for "away" games, harvesting a neighbor's crop when he was ill and in danger of losing his livelihood.

When Glenn was living in Virginia, before becoming an astronaut, the same feelings of responsibility would move him and his family to bring packages of food to a poor black family at Christmastime. The family would not let the Glenns leave until they "repaid" them by singing Christmas carols. It seems clear that Glenn's social conscience was formed before his association with the Kennedys, but the feeling remains, especially among some of his more conservative New Concord neighbors, that the John Glenn they knew years ago has changed, and for the worse. And, they say, the Kennedys were to blame.

"John got tied up with this crazy Kennedy liberal doctrine and veered away from his upbringing as a conservative Democrat," complains former schoolmate Walter Chess. "The Kennedys took John Glenn in as their crowning hero and got him all doctored up. His parents were Byrd Democrats, not part of this screwy Massachusetts mafia." Harold Blackwood, former New Concord postmaster, echoes the same criticism: "He has gone up there to Washington and gotten tied in with all those liberals.... He's not the same boy who grew up in this town, no sirree."

Tom Miller, however, rejects the idea that Glenn has

changed all that much. "I don't think John was nearly the free-giver of welfare Bobby wanted him to be," he recalls. "There's a tendency for rich people, who have felt so fortunate because of what they have fallen heir to, to be more adamant about giving it away to the poor. But a person like John who was poor and has worked himself up and become reasonably wealthy is not so quick to dole out the assets."

Still, Walter Chess, who has remained close to Glenn, recalls a cookout in his backyard in which John listened to Chess's complaints about Washington in the days before Glenn went to the Senate. "One day in the backyard, right out there, I was bitching about something about the government and John said to me: 'Walter, this country can afford anything it wants.'"

Glenn's decision to support Robert Kennedy for the presidency in 1968 was not without opposition among his more conservative colleagues. When he let it be known that he intended to actively campaign for Kennedy, the directors of Royal Crown, the conservative Atlanta-based soft drink firm with which Glenn was still connected, were outraged. They tried to thwart fellow-director Glenn by passing a resolution forbidding any board member from engaging in political activity. But before the board could vote on the measure, Glenn took the floor.

"I understand this resolution is aimed at me," Glenn said, staring intently around the wide conference table. "The fact is Bobby Kennedy is my friend and I intend to campaign for him." He told the board that if they passed the resolution he would be forced to resign. "Then you can go out and hold your press conference, and I'll go out and hold mine—and we'll see who comes out on top." The matter was dropped.

Freed from corporate restraints, Glenn was able to shape his own schedule. He was determined to help his friend become president, no questions asked, much as Bobby and his brother had tried to help him win a U.S. Senate seat regardless of his inexperience five years before. If he disagreed with his friend on the central issue of his candidacy—Vietnam—it didn't matter. Besides, Glenn knew, hardly anyone was going to ask him about it.

❀

It was, of course, the most turbulent year of one of the most turbulent decades of the century. Opposition to the Vietnam War had mushroomed in the years following John Kennedy's death as Lyndon Johnson vowed, "I am not going to lose Vietnam; I am not going to be the president who saw Southeast Asia go the way China went," then escalated the war the way he believed his slain predecessor would have.

Writes Johnson biographer Merle Miller: "It has now become part of the myth of Camelot that John F. Kennedy intended to withdraw from Vietnam after he had won the 1964 election. That myth was launched in an article in *Life* magazine by the president's longtime friend and White House associate Kenneth O'Donnell, who claimed that Kennedy had told him so, and Senator Mike Mansfield had a similar recollection, dating from a conversation with the president early in 1963."

But Kennedy's views on Vietnam were not so clear-cut. Even Kennedy family biographer and historian Arthur M. Schlesinger, Jr., concedes that President Kennedy's "Vietnam legacy was dual and contradictory."

"He had left on the public record the impression of a major national stake in the defense of South Vietnam against communism," Schlesinger writes. "He had left steadily enlarging programs of military and economic assistance. He had left national security advisors who for three years had been urging an American expeditionary force and a total commitment to the salvation of South Vietnam."

But, the historian notes, Kennedy "had consistently refused to send such a force or to make such a commitment. He had left a formal plan, processed successfully through the Pentagon, for the withdrawal of American advisors by the end of 1965.... And he left private opposition, repeatedly and emphatically stated, to the dispatch of American ground forces." Each of these contradictory policies, Schlesinger says, "bore the Kennedy stamp." It was up to Lyndon Johnson to decide between them.

From the time Johnson made the decision to commit U.S. ground forces to South Vietnam's defense in 1965, Bobby Kennedy, then the junior senator from New York, agonized over whether he should challenge Johnson for the Democratic presidential nomination in 1968. In 1967, Allard Lowenstein, the late bespectacled antiwar activist from New York, pleaded with Bobby to run, but he demurred. "I would have a problem if I ran first against Johnson," Kennedy told Lowenstein and a handful of other friends. "People would say that I was splitting the party out of ambition and envy." Kennedy encouraged Lowenstein to find another candidate, saying "it can't be me because of my relationship to Johnson."

The candidate that Lowenstein and others chose was Senator Eugene F. McCarthy of Minnesota. On March 12, 1968, in one of the greatest Pyrrhic victories of modern politics, Johnson barely beat McCarthy, the only avowed antiwar candidate, with a 49.5% plurality in the New Hampshire presidential primary. But the victory was lost in the attention given McCarthy's robust 42.4% second-place showing. Because of the oddities of the primary selection process, he, not Johnson, had won 20 of the 24 convention delegates. Shortly thereafter, lamely insisting that New Hampshire had shown that the Democratic party was already torn, Kennedy announced his candidacy for president. On March 31, Johnson ended a televised address announcing he would not seek reelection.

RFK was pilloried, both in and out of the party, as a late-comer, a ruthlessly ambitious politician whose anti-Vietnam challenge to Lyndon Johnson had come only after McCarthy's antiwar "children's crusade" had begun to attract votes. "He didn't even let Gene and the young people have a few moments to savor their victory," declared Washington news columnist Mary McGrory. Murray Kempton, as acid as eloquent, called Kennedy a coward who had come "down from the hills to shoot the wounded [and in so doing had] managed to confirm the worst things his enemies have ever said about him..." But there could be no turning back. Kennedy began traveling the country with a hastily put together entourage that included a former football player, Roosevelt Grier, to emphasize Kennedy's ties to blacks, and a retired astronaut-war hero, John H. Glenn, Jr., whom he hoped would neutralize his criticism of Johnson's Vietnam policy.

Recalling that decision, Glenn now says simply: "Annie and I had gotten to know Bobby very well, and he was probably one of the most compassionate people I ever knew. And when he asked me to support him for president I did." The effort, which carried the Glenns all over the country in the frantic three months of Bobby's candidacy before he was shot, was based totally on friendship and loyalty to Bobby, and not on any deep-seated opposition by Glenn to the Vietnam War, a view which was the major rationale of Kennedy's candidacy.

If Glenn had any qualms about helping depose an incumbent president who had once ardently supported him in the space program, he did not show it. Johnson, after all, had refused to help Glenn in his first Senate race in 1964. Helping Bobby merely confirmed that Glenn knew who his friends were, not that he opposed Johnson's handling of the war. In fact, says retired General Miller, the closest Glenn came to dissent over the war was his "frustration" that military leaders were not allowed early on to inflict "rapid destruction" that would end the conflict quickly by "convincing the enemy that fighting doesn't pay off."

"I think John understood the Vietnam War better than Bobby because he'd been in Korea," Miller declares. "John understood the importance of the military having the authority to do the thing quickly because of the impatience of the American people. The politician, in his attempts to put the fire out, or get the crisis ended, drags it on and on and on through negotiations. In the meantime people are shooting at each other.

"John and I had considerable conversations about this," Miller continues. "John really didn't support the way the thing was going on in Vietnam. He was also frustrated about the way Korea went. I think John, like a lot of other people who were not necessarily against the Vietnam War, were actually against the way the United States was handling it. They thought we ought to declare war or get the hell out. I think the frustrations that we went through in Korea still had an impression on Glenn. He knew of the political constraints that we felt at the time in Korea. As military men, we just couldn't understand it."

Arthur Schlesinger, at the time one of Bobby's closest advisors, confirms that Kennedy realized the importance of Glenn's support. He confided in a recent interview: "I think that Kennedy felt that having Glenn with him, as an astronaut, would probably help make him more palatable to a lot of people." This tie to an American hero, Schlesinger declares, "would help combat the feeling that in attacking the Vietnam War he was being unpatriotic."

Though his image was valuable Glenn had no practical input in Kennedy's campaign. Remembers Schlesinger: "Bobby liked him personally, but I don't think he took him seriously as an advisor on politics and issues. I don't recall Glenn being identified with issues at all in that period. Bobby had great regard for Glenn. In the first place, Bobby believed in all national heroes and all brave men, and Glenn was all these things."

Bobby made good use of his famous friend. The two would often ride together in the back of an open convertible, separated more often than not by Kennedy's rambunctious springer spaniel, Freckles. It was a time Glenn looks back on fondly—his first prolonged exposure to a national campaign—and one that rekindled his political ambition.

Johnson's withdrawal changed the tenor of the campaign. For the first time it seemed possible that Kennedy could win the nomination by besting not only McCarthy, but Hubert H. Humphrey, LBJ's vice-president, who declared his candidacy shortly after Johnson's withdrawal. A more confident Kennedy led his growing entourage through the primary states of Indiana and Nebraska, winning both by convincing margins. But a determined McCarthy, helped by Kennedy's refusal to debate him, beat Bobby in Oregon, 45-39—the first time any Kennedy had lost an election. The upcoming challenge in California was now that much more critical.

"John Glenn has been a friend of my family in both the happiest times and the hardest hours," said Ted Kennedy at a Democratic party fund-raiser in March, 1983. And the worst of those hours for John Glenn began shortly after midnight, June 5, 1968, when his friend Bobby was shot.

The first shadowy results in the crucial California primary indicated Kennedy would get the win he so badly needed. CBS's poll of voters as they left the booths showed him beating McCarthy by 49 to 41 percent. But Kennedy and those closest to him were cautiously skeptical—and the final margin between Kennedy and McCarthy as it turned out was smaller: only 4.5%. Nevertheless, staffers and supporters in the Ambassador Hotel ballroom were not deterred from an early celebration.

The final days of the California primary race against McCarthy had produced some of Kennedy's best crowds. It made him believe for the first time that despite his late entry into the presidential race he might succeed. The week before, after McCarthy's upset win in Oregon, Kennedy had been forced on the defensive. If he did not win California, Kennedy said, he would bow out, return to the Senate and raise "the next generation of Kennedys." But the crowds were there. Even by Kennedy standards, the turnouts were spectacular, as people thronged his motorcade, trying to grasp the candidate, who, sweating profusely under the bright California sun, grinned broadly and barked, "I need your support!"

But it had not always been a joyful frenzy. In San Francisco's Chinatown, in the midst of a tumultuous welcome, "shots" were heard. Kennedy remained standing in his car, while motioning a friend to help Ethel, who, pale and stricken, had slumped down in her seat. The "shots" turned out to be firecrackers. Earlier, after a day of campaigning in Oakland, Kennedy and a small group that included Glenn and former Olympic decathlon winner Rafer Johnson, held an unannounced meeting at midnight with about a hundred black militants, including members of the Black Panthers, at a local Methodist Church. On the ride over, Kennedy turned to Glenn and warned: "These meetings aren't very attractive. They need to tell people off; they need to tell me off."

They did. Once during the crowded confrontation, amid shouts of "white bigshot," "bastard" and "boy," Rafer Johnson tried to intercede.

"No," Bobby said, "this is between them and me."

"Look man," hollered a local figure known as Black Jesus, "I don't want to hear none of your shit. What the goddamned hell are you going to do, boy.... You bastards haven't done nothing for us. We wants to know, what are you gonna do for us?"

On the drive back to the hotel, the organizers of the meeting apologized to Kennedy. "No, don't," he said. "I'm glad I went."

The next morning, Kennedy returned to West Oakland for a ghetto rally. In the crowd, helping to keep order, were Black Jesus and some of the others, including Panthers, who had vented their anger at Bobby less than 24 hours earlier.

Later on, at rallies and speeches elsewhere across the state, Kennedy was back to the frenzied, exuberant form of his early campaign days. Finally, he declared to the reporters accompanying him in the final days: "If I died in Oregon, Los Angeles is my resurrection city."

At least a thousand supporters, most of them young, cheered the CBS prediction of victory on election night. The cash bar at the Ambassador began doing rush business and one girl assumed the role of cheerleader and took to leading the crowd in spelling out "KENNEDY."

By late evening, Bobby was ready to leave his fifth floor suite, where Glenn and other invitation-only guests had crowded, but he was still reluctant to claim victory in public. The television people were insisting on a statement now, lest Kennedy lose the audience in New York and Chicago because of the time difference. So Kennedy went. Someone told him he should go through the kitchen to avoid the crowds. As he did, he shook hands with the kitchen help; then finally he made it to the jammed ballroom. He began by mentioning Don Drysdale's sixth straight shutout for the Dodgers.

Recalls Glenn: "We were with him in the hotel and I was supposed to go down on the platform with him, but there were so many hangers-on and California people there who wanted to be part of that. We just said we'd stay up in the room."

The little stage where Kennedy was to speak was about three feet high and supported a lectern. It stood against the north wall, and it was here that Kennedy pushed his way through his jubilant fans to speak, trailed by Ethel, dressed in a girlish white minidress and pale white stockings. Pete Hamill recalled at the time that "while Bob was talking, some kid tried to come in through the drapes at the back. I don't remember what he looked like. I don't know whether it was Sirhan Sirhan or not." Bill Barry, Kennedy's bodyguard, saw the youth and ordered him to leave. Hamill recalled that he didn't see Sirhan until Kennedy left the lectern and walked again through the hotel kitchen, where Sirhan started firing with his arms straight out like a practiced pistol shooter, exactly the way John Hinckley would fire his .22 at Ronald Reagan 13 years later.

In the tumult that followed, Glenn rushed to the hospital with the wounded Kennedy and stayed there most of the night. Emergency room doctors at Central Receiving Hospital and neurosurgeons at Good Samaritan Hospital labored in vain to keep the wounded senator alive. Kennedy lingered comatose following three hours of emergency surgery. It was then that Ethel Kennedy asked the Glenns to shepherd the six Kennedy children who had made the trip to California with their father back to Hickory Hill in Virginia. Annie and John went to the hotel where the young Kennedys were sleeping. They were with them when they awoke to the news that their father had been shot.

"Then President Johnson called," Glenn recalls, "and said if we need airplanes or anything like that, why to let him know. We decided the best thing to do, and Ethel agreed, was to bring the kids home." On Glenn's recommendation, President Johnson ordered an Air Force jet flown to Los Angeles. "We brought the kids back to Hickory Hill, went out and stayed the night with them. That was the night that Bobby died."

Glenn rarely speaks publicly of that time. He had been telling this story in a subdued yet controlled voice during an interview in his Senate office. But at the word "died," his voice suddenly caught. His eyes began to redden and by the end there were tears welling in them. "I had to sit on the edge of the bed that next morning and tell each kid that their father was dead. It was one of the hardest things I ever did in my life."

Father Richard McSorley, a Georgetown University priest who served as a companion to the Kennedy children while their parents were campaigning, had been impressed by Glenn as he listened to the astronaut give the children an impromptu lecture on space travel years before, shortly after his flight. After Bobby's death, Glenn was a key figure in planning the funeral. Before the funeral, at Hickory Hill, McSorley recalls, "somebody came downstairs and said that Michael Kennedy [then 11] was upstairs in bed, crying. Did somebody want to come up to comfort him?" Glenn responded that "each of the children has to face this situation personally at some point in their lives." Michael, he said, "has to have some time to face it himself... nobody can really do it for him."

"Glenn was trusted by the family," McSorley says. "He knew each of the children. When he made a decision like that, people would abide by it."

The night before the funeral mass in St. Patrick's Cathedral, at a small dinner gathering in Steve Smith's Manhattan apartment, it was decided that Andy Williams would sing "The Battle Hymn of the Republic." But the singer knew few of the words beyond "Mine eyes have seen the glory." As Williams and a small group of other friends puzzled over what to do, Glenn thumbed through the Encyclopedia Britannica and found the century-old lyrics. Slowly, Glenn recited the words in his flat Ohio accent, as Williams wrote them down on a legal pad.

The next day, hidden in the choir loft, Williams waited until Leonard Bernstein, body swaying, had finished conducting the slow movement from Mahler's Fifth Symphony and led the choir in Verdi's *Requiem*. Then, unaccompanied, Williams' voice echoed through the huge cathedral in what many felt was the most moving moment of the wrenching funeral mass.

That night at Arlington Cemetery, after the day-long train ride from New York, Glenn stood on the sloping hillside near John Kennedy's grave with its eternal flame and watched as his fellow pallbearers folded the flag as he had instructed them hours earlier. Then, with military precision, he handed the red, white and blue triangle to Ted Kennedy, who gave it over to Ethel. Clutching the flag, Ethel walked slowly to her husband's casket and kissed it. And then it was over. That summer, two of the most frequent visitors to Hickory Hill were John and Annie Glenn.

With RFK's death, John Glenn had lost a good, close friend, and the opportunity to reenter the political arena. He would have to begin again if he was to fulfill what he now believed was his destiny.

11

---◆---

FROM THE JAWS OF
VICTORY

If Robert Kennedy had lived and been elected president, one can only speculate how Kennedy would have rewarded Glenn's aid in the campaign. Glenn might have been comfortable as a presidential counselor on science and technology, or the president's science advisor, or possibly even director of NASA. The speculation is intriguing.

Still, the fascination of public service for Glenn has always been in elective, not appointive, office. It is reasonable to assume Glenn would have accepted a high-visibility post from President Robert Kennedy, but only until he could run again for the Senate from Ohio.

For Glenn, that opportunity came in 1970, less than two years after Bobby's death when his old foe, Stephen Young, announced his retirement from the Senate at 80. Glenn was anxious to return to the political arena, and once again, with Young out of the way, he thought the Democratic nomination would be his for the asking. Glenn still had not shed the naive concept that heroism entitled him to public office. That so many other Ohio Democratic politicians seemed to agree only set

Glenn up for the difficulties that lay ahead.

But Glenn still had to contend with what former Ohio Democratic Chairman Pete O'Grady remembers as "a hard core of Ohio Democrats who were suspicious of Glenn's true politics." Ironically, many were Bobby Kennedy liberals who had sided with Young in '64. They continued to view Glenn as something of a closet conservative who, if allowed to reach the Senate, would turn into another Frank Lausche, the conservative Democrat whose positions in the Senate often mirrored those of right-wing Ohio Republicans.

Chief among these skeptics was Young's seasoned campaign manager, the former state legislator Howard Metzenbaum. O'Grady recalls warning Glenn of this "hard core" group in 1969 when Glenn, hoping to try again for Young's seat, called O'Grady up to discuss strategy over dinner. O'Grady, a blunt-spoken man who is now a lobbyist in Columbus, was speaking from experience when he cautioned Glenn about the depth of feeling against him in this basically liberal group.

In 1964, O'Grady had been the grassroots organizer for Young against Glenn. "I never had any feelings one way or another for John until later on," O'Grady remembers. "He was just an opponent. I didn't get into personalities like some of the others did in those days. I heard a lot of that anti-Glenn stuff, and it primarily emanated because of Steve Young's attitude toward John.

"All the campaign people did was mouth or ape whatever Steve was saying in those days. And the feeling carried on. They felt that when John fell in the bathtub that was the end of John in politics. And when he began to stick his head up in the spring of '70, it was an annoyance all over again.

"At the time, I was state chairman," O'Grady continues. "Glenn called me one day and I made arrangements to meet him here in Columbus. We sat down and talked. And I made a commitment to him that if he'd stay off the launching pad for a while, I'd make sure that Steve Young wouldn't run for reelection. Remember, at that time Young already was up into his late 70s. I knew a little bit about Steve and his background. I knew that with the least bit of encouragement, he'd not run for reelection that third time. And nobody figured at that time that

Howard Metzenbaum would jump into the fray."

O'Grady and most other Ohio Democrats simply felt that all Glenn had to do was to keep quiet about it until Young was safely out of the way. "I just knew back in '69 that if John even talked about announcing his candidacy, Steve would've announced himself, so deep was his feeling against John Glenn." On the other hand, O'Grady notes, with Young safely retired, "it would have been a runaway." Or so O'Grady—and John Glenn—thought.

John Glenn did keep his mouth shut, and as expected, Senator Stephen Young announced that after 12 years in the Senate, he would not run for reelection. Glenn rapidly announced that he was a candidate for the post. But rather than getting the nod unopposed as O'Grady had thought, Glenn was challenged for the nomination by Howard Metzenbaum.

Glenn began a low-key, low-financed campaign for the nomination. "Those who were managing Glenn's campaign at the time—and John went along with it—wanted John to spend very little on the primary," O'Grady notes. "They felt that John was well enough known that he didn't have to worry about it. Metzenbaum was an unknown quantity. Nobody was looking for Metzenbaum to win."

After all, O'Grady says, "it was the first time in modern times that a Jew had been nominated, much less elected, for a major office in party politics in Ohio. Metzenbaum was looked upon as a real nonentity in the primary." As a result, O'Grady said, Glenn and his handlers, including some with previous statewide political experience, acted as if the primary was already won. They confidently looked ahead to the general election against the Republicans in the fall.

But while Glenn was pursuing a corporate career, traveling in business circles far removed from New Concord, Howard Metzenbaum had stayed at home in Ohio to resume his political career. He had quietly set his own sights on the Democratic Senate nomination by taking over from the man whose campaigns he had successfully run twice before.

Silver-haired, bespectacled and with a talent for self-promotion, Howard Metzenbaum was a comparative unknown to the average Ohio voter in 1970. He had been a savvy Ohio state legislator for nearly a decade, but he had quit politics in 1952 to make money and by 1970 he had accumulated a great deal of it. "Some people excel at sports," Metzenbaum once observed. "In golf, I can barely break 100. Others have talent in tennis or some other sport. I play them, but I'm not very good at any of them. What I can do is make money."

His financial empire in Ohio began in a parking lot. In the mid-1940s, when the airline industry was barely in its infancy, Metzenbaum began investing in airport parking lots, operating them around the clock. He rejected critics who claimed such an expensive arrangement would never turn a profit. "I knew there would be more people flying airplanes every day," Metzenbaum recalled, "and that eventually it would pay off."

His first lot, which he rented at $400 a month in 1947, was at Cleveland airport. Two years later he joined with Alva T. Bonda, a college classmate, in establishing APCOA, the Airport Parking Company of America. As the firm grew and added other airport concessions, Metzenbaum and Bonda expanded their tiny but growing empire by acquiring 17 Avis rental car franchises, the largest number ever held under a single ownership. The two men continued their controlling interest in APCOA after it went public, then merged the company with ITT in 1966. In the deal, Metzenbaum, who grew up in near-poverty, received some $6 million in stocks out of the approximately $30 million sale price, allowing him to indulge the taste he had acquired for fine things. Once, Metzenbaum, talking to a political acquaintance in his office, remarked: "That problem has many shadings—like that Vasarely hanging over there."

Politically, Metzenbaum had one great asset. In his years as a powerful labor lawyer and key political aide to Stephen Young, he had become a favorite of organization Democrats in Ohio, especially union members. His liberal political views appealed to the state's black and Jewish voters, who appreciated Metzenbaum's strong stand against racial and religious discrimination 20 years before it was fashionable. But in 1970, after an 18-year absence from elective office, Metzenbaum's name was recognized by less than 5% of the Ohio electorate. He knew he had to acquire voter identity if he was going to prevail over such a well-known, and well-liked, personality as John Glenn.

Still, there were hints that Glenn might be vulnerable. Metzenbaum's political consultant was Joe Napolitan, a savvy Washington-based pollster who had established a reputation as a canny interpreter of polling data. Napolitan told Metzenbaum that, on the basis of his soundings, Glenn was weak among blacks, union members and urbanites in the crucial 30-to-49-year-old age bracket, a liability Glenn is still trying to overcome almost 15 years later.

But as he sought to reestablish himself in 1970, Metzenbaum had the disadvantage of being Jewish "in a state that is not known for its liberalism, especially in the downstate ethnic enclaves of Cincinnati and Dayton," as one Metzenbaum man put it. On this point, Metzenbaum was, of necessity, philosophical. "Those people who won't vote for me because I'm Jewish," he said at the time, "will have found ten other reasons for not voting for me."

The stigma of being poor and Jewish had instilled in Metzenbaum not only a will to succeed but the discipline to succeed against formidable odds. He was the grandson of a Jewish immigrant from Hungary and had been raised in a middle-class neighborhood on Cleveland's east side. "My father," he once recalled, "had to sell his 1926 Essex to keep the bank from foreclosing on his house." As a young man, Metzenbaum worked his way through Ohio State University selling Fuller Brushes and magazines. He also earned money by renting bicycles and playing the trombone in a National Youth Administration orchestra.

Metzenbaum was graduated in 1939 and took his law degree at Ohio State two years later. Shortly after passing his bar exam, he placed an ad in a Cleveland newspaper offering to exchange legal services for law office space. The ad was answered by Cleveland attorney Sidney Moss, who ultimately formed an income-tax consulting firm with his resourceful partner. Working in several Ohio cities, Metzenbaum and Moss charged $1 for the preparation of each form. "I earned $10,000 the first year," Metzenbaum recalled proudly. "It was the first real money I ever made."

Money was to figure prominently in Metzenbaum's 1970 primary campaign against Glenn. Metzenbaum organized hard and wisely; the estimated $700,000 he spent on the primary attracted attention even from national news magazines. Metzenbaum opened 15 offices around the state with more than 50 paid coordinators. When the Glenn people tried to hire some workers to distribute literature in Dayton, they were told that Metzenbaum already had them on the payroll. Soon, Glenn, finding himself suddenly surrounded by Metzenbaum advertising and campaign literature, began complaining that Metzenbaum was trying to "buy the election with a million dollars' worth of television spots." Metzenbaum countered effectively with caustic humor.

"I have been on both sides of selling a candidate, with too little or too much to spend," Metzenbaum declared. Yes, he agreed, unequal television exposure was inherently unfair. And that is precisely why he had had to spend so much money to counter the "tax-supported $3.5-billion TV spectacular" that Glenn enjoyed when he orbited the earth. "I have to let people know who I am and what I stand for," the candidate said with a wry grin.

Meanwhile, Glenn was conducting a lackadaisical campaign, what one reporter called a "where do I go today?" effort. The contrast between the two campaigns was stark, and demoralizing to those who hoped Glenn would win. While Metzenbaum ran a union-supported, well-financed campaign that was professional, Glenn and his handlers suffered from political naivete. Ohio reporters, who were getting their first sustained look at John Glenn the politician, were nonplused. For all Glenn had going for him, notes Abe Zaidan of the *Akron Beacon-Journal*, "he flubbed two basic campaign requisites: he never got around to mustering a strong campaign organization and his fund-raising had the ring of tin cups." When reporters complained, for example, that Glenn had a habit of not showing up on time for press conferences, the airy reply was, "What's the difference? This is only the primary."

Glenn's fund-raising apparatus—what there was of it—was laughable. It consisted largely of Annie Glenn's Christmas list.

Warren Baltimore, the Columbus insurance executive and political advisor, recalls: "I tried hard to raise money. I took Annie's Christmas card book and looked for names. I woke up Milton Berle early in the morning. I talked to Danny Kaye." With a laugh, he concedes: "I don't think I raised $300."

Glenn's inexperience cut across every level of the primary campaign, including the desire to do everything himself, even jobs for which he had no background. "Glenn had this thing back then about overseeing all the data, every part of the campaign," recalls Baltimore. "He insisted on doing his own TV ads while Metzenbaum was hiring Charlie Guggenheim to do some of the best TV ads ever commissioned by a politician."

Guggenheim, an Academy Award-nominated cinematographer, was very expensive; but, as Metzenbaum foresaw, he was worth his fee. The producer created gripping cinema verité for Metzenbaum, a form of political television commercial that was then new to politics. "Ohioans witnessed stuff they had never seen before," notes political consultant Steve Avakian. In one of the Guggenheim spots, a hardhat to whom Metzenbaum is talking suddenly breaks down and weeps because he can't afford to buy a home for his family. "It was powerful, gut-wrenching stuff," Avakian recalls, noting that many of the techniques Guggenheim perfected in 1970 were used two years later when he produced television ads for the McGovern presidential campaign. Guggenheim, an old friend of the Kennedy family, would later do the introductory film for the Kennedy Library.

By contrast, Glenn's approach to television commercials was unsophisticated. "He simply figured if he just sat on the edge of a desk and talked directly to the voters, letting them see that a swell guy he was, that's all he had to do," says one professional close to the Glenn campaign.

The problem was Glenn's overconfidence, a confusion between hero worship and votes, an overconfidence he has had to fight over the last decade. "Glenn was co-opted by all the private polls that showed if ten people voted in Ohio, nine wouldn't vote for Metzenbaum under any circumstances," Baltimore maintains. Had Glenn been more knowledgeable at the time, or equipped with a better staff, he might have sensed that he should not have advocated larger budgets for the space program while Metzenbaum talked against Nixon administration social welfare cuts. He might also have realized that an endorsement by the Democratic mayor of Cleveland, Carl Stokes, could signal a large turnout in black areas where Glenn was weak.

By April, 1970, Metzenbaum was fast gaining on Glenn and showing noticeable strength in newspaper and private polls. He was also outspending Glenn four to one, allocating more than $400,000 for television commercials alone. But Glenn could not, or would not, change his tactics. The overconfidence was contagious. Some of Glenn's top people ignored Metzenbaum, convinced that victory was assured. One even went on vacation two weeks before the primary.

An added complication was that Glenn hates pressuring people for campaign money. "I'd rather wrestle a gorilla," he says. Unfortunately his backers were willing to assume that Glenn was well enough known not to need a large campaign bankroll. Supporters who dismissed Metzenbaum, and an even more obscure black challenger, Kenneth Clements, as mere annoyances, kept telling Glenn early in the race: "Come to us for money in the general election; you don't need it now."

But of course he did. He needed it to build the organization he never had, one that would have steered him away from high school civics classes and into party ward meetings. Away from small counties and into places where the Democratic party votes were concentrated, like the heavily populated wards of Cleveland. "John's big problem," said one observer at the time, "was that he met a lot of people. He just didn't meet any Democrats."

There were other problems as well, one close to home, one thousands of miles away in Cambodia. Yet they were related, and Metzenbaum was able to capitalize on both with stunning effectiveness in the final days of the campaign.

On April 30, 1970, American and South Vietnamese forces invaded Cambodia in order to attack Communist bases along the Cambodia-Vietnam border. President Nixon justified the attacks on the grounds that there was no American intent to violate Cambodia's sovereignty, only to harass enemy installations. The action, which many liberal Democrats regarded as an abuse of the president's warmaking powers, set off antiwar protest demonstrations around the country. They prompted

Metzenbaum, long a critic of administration Vietnam policy, to call for a "date certain" withdrawal of American troops.

Metzenbaum's move rankled Glenn, who though privately critical of Nixon's action, could not bring himself to criticize the commander-in-chief in time of war, albeit undeclared war. This position of Metzenbaum's, who had sat out World War II as a legislator with poor eyesight while Glenn was piloting fighter-bombers in the Marshall Islands, further strained Glenn's relationship with his political foe. Metzenbaum did his best to antagonize Glenn by repeatedly running political ads casting aspersions on Glenn's lack of experience as a politician and lawmaker. "The ads more or less said, 'Who do you want to represent you, an astronaut, or a professional,'" recalls Pete O'Grady.

Another, subtler, jibe by Metzenbaum was always to refer to Glenn as "The Colonel." As it happened, this was what many of Glenn's own staffers called him during the race. When Metzenbaum did it, though, it was a clear message to voters—especially the ones Joe Napolitan had targeted—that Glenn was tied to the same military establishment they now opposed.

Steve Avakian, who would later serve as Glenn's press secretary and 1980 Senate campaign manager, says: "I can't see anything that John did right in the '70 primary campaign. He was just a sheep going to slaughter, and Howard Metzenbaum and his manager and law partner, Harold Stern, were playing the tune. The sheep fell into every trap Howard and his political lieutenants laid."

With less than a week to go before the May primary, the Glenn campaign was nearly broke. He spent his last funds on a telethon to raise money for a final TV ad blitz. "The telethon was a slapdash, last-minute thing," recalls a staffer who helped put it on. "Everyone knew Metzenbaum was on the brink of a political miracle." The show had a curious beseeching quality, "as close as one could get to begging," as one viewer said. Callers were unable to get through, and other callers wasted valuable air time talking about controversial issues. This and other blunders led political reporter Abe Zaidan to call Glenn's 1970 primary effort one of the worst political campaigns in Ohio history. Even an eleventh-hour campaign appearance by Ethel Kennedy did not help.

What effect Metzenbaum's jabs at Glenn were having on the electorate was difficult to discern immediately. But what happened on May 4, 1970, the day before the primary, suddenly galvanized the anti-Vietnam War sentiment among the Ohio electorate and brought attention to the views of the staunch antiwar Metzenbaum. It was on that day that four students were shot to death by Ohio National Guardsmen on the campus of Kent State University.

The Glenn-Metzenbaum campaign also became involved in personalities. Spurred in part by scandal sheet stories about ski trips with the Kennedys and hints of romances involving Glenn with both Ethel Kennedy and singer Claudine Longet, rumors began surfacing that Glenn and Annie were soon to divorce. Longet, the willowy, throaty-voiced French singer, was at the time married to Andy Williams, then also a close Kennedy friend. "I think he was very fond of Claudine," says a longtime Glenn associate. But he quickly adds, "I don't think he ever strayed."

Glenn insists his friendship with Miss Longet was just that and nothing more. Longet's career would plummet several years later in 1977, when she was convicted of "misdemeanor homicide" in the apparently accidental shooting death of her lover, ex-ski champion Vladimir (Spider) Sabich, in Aspen, Colorado. Glenn, whose daughter, Lyn, lives in Vail, Colorado, would telephone her regularly during Longet's trial for progress reports on how Claudine was holding up under the pressure and for the press coverage of her trial.

One publication printed an absurd story of Glenn's alleged philandering. "One of those scandal magazines did what I thought was the cheapest thing I ever saw in my life," Glenn recalls. "They wrote up something about how I was having a tryst with Ethel up at some ski resort and ran this picture of the two of us in ski clothes looking at each other, blissfully happy. They said Ethel had fallen on the slopes and I had been careful to pick her up and how we had dinner together every night." In reality, both Robert Kennedy and Annie Glenn had been standing there with their mates when the picture was snapped, but the publication had cropped Bobby Kennedy and Annie Glenn from the photograph.

However, the divorce rumors were persistent enough to convince even some of the Glenns' oldest friends in New Concord that there must be some basis to them. "Gee, John, we're just awfully sorry to hear about you and Annie," one of them commented during a campaign swing back home. Glenn was furious. He became convinced that Harold Stern was spreading the rumors.

Glenn happened to run into Stern at the Neil House. Collaring Stern, the grim-faced ex-Marine pushed him up against a wall. "The next time I walk into the room, you walk out," he said through clenched teeth. "And anytime you see me, walk away from me, 'cause I'll hit you." Reports one witness: "John has arms like triphammers. When he grabbed Stern, the guy turned white as a sheet. I don't think anybody had ever seen John that angry." Today, Glenn confirms every detail of the story but one. "I never said I'd hit anybody," he insists.

Stern, now one of Walter Mondale's key financial backers in Ohio, also confirms that there was a confrontation in which Glenn told him to disappear. But he emphatically denies spreading the divorce rumors. He maintains that Glenn was upset that day because anti-Glenn letters had been sent out by the Metzenbaum campaign over the signature of Senator Stephen Young. The letters charged Glenn with having voted for Richard Nixon in 1960.

"It was at a reception, I think put on by one of the unions," Stern recalls. "Glenn was angry. As I can best remember the incident his anger related to what he thought were some personal attacks on him by Senator Young.

"I know that subsequently, there was a suggestion that somebody thought that I had something to do with rumors relative to his marital relationship," Stern says, lapsing into lawyerly jargon. "I did not. Not only was I not involved in instigating any such rumors, I wasn't involved with the spreading of such rumors. I had no knowledge or information, or in fact desire, to get involved with that type of rumor relative to Senator Glenn."

When the votes were counted, John Glenn, who just months

before had been considered a sure winner, had lost to the once obscure Metzenbaum by nearly 13,000 votes. It was not a large margin, but one that was the more painful to Glenn when he calculated where Metzenbaum had gotten his plurality. By lining up labor and black leaders and spending a tycoon's ransom in advertising, Metzenbaum had managed to carry only 12 of Ohio's 88 counties. But nine of those 12 were among the state's most populous. Glenn had carried 76 of the counties, mainly the rural, thinly populated areas with few Democratic voters.

It was also the heyday of the 21st District Caucus, the Cleveland-based black political machine run by the Stokes brothers, Louis and Carl. On election night there were numerous rumors that the late-arriving paper ballot returns from the heavily black east side of Cleveland may have been doctored in Metzenbaum's favor. But at least one Glenn partisan, Stephen J. Kovacik, does not agree.

"Hell no," Kovacik says, "it was just a case of being beaten organizationally by smart political moves and good television," he says. In fact, Metzenbaum's victory probably would have been greater if not for Kenneth Clements, the black physician who was the third candidate on the Democratic primary ticket. Clements had been intrumental in the Stokes brothers' rise to power, but after a fallout with the Stokeses he announced his independent candidacy. "I don't think Clements's strategy was to nominate John Glenn," recalls a local politician. "I think he was simply trying to break the black vote away from Metzenbaum. The fact that he got about 7 or 8% of the vote indicated his strategy almost worked."

The defeat took a strong personal toll on Glenn. "John Glenn does not like to end up second," says Kovacik. "I think that's obvious. But Glenn not only wound up second, he got beat by an unknown. I mean, in Ohio, for an unknown Cleveland Jew to beat one of the country's heroes is unheard of. I think that when John woke up and found out he really got clobbered, he attributed it not to the fact that he ran a bad campaign, but that Howard ran a dirty campaign. It had nothing to do with Howard being a Jew. If Howard had been an American Indian, John would have hated him."

The primary defeat left Glenn a loser, but a wiser one. It was a lesson he would not forget. Glenn had finally learned that politics was not the simple extension of hero worship. It had its own rules and—not unlike the military—its own traditions which had to be understood, and manipulated, if one were to succeed. Rather than give up after two failed efforts to gain a Senate seat, Glenn decided it was time for the astronaut to become a real politician.

12

PAYING HIS DUES

America, John Glenn told a reporter after his 1970 defeat, had always turned its back on its heroes. His loss to Howard Metzenbaum only confirmed the idea in his mind. After being decorated in two wars, setting a cross-country speed record and being the first American to fly in orbit, the people of his own state had rejected him. It was, he concedes, "one of the biggest disappointments of my life."

The loss, and more, the humiliation, plunged Glenn into a depression. But as with previous defeats, it also stiffened his resolve to try again. "This time, he really felt he had to prove himself," says Monica Nolan, a Cleveland stockbroker and Democratic party official who helped run Glenn's 1970 and 1974 campaigns. "The loss made him all the more determined."

Even the friends of his childhood in New Concord, familiar with Glenn's doggedness, were surprised when he returned to the political arena. Recalls Carl Anker: "When John first tried for the Senate and then had that accident, why, I thought he had missed his opportunity. But to my great surprise, he came back the next time. And then back again. He comes back, fails and fails, and for anyone else, that would have been it. But not John."

Glenn's loss in 1970 was disappointing not only because his margin of defeat was so small but because he believed he deserved to win over a man he viewed as a demagogue. The loss to Metzenbaum also conjured up the private devils of the last "election" he had lost: the peer vote to choose the first American astronaut. In 1970 he was as angry as he had been nine years earlier when he thought a terrible wrong had been done him.

There was no mollifying Glenn about Metzenbaum. "That's one thing about John," notes one political advisor, "If he doesn't like you, it's set in concrete." Even the ritual endorsement of Metzenbaum following the primary was a forced affair. A press conference had been called for 10:00 A.M. shortly after the May 5 primary. Glenn showed up agitated and tense, and as reporters and photographers prepared to record the event, Glenn suddenly decided he could not do it. "I can't go through with this," he muttered. He was dangerously close to bolting when Pete O'Grady muscled the reluctant Glenn into a side room and told him how damaging it would be.

"I was simply looking at it as a political pragmatist," O'Grady remembers. "I encouraged John to get in there and endorse Howard for the purpose of promoting whatever long-range political ambitions he may have had. Yet even so, his endorsement was lukewarm."

Glenn finally stepped to the microphones and said he would support Metzenbaum and urged his election that November. The endorsement, although reluctantly given, was Glenn's first painful lesson in practical politics, one of many he would have to absorb before he could sit in the U.S. Senate. Glenn now realized that if he was to have still another chance at the Senate—and he recognized that it would be his last—he would have to pay his political dues. He would have to make peace with the regular Democratic organization in Ohio.

The political professionals in Ohio were convinced that Glenn held them in a form of benign contempt. Recalls Pete O'Grady: "Even to this day, in putting together his presidential campaign, you'll find that he's got some qualms about professional politicians. He'll pick out some that are very close to him, and they're loyal to him and he's loyal to them. But overall, the professional politician does not fit into John's program."

In the aftermath of 1970, however, Glenn submerged his dislike for those who make their living in the pursuit of influence and power. He agreed to head the campaign committee to elect John Gilligan governor of Ohio that November, beginning a political alliance that would, in its own convoluted way, set Glenn up for a rematch with Howard Metzenbaum four years later. It is a contest that Ohio Democrats still talk of in the hushed tones of fans describing a historic 15-round title fight.

John Gilligan, known as Jack, was a lanky, wavy-haired politician seeking a comeback in 1970 after having lost his House seat in 1966 and a bid for the Senate two years later. This time, fortune, and the peccadillos of his Republican adversaries, favored him. It was revealed that Gilligan's opponent, as well as several other Republican state officials, had received political contributions from a Columbus firm that had previously arranged large loans for their clients from the state treasury.

The scandal seemed to assure Gilligan's victory. But Metzenbaum, who was running for the U.S. Senate that November on the same ticket with Gilligan, was not as fortunate. His opponent was Robert Taft, Jr., the son of the legendary "Mr. Republican" and grandson of the former president. Metzenbaum fought tenaciously and ran ahead of most Democrats in such Republican strongholds as Cincinnati, Taft's hometown, as well as in Columbus and several nonmetropolitan areas. Taft, however, did surprisingly well in Cleveland, Metzenbaum's hometown. By late election night, Gilligan was the new governor of Ohio while Metzenbaum, like Glenn six months earlier, had lost by a nose—by 70,000 votes out of more than three million cast.

With a Republican now in the Senate, Glenn saw that his route to that august body was not permanently blocked. He set about to convince Ohio's political establishment to accept him as one of their own. Glenn put the bulk of his business affairs in other hands and took up permanent residence in Ohio. To make peace with the regulars, he headed the Buckeye Executive Club, a politically influential Democratic organization. Most of the state party leaders soon succumbed to Glenn's combination of persistence and a mild, unaffected manner.

In 1972, he campaigned actively for Senator Edmund S. Muskie during Muskie's abortive race for the Democratic presidential nomination. Glenn missed out on a chance to be a delegate to the 1972 Democratic convention when the Maine Democrat pulled out of the race, leaving the field to George McGovern. In recognition of Glenn's party efforts, Governor Gilligan later appointed him to head a state environmental task force. Glenn chaired hearings throughout the state and soon become known as a friend of the environment. The hearings, which were well attended and heavily covered by the media, produced legislation that Glenn helped draft to create Ohio's own Environmental Protection Agency.

Looking back on the period, Glenn recalls his political chores as if he were ticking off a prelaunch checklist. "I don't think anyone besides the governor spoke at more Jefferson-Jackson Day dinners or fund-raising events," he says. "When Gilligan ran for governor, I did more TV spots for him than anyone else, and he knew it." Glenn has never liked political trench work, but he now realized its value. During all this time, he felt he was amassing political chits that one day he could call in. But when the time came to claim his reward John Glenn was once again sorely disappointed.

In the years following his 1970 Senate defeat, Glenn's time was divided between political drudgery and corporate business. He retained his ties to Royal Crown, exercising stock options and growing wealthier on his hotel holdings. It was during this period that the good fortune that protected Glenn in combat as the "MiG Mad Marine," that shielded him as he plunged back to earth from his space flight, that saved him from permanent injury when he fell in the bathroom, protected him once more. The most dramatic manifestation of Glenn's luck came Saturday, May 29, 1971. On that Memorial Day weekend, John Glenn was nearly killed in a car crash before a stunned crowd of racing fans at the Indianapolis Motor Speedway.

Glenn has always loved speed, on land and sea as well as in

the air. As an adult, one of his favorite sports is waterskiing. He is equally intrigued with the Indianapolis 500, where scores of racers scream round the famed track at more than 150 miles per hour. Once, sitting in his Senate office, Glenn spoke candidly of the lure of speed. "You can emote with an Indy race car driver," he said, "because you've been in a racing car yourself. You've skidded and you know that it's a very delicate balance holding that skid in a turn."

Glenn learned of the "delicate balance" that Memorial Day weekend. Annie Glenn, who summarizes that day with a single word—"horrible"—relates that she and her husband had gone to watch the Indy several times, but on this particular Saturday John was not in the stands with her, but in the pace car. He had been asked to ride in the lead vehicle as it sped around the track allowing a field of 33 racers behind it to gather in formation according to pole position, waiting for the green flag that would start the race.

"I was sitting in the front row in the upper deck," Annie recalls. "They gave me a very good seat. John was all excited about being in the pace car." With the 33 cars roaring behind it, the Dodge Challenger convertible began its circuit, preparing to circle once, then veer off into the pits as the rest of the cars accelerated explosively to racing speed. But as the pace car was finishing its round, Annie Glenn realized that something was wrong. "They were preparing to come off and I could see that the pace car was not slowing down. If anything it was picking up speed," she says, the dread of the day returning in her voice. "I could see that it was going to crash into a truckbed down near the end, where the cars come in to refuel."

Metal and wood risers had been placed there for reporters and TV crews. As the driver of the pace car tried frantically to bring it under control, Annie watched in terror; the car began to skid from side to side, then straightened out, only to crash into the stands where the journalists sat.

Annie turned around and grabbed a pair of binoculars from a nearby spectator. She trained them on the mangled pace car, now wedged under the truckbed. She heard screams, but could not see her husband.

"I could see that there were broken legs and arms," she

recalls haltingly. "There was one person with blood all over him." Her normally dormant stutter, triggered by the disturbing memory, suddenly makes each syllable a struggle. "You've ...got me..quite...e-e-e-e-e-emotional," she says. "I've...got ...to...get myself under...control." She pauses for a moment, then resumes her narrative.

Staring intently through the binoculars, Annie could now see her husband. He was pulling himself out from the wreckage. "John crawled out and put both thumbs up. I could see he had both thumbs up, so I knew he was all right," she says, her voice returning to normal. "He knew I'd probably be watching to see if he was OK."

Miraculously, the four people in the pace car, Glenn, Speedway owner Anton Hullman, TV commentator Chris Schenkel, and the driver, an Indianapolis auto dealer named Eldon Palmer, were unhurt. But some two dozen others on the field were injured in the crash, including nine who required hospitalization. The most seriously hurt was a prominent Brazilian physician, Dr. Vincent Alvarez, who was covering the race as a photojournalist for a Brazilian magazine. He sustained serious head injuries and was probably the person Annie saw covered with blood from the grandstand. Alvarez eventually recovered from his injuries.

Following the crash, Glenn said: "I've been around the world, but I've never been in anything like this."

The following year, 1972, was a political watershed for Glenn, though at the time, he was not aware of it. Exactly ten years before he had burst upon the world stage as a space hero. Now, he was a political has-been. But despite his defeats, Glenn remained in the public mind and was surprisingly popular. "He still receives daily batches of fan mail at his comfortable apartment in the high-rise building on the outskirts of Columbus where he lives with his wife, Annie," said a newspaper profile on the tenth anniversary of his flight. "He is a popular speaker on college campuses where, he says, he talks 'about how this country has developed. My reception is very, very good—more than I expected.'" The article noted that Glenn "is an executive with Holiday Inn Corp., charged with developing new motel projects" and also "serves as a director of Royal Crown Cola, for which he once worked as head of the international division."

The final paragraph of the profile is the most significant. "It's no secret that one reason Glenn has continued to be so active in the Democratic party is the fact that two years from now, Republican Senator William Saxbe will be up for reelection and Glenn wants to establish good credentials within the party."

The article was accurate. As spring turned to summer in 1972, Glenn continued to work as a loyal Democratic party man. But in the humid predawn of June 17, five men wearing business suits and blue plastic surgical gloves were arrested at gunpoint after they had broken into the Democratic party's headquarters at the Watergate office building in Washington. What followed from that "third rate burglary" would topple a sitting president in one of the worst political scandals in the nation's history. For John Glenn, however, it would be providential, altering both Saxbe's and Glenn's prospects and ultimately give Glenn the opportunity for a rematch against his political nemesis, Howard Metzenbaum.

Saxbe, formerly Ohio's attorney general and speaker of the state house of representatives, was an enigma to many of his fellow Ohio Republicans. He was a bluntly outspoken man characterized by two attitudes unusual in politics. The first was that he did not look forward to running for a second term in the Senate in 1974. The second was that, since his election in 1968 was a fluke, there was no need for him to be nice to anyone, least of all the president of the United States, Richard Nixon.

Certainly, few in Ohio politics had expected Saxbe to make it to the Senate in 1968 when he was tapped as the GOP candidate to face the staunchly conservative and seemingly indomitable Democrat, Frank Lausche, then seeking reelection to a third term. But 1968 was the year Jack Gilligan, backed by Ohio's powerful labor lobby, had defeated Lausche, the conservative Democrat in a primary race. Lausche, a whitehaired, craggy-faced curmudgeon, had been virtually unbeatable in general elections, drawing thousands of Republican votes away from his opponents. The more liberal Gilligan could perform no such miracle against Saxbe, and in the general election that fall, Saxbe won the once-secure Democratic Senate seat by 114,000 votes out of nearly four million.

Having arrived in the Senate unexpectedly, the *Almanac of American Politics* noted, Saxbe "appears to act as if his seat was a windfall." His barbs at his own president were especially sharp. When Nixon unleashed the bombing of North Vietnam during Christmas 1972, Saxbe declared with scathing frankness: "The president appears to have left his senses."

Nixon had already begun his downward slide in the Watergate maelstrom by the time William Saxbe came to public attention again in the fall of '73. It came to be known as the Saturday Night Massacre. For months, it appeared as if the president was staying one step ahead of the law. But each time the White House sought to contain the political damage, some new revelation brought investigators closer to the Oval Office.

Public outrage soon forced Nixon to name a special prosecutor to independently investigate the Watergate affair. He chose Harvard law professor Archibald Cox, a lanky, crewcut man who favors bow ties. When it was revealed during televised Senate hearings that Nixon had secretly taped his White House meetings and telephone conversations, Cox and his lawyers demanded the tapes. Rebuffed by the president on the grounds of "executive privilege," Cox went to court to compel their release. When he balked at Nixon's proposal to keep the tapes but to release "summaries" instead, the president fired the prosecutor on an unseasonably warm Saturday night, October 20, 1973. Immediately after, Elliot Richardson, the attorney general who had studied under Cox at Harvard, and the number-two man at the Justice Department, Deputy Attorney General William D. Ruckelshaus, both resigned in protest.

Nixon moved quickly to replace the attorney general. His surprising choice was the outspoken Bill Saxbe, creating a vacancy in the Senate that Governor Gilligan was required to fill. Gilligan also acted quickly with a strategy that he thought was brilliant—one that might land him in the White House by 1976. Instead, it unwittingly set him on the path to political oblivion.

Glenn's relationship with Gilligan was always correct, if not especially cordial. The styles of the two men were certainly markedly different. Jack Gilligan was a politician, precisely the type of politician John Glenn disliked. He was the "professional" who could burst into a room, work it to the corners, and be gone in ten minutes, looking forward to his next appearance. Neither did Gilligan share Glenn's qualms about the political company he had to keep to succeed. "There are," Gilligan once said, "a lot of people in politics whom I must meet on the street, and whose hands I must shake whom I would not necessarily recommend to the College of Cardinals."

One of these people was Howard Metzenbaum, whom Gilligan disliked intensely; he had even fired him from his gubernatorial campaign staff in 1968. Metzenbaum, who was finally elected to the Senate in 1976 in a rematch with Robert Taft, Jr., inspires strong, sometimes conflicting, feelings among his fellow politicians. "He's a mixture," declares a veteran Democratic lawmaker. "He is obnoxious and tenacious and quite arrogant. He's not very popular in the Senate, yet from a liberal Democrat's point of view, he's very effective." Few other senators have so strong a record on consumer issues as Metzenbaum, one that extends back to his days in the Ohio legislature and the Metzenbaum Act, which became a model for the federal truth-in-lending law.

Few politicians can claim such unwavering labor support, endorsements that have garnered Metzenbaum votes and funds in every one of his political campaigns. His liberal stance on public issues was obvious as far back as 1943 when, as a freshman Ohio legislator, he introduced a measure that would have banned discrimination by employers and unions on the basis of race, religion or national origin. The bill failed, but Metzenbaum did manage to win expansion of Ohio's unemployment and workman's compensation programs.

He came to politics the hard way, running for the legislature as a 25-year-old Democrat without the endorsement of the local party organization. And at the time he took his oath he was the youngest person ever to serve in the Ohio House of Representatives. But his obsessive drive to succeed, in politics and business, has made him a controversial personality. "I don't want to say anything bad about Howard," notes party official Monica

Nolan, citing Metzenbaum's 1980 support of her idol, Ted Kennedy, for president over Jimmy Carter, "but he can be hard to get along with." Others are not as kind. "Howard Metzenbaum is interested in just one person—Howard Metzenbaum," declares another Ohio Democrat.

Following his upset win over John Glenn in 1970, as well as his creditable, though losing, showing in the general election against Taft, it seemed obvious to Metzenbaum that William Saxbe's vacated U.S. Senate seat from Ohio belonged to him. He so informed the governor, bringing with him the backing of his powerful friends in organized labor.

John Glenn had the same thought. He believed he had just as much right to the vacancy since Metzenbaum was now also a political loser. Glenn was heartened by the fact that Gilligan disliked Metzenbaum, while he and the governor had a working accord. At the very least, Glenn believed, Gilligan should appoint a caretaker to the post—someone like A. J. Lancione, the aging speaker of the Ohio house—and let him and Metzenbaum fight it out on an equal footing in the 1974 primary.

John Gilligan was self-absorbed when the two would-be senators battled for his ear at the end of 1973. In fact, Gilligan's thoughts were on 1976, when, he sensed, there would be an excellent chance for a progressive, telegenic governor to capture the Democratic presidential nomination, or failing that, the vice-presidential spot. (As it happened, Gilligan was half right. The progressive, telegenic governor who marched to the nomination was Jimmy Carter.) But for Gilligan's plan to work he had to get reelected governor in 1974. To accomplish that, he needed to run with a popular lieutenant governor, someone who could take over the state once Gilligan was tapped for higher office. His choice for his 1974 gubernatorial running mate was John Glenn. To name Glenn to the Senate now would make him unavailable for the state post in '74.

Gilligan approached Glenn with the following offer: to give up the idea of the Senate now and run on his ticket for lieutenant governor in 1974. In return he would have a clear shot at the 1976 Senate nomination. In the meantime, Gilligan told Glenn, he intended to appoint Metzenbaum to fill out the remainder of Saxbe's term. He also told Glenn he did not want a messy primary fight between Glenn and Metzenbaum in 1974 to detract from his image as a strong Democratic vote getter. Besides, there would be no need for a primary squabble if Glenn signed on for the state ticket and held his senatorial ambitions in abeyance until '76. Abrasive though Metzenbaum admittedly was, Gilligan realized he had the support of powerful Democratic voting blocs in Ohio: labor, blacks and liberal Jews. These were the groups Gilligan needed if he wanted to impress national Democrats with his drawing power.

"It wasn't hard for labor to convince Jack that if he'd appoint Metzenbaum to the Senate, they would financially support his re-election for governor and support him in any future national ambitions that he may have," Pete O'Grady notes. "Remember the decision was made by national labor, not Ohio labor, to appoint Metzenbaum to the United States Senate." It was an indication of the formidable extent of Metzenbaum's backing from the union movement.

Gilligan did not mention one other factor to Glenn. He was wary of Glenn. Gilligan was afraid that if he appointed him senator, that when Glenn ran in 1974 for a full six-year term he would siphon away publicity badly needed to fuel Gilligan's own national ambitions. "Gilligan had a group of people around him who had him convinced that he was going to spring onto the national scene if he could get himself reelected governor," remembers O'Grady. "Anything that would encourage Glenn to success in a Senate race that year would overshadow Jack Gilligan's personal ambitions. So they did everything they could to discourage John."

On paper, Gilligan's plan looked fine, but he had overlooked one contingency: John Glenn would have no part of it. John Glenn's dislike of Metzenbaum was so intense that he would challenge the Clevelander regardless of any deal Gilligan might propose. Glenn was now savvy enough to realize that a promise of support for a Senate race two years distant meant very little in the changing alliances of Ohio politics.

What might have happened if Glenn had gone along and run with Gilligan for lieutenant governor? "I think he would have been stuck," declares Pete O'Grady. "Stuck as lieutenant governor. And he probably would have wound up becoming governor of Ohio—something he wanted no part of. At no point in John's political career did John ever want to be governor of this state. His interest was always at the national level."

This was what Glenn told Gilligan in the waning months of 1973. Seeing his aspirations to national prominence threatened, Gilligan pressured Glenn hard. At a closed door meeting at the governor's mansion with the state's top labor leaders present, Gilligan looked hard at Glenn as each labor chieftain vowed to oppose Glenn if he decided to fight their ally Metzenbaum in the 1974 Senate race. Gilligan told Glenn that he had lined up the 12 top county chairmen in Ohio to oppose Glenn in '74 if he didn't accept Gilligan's offer to run for lieutenant governor. The alternatives were clear: either Glenn played ball or the combined influence of the state party machinery and organized labor would see to it that his political career was over.

It was the wrong thing to say to John Glenn, the ex-Marine fighter pilot. "I warned Gilligan that we were either going to come to a peaceable agreement or I was going to come out swinging," Glenn recalled. "The governor's people evidently thought I was going to knuckle under, but I didn't."

Today Glenn looks back on that confrontation. "It had really gotten beyond the realm of what I thought was proper in politics," he says. In reality, Gilligan's action was no less self-serving than Glenn's attempt to force Stephen Young out of office in 1964. What Glenn's reaction did demonstrate was that he was finally learning a basic political lesson: when to go public with a private quarrel.

Several days after the meeting at the governor's mansion, armed with the presence of newsmen, Glenn stormed before the state party executive committee and took on the governor and the Democratic party establishment. No, Glenn thundered, he wasn't going to settle for lieutenant governor. He was going for the Senate nomination whether or not Metzenbaum was appointed to fill the remaining months of Saxbe's term. "Suddenly, inexplicably, I am alone and marked for political extinction," Glenn declared to the group. He accused Gilligan and the state party leaders of "trying to stamp me into political mud."

Then, with a patriotic bravado he would later use again with brilliant effect, Glenn stared hard at the politicians who opposed him and said: "I never pulled out high over targets. I was the one that went in low and got them! As a result, I was known as 'Old Magnet Tail' because I happened to pick up more flak than anyone else doing it."

The message was clear: John Glenn, who had entered politics believing the old rules did not apply to him, was letting his party hierarchy know he had not changed his mind. If the party leaders had abandoned him, so be it. He was ready to go to the public and take on the organization alone. Nearly four years before, Glenn had been the darling of the party establishment and Metzenbaum a virtually unknown quantity. Now, the positions were reversed. Glenn was the lone challenger against a well financed, and soon-to-be-incumbent senator, Howard Metzenbaum.

John Glenn realized there would be no more chances in the political arena if he lost this one. To no one's surprise his fight with Howard Metzenbaum brought out the Marine in John Glenn and turned into a historic political brawl.

13

"I'VE HELD A JOB"

It was perhaps the bitterest and surely the most expensive primary race in the state's history. It proved the old adage that in Ohio, when Democrats need a firing squad, they form a circle. Glenn had hoped his show of bravado before the state executive committee would force the governor to reconsider his plan to appoint Metzenbaum and instead name a caretaker senator. It was a faint hope and Glenn did not count on it as he began his own campaign for the '74 Senate nomination on a raw December day in 1973.

It was in Howard Metzenbaum's hometown of Cleveland. There were few reporters assembled at a local hotel as Glenn showed up in a blue doubleknit suit and patterned tie to read his announcement of candidacy. Most of the journalists wanted to know how much money Glenn would have to spend on his campaign. Metzenbaum, backed by the state organization and big labor, and shored by the prospect of being named to the Senate in a matter of days, was again primed to spend lavishly.

Glenn answered that Matthew A. Reese, the Washington political consultant he had hired to run his campaign and help him shed his image as a loser, had told him it would cost $605,000 to run a "shoestring" campaign. Metzenbaum, of course, had spent $700,000 four years earlier and was prepared to raise even more this time.

Just as in 1964, when he first entered politics, Glenn's campaign team stood in the background as he made his announcement with grim earnestness. Gone were Wayne Hays and Bob Voas, replaced now by intense young men like Andy Vitali, a 35-year-old political staffer out of the Kennedy farm who had worked on JFK's 1960 effort and had spent the previous six years as executive assistant to Ted Kennedy. On this chill windy day, as he held onto his lengthy outline of the week's events, Vitali looked confident and sounded impressive.

The 1974 campaign was, in the words of Steve Avakian, to become one of the most "rockem, sockem, nasty, personal, vindictive, hateful campaigns any two politicians have ever been through in this country."

"You can have your Carter-Ford, your Reagan-Carter campaigns," Avakian insists. "We just haven't witnessed on a national level what these two guys did to each other in Ohio. These guys would stand chin to chin, night after night and drop bags of crap on each other for months. In the end they both showed an ability to slug it out."

The tenor of Glenn's vehement attacks on Metzenbaum, which began shortly after Metzenbaum had been appointed by Gilligan to fill the remainder of Saxbe's Senate term, highlighted the fundamental differences between the two politicians. It would be difficult to find two men more culturally and socially divergent. Metzenbaum, the scrappy, liberal, big-city Jew who because of his poor eyesight sat out the war as a 4-F and who struggled to make himself a millionaire, versus Glenn, the Presbyterian small-town boy who left college to be a war hero, sailed around the earth and into the world's admiration, and who capitalized on that fame in politics and the corporate boardroom.

Inevitably, Glenn's dislike of Metzenbaum, which would be even stronger in '74 than in '70, prompted rumors that Glenn was anti-Semitic. Glenn obviously denies this, but so too do many of Glenn's political foes. What the '74 campaign against

Metzenbaum did establish was that Glenn could be as obdurate and passionate in his dislikes as he could be unwavering in his beliefs. The feud between the two men continues to this day, but in a 1981 interview with the *Cleveland Plain Dealer,* Metzenbaum, by then a senator himself, tried to downplay the stories of tension, calling published references to his feud with Glenn "a figment of the media."

"Certainly we're not close," Metzenbaum conceded. "We both come from very different backgrounds. Our upbringing is totally different [but] there are very few relationships in the Senate that I know of where there is a close personal relationship. I don't think there has to be an explanation of why there isn't a close relationship of a personal nature, but that's a long way from being a feud, or having a contentious relationship. John and I haven't had an unpleasantness since the days we campaigned against each other. I think I honestly believe the story of a feud is a nonstory and I would guess John Glenn would say the same."

When asked if he and Metzenbaum will ever end their feud, Glenn responds "I don't know," but the grim set of his face suggests that it will never totally end. At least one of Glenn's advisors concedes that in his struggle to picture himself as the one "centrist" among those seeking the 1984 presidential nomination, it serves Glenn's purposes every time the differences between him and the liberal Metzenbaum are mentioned. Still, Glenn did invite his Senate colleague to New Concord when he announced for president. Metzenbaum begged off, citing family commitments.

At the podium that gray December day in 1973, Glenn sounded the patriotic theme that he knows is politically effective. Yes, he said, he could have been a millionaire several times over after his space flight, but he chose instead to serve his country by seeking public office. Glenn tried to minimize the 1970 debacle against Metzenbaum. "In 1970," he insisted, "we got a late start, we didn't get the right people and we had no money. It wasn't that we were so naive that we didn't recognize things were going wrong; it's just that we couldn't do very much about it. This time we hope to convince people who will contribute that we are worthy of their contributions."

This time it was different. Glenn's 1974 campaign for the Democratic nomination for U.S. Senate started out from Cleveland in a custom-decorated bus, not unlike a rolling hotel suite. There was a TV, stereo, cushioned chairs and sofa, bar, refrigerator, electric typewriter and mimeo machine.

The week-long tour of such cities as Piqua, Toledo and Lima found Glenn making the rounds of shopping centers and senior citizens' homes, factories and storefronts. As in 1970, the reception was friendly and at times enthusiastic. In Akron, a prominent union town that Glenn needed desperately, he heaped praise on Peter Bommarito, then president of the rubber workers union, one of only two major labor unions backing Glenn at the time. Just how important Bommarito's support was to Glenn would become apparent only at the end of the campaign, when Glenn began to break Metzenbaum's viselike grip on big labor backing. For now, though, the political highs for Glenn came in small, but welcome, bursts.

"John Glenn! My main astronaut!" a black girl exulted in Steubenville. "Do these space shots really cause all the flooding we've been having?" asked a little old lady in Fort Findlay. At a Citizens for Glenn gathering at an Akron Holiday Inn, Glenn characteristically lingered too long in a friendly crowd, and Warren Baltimore had to drag him from the room to stay on schedule. "What are you trying to do to me, Warren?" Glenn joked as they bounded onto the campaign bus. "I've got a hot crowd hanging on every word, old ladies weeping in the back row, 30,000 people rushing out to volunteer, and you want me to cut and run!"

To anyone witnessing such a spectacle for the first time, the enthusiasm showered on Glenn seemed an excellent beginning for a political campaign. But to the few professionals like Steve Kovacik, then a wealthy Columbus attorney who first learned about politics in his native Chicago, the John Glenn road show was just that: theatrics. Where, for example, were the party officials, the labor people? Was there any effort being made to undermine the united opposition to Glenn from these groups, to sit down privately with them—certainly not in a motel room on wheels—to convince them to bolt Metzenbaum or at least stay neutral? And, most important, who was raising money for TV and where was Metzenbaum vulnerable?

It was as if Glenn hadn't learned anything from his previous campaign. Doug Ash, then a fresh-faced political aide to Glenn's chief of staff, Matt Reese, noted: "When we got in here, there wasn't even a list of contributors from the last campaign. Last time, Glenn registered 95% recognizability in the polls, but his base was a mile wide and an inch deep. We're trying to make it a foot deep.

"He's a good man," Ash said, shaking his head, "but he's got to knock off things like stopping at that mall earlier today to buy fudge."

Recalls Kovacik: "They started their 'whirlwind announcement week'—you heard about that?—they hired a bus and hit every city in Ohio, and I thought, 'what a waste!' " For two months, though, the campaign went on like that, Glenn appearing before various groups, smiling and shaking hands. To be sure, it was more than he had done in 1970, but the early movement in the polls was all toward Metzenbaum, who had now been appointed to the Senate to fill Saxbe's unexpired term. Something needed changing.

In Washington, Matt Reese could see that things were not going well even if his client could not. The campaign was two months old and Glenn had yet to draw blood. Vitali, game though he was, did not, as one local Democrat put it, "know the territory." By early February, Reese was on the phone looking for a replacement for Glenn's campaign manager. He was looking for Kovacik, and found him in New York.

"The campaign was flat on its ass when I came aboard," declares Kovacik. "I knew that John could be a great candidate if he was directed, and that's what I set out to do." Kovacik's version of events is self-serving, but there is a near-unanimous verdict from both sides that Kovacik was the man who turned things around for Glenn and provided the margin of victory. "Steve Kovacik, more than anyone," declares one of Metzenbaum's top aides today, "is the guy who got John Glenn elected in 1974."

"I happened to be in New York," Kovacik recalls, "and Matt Reese tracked me down. We had a breakfast for about four hours, as I recall, and he finally said, 'why don't you go in and take over the campaign?' I said, 'Well, it's late' because at that time the primary was in May. I also said, 'I'll have to talk to John.' " Reese nodded and said he'd arrange the meeting.

"So when I got back to Columbus, I sat down with John and I said, 'Look, John, I've got to run it my way. I've got to bring in my people, and you've got to give me carte blanche.' I said, 'I give you my word there'll be nothing done illegally, but you're going to run your ass off.' And he said, 'Fine.' "

In the weeks that followed, Kovacik ran the show in everything but name. "I never claimed to be campaign manager. That surprised a lot of people. I tried to run it from behind the scenes. Andy maintained his title as campaign manager and John didn't want to fire him, so he had him travel with him, and that's how we worked it out."

The humiliation of 1970 coupled with a slow start in '74 had taught Glenn that a winning political campaign did not just happen by itself. Glenn's campaign was also heavily indebted to Kovacik financially. Kovacik's personal contributions to Glenn in 1974 totaled $80,000, the largest single gift to any 1974 Senate candidate in those pre-Watergate reform days.

Kovacik had married money. His wife at the time was Laurel Blossom, whose family was one of the wealthiest in Ohio. A direct descendant of one of John D. Rockefeller's original partners, Laurel Blossom was estimated in 1974 to be worth $10 million. During his marriage to Laurel, which has since dissolved, Kovacik shuttled between New York, where Laurel spent much of her time, and Columbus, where he preferred to be, ensconced in a lavish duplex condominium that cost more than $300,000. He drove one of the most expensive cars in the world, a Rolls Royce Corniche.

Glenn's reliance on Kovacik seemed out of character. In fact, many Ohio political observers wondered at the time if Kovacik was merely using Glenn, then on the outs with Jack Gilligan, to get back at the governor for firing him from his organization in 1970. "If nothing else," wrote Myra McPherson, a *Washington Post* staff writer, "Glenn, the man of simple tastes and pleasures, does seem out of place when you see him out to dinner with Kovacik and an entourage of a dozen Kovacik camp followers."

But Glenn had an answer to those critical of his relationship with the high-living Kovacik. In essence, it was that Kovacik and his wife were so rich they did not need to buy Glenn's influence as a legislator; neither did they have an ax to grind. They were, as Glenn maintained at the time, "old money." "Steve and Laurel don't represent any special interests or business," Glenn declared. "If he had been an executive of General Motors or Ford or some major industry, I would not have accepted his help. He is independent financially, and I have made no commitments to him."

In fact, Kovacik's $80,000 in contributions, though large, represented barely a tenth of what the campaign needed. While Metzenbaum tapped both his personal and political resources, Glenn's people turned once again to Annie's Christmas list. "We were broke," Kovacik maintains. "Christ, who did we call? Milton Berle gave us a hundred bucks, or his wife did. We got turned down by people such as Andy Williams, and Lorne Greene, who said he couldn't give because he was a Canadian citizen. Then surprisingly, we got a very nice check from Steve Lawrence and Eydie Gorme. They sent us a grand, or two grand."

But the results were not spectacular. At one point, rather than try to persuade celebrities over the phone, Kovacik and two others flew to the West Coast to solicit contributions. "We didn't turn up much," he concedes. By contrast, while the Glenn camp was struggling for every dollar, Metzenbaum, backed by almost all the Ohio Democratic county chairmen, was able to hold $100-a-plate fund-raisers throughout the state. In addition, notes one Glenn worker, "labor gave him gobs of money."

If he couldn't top Metzenbaum dollar for dollar, Glenn decided to make political capital out of "taking our campaign to the people." In doing so, he pictured Metzenbaum to be in the pocket of the bosses and big labor. Another aspect of the new strategy was to ignore most of the Ohio's 88 counties and concentrate on the big cities Glenn had lost in 1970. It was a calculated risk that Glenn and Kovacik deemed worth taking.

"We traveled the 14 major counties exclusively; we knew he was going to win the other 74," Kovacik recalls.

This time Glenn concentrated on Ohio's large ethnic vote. He attended every ward club meeting from Toledo to Youngstown. "I'm an eastern European," Kovacik says, "and I know how my people feel about John Glenn. They like him. We hit every place there was kielbasa—and all the Italian wards. We had John going from six in the morning till two the next morning."

"I'm a big believer in organization," Kovacik adds, "and we took John and scheduled him in one half of the state and we had Annie—who was a great campaigner—doing the other side. She did a superb job. People loved her." Recalls another veteran of the campaign: "It was just the thing we should have been doing in '70."

The 99-cent corned beef dinner night at the Flat Iron Cafe in Cleveland was typical of Glenn's attempt to generate, if not big dollars, then the kind of favorable publicity that would translate into votes for the May primary. And Glenn had an opportunity to show the warmth sometimes hidden behind his "official" demeanor. He did seem to enjoy it. Noted one reporter at the time: "If a man can have fun trying to munch corned beef while smiling, writing his autograph on a woman's arm and having people stare at him while he chews, Glenn appeared to have fun."

After someone rapped his beer bottle on the counter, Glenn hopped onto a formica-topped table to address the crowd that filled the popular restaurant in Cleveland's "Flats" area and spilled out into the street and into an adjacent parking lot. "This is what we've been doing throughout the campaign—I don't mean spending all of our time at the Flat Iron Cafe," Glenn cracked as the crowd laughed appreciatively. "We said we were going to take our campaign to the people," he went on, looking out over a crowd of some 500, "and there's no better example than tonight.

"In this year of Watergate," Glenn declared, finally delivering the not-so-subtle message he had been planning all along, "it is important to send to the Senate someone with integrity. The country can get over Watergate, but only if we have honest people in public office."

There it was: the nub of his campaign against Metzenbaum. Metzenbaum, the politician. Metzenbaum the multimillionaire who had held another $100-a-plate party fund-raiser the night before Glenn rubbed elbows with the common folk. That night in the Flats, Glenn—who by this time was wealthy—was not alone as he delivered his message. Standing with him, dwarfing him actually, was former football professional Rosey Grier, whom Glenn introduced as his friend from the Bobby Kennedy campaign. He was conjuring up support not only among blacks, but among the blue collar, largely Catholic, audience with their undying sympathies for the departed Jack and Bobby.

But if Glenn had relied only on symbolism, his campaign would have gone nowhere. It would have almost certainly been swamped by Metzenbaum's canny use of media and advertising. As it happened, the fact that the primary race took place during "Watergate summer," gave the campaign a moral theme. It proved to be all Glenn needed to gain critical ground on his opponent. In a way, it enabled Glenn to get back at Metzenbaum for the way he had used his money to defeat him four years earlier. For in the end, it was Metzenbaum's wealth—and the lengths he went to to keep it from Uncle Sam—that made the difference on primary day.

The accusations that flew between Glenn and Metzenbaum seemed unending. Metzenbaum charged, and Glenn denied, that Glenn was getting money from the oil industry. Metzenbaum charged, once again, that Glenn had voted for Nixon over Kennedy in 1960. But the two most effective ripostes were made by Glenn: they involved Howard Metzenbaum's tax returns and John Glenn's rip-roaring patriotic response to his opponent's claim that he had "never held a job." Both would say volumes about John Glenn the man and John Glenn the politician. They would prove to a concerned public that Glenn could gut-fight with the best.

In other times, the fact that a millionaire politician like Metzenbaum had been able to shelter so much of his income from federal taxes might not have been a fatal blow. But not in the spring of '74. Watergate disclosures were at their peak, and stories of chicanery by the Nixon White House and reelection committee were standard fare on the evening news.

Metzenbaum's tax status soon became the central issue of the primary campaign. It was quietly engineered by a crafty Steve Kovacik with a compliant Glenn providing the lung power. Early newspaper stories first revealed the extent of Metzenbaum's tax sheltering. In 1969 Metzenbaum had earned a near fortune but had not paid a penny in federal taxes. Glenn's tax returns, which he had willingly made public, also showed huge income. But in contrast to Metzenbaum, they also showed huge tax payments. In 1972, for example, Glenn had paid more federal income taxes than Metzenbaum paid for all of 1968, 1969, 1970, 1971 and 1972 combined, while Glenn's adjusted gross income was not even a third of Metzenbaum's. "My accountant thinks I'm crazy," Glenn said, adding that he didn't think it "fair" for people "to work their taxes down to zero when they've earned hundreds of thousands of dollars."

The tax issue was made for Glenn. It not only gave him a chance to cast numberless aspersions on Metzenbaum's honesty and character, but made Glenn appear pure by comparison. Early in the '74 primary race, Glenn released copies of his income tax returns from 1965 through 1973, the years in which he made the first big money of his life. Metzenbaum also released his 1973 return, but he provided only summaries of the years 1967 through 1972, calling the disclosure "the most far-reaching of any by a federal officeholder."

The partial records showed that through the years 1967 to '72, Metzenbaum paid only $164,000 in federal income taxes on an adjusted gross income of more than $1.2 million. They also revealed that Metzenbaum, his wife, Shirley, and two dependent children had total assets, as of December 31, 1973, of $6.9 million and total liabilities of $3.3 million, for a net worth of $3.6 million. And, the summaries showed, because of a series of business loss deductions, it turned out that Metzenbaum had paid no federal taxes at all in 1969.

It was a revelation Glenn used gleefully. "This year," Glenn declared, "everybody ought to release their income tax returns." He added: "I haven't used tax shelters, even though they may be legal because I don't think it's right. And I think he [Metzenbaum] should tell us more about his liabilities. He admits he owes more than $3 million. Who does he owe it to? What for?

"He's hiding it," Glenn charged, adding, "that suggests a conflict of interest. If we're going to debate the issues, he should come right out with all the information so we'll know what this is about." In case anyone missed the moral point, Glenn declared that "the facts about [Metzenbaum's] tangled financial background are dribbling out just like the facts about Watergate."

Metzenbaum knew he had a publicity nightmare on his hands. He tried to deflect some of the bad news by accusing Glenn of failing to pay, until 1972, any state taxes on intangible personal property. Ohio residents, under state law, have to pay taxes on stock dividends and the like. But Glenn managed not only to parry the criticism, but to come out heroic. He argued that until 1972, his tax accountants in Houston were unaware of the Ohio law. When he moved back to Ohio, he retained a local firm which determined that he owed a total of $11,000 in back taxes, a sum he promptly paid. As it turned out, he had been too eager. The figure was high and Glenn received a $3,000 refund from the state. "Remember," one of Glenn's advisors noted, "he didn't have to be ordered to pay it. As soon as Glenn found out he owed it, he paid."

What made the incident especially harmful to Metzenbaum in the eyes of the voters was that in April of 1973 the Internal Revenue Service had charged Metzenbaum with a tax "deficiency" of $118,000. Rather than pay immediately, Metzenbaum took the perfectly legal step of challenging the IRS ruling in tax court. In fact, he eventually won his case against the IRS, but not before the political damage was done.

Investigative reporter Jim Perry, commenting on the charges flying back and forth between the Glenn and Metzenbaum camps, declared, "You wonder if maybe the difference between these two candidates isn't that Metzenbaum, a lawyer, had handled his money a little more cleverly than Glenn. He was clever enough to get into political trouble. Glenn was dumb enough to stay out of it."

With the primary election in its final weeks, Metzenbaum took a gamble. He purchased TV time to try to "explain" his tax problems to the voter. Noted Abe Zaidan in the *Beacon-Journal:* "Metzenbaum is not satisfied to panic in private: He buys television time to explain that he has done nothing wrong. He seems nervous, defensive. To make matters worse, when newsmen stop raising the tax issue at press conferences, Metzenbaum volunteers the information." Not lost on the political pros who once had dismissed Glenn as a lightweight was the fact that now it was Metzenbaum, not Glenn, who looked foolish in an eleventh hour television appearance.

For weeks, Glenn's continued reservoir of good feeling among voters—not to mention his effective exploitation of the tax issue—had put him ahead in the polls. But the same thing had been true in 1970, when Glenn had lost the election.

The behind the scenes fighting became even more intense. Monica Nolan recalls that the united front against Glenn by the state Democratic party and organized labor had produced its share of political hardball. "I can remember people would cancel meetings rather than let me speak on behalf of John," she says.

Steve Kovacik's memories are even more vivid. "Oh, Christ," he declares, "Paul Tipps, who was then the chairman of Montgomery County, did everything but throw roadblocks up leading into Dayton. It's ironic now, since he's working for Glenn. But he really was bad news back then. Dayton was always a Metzenbaum stronghold, and so we set out to beat his ass out there just for vengeance and we did. We doubled our vote and beat Metzenbaum two-to-one in Tipps's own county."

Kovacik also recalls, "We were just shut out of any kind of political activity with the organization. They would cancel meetings on us, tell us one time for a meeting and then hold it at another place. They hassled our volunteers. We'd put out literature and then they'd pick it up and throw it away and deny that they did it, that kind of thing."

Aside from contributing heavily to Metzenbaum, organized labor also distributed literature trying to portray Glenn as a closet Republican. Notes Kovacik: "There was a piece run in the *Akron Beacon-Journal* in '64 which accused Glenn of being a

Republican. [The article actually referred to attempts by the then Ohio Republican chairman Ray Bliss to woo Glenn into the Republican camp when he first considered politics.] They reprinted the article and we would find them under everybody's windshield in factory parking lots."

Glenn had always assumed that his bona fides as a Democrat had been firmly established by his close ties with the Kennedys, especially Bobby. In 1970, Ethel Kennedy had campaigned for Glenn, and now, with the campaign nearing its close, Glenn looked forward to having her appear for him again. But Ethel suddenly backed out with the excuse that to speak for Glenn would set a precedent for other office-seekers asking her aid.

The refusal floored and angered Glenn, who suspected that Metzenbaum was behind it. In closed door meetings with Kovacik, Glenn fumed that Metzenbaum, long a friend of the Kennedy family himself, had brought pressure to bear on Ethel through Ted Kennedy. Ethel's grounds for turning Glenn down were obviously specious; hardly anyone alive had the claim on her friendship that Glenn did. He had even performed the difficult chore of comforting her children after their father was killed. "I always thought the Kennedys were supposed to be so loyal," declares Monica Nolan.

As it turned out, some of the Kennedy bonds did hold and ended up helping Glenn more than he expected. The unexpected Kennedy who came to his aid was Jacqueline Kennedy Onassis. "We were, I believe, in Cincinnati at the time and we had just been turned down by Ethel and we were very disappointed," recalls Kovacik. In the room were Kovacik, Glenn, Jim Dunn, the audio technician who helped prepare radio spots for the campaign, and Rosey Grier. "Then Rosey says, 'What the hell, let me call Jackie.' And John says, 'Wait a minute, I'll do it.' "

According to Kovacik, Glenn did not mention Ethel's rebuff to Jackie. "He called Jackie very nicely and she took the call. He said, 'I'm running.' She said, 'I know, I'll help you, whatever I can do.' We tried to get her out to Ohio, but we couldn't do that. But she did tape a commercial for us." It was Jackie's first political statement since the death of her husband, and it created a small sensation in the campaign's final weeks. The endorsement noted the affection both Jackie and her late husband had felt for Glenn, as "an outstanding American."

"She in effect said that if JFK were alive today, he'd probably endorse John," Kovacik says. "It was nicely done." Later, asked his reaction to the "Jackie" endorsement, Metzenbaum replied airily that on the same day he had been endorsed by United Auto Workers President Leonard Woodcock.

Almost four years earlier, Metzenbaum had been poised on the verge of a stunning win against John Glenn. Now the situation was dramatically reversed with Glenn surging ahead in the polls. Four years earlier, events in Cambodia and Kent State had seemed to conspire against Glenn to ensure his defeat. Now, as the campaign entered its final two weeks, events were conspiring against Metzenbaum. But Metzenbaum had only himself to blame for giving Glenn the final, hammering blow of the long, bitter primary race.

It was at a cheering Metzenbaum fund-raiser at the Sheraton Cleveland. The appointed senator had his script ready. It was a sign of desperation, a poorly calculated attack on Glenn's military career. Glenn, Metzenbaum charged, had spent his entire career at the federal trough. He had never had to meet a payroll, as Metzenbaum had on so many occasions in private business. Amid the tumult and the extravagant statements, Metzenbaum's charges came out more nakedly: John Glenn, war hero, and astronaut, had "never held a job."

As soon as they heard reports of what Metzenbaum had said, Glenn and his people knew the election was won. But they let the issue lie dormant for two weeks, while Glenn and his speechwriters crafted a response. They made sure not one word would be wasted when Glenn, figuratively draped in the flag he had served so well, would loose his thunderbolt personally at Metzenbaum during the climactic debate at Cleveland's City Club the Friday before the election.

By tradition, the City Club is the last major forum before an Ohio election. Since the turn of the century, political adversaries have exchanged closing blows at the club's podium. And so it was on May 3, 1974, when Howard Metzenbaum and John Glenn squared off. Ironically, Glenn had almost boycotted the debate because Metzenbaum refused to accede to Glenn's demand that he make public all his financial records. Then, realizing that the club intended to give Metzenbaum an hour all to himself if he did not show up, Glenn "released" Metzenbaum from the condition and agreed to debate.

An audience of 600 watched as 100 supporters from each section cheered and catcalled at the appropriate moments. Once during the program, when Glenn was asked about his relations with the state UAW in connection with seeking its endorsement, he said he had been refused admittance to a UAW meeting in Toledo. "That's a damn lie!" shouted UAW regional director William Casstevens from the audience, insisting that Glenn had been interviewed several times by auto union leaders.

At another point, a spectator sitting with Glenn supporters asked what each candidate was doing in 1943. Glenn replied that he had been in Marine pilot training; Metzenbaum said that he was in the Ohio General Assembly after having been classified 4F for "bad eyes." Glenn later denied that the question had been planted.

On the issue of school busing, Metzenbaum said: "It is a partial answer, but we should do it as Cleveland has done it, by widening school districts. I think there are better answers." Glenn was against the idea: "Most of the minority leaders I have talked to favor what I propose—upgrading the schools where the kids are. This way we don't take a kid out of his area and make him feel like a foreigner."

What followed made Ohio, and possibly national, political history. An observer who was at the City Club that day recalls the details: "Glenn was the last one to speak. Frankly, it had been boring as hell, just a rehash of what these two had been saying for the past several weeks. Then, while Howard was sitting in his chair and Glenn was at the mike, Glenn said he was dismayed to hear two weeks before that Metzenbaum said that he, Glenn, had never held a job.

"Then Glenn turned toward Howard and said: 'Howard, I can't believe you said that.' "

Glenn began in a low, yet deadly earnest tone, that rose in

intensity—and sincerity—as he spoke.

"I served 23 years in the United States Marine Corps. I went through two wars. I flew 149 missions. My plane was hit by anti-aircraft fire on 12 different occasions.

"I was in the space program. It wasn't my checkbook, it was my life that was on the line. This was not a nine-to-five job where I took time off to take the daily cash receipts to the bank.

"I ask you to go with me," Glenn told Metzenbaum, his voice starting to rise and fall dramatically in almost military cadence, "as I went the other day to a veterans hospital, and look those men with their mangled bodies in the eye and tell them they didn't hold a job. You go with me to any gold star mother and you look her in the eye and tell her that her son did not hold a job.

"You go with me to the space program, and you go as I have gone to the widows and the orphans of Ed White and Gus Grissom and Roger Chaffee, and you look those kids in the eye and tell them their dad didn't hold a job.

"You go with me on Memorial Day coming up and you stand in Arlington National Cemetery—where I have more friends than I like to remember—and you watch those waving flags and you stand there and you think about this nation and you tell me that those people didn't have a job.

"I tell you, Howard Metzenbaum," Glenn said, his voice now a thunder of indignation at the 4-F sitting beside him, "you should be on your knees every day of your life thanking God that there were some men—some men—who held a job.

"And they required a dedication to purpose and a love of country and a dedication to duty that was more important than life itself. And their self-sacrifice is what has made this country possible.

"I've held a job, Howard."

A standing ovation followed. When it was over, Metzenbaum lamely responded, "I was talking about a job in private employment."

That weekend, the Glenn campaign used radio spots purchased well beforehand and saturated the stations with excerpts from the speech, which had become front page news in all the papers. On primary day, Glenn beat Metzenbaum by 95,000 votes, repaying him handily for the humiliation of 1970. In the general election that November, Glenn vanquished Cleveland mayor Ralph J. Perk, beating the Republican by a margin of better than two-to-one out of nearly three million votes cast. It was the first time that anyone had carried all 88 Ohio counties. The ambitious astronaut had scored his first political victory. John Gilligan, in trouble from the start and spurned by the ascendant Glenn, lost his bid for reelection, which ended his national ambitions.

It had taken more than a decade, but after three elections, John Glenn—Senator John Herschel Glenn, Jr.—was finally going to Washington.

14

YEARS IN THE SENATE: A LIBERAL OR CENTRIST?

John Glenn walked through the ornate mahogany doors leading into the Senate chamber and, following custom, was escorted down the center aisle to the well of the chamber by his senior colleague from Ohio, Robert Taft, Jr. Shortly past noon, January 14, 1975, as the first session of the 94th Congress convened, the vice-president of the United States, Nelson A. Rockefeller, the Senate's presiding officer, administered the oath of office to Glenn as Annie held the Bible.

The short, one-sentence oath, written by the Founding Fathers, was virtually identical to that taken by every incoming president. "I, John Herschel Glenn," he intoned, "do solemnly swear that I will faithfully execute the duties of the office upon which I am about to enter, and will to the best of my ability, preserve, protect and defend the Constitution of the United States."

With that, Glenn became a U.S. senator. Later, at a reception for incoming members, all the attention seemed to focus on him. Family, reporters, and other senators flocked to Glenn to wish him well. Recalls fellow freshman Senator Wendell H. Ford of Kentucky, a craggy-faced former governor: "If any of us wanted to get our picture taken, we stood next to John."

Shortly before the ceremony, Glenn's daughter presented her father with what she thought was the perfect gift: a small print of the Flemish painter Peter Paul Rubens's masterpiece, "Daniel in the Lion's Den." "Lyn thought that must be how I was feeling, so she got it for me," Glenn says. He had the print framed, and it now hangs near his desk in his Senate office. Glenn's attachment to the painting is instructive. In the eight years he has served as a senator, Glenn has never been truly comfortable with his colleagues in the daily drama of the arena.

An arena is precisely what the Senate chamber looks like from above, dotted by a hundred mahogany desks and encircled by galleries for the press and public. The political give and take, the "get along, go along" atmosphere that dominates the chamber, seems alien to Glenn, a man accustomed to staking his future on his own decisions. Though he had dreamed of the Senate from the time he first wrote an essay about that body in high school, Glenn, once arrived, found he did not fit in.

At least Glenn did not fit in the way others wanted him to. "He was not raised as a politician," notes a congressional staffer to a senior House Democrat. "You have to remember that. He thinks differently about things and he approaches things differently. There is no feeling of camaraderie with him. He's considered an isolated person whom people do not get to know or to talk to."

It was as if Glenn were back among his seven fellow astronauts as odd man out. Charming in public, gracious in private, he soon came to be known in the Senate as someone who could not be swayed from a position he judged to be correct no matter how compelling the political argument for compromise or delay. In the case of one package of legislation—President Jimmy Carter's first energy conservation program—Senator Glenn thought some parts of it so worthwhile that he argued on their behalf even after the administration had abandoned or compromised them away.

In creating the Department of Energy, Carter had originally proposed that it be headed by a powerful Secretary of Energy empowered to set natural gas prices. The goal was to overcome the defects of a bureaucratically stymied Federal Energy Regulatory Commission. Glenn strongly supported the notion, contending that no major change in U.S. energy consumption habits could be made without a strong federal energy executive. But when the administration decided that the energy "czar" idea would not be ratified by Congress, they discarded it. Undaunted, Glenn tried to get the measure passed on his own, placing him in the uncomfortable position of opposing the new president of his own party on his first major legislative initiative.

In a body that thrives on the formulation of public policy through deals and compromises, Glenn is one of the few members who, a former staffer says, "has had difficulty with anything that smacked of a maneuver, even if it meant easing the way for his own legislation to get close attention on the floor."

The self-imposed distance has not seemed to diminish Glenn's effectiveness as a legislator. During his first year, Glenn, who is not a lawyer, won Senate approval of more than 30 consecutive floor amendments to legislation covering energy, civil rights and foreign policy. Political professionals were impressed because included in that unbroken string of successes were ten amendments on which Glenn had to confront senior Democrats with roll-call votes. And he won every time.

A former Glenn aide explains the significance. "When you go to a vote on a floor amendment, you generally lose. That's because when you offer a floor amendment, the first thing you do is go to the floor managers of the bill. If it is acceptable to them, your amendment is usually passed by voice vote." But, the aide notes, when a floor amendment goes to a vote, it means that the floor managers disapprove of the amendment and insist on a vote because they want to stop it. In such cases, the other senators normally vote with the committee originating the bill. "But of Glenn's first 35 or so amendments," the aide recalls, "I'd say about ten of them went to floor votes, and we won them all. It kills me when I hear that Glenn is not much of a legislator."

❀

He came to the office early and stayed late, determined to become, in his own words, "the best senator Ohio ever had." His first office, in which he stayed only briefly before moving to larger quarters in the building, was on the first floor of the Dirksen Building, within yards of the building's main entrance, next to the pay phones and a bank of elevators. It had been vacated just a few weeks before by a reluctant Howard Metzenbaum, the appointed senator whom Glenn defeated in the bitter May '74 primary.

Glenn could frequently be found sitting at his desk on weekends, poring over papers and manuals the way he once had waded through arcane books on spacecraft, or earlier, the challenging calculus texts of his test pilot training. When he learned that one of the perquisites of congressional membership was a private gym facility, he vowed to structure his days so there would always be time for a workout. The plan failed dismally. One former aide can't recall Glenn ever using the gym. (Instead he gets up early most mornings and jogs two or three miles before setting out to work or campaign.)

One of Glenn's closest aides during his freshman year was a young lawyer named Leonard Bickwit, whom Glenn hired as his legislative assistant. Bickwit, a graduate of Yale, Oxford and Harvard Law School, is a softspoken young man now in private practice who supports Glenn's presidential hopes. Before joining Glenn, he had worked on the staff of the Senate Commerce Committee for liberal Democratic Senator Philip A. Hart of Michigan. Hart, one of the Senate's most respected members until his death from cancer, set high standards for himself and his staff. When Bickwit went over to work for Glenn he wondered what it would be like.

"He was an incredibly intellectually curious person," Bickwit recalls of Glenn. "It was really fun to see somebody as excited as he was about the opportunities to learn and contribute. I had grown used to a system where most of the ideas came from the staff. The major function that senators served was to weed out the good ideas from the bad ones.

"One favorable comparison I'd made between Glenn and Hart," Bickwit notes, "is that Glenn was really thinking all the time, trying to come up with new ideas and behaving in a creative way." Sometimes, though, the freshman senator's zeal to "contribute" rankled his more senior colleagues. Once, during a heated debate on the Senate floor between Texas's two senators, Republican John G. Tower, chairman of the Armed Services Committee, and Democrat Lloyd Bentsen, Glenn kept standing up asking for time to speak. Finally, Bentsen turned toward his junior colleague and said with icy politeness: "May I say to the distinguished Senator from Ohio I mean no discourtesy, but I would suggest that he make himself comfortable."

Glenn deliberately tried to avoid the limelight during his freshman year of 1975 and into the presidential election year that followed. He declined hundreds of speaking invitations from around the country, preferring to stay in Washington and amass an impressive attendance record. He even lectured his fellow Democrats during a meeting of the Democratic caucus that it was "unconscionable" for the Senate to take a two-week recess in March 1975 without having voted on pending tax legislation. He passed up the chance to make three "fact-finding" junkets during the recess, one to Mexico and Central America, another to Europe and a third to Russia. He deliberately held no formal news conferences, preferring individual interviews, mostly with reporters from Ohio.

On legislative matters, Glenn did not make headlines, but he did manage to make his influence felt. Barely two months after he took office, Glenn "got disgusted and left" a Democratic caucus meeting after extended debate on whether to support President Ford's request for emergency aid of $222 million to Cambodia and $30 million to South Vietnam. In his absence, the lawmakers voted overwhelmingly against supporting both measures. Glenn, who had grown increasingly skeptical of the American role in Southeast Asia, said after the vote that he would have opposed any aid to Cambodia but would have approved it for South Vietnam. Of his objections to the Cambodian aid, Glenn declared: "We never should have got involved in Cambodia at all."

These were sentiments he had not expressed in 1970 during his unsuccessful primary race against Howard Metzenbaum, after President Nixon ordered the controversial Cambodian "incursions." One month after Ford tried to get the additional aid through Congress, Saigon finally fell to the Communists. Like so many of his countrymen who were glad the war was finally over, Glenn all but washed his hands of the tragedy. "Most Americans felt we had a commitment to South Vietnam," Glenn said at the time. "I along with 80% of the American people changed my mind. We got overcommitted."

On domestic legislation, Glenn proved to be a methodical plugger rather than a headline maker. Named to the Senate Interior Committee, Glenn was dismayed when the panel voted, over his lone objection, to allow oil-producing states to increase prices on the first 20,000 barrels of oil produced each day. Following the 4-1 vote in committee, Glenn circulated two "Dear Colleague" letters to the entire Senate and personally lobbied several of his fellow senators on the floor. The key vote on the measure was 63-33 in favor of Glenn's position.

But perhaps the most dramatic demonstration of Glenn's early ability to quietly muster votes came in December 1975 during debate on an appropriations bill. Glenn, reflecting an interest in energy-related technology that grew out of his astronaut background, proposed to raise from $3.1 million to $10 million the amount for development of fuel cells, energy storage devices he first encountered in his NASA days. The amendment immediately ran into strong opposition from Senate Majority Whip Robert C. Byrd of West Virginia, a courtly Democrat with a hawklike visage and an incongruous pompadour who was then a key appropriations subcommittee chairman. Few would have thought that a freshman senator would take on one of the Senate's most powerful men. But in a dramatic showdown on the Senate floor, freshman Glenn bested veteran Byrd with votes to spare. The amendment passed 50-43.

During his first years in the Senate, Glenn sought a low profile, but his astronaut fame made it impossible to be anonymous. His mail ran to more than 6,000 pieces a week. Glenn's first year in office was also the 13th anniversary of his 1962 orbital flight. He received numerous requests to send greetings to boys who were about to be Bar Mitzvahed, 13 being the age that young Jewish males pass ceremonially into manhood. All the requests were honored, even if most were signed with robot pens that exactly reproduce Glenn's signature. The odd-looking devices, which grasp a pen in a disembodied metal claw, are programmed to write a signature with uncanny accuracy. So exactly can the "Robo-Pen" reproduce a signature that most congressional offices make sure the machine is locked up each night to prevent unauthorized use.

Publicity seemed to seek him out, even when he hoped to avoid it. A few days before he was sworn in, the *Washington Post* magazine ran a lengthy cover piece on Glenn over the headline "Hero as Politician." A somewhat discomfited Glenn noted that "there are a lot of senators who have been here twenty years who haven't been on the cover of the magazine. Some of them would be happy just being mentioned on a back page."

The author, Myra McPherson, spoke glowingly of Glenn's good manners and upbringing. "The years have been kind to John Glenn," she wrote, "which is not always the case with men whose features are perpetually Joe College. He is not like Mickey Rooney or Jackie Coogan; old men who run round with ill-fitting little boy faces. There are deep waves of wrinkles on his forehead, and the green eyes are encircled in crinkles, but there are no jowls and, of course, no marks of dissipation." The article was a generally favorable one that helped perpetuate the idea that Glenn would tend to be a conservative since he came from a hometown where, according to a boyhood friend, "nobody is liberal."

But during that first year in the Senate, 1975, Glenn surprised his conservative admirers by rapidly assuming a liberal philosophic stance. He voted an almost straight liberal Democratic party ticket. During the 1975 session, Glenn voted for higher spending, refusing to cut the budget by $25 billion; he voted against a $31-billion Pentagon request for weapons; he voted for the New York City multibillion-dollar bailout.

Over business lobby opposition, he voted for the Federal Consumer Protection Agency. He voted to continue federal aid to abortion, and alongside Teddy Kennedy, to dismantle the "Safeguard" anti-ballistic missile installation at Grand Forks, North Dakota. In the field of education, he supported a HEW plan to require the sexual integration of physical education classes, fraternities and sororities.

Glenn calls himself a centrist, proudly and without hesitation. But the Glenn of actual voting record is a decidedly liberal politician who often runs counter to his insular small-town upbringing. This Glenn, an eight-year Senate veteran, has a voting record that for the years 1981 and '82 has earned him praise and an average 75% score from the left-liberal Americans for Democratic Action. It was a liberal accolade for his opposition to such things as the MX missile, school prayer and the three-martini lunch, as well as for his support of the ERA, public works jobs, federal funding of abortions and political action by trade unions. More recently, liberals have praised his opposition to President Reagan's Central American program.

To be sure, the ADA heaps less praise on Glenn than on such ultra-liberals as Kennedy of Massachusetts or Cranston of California, but its rating still confers on him the title "liberal" and lists him among the top 20 liberals in the Senate. Though Glenn bitterly fought his political foe Howard Metzenbaum, a liberal Democrat who has twice in his career earned a perfect 100 from the ADA, on the Senate floor Glenn votes with Metzenbaum nearly eight times out of ten.

By contrast, the American Conservative Union sees Glenn as a political villain. On key domestic and foreign issues selected by the group, the ACU scored Glenn a relatively low 28% for his 1982 voting record. Still, from the ACU's conservative vantage point, Glenn has been improving: His cumulative Senate career score is 9 points out of 100. In the ACU's constellation, Glenn is a liberal star whom it ranks as the chamber's 11th leading liberal, more liberal by one percentage point than even Howard Metzenbaum.

Glenn is scored somewhat more conservative than such liberal leaders as Kennedy (cumulative score of 3) or Cranston (6), but not nearly as centrist as such moderate liberal Democrats as Senate Minority Leader Robert C. Byrd (28) of West Virginia.

Why does Glenn seem to have a double identity? Why does one veteran congressional staffer say flatly of Glenn: "He obviously is much more conservative than a lot of Democrats," while Senator Jake Garn of Utah, a conservative Republican who came to the Senate the same year as Glenn, says just as flatly: "On many issues, John is liberal—sincerely so. He surprises me because usually someone with his kind of background is more conservative."

The answer is that Glenn unexpectedly confounds his critics, and sometimes his supporters, on both sides of the aisle. Occasionally he will veer from the Democratic party path to follow a more centrist, or even conservative, direction that is more consistent with his upbringing and military service. Although a staunch foe of the MX missile, Glenn has been one of the Senate's most forceful advocates of the B-1 bomber. In the 1970s, he figured prominently in blocking President Carter's plan to withdraw our troops from South Korea, a move that may have saved that country from Communist invasion.

But again the question: Is Glenn a centrist?

In his political dictionary, columnist William Safire notes that the term centrist "is of relatively recent political coinage, and is gaining in use as a more sophisticated self-definition than 'middle-of-the-roader.'" He adds that "the phrase is now used to define the area where the swing voter lies and where the big decisions are made; a politician who is a centrist can attract both mildly liberal and mildly conservative votes, and can develop a pattern of positions that encompass points on both sides of an ideological fence."

Many positions favored by Glenn that he views as centrist are in the area of military spending and procurement. He regularly tells audiences that defense budgets often seem based on the sales pitch of "the last contractor walking through the Mall entrance of the Pentagon." Though often criticized for his strong support of the B-1 bomber, Glenn maintains that the plane is a better gamble than the sophisticated Stealth bomber that is scheduled to replace it. Glenn insists that Stealth will take longer than advertised to come on line. Once it does, he feels, it will be only a matter of a few years before it becomes obsolete.

Glenn's most controversial view as a "centrist" is probably his recent vote in favor of replacing American stockpiles of deadly nerve gas. At issue was whether the United States, which has not produced chemical weapons since 1969 and which has renounced their first use, should replace existing stockpiles of 155-millimeter shells containing so-called unitary nerve gas with binary nerve gas, consisting of two agents kept separate until use. The Reagan administration maintained that the old shells were deteriorating; opponents dismissed the notion, saying they were good at least through 1990.

The initial Senate vote on the matter in July 1983 was 49-49, with vice-president George Bush casting the deciding vote in favor of the proposal. Only a handful of Democrats voted for it, including Glenn and Senator Fritz Hollings, the only two Democratic presidential candidates to do so. Immediately after the vote, Walter Mondale criticized supporters of the measure for voting in favor of one of the cruelest weapons in any nation's arsenal. Glenn testily countered through a spokesman that his vote was "not for nerve gas, but for safety."

Issues of national security sometimes place Glenn in the centrist column, but a senator such as Democrat Lloyd Bentsen of Texas, for example, might lay better claim to the label. His ratings at either end of the political spectrum are nearly equal (a 39 from the ADA in 1980; a 38 from the ACU that same year), while Glenn's liberal ratings are high and his conservative scores generally low. Glenn does try, with notorious slowness at times, to seek the middle ground in many policy debates, but he comes by his personally defined centrist profile not by a deliberate tack to the center, but by a blending of two extremes. His staunch liberalism in most areas, especially social welfare and labor policy, is tempered by his more conservative views on a small but important handful of other issues, including military and economic policy.

Glenn was, for example, an early supporter of Reaganomics, voting—along with many of his Democratic colleagues—for the president's budget and tax cuts. He has often voted pro-business, as when he opposed a law that would have restricted oil companies from both refining and marketing gasoline. He angered usually friendly labor with his opposition to "common situs" picketing, a form of secondary boycott that permits union construction workers to picket striking firms for which they do not work. In a recent attempt to solidify his anti-crime credentials, Glenn has advocated abolishing virtually all parole for criminals.

But to view Glenn, as some do, as a conservative with a saving touch of liberalism is to skew the truth. In fact, the evidence is overwhelming that Glenn is a liberal with a mitigating touch of conservatism. "Glenn may be a centrist," writes Morton Kondracke in the New Republic, "but his position is center-left." If Glenn "is an Eisenhower," Kondracke goes on, he "would be a Democratic Eisenhower, a cautious progressive rather than a conservative." Differences of perception notwithstanding, both Glenn and his organizers realize that being viewed differently by different parts of the electorate could help Glenn immeasurably in a campaign for president. Of course, the reverse could also be true if he were perceived as trying to be all things to all people.

Glenn's liberal record, peppered with diverse opposing stands, has prompted critics to ask if he has any guiding ideology at all, or whether he is merely a "tinkerer" on major issues. "The perception and the reality of Glenn as a follower rather than aleader on social and economic issues stems in large part from the committee assignments he has sought and received in the Senate," declares a comprehensive analysis of Glenn's record by the Institute for Socioeconomic Studies in White Plains, New York. "Unlike Senator Bill Bradley of New Jersey or Senator Daniel Patrick Moynihan of New York, Glenn does not serve on the Finance Committee, and thus is not naturally drawn into the myriad socioeconomic issues that panel covers—tax policy, Social Security, Medicare and Medicaid, unemployment insurance, welfare.

"By not being a member of the Labor and Human Resources committee like Howard M. Metzenbaum," the study goes on, "Glenn is deprived of jurisdiction over education and health programs and the training of public jobs programs of the Labor Department. Nor does he hold a seat, as Kennedy does, on the Judiciary Committee, the principal battleground for civil rights legislation."

Of course, the committees on which Glenn does sit provide him with ample opportunity to show off his credentials in equally important international and domestic areas. He is a ranking Democrat on the Senate Foreign Relations Committee and until the GOP takeover of the Senate, was chairman of its critical East Asian and Pacific Affairs subcommittee. The Foreign Relations Committee does not initiate legislation. Still, the institute study notes, "one of his principal strengths as a senator and a presidential candidate is his knowledge of international affairs."

Glenn's second major committee assignment is to the Governmental Affairs Committee, where he has continued a strong and visible interest in promoting energy legislation, an interest that reaches back to his earlier tenure on the Senate Interior Committee. Glenn also is the ranking Democrat on the Senate's Special Committee on Aging, a panel that serves largely as a sounding board for the grievances of the elderly and does not have the power to send legislation to the Senate floor.

But despite the Institute for Socioeconomic Studies assessment of Glenn as a "follower rather than a leader," no one can doubt his leadership role in foreign relations. During his eight-year Senate career Glenn has become, in the opinion of the *Almanac of American Politics,* "an important senator," who has risked the loss of support from various political groups, including some American Jews, to express his views on foreign policy.

In 1981, Glenn was a leading figure in seeking a safe compromise on the sale of AWAC jets to Saudi Arabia. He ultimately opposed the sale to the Arabs, but his initial efforts at compromise angered some Jewish groups, who remain wary of his attitude toward Israel. Two years earlier, Glenn had supported the sale of F-15 fighter jets to Saudi Arabia, a move that did not help his prestige among powerful Jewish Democrats, who pressured him to change his mind. Insisting the sale was in the best interests of both countries, Glenn refused to alter his position.

Glenn's troubles with American Jews do not stop with the F-15s or the AWACs. He was one of Israel's harshest Senate critics following its 1981 bombing of an Iraqi nuclear reactor, calling the attack "one of the most destructive events in recent history." His statements over the years calling for the inclusion of the Palestine Liberation Organization in Middle East peace talks and his opposition to Israeli West Bank settlements have soured his relations with portions of American Jewry.

Glenn angrily repudiates any charge that he is anti-Israel. "I think that American threats against Israel are counterproductive. All they do is lessen Israeli confidence in our resolve to back them and see the whole Camp David process through," he says. "The time has come, finally, when everyone should realize that Israel is there and is going to exist. That is not negotiable. Let's follow the Camp David process, including representatives of the Palestine people, and bring peace and true representation back and forth nationally between Israel and all of its neighbors."

Glenn's idea of political horse-trading in the Senate has been unique. It is to come to a position, articulate it to his colleagues, either privately, on the Senate floor or in committee, then wait for them to come around to his way of thinking. One of his aides concedes that Glenn "is not a horse-trader," but insists that this somehow makes it easier for other senators to deal with him because they know he has "no ulterior motives" when he refuses to budge on an issue.

Another close Glenn advisor explains his behavior this way: "I think it was an application of normal morals to the political scene. Say someone comes to you and says, 'I'd like you to come to my daughter's wedding,' and the response is, 'I'll do it if you will lend me some money.' Obviously, the reaction would be negative." In Glenn's case, he continues, the senator uses the same standard to reject supporting someone else's legislation—or changing his own—in return for political gain. "He just doesn't respond to threats and doesn't respond to deals."

This attitude, which some describe as "stiff-necked" and "stubborn" and others as "principled," has, on a number of occasions, gotten Glenn into trouble with groups whom he must court if he intends to win his party's presidential nomination, much less the presidency. Glenn's critics point to a 1977 confrontation between Glenn and some of Ohio's most prominent black politicians as evidence of his intransigence when he fails to get his way.

At issue was the appointment of a new U.S. attorney in Cleveland, a seat that has traditionally been black since the days of the Kennedy administration. Following custom, both Ohio senators, in this case Glenn and Howard Metzenbaum, were to have collaborated on a nomination. But Glenn had his own black candidate, an Ohio judge named George White, while Metzenbaum backed Carl Character, a former law partner of Congressman Louis Stokes. In an angry confrontation with Stokes and other black Ohio leaders, Glenn said that the black community was not going to dictate to him its choice of the new U.S. attorney.

Stokes, one of Cleveland's most powerful politicans, replied in kind. He called Glenn's remarks "a slap in the face of the black community and an insult." Despite Stokes's fiery rhetoric six years ago, he speaks about the incident today as if it were a minor annoyance. More significantly, Stokes now heaps praise on Glenn's civil rights record. "We didn't harbor any grudge about it," Stokes maintains. "I said what I had to say to him about it at the time, and took my position, both publicly and privately. We continued to work together.

"Glenn has an excellent civil rights record," Stokes emphasizes. "In terms of affirmative action and equal employment opportunity, he is outstanding. The problem is that Glenn's record is not known in the black community the way Metzenbaum's is. Fritz Mondale's record in the black community is also well known and identified, but John Glenn's is probably just as good. After all, John Glenn is the one who exposed the Senate and its lack of equal opportunity in congressional offices. He's the one that opened up that Pandora's Box and gave the Senate hell about it."

What Glenn had tried to do was force the Senate, which can and does exempt itself from many of the laws it passes, to live up to the dictates of the Equal Employment Opportunity Commission. He even proposed that a special board be created to hear complaints about job discrimination against senators. The effort failed, but it generated a great deal of publicity and some action. Glenn's own Senate and campaign staffs are fully racially integrated. Reportedly, they even include a homosexual.

"Right now," Stokes charges, "Glenn's got way more blacks than Fritz Mondale. Glenn's people came over to see me one day, a whole crew of them. Glenn must have fifteen or twenty top young black people in his minority complement in the campaign. And to my knowledge, Fritz is only carrying two." Mondale does have only two blacks on his senior staff, says his press secretary, Maxine Isaacs. But she adds that Mondale's contingent of black advisors is fully the equal of Glenn's and includes mayors Andrew Young of Atlanta and Coleman Young of Detroit.

Glenn can also lay claim to at least one significant domestic program aimed at easing racial tension. In 1977 he was the author of a program to provide money for so-called magnet schools designed to promote integration by attracting talented students from out of the school neighborhood. The program, which is undergoing its first in-depth review by the Department of Education, was conceived, says a Glenn staffer, "as a way of getting around the whole busing issue and the problems of desegregation by establishing schools that would attract white as well as black kids to them."

Glenn's position on another controversial social issue, abortion, is unequivocal. He favors federal funding of abortion and believes it is an individual woman's right to decide whether or not she will give birth. Abortion, Glenn says, is a "health action." Though he supports the Roe v. Wade Supreme Court decision permitting abortion on demand in the first three months of pregnancy, Glenn concedes, "I don't have any magic number of a specific number of days [when a fetus is viable] any more than anyone else, but I have felt that whatever a woman's personal beliefs with her priest, pastor, rabbi, it is a moral, ethical and religious decision for her and that judgment should remain in her hands.

"For those who believe that they know the exact moment when life starts and when it's sacred," Glenn continues, "I certainly encourage them to live out their beliefs. But for those many others who do not share those beliefs, and who feel that there is a time period after conception when those cells that are together are not identifiable as a specific human being, then I don't think you can force the opinions of the first group, by law, onto the people who do not share those beliefs.

"If you look at it that way," Glenn declares, "then it becomes a health matter. The question is, are we only going to permit that health action to be taken by those who are wealthy?"

In the Senate, Glenn has voted for abortion no fewer than 40 times over the past eight years, making nearly every record vote on the issue. Like other pro-choice lawmakers, Glenn says he opposes abortion "when a baby gets to where it's a viable entity outside the mother's body." On the other hand, he is of two minds on controversial "squeal rules," which would require notification of parents when minor children seek birth control help. "I don't have extremely strong feelings on it one way or the other," Glenn confesses. "I guess that with the extreme number of unwanted pregnancies, we should do everything we can to prevent them. On the other hand, you can argue that we don't want to encourage promiscuity that leads to more pregnancies. So I don't know."

Asked if he would have wanted to be notified if his own children sought birth control help, Glenn admits, "Sure. I would prefer to be. But should that be a matter of law? Don't we have better things to consider than that? I think we do."

Glenn critics in Ohio have spent more time examining his political style than his stand on issues. As he has learned painfully, no politician—even one as popular as Glenn—can long ignore charges that he is "out of touch" with his constituents, unable to make up his mind and disorganized. All three charges were aired during Glenn's first term. The "out of touch" charge was made by the *Cleveland Plain Dealer,* but could have been averted if Glenn or his staff had mended the damage before it made its way into print.

A *Plain Dealer* reporter had received a phone call from the minister of a Mansfield, Ohio, church, complaining that Glenn had forgotten to telephone a group of students waiting to talk to him on a prearranged conference call. The minister was upset. After trying several times to get through to Glenn's office, he gave up and called the newspaper to see if it could help. The reporter obliged, called Glenn's office and, saying in effect, "Hey, you better give this guy a call," then forgot about the matter.

A few days later, the minister called again, wanting to know if the reporter had ever gotten through to Glenn. This time, Glenn's seeming indifference intrigued the reporter, who wrote a short unsigned piece about it. "But the state editor saw the piece and decided to run it six columns across the top of the page," the reporter recalls. The big black headline over the piece read: "Out of Touch." Glenn, confessing, "I goofed," apologized to the students.

There were other incidents. David C. Hetzler, director of Common Cause in Ohio, tried unsuccessfully for two years to sit down with Glenn to discuss the issue of campaign finances. The Washington headquarters of the group finally suggested that Hetzler go public on Glenn's failure to respond. Immediately after talking with reporters, Glenn was on the phone to Hetzler saying, "I understand you have been trying to get hold of me."

Much of the blame for such embarrassing incidents has been laid on Glenn's top aide, Bill White, who supposedly acts as a palace guard to keep his boss isolated. A group of Ohio reporters once sent Glenn's press secretary a phony birthday telegram signed with White's name, saying: "As a special present, I've arranged for you to meet Senator Glenn."

Glenn's campaign disorganization has produced more than occasional bad press. One glaring error came last April when Glenn passed up meetings of black and women's caucuses at the Democratic State Convention in Springfield, Massachusetts. Glenn's headquarters tried to blame the mixup on "missed communications," maintaining that Glenn had not been told the precise time of the meetings.

Glenn's Senate career has spanned the administrations of three presidents, Ford, Carter and Reagan. Carter, the only Democrat, was also the president with whom Glenn had the most difficulty, both personally and professionally.

"I still see him occasionally," Glenn says. "I've run into him a couple of times." Glenn, in fact, made it a point to visit Carter in Georgia early in his campaign, as if to emphasize the distance Walter Mondale seemed to be putting between himself and his old boss. The meeting was cordial enough, and Carter, who ostensibly had endorsed Mondale for president, astounded reporters—and delighted Glenn—by saying he could live with either man in the White House.

Glenn, who says it is a "disgrace" the way America does not take advantage of its past presidents' expertise, is nonetheless privately candid about his own lack of enthusiasm for the Georgian. Carter's presidency, Glenn says, "is difficult to assess. Maybe we need a longer lapse of history here before we look back and see what happened or did not happen. "I don't think there was ever a better intentioned U.S. president..." Glenn says, his voice trailing off, obviously uncomfortable with having to praise a man for whom he cares little.

Glenn's difficulties with Carter began before the Georgian entered the White House. The conflict dates from 1976, when Glenn had completed over a year in the Senate and was rejected by Carter for the number-two spot on the ticket. Even before Glenn took the oath of office as senator, his supporters were touting him as a 1976 vice-presidential possibility. In late 1974, shortly after Glenn's election, the Democratic miniconvention saw thousands of orange "Jackson for President/Glenn for Vice-President" cards circulated among the delegates. Glenn was a natural political ally of Senator Henry M. Jackson of Washington, then the chairman of the Senate Interior Committee, on which Glenn served during his first two years in the Senate. Like Glenn, Jackson was considered an expert on military affairs who also harbored presidential ambitions. One observer was prompted to comment that Jackson only invited Glenn to join his committee to keep an eye on him.

As presidential 1976 neared, Glenn began thinking of himself as a logical nominee for the second position, but only if the party sought him. "I don't mortgage my future in any direction," Glenn said at the time. "I've got all my options open, and that's a great spot to be in."

The option Glenn's political mentor Steve Kovacik sought was not the vice-presidency. Kovacik wanted Glenn to go all the way. "There was, as we saw it," Kovacik recalls, "a wide open field for the '76 presidential nomination. When I say 'we,' I'm talking about Milt Wolf, who is now his finance chairman, and myself. We suggested to John that he do a Nixon, travel around the country speaking and picking up Democratic support in key states, much as Richard Nixon had done in the years after his losing the 1962 California gubernatorial race. States like Georgia and Arizona wanted Glenn for Jefferson-Jackson Day dinners. We encouraged him to do it, figuring that if he went into the primaries, that was the kind of territory where he could do very well."

Kovacik was instrumental in orchestrating the Glenn boomlet at the 1974 Democratic miniconvention. The only thing Kovacik lacked in '76 was a willing candidate. "What John did, essentially, was decide against it," Kovacik says. "He said he wasn't ready and didn't want to do it. He didn't want people to think he was that ambitious so soon after being elected to the Senate. So we didn't pull it off."

One Democrat who had no reservations about starting early was former Governor Jimmy Carter of Georgia. Campaigning quietly for nearly two years before the first primary, Carter and his brilliant campaign strategist Hamilton Jordan managed to steal a march on every major Democrat seeking the party's nomination. By the time the first ballots had been counted in the Iowa precinct caucuses and in the New Hampshire primary soon thereafter, Carter had emerged as "the man to beat." As it turned out, no one could.

Carter's last significant primary win—in Ohio—was the cap on his triumphal six-month primary and caucus campaign. Though Carter theoretically could have been denied the nomination at the convention by a coalition of opponents, Chicago Mayor Richard J. Daley in essence pronounced Carter the nominee after Ohio. Within twenty-four hours all opposition to Carter vanished. He would go to New York the following month with his nomination assured; all he needed was a running mate. By this time, John Glenn was a willing candidate.

Glenn came to New York convinced he had as good a chance as anyone to win the second spot. Jimmy Carter's own confidant, Atlanta attorney Charles Kirbo, had spent two hours in private talks with Glenn, fueling Glenn's hopes. Kirbo was, in fact, Glenn's staunchest ally in the Carter inner councils, arguing that the former astronaut was more politically in tune with Carter than the other candidates. Certainly he was the most widely known figure among the choices.

But as the convention opened, there were disturbing rumors

about Glenn's finances. Glenn was surprised. His financial history, particularly the huge amount of tax he had paid, had been thoroughly divulged in his 1974 campaign against Howard Metzenbaum. What some reporters were beginning to suspect was that a signal was being passed by the Carterites to deflect or defuse pro-Glenn stories that would take away from Mondale, the presumptive choice for vice-president.

Political reporters who ran into Carter's press secretary were told by Powell that *Parade* magazine was coming out with a piece that Sunday on Glenn. It dwelt heavily, Powell told them, on Glenn's relationship with millionaire Steve Kovacik. Meanwhile, Carter's people were questioning several Ohioans about whether Glenn and Kovacik had ever had any business dealings. Through all of this, Powell, and later Carter himself, kept insisting that they did not mean to cast any aspersions. Carter even offered the opinion that Glenn's use of certain tax shelters "was perfectly proper." "In fact," Carter declared, "it was a very conservative approach on his part to the amount of tax money that he did pay. He could have cut corners, but he did not."

Bill Boyarsky of the *Los Angeles Times* wrote: "It seemed a lot of noise over what happened to be a minor matter, but at a national convention without much news, the incident provided a difficult problem for Glenn, who did not want a promising political career hurt by what he considered rumors. Some Glenn advisors, believing the senator was being unfairly smeared, told him to take it up with Carter. But Glenn, at a Sunday night meeting with some of his closest advisors, decided to handle the problem by ignoring it."

Besides, Glenn said tersely, he had a speech to finish. The next day, having completed his keynote speech just in time for it to be transcribed onto the Teleprompters, Glenn opened the Democratic National Convention. The reception he received demoralized, then angered Glenn.

At a party for Glenn given afterward by Ohio Lieutenant Governor Richard Celeste, Glenn was subdued. Most of those who attended had a few drinks and left. "There were people in the room," wrote Richard Reeves, "who knew that the senator, despite his public diffidence, very much wanted the vice-presidency, and there were a couple who had heard a rumor that

Hamilton Jordan, Carter's manager, had reacted to Glenn's keynote performance by saying, 'I guess that eliminates one guy.'"

At the Glenn party, Walter Cronkite stopped by for a short visit. He was sought out by Socko Wiethe, who told Cronkite he thought he had gone a little overboard in calling Glenn's performance "dull." Had David Brinkley showed up, Wiethe could have berated him for calling Glenn's speech "the political equivalent of a sales manager talking to his salesmen."

"The whole atmosphere [in the Carter camp]," recalls Jody Powell, was "'Wow, that's a bad speech.'" But he quickly adds that "the speech really didn't have anything to do" with Carter's final choice.

Despite his poor reception in the convention hall, Glenn still ordered a special phone from New York Telephone for $229.49 to give Carter immediate access when he called. As it often does when dealing with politicians, the company wanted cash up front. Glenn paid, but the expensive special phone did not work when Carter finally called.

Steve Avakian, then Glenn's press secretary, was assigned sentry duty by the special phone on Wednesday evening, July 14, while Glenn and his wife were out to dinner. "Greg Schneiders [then working for Carter] called me at around 9:30," Avakian recalls, "and said, 'the call will come at around 8:30 tomorrow morning. Will someone be there to take it?'"

"I think that can be arranged," Avakian replied, laughing.

The first indication that it was not going to be Glenn was when 8:30 came and went without a call. As Glenn and his family waited anxiously in their suite at the Sheraton and a crowd of reporters milled about in the corridor, Jimmy Carter was offering the job to Fritz Mondale. Then at 8:40 Schneiders placed the call to Glenn.

There was no answer. Everyone in Glenn's suite was poised to grab the $229 phone when it rang, but nobody, it seemed, was calling. The phone did not ring when Schneiders called. Meanwhile, Schneiders, looking over his shoulder at his impatient boss, wished someone would pick up the damn phone in the Glenn suite. Finally, he called the Sheraton switchboard and asked if there were another number for Senator Glenn. "We're not allowed to give out that information," the operator said. Schneiders told the operator this was a very important call from Jimmy Carter, the Democratic nominee for president of the United States, and could she try the other number.

"It's busy," the operator said.

Stifling a curse, Schneiders asked the operator if she could break in on the call. "This is an urgent call from Jimmy Carter," Schneiders repeated, emphasizing the last two words. "I'm sure Senator Glenn would like to talk to him." But the operator still demurred.

Growing desperate, Schneiders asked if someone could be sent to Glenn's room to tell him about Carter's call. No, he was told, hotel policy forbade that too. After Schneiders hung up, Carter told him that if he did not get through in five minutes he was to take a cab to Glenn's hotel and personally tell Glenn to call him. Five minutes later, Schneiders finally got through. It was 8:51.

Glenn was in his shirtsleeves. When he came to the phone, which was now working, Schneiders said the governor would be right there. After a few moments, he asked Glenn if he could wait; President Ford had just called to offer Carter his congratulations on winning the nomination.

Glenn waited. Jimmy Carter finally came on the line. "John," he said, "I've called to let you know that I've picked someone else. I enjoyed meeting you, John, and I want you to be my lifelong friend. I'd also like to count on your help in the campaign." "I'll do whatever I can," Glenn said gamely, then hung up.

He walked into the other room where his family and staff waited expectantly. "He sort of shook his head, then sat down," Steve Avakian recalls. "Well," Glenn said to his wife, "we wondered who was going to cut the grass at home this weekend. It's going to be me."

Glenn and Annie were not only disappointed; they were resentful of the way they felt they had been treated by the Carters. Their anger was centered less on Glenn's failure to be chosen than on their suspicion that Glenn had been passed over by Jimmy Carter because of Annie Glenn's stutter, which was not cured until two years later.

Rumors of this had circulated at the convention, but had not been discussed by the press. Shortly after Carter's election, however, Richard Reeves reported in his book *Convention:* "One of the negatives in the consideration of John Glenn for vice-president, according to Carter staff members, was that his wife Annie stutters and Mrs. Carter did not believe that she would be an effective campaigner."

Glenn viewed the Carter attitude as an unconscionable smear on his wife. "Glenn still seethes," wrote Betty Cuniberti of the *Los Angeles Times.* Of Reeves's charge, Glenn has simply stated: "It has never been denied."

Today, Carter press secretary Jody Powell strongly denies the allegation. "I never heard it come up anywhere in the campaign." Greg Schneiders, who has served both Carter and Glenn, agrees with Powell.

Glenn, who has recently attempted a rapprochement with Carter, is now slower to repeat the charge against the former president. But when Annie Glenn is questioned about what happened in 1976, all the vitality drains from her eyes. It is clear that the Glenns still look back in anger.

Glenn's relations with the Carter presidency were never cordial. In fact—though it would be impolitic for him to say it—Glenn probably had an easier time talking with former President Nixon than with Carter, particularly about foreign and military affairs. Glenn does say that he and his wife had a surprisingly cordial exchange with Nixon at the White House, when all were Jimmy Carter's guests at the historic state dinner honoring Chinese premier Deng Xiaoping following Carter's announcement of normalization of relations with China in December 1978.

The following year marked the beginning of the demise of Jimmy Carter's presidency. It was in 1979 that the government of the Shah of Iran fell. In October, the American embassy in Tehran had been seized and American hostages taken. In the end, frustration over Iran, anger over the economy and, sadly, derision, combined to overwhelm the pious Georgian.

Glenn knew that the first American casualties of the Iranian revolution were two radar installations in northern Iran that were rendered useless with the forced departure of American personnel. The two listening posts, equipped with sophisticated radar, were to have been key verification points for any Soviet violations of the SALT II treaty the Carter administration was then painstakingly negotiating with the Soviet Union.

Glenn, who had made nuclear nonproliferation one of his primary concerns in the Senate, believed that the loss of the two stations made verification of SALT II impossible. He quickly became a major obstacle to the treaty's ratification in the Senate. The coolness between Carter and Glenn that had begun in 1976 would erupt into open hostility on an April day in 1979 when the two men engaged in a bitter shouting match over the phone. It was shortly before Glenn was to make a speech about the SALT treaty in Groton, Connecticut. The speech, in which Glenn denounced the idea of approving a treaty he felt could not be verified, set the stage for an odd confrontation between Glenn and Rosalynn Carter as the two took part in christening ceremonies for the Trident nuclear submarine, the USS *Ohio*.

"Rosalynn read an advance text of the senator's speech," Carter writes in his memoirs, "and was appalled to discover that he [Glenn] was going to denounce the SALT II treaty, which we were still negotiating, and to demand that the Soviets not only give us advance notice of all missile test firings, but also permit American planes to fly over Soviet test sites during the launchings.

"Furthermore, he planned to say that there was no other way for us to verify Soviet compliance with the prospective agreement. I was furious." The former president notes that his wife persuaded him not to call Glenn while he was so worked up. Instead, he dictated new language into Rosalynn's remarks to refute what Glenn planned to say.

The next morning, as Glenn prepared to leave for the airport to fly to Groton, the phone rang at his home. It was the White House, informing Glenn that the president was on the line. "I've never had a president talk to me that way," Glenn recalls today, "and I've never talked to a president that way." The two men exploded at one another during a conversation that lasted half an hour. Carter angrily accused Glenn of "trying to kill the nuclear arms limitation process while still claiming to be a supporter of SALT." Glenn, equally angry, replied that there was no way he was going to vote for a treaty that could not be verified.

Finally, Glenn agreed to remove the most provocative language from the text of his speech, the remarks concerning his new demands about flyovers and advance Soviet warnings of missile tests. "When the president makes a personal plea," Glenn told reporters afterward, "I have to honor that. I don't want to be the guy who wrecked the SALT talks."

Because of the prolonged phone call with the president, Glenn was late getting to the airport. The plane carrying the copies of his prepared text had already taken off. Inflight, Glenn radioed ahead, trying to stop distribution of his speech in Groton, but copies of the complete text were passed out anyway. Under chill gray skies in freezing winds, as Mrs. Carter stared at him hostilely, Glenn told the audience at the Trident christening: "I talked with the president at some length before coming up here. Due to the delicacy of the [SALT II] negotiations, I agreed that some of the remarks not be made." But even without the excised remarks—which were printed in the next day's news reports—Glenn made his strong objections clear.

"I believe verification must be better defined prior to a signing of the treaty," Glenn declared, "and prior to submission to the Senate, or we risk having this vital treaty disapproved or sent back to the president for further directed negotiating."

Either action, Glenn continued, "would have the effect of placing the Soviet Union before the world as being of greater peace-loving, arms-control intent than the United States. I do not want to see our nation placed in that position."

When Mrs. Carter took the podium, she said she wanted to "say a few words" about the treaty.

"Jimmy is not willing to accept a SALT treaty that is not in the best interest of our country and not verifiable," she declared. "If he had been, he could have done it in the past two years. But he had persisted. It is my feeling, and Senator Glenn understands this, that premature public debate on issues such as this can be very damaging." With that, she turned to look at

Glenn, who sat expressionless. "And also," Mrs. Carter said, "there are some matters pertaining to verifying the treaty that can't be talked about. They're too sensitive."

The "matters" to which Mrs. Carter referred concerned secret U.S. talks with China that were designed to give the United States the verification capability it had lost in Iran via a Chinese monitoring station. Administration officials maintained that public discussion of alternative monitoring posts would put the U.S. "in a bind" and "only make any negotiations to replace our listening posts more troublesome."

Carter's press secretary, Jody Powell, later charged that Glenn knew about the Chinese listening post at the time he made his speech, but Glenn strongly denied it. By year end, the whole question had become moot. Carter abandoned efforts to have the treaty approved following the Soviet invasion of Afghanistan. He called it "the most profound disappointment" of his presidency.

For John Glenn, the years between 1975, when he came to the Senate, and 1979, when he looked forward to his first reelection campaign, were some of the more rewarding, and frustrating, of his life. He chafed under the arcane rules of the Senate and the inherent slowness of the legislative process. But in the five years he served on Capitol Hill he had established himself as a national political presence, a man who could take on his political elders—even his president. If not always victorious, he was at least a force to be reckoned with.

Nineteen-eighty would be a watershed for Glenn. It would be the year that Jimmy Carter would lose in a landslide and a year that Glenn would be reelected in a landslide. The same determination that had propelled him into the space program and into the race for the Senate would now move him that final step.

15

MISSION WHITE HOUSE

"In the wake of his landslide reelection, Sen. John H. Glenn (D-Ohio) said yesterday he is at least thinking about running for president in 1984," wrote Tom Brazaitis in the *Cleveland Plain Dealer* within days after Glenn's 1980 Senate reelection triumph. Brazaitis, a lanky reporter who has known Glenn for years, wrote that the senator would now start accepting speaking invitations around the country and "base a decision on whether to run on a thorough assessment of Ronald Reagan's handling of the presidency."

But Glenn, who leaves little to chance, had already done more than think about his bid for the White House. He had made sure that sufficient funds would be available, money he had quietly generated and set aside for this purpose. It was an over-$100,000 surplus from his 1980 campaign, funds he would use to become a fixture at Democratic party dinners and functions around the country. His appearances were ostensibly being made to help congressional candidates in the '82 off-year elections, but they simultaneously laid the groundwork for his own unannounced presidential race. By election night '82, amid significant gains by Democrats in Congress and the statehouses, Glenn had become convinced that Ronald Reagan was vulnerable. He also knew that his own political appeal would never be as strong.

The task of piecing together the early Glenn campaign fell to William R. White, the 42-year-old Columbus attorney who was then Glenn's administrative assistant. A tall, well-built man with deep-set eyes and perfect teeth, White has a reputation in Washington as an overprotective worrier who has to approve anything involving his boss. As was the case with Jimmy Carter and Ham Jordan, Glenn has complete faith in White and treats him much like a son. Just as Jordan did for Carter in 1976, in 1982 White prepared a book-length strategy memo for Glenn detailing how to win the Democratic presidential nomination. Should Glenn gain the White House, White would assuredly be a key member of his White House staff.

"I practiced law in Columbus for seven years, and the firm I was with were his lawyers, which is how I first met the senator," White recalls. "I actually represented him personally. I still do. And I got involved in his '70 campaign as his research director and was his treasurer in '74—still working in the law firm."

White's work on Glenn's will—in which Glenn leaves the bulk of his holdings in real estate and stock to his wife and children, and his papers to his alma mater, Muskingum College in New Concord—led to his doing legal research for Glenn's unsuccessful 1970 primary campaign against Democrat Howard Metzenbaum. The relationship quickly flourished. When Glenn was finally elected to the Senate in 1974, White went with him to Washington as his administrative assistant.

After six years as Glenn's AA, White became the overall strategist of Glenn's 1980 reelection drive, along with Ohio campaign manager Steve Avakian. If in public Glenn was coyly deflecting talk of a presidential race, the private Glenn was putting out a far different word. "I was under strict orders to develop a surplus," remembers White.

The campaign surplus enabled Glenn to freely accept invitations to Jefferson-Jackson Day dinners and other Democratic party affairs around the country. Increasingly he found himself sharing the dais with Democrats Ted Kennedy and Fritz Mondale. It was, White maintains, a time when Glenn was "trying on the idea of running for president," though he admits his boss was "receptive to the idea of exploring" for support even while Jimmy Carter was still in office.

A swing through Washington state in the fall of '81 showed how rapidly Glenn could adapt to local political climates. The first night, speaking at a fund-raiser in Olympia, it was standard middle-road Glenn, asking that Reagan and his economic program be given a chance to work. But state Democratic Chairman Karen Marchioro complained that that would not do in the economically depressed Pacific Northwest. The next night Glenn blasted Reaganomics to the enthusiastic cheers of local Democrats.

Shortly after in New Hampshire, without prompting, Glenn showed partisan colors. He called Reaganomics "economic laetrile," characterizing budget director David Stockman as someone who "has broken faith with the country as well as Congress." Stockman's frank "confessions" about the failings of the plan, reported by William Greider in the *Atlantic Monthly,* reveal him to be, said Glenn, "one of those who know the cost of everything and the value of very little ... One million Americans have lost their jobs, and I see no earthly reason why David Stockman should keep his." In savaging Stockman, Glenn was serving his audiences what they wanted to hear. It was in sharp contrast to his 1976 convention speech in which he pleased himself but hardly anyone else.

One reason Glenn has even considered the presidency is the nature of Ohio itself, and the breadth of his 1980 victory there. "If you wanted to send a foreigner to a single state that had within it most of the varying ways of life in America, you could not do better than Ohio," says the *Almanac of American Politics.* Indeed, the state, situated squarely between the industrial Northeast and the agricultural Midwest, is a varied mixture of small towns and boom towns, slums and farms, industry and agribusiness.

A varied type of people and political opinion accompany

such a mix. Says Glenn: "There are liberals and arch-conserva-
tives, a wide spread of ethnic and religious groups, stripmining
areas in the east and, to the west, some of the richest farming
land in the country." In the 1976 and 1980 presidential elections, Ohio came as close as any state to mirroring the national
results. Politicians in both parties bow down to the truism: If you
can do well in Ohio, you can do well anywhere.

And in 1980 Glenn did very well. He carried the black and
Italian wards of Cleveland and the Polish wards of Youngstown.
His heroism in two wars and identification with a strong defense
brought him votes by the thousand from Germans in Cincinnati
and WASPS in Columbus. Only in the conservative Republican
enclaves of Paulding County near the Indiana border, whose
representatives in Congress include onetime Nixon diehard
Delbert Latta, did he falter. And when all the votes were
counted, Glenn had carried 87 counties out of 88.

"There was no one big event that made me decide to run for
president," Glenn says today. "I was looking into it, considering
it, all during '82, and I was all over the country during the
congressional campaign. We were getting a very good reception
wherever we went, and people were very favorably disposed
toward the ideas I was putting forward. So we decided—I decided—shortly after the '82 election that we would start moving.
We had thought earlier that it would take some 14 to 16 months
ahead of the early caucuses and primaries to put together whatever organization, whatever fund-raising, was necessary—and
that's the schedule we're on."

To make the transition from senator to presidential candidate, Glenn began joining the rest of the hopefuls at Democratic
"cattle calls." Whether miniconventions, party conferences or
state party dinners, they all had the same purpose: to show off
the talents—and deficiencies—of the men actively seeking the
1984 Democratic presidential nomination. One of the earliest of
these cattle shows was in June 1982, in Philadelphia, at the
Democratic party's mid-term convention. The three-day conference had been tightly orchestrated by party Chairman Charles
Manatt, a canny millionaire banker from California. It was to be
a demonstration of solidarity in the wake of the 1980 Jimmy
Carter debacle.

The star of that gathering was Ted Kennedy, who was then still a possible 1984 candidate, and the clear favorite of many who crammed the red, white and blue confines of Philadelphia's Civic Center looking for a leader. Teddy obliged. Reading his text through new wire-frame glasses, he delivered a telling diatribe against Reaganomics, vowing to help lead the party to a more equitable tomorrow. The former vice-president and second favorite, Fritz Mondale, called to mind the style of his late political mentor Hubert H. Humphrey, to the audience's raucous delight.

When Glenn's turn came to speak, the crowd expected little in the way of eloquence. They were not disappointed. The Ohio senator delivered a pedestrian speech attacking the Reagan administration. If a straw poll had been taken among the delegates, Kennedy would have been the obvious leader, Mondale second, and Glenn only one of several runners-up.

Glenn's strength was obviously not inside the room with the politicians. As always, it was with the populace outside, to whom his face was as familiar as his silver spacesuit. One high Democratic party official recalls being outside the Philadelphia headquarters hotel, the Bellevue Stratford, when John Glenn left the building and walked down the street. It all but made this shrewd political observer forget Glenn's pedestrian oratory just a few hours before.

"When we walked down the street, construction workers, remembering more than 20 years back, would turn their heads and say, 'Isn't that John Glenn?'" the party official recounts. "Women, men, old and young, would see Glenn and think, not 'Senator from Ohio,' but 'hero.'" To a political professional looking toward 1984, it was subtle but striking evidence of popularity that had nothing to do with the kind of party enthusiasm that had been generated for Mondale and Kennedy. "That's the yeasty kind of public juice that follows a John Glenn," said the official, who cautions: "But remember, it has nothing to do with his ability to be president."

Glenn returned to Washington pleased, though hardly overwhelmed, by his reception. The dewy-eyed response Kennedy had received from the party rank-and-file only confirmed Glenn's belief that it would be near-impossible for anyone to get the nomination as long as Kennedy remained in the race. The situation remained unchanged until that December, when Ted Kennedy made a sudden and unexpected announcement. At a jammed news conference in the Dirksen Senate Office Building on December 1, 1982, Kennedy stunned—and relieved—many Democrats, not the least of whom was Glenn, when he dropped out of the presidential race for 1984, and possibly forever.

Luck, which had been such a vital part of John Glenn's career in the past, seemed to be guiding his future as well. But there were problems. Glenn and campaign manager Bill White realized that Kennedy's departure would raise expectations for Glenn's relatively unformed campaign. In his 191-page campaign manual—two looseleaf books and a separate index—White had noted that Kennedy's continued presence made Walter Mondale, not Glenn, look bad. For all of Mondale's early organizing, he consistently ran far behind the Massachusetts senator in the public polls, and only slightly ahead of the less organized Glenn. The longer the race lasted between Kennedy and Mondale, the less public scrutiny there would be of the relatively unsophisticated Glenn operation.

It was a disarmingly frank Glenn who sat before a crowd of reporters in the Senate press gallery hours after Kennedy's withdrawal speech. "I haven't tried to analyze whether [Kennedy's move] is good or bad for me," he claimed. He echoed White's view that it would have been preferable for him to sit back "watching the fray"—that is, letting Kennedy and Mondale compete for liberal Democratic support. But Glenn had to admit that as long as Kennedy stayed in the race, it would have been hard, if not impossible, to deny him the nomination.

Still, the irony was that for all of the avid support for Kennedy among party liberals, it seemed clear that he could never win a general election. The evidence was apparent in his own 1982 reelection to the Senate. Kennedy's 61%-39% victory margin over a well-financed but obscure Republican, Ray Shamie, was large. But in a state where Kennedy was accustomed to reelection percentages ten to 15 points higher, it indicated an erosion in his political base. His percentage of victory was lower even than the 63% he drew in 1970, a year after Chappaquiddick. To many that proved the stigma of the tragedy lingered, an invisible burden, as Theodore White called it, having at its core the charge that in 1969 he abandoned a woman in distress, leaving her to drown in a car he was driving; and then lied about it.

His hapless 1980 campaign against Jimmy Carter—in which Carter's minions savaged Kennedy's character at every opportunity—proved to Kennedy how potent an issue Chappaquiddick remained. In '82 he sought to counter it with a series of TV ads that emphasized his family ties (though he was soon to divorce), while conceding he was was not "a plaster saint." The ads were widely viewed as test marketings of the media strategy Kennedy would use in his '84 presidential campaign. But even those close to him wondered if, in light of his '82 numbers, Kennedy's appeal as the heir to Camelot was gone.

Glenn's own relationship with Ted Kennedy was never close, despite the genuine affection he felt for older brothers Jack and Bobby. In fact, Glenn came to resent Ted. He strongly disapproved of his life-style, of the reports of womanizing and of the toll he saw it take on Kennedy's wife, Joan, during vacations with the Kennedy clan in the sixties. More galling personally was Glenn's belief that Kennedy had prevailed on Bobby's widow, Ethel, once a close Glenn friend, to cancel a 1974 Senate campaign appearance in Ohio on his behalf.

Kennedy had done this, Glenn believed, at the urging of Kennedy's liberal ally in the Senate, Howard Metzenbaum. Despite a handwritten letter from Ethel after Glenn's successful campaign, in which she professed her love for both John and Annie, Glenn's friendship with Ethel never revived. What little closeness there was to Ted Kennedy vanished entirely. Links forged over two decades with the Kennedy clan had been finally broken.

Despite Kennedy's withdrawal, few were sanguine about Glenn's chances, and early criticism mounted. Bill White contends that after the Kennedy announcement the bad press the Glenn organization received was similar to "somebody putting the light on suddenly and finding that we weren't dressed."

Tales circulated in Washington about the lackluster caliber of the Glenn staff and its internal rivalries, mostly centering around White and his seeming inability to sign up even low-level staff people for the long haul.

Others were equally negative about the Glenn candidacy for different reasons. "It would be the height of naivete for Glenn to think he can take the nomination because he was in space and Korea," noted a Mondale man. "Those are good tickets to the poker table, but you still gotta play."

There were dire predictions for Glenn, whom many party regulars still considered an astronaut intruding in professional politics rather than an eight-year veteran of the Senate. The Mondale man, echoing the view that people only liked Glenn for nonpolitical and nonideological reasons, added a pessimistic assessment: "You have to have plans and people for over a 12-month period. If it's going to be a war of attrition—and the chances of that increase now that Teddy's out—then Glenn, in my judgment, is on the verge of being out of it."

If hero Glenn was to seize the nomination, pundits believed, he would have to couple his favorable name recognition with early financial support from key backers in Ohio. To win, they said, he would have to make a "quick kill" of Mondale, Hart, Cranston, and others in the early Democratic caucuses and primaries and force the party to coalesce around him. But in fact, Glenn and his strategists had already abandoned the "quick kill" theory. Instead, Glenn began to plan for a nationwide effort in whichhe would compete for delegates in all 50 states. John Glenn is strongly convinced that, as the only well-known centrist among the hopefuls, he is the most electable Democrat in the crowded field. Eventually, Glenn believes, the party will come to see that.

Creating a presidential organization was more vital than ever in late '82 and early '83 because of the new exigencies of the campaign calendar. Glenn's lack of organization in the early days gave rise to numerous stories that he was wasting valuable time, stories that only stopped when Glenn surged forward in polls in the spring of '83. The Democratic party, in its zeal to shorten the absurdly long election process, had managed instead to lengthen it even further, forcing candidates for 1984—Glenn,

Mondale, Cranston, Hart and others—to publicly commit themselves earlier than ever before. The party had shortened the old
five-week window of time between the Iowa precinct caucuses
and the New Hampshire primary, persuading several states to
hold their primary contests in March '84 rather than over the
next three months.

As a result, the five-week "fallow period" after the Iowa
caucuses would now see an explosion of political activity in
which as many as half of all the 1984 Democratic convention
delegates would be selected before April. Staring at just such a
front-loaded political schedule, Arizona Congressman Morris
Udall, who had run a convincing race for the 1976 Democratic
presidential nomination against Jimmy Carter, aborted his own
campaign. "To come in now would be a day late and a few
dollars short," he told a jammed press conference on February
9, 1983.

"The compression of the primary and caucus calendar
means there will be no time for a candidate to work the next
state," explains one Glenn insider. "When you think about it,
we're halfway between what we had in 1976 and a national
primary. This poses serious questions for the less well-known
candidates. Guys like Reuben Askew and Fritz Hollings and
Gary Hart can only raise just so much money, and if they have
no tangible victories, it's going to take a hell of a lot of confidence to keep the money coming in over the next year. To try to
use a 'Jimmy Who?' strategy in 1984 would be like a general
fighting the last war. Remember, Carter already did it. Now it's
going to be much harder for any candidate to sneak up on the
opposition.

"The first thing that has to be achieved in any campaign,"
the Glenn staffer continues, "is to cross the threshhold of credibility—people have to believe your candidacy is possible. Carter
never crossed it until after the Florida primary. The question
now, with everything moved forward, is how do you cross that
credibility threshhold? I don't know how you do that if you are
relatively unknown."

Glenn, of course, is not unknown. To the contrary, he has
instant voter recognition. During his pre-announcement appearances, any observer would have been impressed by the

friendliness of the crowds. There is an ease with which people approach him, as if they have known him for years, which in a sense, of course, they have. It is natural for a politician to equate such a warm response with political support, though Glenn himself had learned in 1970, after a disastrously inept Senate primary loss, that a hero's welcome does not always translate into votes.

The development of Glenn's campaign apparatus was a comparatively low profile affair, creating the impression of an effort begun too late with too little. Some of the criticism was warranted, but while national attention was focused on Mondale and Kennedy, Glenn was assiduously putting together an organization that, after a slow start, has managed to raise more than $1 million in campaign funds, second only to Mondale.

One of Glenn's fund-raising problems has been among Jewish Democratic contributors, which has some of his aides concerned about the long-term effect of a Jewish boycott. "Fundraising has been good, not great," a Glenn advisor confided in July 1983. "His positions on Israel have really cost us, maybe as much as 60% to 70% of our early fund-raising." So concerned was New England coordinator Richard S. Sloan over Glenn's repeated unwillingness to openly court Jewish and other special interest groups, as did Mondale, that Sloan gave Glenn a blistering private memo warning of disaster unless he changed his independent course. "Unless this campaign is prepared 'to pander' to the various special interest groups within the Democratic party," warned Sloan, who had been a top Carter fieldman in Ohio, "it will never have the opportunity to employ a general election strategy. John Glenn must understand the Democratic nomination will not be handed to him."

To bolster his staff, Glenn signed on political experts like Paul Rosenberg, a management consultant on leave from McKinsey and Co., Inc., who envisioned a modern campaign that would call on high technology. During a campaign flight, for example, Glenn would be able to punch up the names and backgrounds of the people who would be waiting to greet him on an airport runway. The idea appealed to Glenn, who, as a former test pilot and astronaut, is fascinated by electronics and can use them effortlessly. In fact, Glenn helped design fingertip lights for his spacesuit 20 years ago and today displays real enthusiasm for miniaturized tape recorders and similar electronic gear. His campaign headquarters has telephone consoles with digital readouts and state-of-the-art call forwarding that sometimes baffle his own staffers and receptionists.

Besides Rosenberg, Glenn retained Bob Farmer, a bespectacled, roundfaced direct mail fund-raiser who had been working for Ted Kennedy up until the day he declared himself out of the race. With Farmer came additional computer lists. Glenn also held onto a boyish direct mail wizard, Vann Snyder, a rapid-talking New Englander who had helped put Michael Dukakis back in the Massachusetts statehouse. Snyder was convinced that the same Silent Majority that elected Richard Nixon would mobilize now behind middle-American Glenn, whom they saw, rightly or otherwise, as a confirmed middle-of-the-roader.

A sure clue to where a politician thinks his strengths lie is in his quest for money. Glenn looked both ways: to Republicans as well as Democrats. Initially, Snyder began his prospecting where one would expect: among Glenn's previous contributors, among supporters of Ohio Governor Richard Celeste, a close Glenn ally, as well as among previous contributors to the "D-triple C," the Democratic Congressional Campaign Committee. The first two fund-raising letters, bearing the legend "Senator John Glenn" at the top, went out in mid-April 1983, shortly before Glenn announced.

"The letters could have been signed by any of the other Democratic candidates, with the possible exception of Hollings," admits Snyder. "It was your basic litmus test of Democratic issues, and portrayed Glenn in his most liberal light, as a supporter of the voting rights act, ERA, abortion, and making Martin Luther King's birthday a national holiday." Glenn, who long has favored freedom of choice on abortion throughout his eight years in the Senate, did not come right out and say "I favor abortion on demand." Rather, his letters couched the issue in two ways, one as "the right of women to choose"—he didn't say what—the other "guaranteeing women their right to freedom of choice in matters of procreation."

In addition, says Snyder, Glenn "went prospecting where no other Democrat could look." His staff bought lists of Republicans in an attempt to "mine" funds from them. The initial mailing, however, produced only a half of one percent response, not enough to pay for itself. This was not as dismal as it sounded. In the high-volume, low-return business of direct mail, a response of 1.5% is considered excellent. But the effort foundered in the early going for two reasons. First, the "cream" lists, as Snyder called them—contributors to such moderate Republican senators as Lowell P. Weicker of Connecticut and Robert Packwood of Oregon—were unavailable to Democratic candidates.

Secondly, there was a suspicion among Glenn's hierarchy that a moderate candidate could never do well in direct mail, a medium that traditionally appeals to people on the left and right extremes. Glenn did not help the effort when, to Snyder's chagrin, he toned down the anti-Reagan rhetoric in his "liberal" fund-raising letters. Snyder's original draft had Glenn speaking of Reagan's "mean-spirited and misdirected policies." On seeing the draft, Glenn reached for his pen, crossed out the phrase and substituted "misdirected and misdrawn policies."

"I don't think we can say Reagan is mean," said Glenn, who in early 1981 supported the Reagan economic program because, as he said, "there was a chance it might work."

Inhouse misgivings over direct mail prompted frustrating delays, which at one point cost the campaign $15,000. Snyder originally had wanted to send out Glenn's first direct mail solicitations in early '83, but he could not get the go-ahead until mid-April. He then had to spend an extra $15,000 in postage in order to send the 150,000 letters out by first class mail. Otherwise there was a danger the pleas for money would arrive at an awkward time: income tax day, April 15.

If Glenn's direct mail effort shows him trying to garner support from both left and right, another, less publicized, phase of his fund-raising shows him to be ardently pro-business. Glenn's financial men reflect the new breed of Washington superlawyer and superlobbyist. Their presence reflects Glenn's determination to avoid the mistakes of his 1970 Senate primary campaign in which he lost to fellow Democrat Howard Metzenbaum after literally running out of money.

Glenn's Ohio angels, who have been supporting him for years, are well known in national politics. Ohio construction magnate Milton A. Wolf is Glenn's national finance chairman. Wolf's potency is illustrated by the legend, apparently true, that without leaving his living room he personally bailed out the Carter campaign in 1976 by raising a desperately needed $80,000. Not surprisingly, Wolf was named Carter's ambassador to Austria.

Another Glenn financier is Marvin Warner, a wealthy Cincinnati businessman and former ambassador to Switzerland. Warner, who accumulated a fortune in real estate and banking, also breeds racehorses and dabbles in sports teams. Chief among Glenn's moneymen is Thomas H. (Tommy) Boggs, whom the *Wall Street Journal* has referred to as "the prototype of the high-powered Washington lobbyist.... [He is] cunning, calculating and seemingly devoid of any real moral compass, driven mainly by money and success." Boggs, *primus inter pares* in Glenn's fund-raising apparatus, began hosting private luncheons for Glenn in which a blank check accompanied the coffee. He is partner in a firm that employs 80 lawyers and represents upwards of 500 clients. The Association of Trial Lawyers of America has employed him to battle no-fault insurance, while Lee Iacocca of Chrysler hired him to lobby for approval of its $1.4 billion in federal loan guarantees.

Glenn's pro-business attitude is a natural outgrowth of his small-town Ohio upbringing as well as his brief, but highly profitable, experience as a corporate executive in the years after his space flight. Bill White has cautioned Glenn that the business-oriented Republicans who had happily supported him for the U.S. Senate were the same people who played golf with Jerry Ford, dined with George Bush and who would probably not support him for president on the Democratic ticket. To these people, White suggested Glenn make a simple proposition: It is in your interest, and in your shareholders' interest, and the nation's interest, to nominate the best possible Democrat. Would you rather choose between Ronald Reagan and John Glenn or Ronald Reagan and Fritz Mondale? To many in the business community, this is a persuasive argument.

This is as critical as Glenn has gotten about his fellow Democratic candidates. His campaign strategy is to say as little as possible to antagonize supporters of other candidates, people whom Glenn ultimately hopes to bring to his side. In every case, says White, Glenn should approach all elements of the Democratic party for support. This is not necessarily sportsmanship; it would make it easier for Glenn to steal delegates at the 1984 convention as candidates weaken.

The new party rules favor Glenn. In 1980, delegates were tightly bound to their candidate, while the '84 rules simply state that delegates should "in all good conscience reflect the sentiments of those who elected them." The insipid nature of the rule—not to mention the absence of a sanction for its violation—could signal open convention warfare over delegate bodies. White has told Glenn he should create every opportunity for delegates to come to the belief that "the sentiments of those who elected them" have swung to him. If you don't do it, White warned, you can bet the other candidates will.

Seen as a whole, Glenn's campaign revolves around two superstrategies. The first is that he can win a general election; the second that he is a hardworking, loyal Democrat. The latter reflects the difficulty Glenn still has convincing some Democrats that he is not just a superstar loner, or even a closet Republican. In private strategy meetings, White has warned Glenn that it could be fatal to his campaign if party regulars suspect that he feels he is "entitled" to the nomination because of his reputed electability, a real danger in a man of Glenn's temperament. That would only conjure up invidious comparisons with the last "outsider" to win the nomination—Jimmy Carter. Such an error could be reason enough for delegates to stick with a nominee like Mondale, whose party credentials are perfectly in order.

To counter claims that he has a poor political staff, Glenn has brought in experienced staffers of national reputation. In January 1983, he hired Greg Schneiders as his 1984 campaign press secretary. Glenn also signed veteran operative Joe Grandmaison as political director. Grandmaison's appointment ostensibly was made to free up Glenn's chief of staff, Bill White, for other duties. But within the Glenn camp, there is the hope that the appointment will reduce White's enormous power. Meanwhile Bob Keefe, a beefy, cigar-chomping strategist who has worked both for Jimmy Carter and Birch Bayh, is on the periphery as the campaign's "faculty advisor."

The belated naming of Schneiders, a bespectacled political junkie with a nasal baritone and wry wit, was widely seen by political reporters as the "official" start of Glenn's campaign. It finally provided the press with a reliable source of information about what was going on. Glenn had been casting about for a "wartime" press secretary with little success before Schneiders was recruited out of the Senate Democratic Policy Committee. It was a happy choice. A Detroit native whose love of politics is exceeded only by his fondness for sailing, Schneiders gives the campaign a professional patina it badly needed. His appointment nearly two years before the '84 election also confirmed that the public part of the 1984 presidential race would be longer, and start earlier, than any before it.

Kennedy's withdrawal from the 1984 sweepstakes and the building of a professional organization helped advance Glenn in the polls, but did nothing to solve a sore lingering problem: How could he alter his image as a boring, even banal speaker? His attack on the problem was typically Glennesque: dogged, plodding, and in the end, reasonably successful.

The change from John the Dull to John the Occasionally Eloquent began during 1982, largely out of view of reporters. Special reading texts were prepared for the candidate when he was out speaking. Large, "Orator" type made the words easier to read. Detailed stage directions were included in parentheses. ("Pause—and look over knowingly at [Virginia Governor Charles] Robb.") Only the top half of a page was used. Glenn would thus have more time to face his audience and less to look down at his text. Not incidentally, the audience would also spend less time staring at Glenn's bald head.

His staff worked feverishly to help Glenn shed his square image, but in his quest for new sophistication, Glenn sometimes produced discordant results. At a 1982 birthday party for Reps. Steny Hoyer of Maryland and Tony Coelho of California, Glenn noted that in his first year in Congress, Hoyer had become known as a big Coca-Cola drinker. "In fact," said Glenn, "he's probably the only person on Capitol Hill with a Coke habit that's legal." Then Glenn, known as one of the Purity Twins because neither he nor Annie ever smoked or drank as youngsters, said, "You know, this drug business is getting serious. It's gotten so bad that when I asked one of my colleagues if I could borrow a few of his lines tonight, he handed me a mirror and some powder."

Glenn was straining to bring excitement to his delivery. It galled him to be tagged a poor speaker. He kept reminding the press that his first major public appearance, an address to a joint session of Congress shortly after his space flight, had been hailed as an oratorical tour de force. Arthur Krock in the *New York Times* had then commented that Glenn had the stuff of national leadership.

If only the 1976 keynote speech had never happened. Glenn realized the public perception of him as a poor speaker could seriously hurt his chances for the 1984 nomination, especially when compared with the marked improvement in Mondale's delivery. Mondale, only a journeyman speaker, had managed, through professional coaching, to tame his inherently whiny voice and speak in a lower register. When he combined choked emotion with seemingly genuine rage, the new Mondale was almost a reincarnation of his political mentor Hubert Humphrey, the Democrats' best stump speaker until his death in 1978.

The contrast with Glenn was now more obvious. It did not make Glenn feel better when one political consultant told Bill White that the only reason the press harped on Glenn as a poor speaker was that there was nothing else negative to write about him. White dismissed the idea, but included the consultant's view in the appendix to his strategy memo. By December of '82, shortly after Kennedy's withdrawal, Glenn had begun his own private tutoring, an ambitious undertaking that White and Glenn were anxious to keep confidential lest Glenn's "natural" image suffer.

The sessions were quietly organized by D. H. Sawyer and Associates, a New York public relations firm with a long list of

Democratic clients including House Speaker Tip O'Neill, New York Senator Daniel Patrick Moynihan, and several governors. The initial sessions were done cost-free in an apparent effort to lure Glenn as a client. It was only months later, on April 20, 1983—the day before Glenn formally announced for president —that White announced that Sawyer had been retained "as the campaign's media consultant."

Working out of a studio on Massachusetts Avenue in Washington, Sawyer and his people created a prop television set and had Glenn field questions as if he were appearing on *Meet the Press.* When his answers were videotaped and played back, it was obvious that Glenn was not answering quickly or succinctly enough. Glenn carefully followed the imagemakers' instructions on how to recast his answers to make them shorter and more punchy.

Sawyer had proposed these "video workshops" as a way "to let [Glenn] see his own performance, and also cover controversial areas that might trap the senator in the first months: busing, Social Security, abortion, Taiwan, South Africa." These, Sawyer said, were "the treacherous pushbutton issues" that could activate single-issue voters for or against a candidate on the basis of one inept sentence. The important thing was to keep Glenn from repeating ad lib mistakes such as those he had made the previous summer. Over breakfast with reporters, he suggested the nation consider a voluntary alternative to Social Security, a proposal that was anathema to liberal voters.

His coaches then concentrated on what came to be called "the Roger Mudd question." Nothing was more devastating to Ted Kennedy's 1980 presidential campaign than his response to correspondent Mudd's blunt question during a filmed TV interview, "Why do you want to be president?" Kennedy's answer was disjointed and unclear.

Bill White's strategy memo reprinted Kennedy's entire response to Mudd with the admonition that Glenn memorize a simple, three-part answer. Basically, it stated: "I want to be president because (1) I am concerned about America and the direction it is heading, (2) I have served it all my life and want to continue, and (3) I have some distinct ideas how to improve things."

White counseled Glenn that he did not have to recite an armload of specific ideas early in the campaign. He merely had to be perceived as having some. Reflecting a cynical view of the press, White noted that reporters—and by implication, the public—did not care a whit about specific issues, much less legislative proposals, so early in the race. But if a candidate was perceived as not having ideas, he would be crucified. Glenn proved an apt pupil, and now uses the strategy paper phrasing whenever he is asked the "Mudd" question.

Armed with his new-found sophistication and facing a radically altered political landscape, Glenn took his presidential show on the road. Glenn's early campaign travel, which had taken him all over the country on behalf of fellow Democrats in 1982, took on far greater significance after the midterm elections and Kennedy's announcement. Now Glenn would come under much close scutiny, not only from party professionals and activists looking for someone else to support, but from reporters who realized that the race for the 1984 nomination was going to be a real contest.

In early December 1982, Glenn flew to Texarkana, where he began his unannounced pursuit of the presidency. In the first class section of American's flight 271, on Pearl Harbor Day, December 7, Glenn studied his notes for the day ahead. The news of Kennedy's withdrawal was still fresh in the air and Glenn was intent on capitalizing on it. All through the two-and-a-half-hour flight, Mary Jane Veno, an attractive, sharp-featured blonde who grew up in Zanesville, Ohio and has been Glenn's aide since 1975, padded back and forth in stockinged feet from the rear cabin with speech texts and factsheets on a day that would begin and end in Texarkana, on the Texas-Arkansas border. It would cover no fewer than six separate appearances before some of the most influential and wealthy Democrats in both states.

Glenn was truthfully able to say that the trip had been planned long before Kennedy's move. But as originally scheduled, the Texarkana foray was to have been a perfunctory fence-mending exercise. Now, it had suddenly been transformed into a practice presidential campaign trip.

Arriving at the sprawling Dallas-Ft. Worth airport, Glenn walked off the plane with his hands stuffed into the pockets of his tan topcoat. "You wanna see a tragedy?" he said. Glenn pointed to the toe of an expensive new pair of black buckle loafers that he had somehow managed to gouge. Characteristically, Glenn did not "work" the passengers during the commercial flight, preferring to concentrate on the papers "MJ" kept bringing to him from the rear. As he waited for a private plane to pick him up for the short hop to Texarkana—staring occasionally at his shoe—most of Glenn's fellow passengers filed past him, oblivious of his presence. But those who did see him recognized him immediately. "He's shorter than I thought," said one woman, viewing the senator for the first time.

In the crowded twin-engine Beechcraft to Texarkana, Glenn munched on a doughnut as he spoke easily with his host, Ed Miller, a round-faced county judge and a power among Texas and Arkansas Democrats. When Miller remarked that the people in his conservative, though heavily Democratic, area "are going to be looking to you for leadership," Glenn smiled in appreciation but said nothing.

As the plane landed at a well-tended small airfield on the edge of Texarkana, Miller was embarrassed to find his prearranged reception party, the mayors of Texarkana, Texas and Texarkana, Arkansas, had not yet arrived. Only Miller's wife was there to greet Glenn, along with a lone TV reporter from Channel 6, carrying a heavy minicam, a microphone and a videotape machine. Seeing the young man struggling with his gear, Glenn offered to hold the mike during the obligatory planeside remarks.

"If I run, it'll be for cause," Glenn said, staring intently into the lens. But holding the microphone out of politeness, Glenn looked more like a reporter than a hero who had once commanded world attention. After his statement, Glenn returned the mike to the flustered newsie, who nearly dropped his camera. Glenn was already in Miller's car driving off to his first appearance when the two tardy mayors arrived, breathless and chagrined.

That day Glenn clearly displayed to his hosts his strengths and his weaknesses, each centering on his speaking style. During a lunch meeting with Texarkana business and civic leaders, Glenn took more than five minutes to answer a simple question. "You asked me the time of day and I built you a whole watch," he sheepishly admitted. He was considerably more adept at a later news conference, but the questioning from the local press was uncritical and polite. At a cocktail party at the home of a wealthy backer, Glenn displayed his talent as a gracious listener. But it was his last appearance in Texarkana that day that offered the greatest political dividend by demonstrating that his speech-making lessons were paying off.

It was the 70th annual meeting of the Texarkana Chamber of Commerce. Glenn sat straight in his chair on the stage of a cavernous, 1924 vaudeville theater that had been restored to its art deco brilliance by billionaire H. Ross Perot. The flags of the 50 states formed a backdrop as Senator David Pryor stepped to the podium to begin his introduction in a languid Arkansas drawl.

"Whoever we are, and whatever we are and wherever we are," Pryor said, "Americans are a unique people that loves its legends, loves its history, and, yes, loves its heroes. Tonight, I'm honored to introduce one of those legends...truly, I think one of the finest human beings that has ever graced our country and certainly one of the finest human beings who has ever been a member of the United States Senate.

"You remember that day, February 20, 1962, when John Glenn became the first human being to orbit our earth—seventeen thousand and five hundred miles per hour—around this earth on three occasions, in a small and minuscule capsule, not much bigger than a Texarkana washtub."

In private, Pryor has a disarmingly insouciant air and seems always to be suppressing a grin. Governor of his state at 41, senator at 44, he knows what plays well to a homestate audience. In Texarkana his southwest drawl seemed to gain in richness as he lauded Glenn, mistakenly calling him the first human being in orbit (cosmonaut Yuri Gargarin was first by ten months). A Southerner with a reputation as a progressive, Pryor had already been mentioned as an ideal running mate for Glenn, both geographically and ideologically. His performance in Texarkana indicated that he thought so too.

Finally, to thunderous applause, Pryor gave the floor to Glenn. The unannounced candidate spoke for roughly half an hour in a sometimes disjointed effort nicely held together by a folksy, avuncular style. It was a different presentation from his usual preachy manner, and the crowd was soon murmuring approval and chuckling in response at the right places. It was a rough cut of "The Speech," a lecture that Glenn was to practice and deliver so often that he could recite it with sufficient humanity and sincerity to impress even the most cynical reporter.

Glenn's version that night was an informal summary that combined protectionist rhetoric against foreign imports with a short history of U.S.-Soviet relations. He noted in particular Russia's staggering loss of 20 million people in World War II and her subsequent "paranoia about absolute security." He angled for applause and got it with a low-key yet fervent pitch on America's lost greatness and the need to restore Reagan administration budget cuts in education and federally funded basic research.

It was the ending, though, that touched these people, citizens whose roots in American patriotism remained strong despite a generation of national self-doubt. This was not a crowd in which to preach ERA or abortion. It was a crowd that loved the flag as it was and reveled in having it waved resplendently before them. And Glenn obliged. "Whatever other problems we have, this nation remains today exactly what it was at the time of its founding—a land of unparalleled blessing, of unparalleled hope, of unparalleled opportunity," the former astronaut said, in an obvious reference to own exemplary career. "We remain that beacon of freedom that stands before the rest of the world.

"Do you remember that horrible scene on the beaches of Florida about a year and a half ago," Glenn continued, his voice suddenly gaining passion. "Those were not Americans trying to hide little boats under the palm fronds and get out of the United States. Those were people who were willing to risk death at sea—and they lost!—just trying to get into this land that we have become so caustically critical of."

Glenn then paraphrased Ralph Waldo Emerson: "The new

horizons, the future that we can have, can eclipse anything we have ever known in the past.

"This time, like all times, is a very good one," Glenn said, his voice now almost a whisper, "if we but know what to do with it. Thank you very much."

The crowd was silent for a second. Then, it rose as one. The noise and the approval were deafening.

The turn of the year brought relatively good results for Glenn from the nation's pollsters. Despite Glenn's late emergence into in the race, George Gallup reported that both Glenn and Mondale had taken early leads in test heats against Ronald Reagan. Glenn was popular nationwide and gaining among Democrats, but the former vice-president enjoyed a comfortable two-to-one advantage over Glenn among party members. In his first "post-Kennedy" survey, released January 13, Gallup noted that "when the race for the 1984 Democratic nomination is narrowed to two frontrunners, Mondale is the choice of 59% of Democrats...while 28% pick Glenn and 14% are undecided."

Going into 1983, Mondale had reason to feel confident. A politician noted for his methodical caution and undisputed credentials with key Democratic constituencies, he had put together a campaign organization that was the envy of his rivals. Operating out of a large suite of offices on Wisconsin Avenue, just above Washington's fashionable Georgetown, the former vice-president's workers moved quickly to cement their man's advantage as the leading candidate.

To broaden his political base and appeal to those Democrats who abandoned the Carter-Mondale ticket in 1980 to vote for Ronald Reagan, Mondale made a move to the right early in his campaign. He showed up on the 700 Club, the evangelical TV talk show whose fans include many in the Moral Majority and New Right. He aligned himself with centrist politicians such as Mayor Ed Koch of New York who, until losing the race for the governorship, had increased his political capital tenfold by moving toward the right. Most significantly, Mondale, whose ratings from liberal groups exceeded even those of his late mentor Hubert H. Humphrey, began to criticize the social programs he had so long advocated. "Where we overregulated, we should cut back," Mondale declared. "Where we fueled inflation, we should push for tax relief. Where government has been clumsy or expensive or intrusive, we should make government better."

It was effective, but if Mondale had looked behind him, he would have seen an ambitious former astronaut taking painstaking steps to close up the distance. John Glenn was starting to move, even managing to look good in enemy territory.

John Glenn eased his burgundy LeBaron into the VIP slot, avoiding a maze of roads leading to more distant parking and walked casually to the entrance door, under the recognizing stare of porters, cabbies and passengers.

Butler General Aviation Terminal at Washington National sits to the north of the airport's main buildings and resembles a doctor's waiting room more than a busy airport lounge. There are comfortable seats, beige carpeting, subdued lighting, and none of the petty annoyances of commercial air travel. There are no metal detectors, no X-ray machines, no zealots with carnations or clipboards touting Reverend Moon or nuclear energy. Above all, no crowds. For those who can afford it, it is the only way to travel. Just beyond the waiting room's large glass windows, a half-dozen private planes sit waiting for their clients —business executives, network television crews, an occasional celebrity.

On this pleasant day of March 3, 1983, the client was a presidential candidate on his way to a another political cattle show. Glenn had been to these exercises before. Tonight's in Boston would be no different: a Democratic state party fundraising dinner at which he and his fellow candidates would speak to other politicians. But it was Kennedy country and Glenn was seeking to impress potential delegates in perhaps the most liberal state in the nation. Shaking hands with his pilot—Glenn would be too busy to fly himself—he boarded the tiny twin-engine Beechcraft and strapped himself in for takeoff.

The afternoon sun streamed through the round polarized windows of Glenn's plane as it banked left, following a compass pointing north. "At this early stage in the race," Glenn told his seatmate," your status as a candidate depends less on your stand on issues than on how well you can tell a joke. Big deal." Nevertheless, during the hour-and-45-minute flight to Boston, Glenn would labor over his prepared text and more than once ask Greg Schneiders if he thought the gag lines would work.

Bob Farmer, one of Glenn's fund-raisers, watching his new boss shuffle papers in his battered leather briefcase, told Glenn that when he got to the night's affair at Boston's Park Plaza Hotel, he should seek our Senator Paul Tsongas's twin sister and tell her he wanted to sit down with her. Senator Tsongas, a liberal Democrat who had looked forward to supporting Kennedy, was now professing his nonalignment. His sister had been very active in Massachusetts politics and both were viewed as valuable allies in siphoning off liberal support from Mondale. Glenn looked at Farmer and nodded. "I didn't know Paul had a sister," he said. (Several months later Tsongas not only endorsed Glenn, but made his views known in a newspaper op-ed piece that was reprinted widely.)

The hotel was packed with candidates and politicians. As black-suited waiters bustled about in the main dining room, hundreds of Massachusetts pols mingled outside on an ornate balcony overlooking the hotel's lobby. It was a time of overheard conversation and surreptitious looks. Everyone was craning to see who was there, who was not there, who was talking to whom.

In one small room commandeered by the local TV station, candidates trooped in and out for their few seconds of footage on the evening news. Senator Fritz Hollings, 61, a congenial man with little name recognition outside his home state of South Carolina, handed out pamphlets about himself with the headline: "What a Difference a Hollings Might Make." He weaved through hundreds of people, his eyes darting, searching for a friendly face or a flicker of recognition. Senator Gary Hart of Colorado, 15 years younger than the white-haired Hollings, seemed more relaxed, mingling easily with the crowd, laughing occasionally and moving expertly through the human sea. That night, anyway, he was not the standoffish Gary Hart many had come to know in Washington, a man who could turn off potential supporters with a distant, distracted air reminiscent of former Senator Eugene McCarthy.

When he arrived, midway into the crowded cocktail hour, Glenn was told that the speaking order for the affair had been changed. Mondale would be speaking first, before dinner, and leaving early. Mondale said he had another commitment that evening. Glenn was not buying the excuse. "That's the third time he's pulled that," he groused to Schneiders. (It turned out that Mondale had to leave to make the last commercial flight back to National Airport before 11:00 P.M.)

For all his expert maneuvering, Mondale was outfoxed by circumstance. The dinner started late. MC Ted Kennedy's opening remarks lasted far longer than expected, and the faulty sound system seemed devised by a Republican. Mondale was forced to talk through the $150-a-person main course, shouting to be heard through the faulty mikes and over the clatter of cutlery. "The 1,500 diners seemed not to feel that their inattention constituted any breach of hospitality," syndicated columnist Mary McGrory wrote later.

The introduction by Kennedy set the tone for Mondale's discomfort. "Now, of course, Fritz Mondale has been making a lot of news lately," Kennedy said. "Did you see that story last week in the *Boston Globe*, where Fritz said that during the Carter administration, he disagreed with the grain embargo, the MX missile, the F-15 sale to Saudi Arabia, the high-interest rate policy and even the malaise speech?

"You know," Kennedy went on, "maybe I could have saved myself a lot of trouble in 1980. I should have asked Fritz Mondale to run against Jimmy Carter!" When he had finally struggled through his remarks and hastily departed, Mondale was perturbed.

By the time Glenn rose to speak, it was close to 10:00 P.M. The dinner had gone on too long, and Glenn was not even the last candidate on the agenda. He cut his remarks drastically, but unlike Mondale, he did not lose the crowd. Ignoring Bill White's admonition to placate Kennedy now that he was out of the race, Glenn twitted the Massachusetts senator for endorsing loser

Mayor Jane Byrne in the Chicago mayoral primary. He then went through an abbreviated version of his anti-Reagan litany ("let him stop confusing the epistles of the New Testament with the apostles of the New Right..."), ending with what was becoming his standard philosophical pitch for "new horizons... guided by the light of old values." As Glenn too ducked out of the ballroom to catch his plane home, he was upbeat, convinced that Mondale's performance would hurt him in the months ahead.

Glenn's car pulled up to the general aviation terminal at Logan. Although anxious to get home, he lingered in the waiting room when a man and his wife, recognizing him immediately, stopped to say hello. Finally, he made his way toward the gate as a young white-suited medical technician rushed past, pushing a blue plastic container on wheels holding a reddish-blue object awash in blood.

"What's that?" he was asked.

"A kidney," the technician replied with a grin. Then, suddenly realizing whom he had almost rushed past, the technician stopped. With his hand resting casually on the kidney box, he watched for several precious minutes as the former astronaut disappeared through the hatch of his plane. Once Glenn was gone, the technician broke into a run to a waiting ambulance, hoping to make up the time he had lost gawking at a man who had been a childhood hero.

On the flight home, Glenn was pleased with the reception he had gotten that night. But his thoughts soon turned to the announcement address he would make the following month—and to the off-the-record address he would make several weeks before that. For him, the latter appearance would be as important as his formal announcement for president.

On Saturday evening, March 26, Glenn had to face his sternest audience of all: the Washington press. For years they had dubbed him a poor speaker, and by implication, a dullard. They acknowledged that his record as a hero, his boyish grin and middle-American life-style gave him enviable national appeal and voter recognition. But the consensus among the opinion-makers was still that Glenn could not hold an audience. They had not forgotten his 1976 keynote fiasco, and saw little reason in 1983 to change their opinion. Now Glenn would be put to the test before these very skeptics. As Glenn later conceded, a poor performance that March night could have destroyed his presidential campaign before it formally began. Such was the power and influence of the Gridiron Club.

Not a "club" at all, the Gridiron is a tightly knit group of Washington's 50 most senior and respected print journalists. Once a year they meet for a formal dinner and musical revue that features, among other things, Washington's ruling elite dancing, singing and poking fun at itself.

It had begun in 1885. Every year since, the president of the club has opened each dinner with the admonition: "Reporters are never present; ladies, always"—a reference to the fact that everything said must be off the record, and in good taste. The rules have been observed for the most part. In recent years, as pressure grew for equal rights, women reporters have been accepted into the Gridiron's once exclusively male ranks.

The Gridiron meetings have made political history. In 1907, President Theodore Roosevelt almost came to blows with his longtime political nemesis, Senator Joseph B. Foraker, when the two angrily confronted each other in what was to have been a genteel exchange at a Gridiron dinner. Decades later, another Roosevelt—FDR—left mouths agape with his blistering comments about the stupidity of the American press. "It is this vast and militant ignorance, this widespread and fathomless prejudice against intelligence that makes American journalism so pathetically feeble and vulgar, and so generally disreputable," the president said. Only after everyone in the room felt thoroughly insulted did Roosevelt reveal that the remarks were not his, but the words of the dean of American political reporters, H. L. Mencken.

In the late sixties, President Nixon and Spiro Agnew sat back to back at twin pianos and sang Dixie to each other in an unsubtle reference to the "southern strategy" that had helped put them in office. In 1972, former New York Mayor John V. Lindsay, long on looks but short on political intuition, helped destroy his legitimacy as a presidential contender by regaling his influential audience with off-color jokes.

It was into these potentially hazardous waters that Glenn was invited as the Democratic party's chief "spokesman" when the Gridiron Club convened that Saturday evening. "We recognized that it was a high-risk venture," recalls Dale Butland, Glenn's chief speechwriter, who noted that Glenn had received the invitation after Walter Mondale had declined the honor. Before the meeting James Reston of the *New York Times,* himself a Gridiron member, had publicly called Glenn's decision to speak "a mistake." But Glenn realized it was the best opportunity to turn around his reputation as a dismal orator.

To prepare for the night, Glenn developed a Gridiron team. He called upon professionals, including humorist Art Buchwald, to write the text. "A Gridiron speech is a group effort. It's like writing for *Your Show of Shows,*" says Buchwald, the columnist who has been writing humorous Gridiron speeches for politicians for two decades. "I did a Lyndon speech that he never gave," recalls Buchwald. "He got mad. It was the first time he was president, and we had worked on it for about two or three weeks. He just sat through the sketches and didn't like the whole idea. When it was his turn to speak, he just got up and said: 'Ah wanna thank you for this fahn dinner' and sat down."

But Glenn was in a different position than an incumbent president. He had to take a risk in order to make a much-needed good impression with Washington's media elite. "He was aware of the importance of it, and so were we," says Buchwald. "We said, 'if you're a success, it's gonna help you a little. But if you bomb out, it can killya. It turns out it helped him a lot."

There was certainly no lack of talent involved in the preparation. Besides the help from Buchwald and Glenn's speechwriters, Butland and Dennis Fitzgibbons, there were contributions from such old Washington hands as Frank Mankiewicz, Dick Drayne and Mark Shields, veteran members of the New England political mafia. Shields is an ex-Bostonian and a political columnist renowned for his wry wit; Mankiewicz had been Bobby Kennedy's press secretary; Drayne served in the same capacity for Teddy. They pooled their ideas and produced a first draft that ran much longer than the 15 minutes allotted.

"Then," says Buchwald, "you start throwing out the stuff that won't work, the stuff the candidate doesn't like, or the stuff that somebody objects to because of taste, and you keep whittling and whittling it down."

Because of time, recalls Dale Butland, they reluctantly discarded one part of the speech in which Glenn was to give a convoluted explanation of the disarmament process, getting more and more confused—and presumably growing funnier and funnier—as he went along. "The funny thing about disarmament," Buchwald notes, "is you don't know when to laugh." So the bit was discarded.

Another problem was Glenn himself. "John is pretty straight," notes Buchwald, "and the idea of making people laugh, I think, was a bigger trip for him than going to the moon." In the early sessions—which Glenn attended even when he had to cancel other appointments—he read his lines with forced theatrics. "We told him he was hammin' it up too much," Buchwald explains. "We said, 'look, just be natural. Use your own natural voice.' When somebody's not used to this, they tend to think they're supposed to take on a different role, when in fact the jokes are supposed to be funny and not the person."

Glenn took direction well, and contributed a line here and there. He even swallowed hard and included a mocking reference to his disastrous 1976 convention speech. The text was put on tape and Glenn practiced it incessantly.

With three hours to go before the dinner, however, Buchwald and others were still not confident. "The final rehearsal was at our house," Buchwald remembers. "We had heard it too much. We were sittin' around and didn't know what the hell was workin' and what wasn't. So there's a lady who takes care of our pool and my wife, Ann—they hadn't been in the room—and we said, 'Okay, John, you've gotta read it one more time.' So we brought in my wife and this lady who cleans the pool. First she walks in and sees it's John Glenn and she's thrilled just to be in the same room. And then when she's asked to sit down and listen to his speech, it blew her mind."

Did they like it?

"Oh yeah, they both did. They roared in all the right places and it really was a big boost to John and his own confidence."

Three hours later, Glenn delivered the speech and stole the show. "As many of you may know, Scotty [Reston] thinks it was a mistake for me to accept this invitation because I can't give a funny speech," Glenn began his address. "So after reading his column, I turned to Bob Strauss for advice. Bob said, 'John, don't worry. Just give the same speech you gave at the 1976 Democratic convention. The whole damn country laughed at that one.'

"First, let me say that I am not dull. Boring maybe, but not dull. Frankly, I'm getting sick and tired of hearing about how dull I am. So my staff has launched an organized campaign to stop those rumors once and for all. As you may have noticed, it's the only organized campaign I've got..."

It went on like that for 15 minutes. The powerful media chiefs, charmed by Glenn's delf-deprecating humor, roared their approval. Midway into the speech, after saying that "Republicans have done for balanced budgets what Orson Welles has done for designer jeans," Glenn peered down into the audience at Reston and cracked, "How'm I doing, Scotty?" More howls.

"We had that line in there," Buchwald recalls, "and then we decided that if he wasn't doin' that good, not to use it, let him use his own judgment on it. And he had 'em on a roll so it came naturally. I was sorta pleased with that because it showed he had some sense of timing."

For Glenn, the Gridiron humor was not frivolous. It was a political life-or-death battle against his reputation for dullness. Within days, little asides and appositional phrases began appearing in the copy of Washington's journalistic hierarchy, noting Glenn's big improvement as a speaker. David Broder of the *Washington Post* went so far as to say Glenn's Gridiron performance may have lifted his dullard's mantle "forever."

It was a relaxed and outwardly confident Glenn who plunged into his formal campaigning as spring of 1983 arrived and scrutiny increased not only of him but of Walter Mondale. His top staff were convinced that Glenn's unwillingness to criticize his Democratic opponents could ultimately hurt him, but there was no arguing with the results of the national polls that May.

"A new *Los Angeles Times* poll shows Ohio Sen. John Glenn overtaking longtime frontrunner Walter Mondale in the contest for the Democratic presidential nomination, suggesting that voter preferences for 1984 may be more volatile than many politicians and analysts have believed," wrote *Los Angeles Times* political correspondent Robert Shogan on May 15. The surprising figures on Glenn had been buried in a welter of other polling data until Shogan pulled them out for a story that made headlines across the country.

Predictably, it prompted an angry reaction from the Mondale camp. "We have been saying all along that we don't put any stock in presidential preference polls," declared Mondale press secretary Maxine Isaacs. She added that the L.A. *Times* survey was "fundamentally out of step" with other polls, which consistently showed Mondale to be the frontrunner. Just four days later, however, George Gallup weighed in with findings showing Glenn gaining on Mondale among Democrats, and noting that "Senator John Glenn is now seen as a stronger vote-getter than former Vice-President Walter Mondale."

The twin findings seemed to confirm the central theme of Glenn's candidacy. Here was a candidate who not only could appeal to fellow Democrats, but to the electorate as a whole. In short, here was a candidate who could win in 1984.

The political calculus that once seemed weighted heavily toward Fritz Mondale started to shift toward Glenn. It was helped by the fact that the former astronaut retained an unbelievably large measure of public approval. Public response to Ted Kennedy, for example, was mixed: 53% favorable, according to the L.A. *Times,* against 46% unfavorable. Mondale's numbers were better—69% favorable versus 27% unfavorable. But Glenn's popularity was near-unprecedented: 80% favorable, versus a scant 11% unfavorable.

Glenn could not help but gloat over the poll results. At a small dinner party at his home just days after the polls were published, Glenn was all smiles. He bantered about the results until the stroke of 8:00 P.M., when Ronald Reagan had scheduled a news conference. Looking at his watch, Glenn walked from his patio into the living room and sat down with notepad in hand directly across from the huge Sony that dominates one corner of the comfortable room to listen to the comments of President Reagan, the man he now felt he had at least a 50-50 chance of facing in the November 1984 election.

July is the start of dog days in Washington when everything seems to stop under the city's ferocious humidity. But this July Glenn and his fellow presidential hopefuls remained active not only in Washington, but around the sweltering nation. As in earlier months, they tripped over each other at party gatherings and special interest group caucuses. Only now, the goodnatured jibes grew more pointed as the inevitable sorting out of the candidates began.

Gary Hart, the Colorado senator, was finding it difficult to meet his campaign payroll. Predictably, his supporters accused opponents, especially those working for Californian Alan Cranston, of spreading rumors that Hart's campaign was in disarray.

Fritz Hollings, who had often been the political court jester on the hustings, turned sarcastic, belittling a John Glenn proposal to control acid rain through special taxes funneled into an overall "superfund." Calling it "incredible and naive," Hollings accused Glenn of being in the pocket of "big power companies back in Ohio." In rebuttal, Glenn confronted Hollings on the Senate floor and accused him of deliberately distorting his position.

Alan Cranston, trying hard to be perceived as something other than a one-issue candidate supporting the nuclear freeze, declared he would be willing as president to withhold federal funds for bridge repairs from states refusing to ratify the Equal Rights Amendment. In a column headlined "The Giant Panderer," columnist Mark Shields noted that if President Reagan had tried the same maneuver to force compliance with legislation supporting prayer in schools, he would have been pilloried.

And Walter Mondale accurately complained that everyone was taking potshots at him.

As he ended the first three months of his formal campaign, Glenn and his top staff held a private "retreat" to assess what they had accomplished and where they were going. The two-day session took place in the Concord room of the Hyatt Hotel on Capitol Hill. Most in Glenn's staff were convinced Glenn had won the first battle of his campaign. He was now perceived as substantive enough to become president.

His staff were also figuring another factor into Glenn's equation. It was the release of the film version of Tom Wolfe's *The Right Stuff*, which has been timed to coincide with the true beginning of the 1984 presidential primary campaign. It is an understandable move by the producers that also delights Glenn's campaign staff. Glenn, however, is less sanguine about it. He was shown the shooting script beforehand, and thinks it is a frivolous film, what he calls a "Laurel and Hardy Go to Space" affair. Glenn was advised by his staff never to see the film, fearful that, as Greg Schneiders says, "he'd spend the rest of the campaign being a film critic." The picture's merits notwithstanding, columnist Jimmy Breslin calls it "the greatest break any modern politician has had in a campaign."

"Voters in primaries are not going to make judgments of the candidates based on their own perceptions," declared one Glenn strategist at the assessment conference. He explained: "In the early months, by January '84, they will make their judgments about his character and his values based on what they have seen of him in the evening news and read about him in the papers. Is he substantive enough is a 'received' distinction, passed on by the media elites who will render a judgment by January 1984 with respect to whether he is saying enough about the issues to be taken seriously as a potential president."

Of particular interest to Glenn's campaign staff as they sat around the conference table were the results of a face-to-face "focus group" poll commissioned by the campaign and designed to probe deeper than the usual telephone polling. On one important point, the focus group seemed to confirm Glenn's and Bill White's instincts, as well as the findings of the L.A. *Times* and other polls—findings that had been largely ignored. Namely, it was that Glenn was the only Democrat who would benefit by an upturn in the economy.

"What people were saying, in effect, was that we wanted too much, we were greedy," a Glenn aide explains. "The Democrats gave us too much in the past, and that led to overspending, deficits and out of control inflation. The feeling was that we got caught with our hands in the cookie jar and we needed some strong medicine. And Reagan was that strong medicine. But now, with the economy improving, they don't want him around any longer. He was never viewed as someone with a vision for the future, he was only a transitional president."

The L.A. *Times* results put this unusual conclusion somewhat differently, but with the same result. "A flurry of statistics indicated the end of the recession may also have helped Glenn and hurt Mondale," the *Times* said. "The apparent end of hard times might have made the traditional liberalism to which Mondale is linked in many voters' minds less appealing."

One week after his assessment meeting, Glenn joined the other candidates in Detroit to address the Democratic National Committee. By this time, it had become clear that the Democratic contest—even with six months to go before the first presidential primary and caucus balloting—had become a two-man race. "Back-to-back speeches [by Mondale and Glenn]," wrote David Broder in the *Washington Post,* "produced no clear victor, but they drew a sharp contrast between the polished veteran of political wars and the earnest newcomer to the presidential struggle."

Adam Clymer in the *New York Times* was more critical of Mondale. "Mr. Mondale is just protecting the plate, trying not to make mistakes, and comes across as awfully diffident about giving people a strong reason to be for him," Clymer said. He added that much of what Mondale said "lacked passion and seemed glib."

Glenn, talking to his fellow Democrats in Detroit, finally seemed to have found his voice. He jabbed subtly but effectively at Mondale and the others without ever appearing strident, simultaneously trying to reinforce the impression of himself as a man of substance and ideas. "We can't revive the economy any more than we can end the arms race with a single phone call," Glenn declared, in an obvious reference to Mondale's breathless assertion that once elected president, he would immediately call Yuri Andropov and ask "if we can't please" end nuclear escalation.

Glenn refused to salivate after the AFL-CIO's endorsement —which Mondale appeared destined to get anyway—noting that "it would not be a complete albatross around the neck of a candidate." On the issue of peace, Glenn used his military experience as deftly as he had nearly a decade earlier in his climactic debate with Howard Metzenbaum, and spoke with a passion: "I don't have to turn on late night TV to see what combat is like. It's tough, it's awful, it's terrible."

"I've written some of those next-of-kin letters," Glenn declared to the hushed group, "knocked on the door and wished that the lady of the house was not coming to the door because of what I had to tell her. I know what the horrible side of war is. You're never going to have anybody that's going to negotiate harder for peace than I am."

When he was finished, Judy Henning, a DNC member from Colorado, said Glenn "was projecting us into the future, while Mondale was still addressing issues Democrats dealt with in the past." Added another Democrat: "Mondale has great emotional appeal, but he did not articulate any new programs. Glenn probably reflected better the pragmatic mood of the country."

It was far too early to grow confident, far too early to run anything but frightened. But that day in Detroit in July 1983, John Glenn could be forgiven if he dreamed of the Oval Office.

16

WHAT KIND OF
PRESIDENT?

John Glenn's voting record, his person, and his history add up to more than a small-town clean-cut American hero seeking to enter the White House. He has evolved into a politically complex man whose administration—if it assumed the shape now being indicated—would be one of the most surprising in American history.

It would be surprising to conservatives and middle-of-the-roaders for its strong advocacy of ambitious federal social programs reminiscent of the Great Society, programs geared to a concept of "national compassion." For liberals, it would be surprising, perhaps distressing, for its ardent, open pro-business posture. In the areas of defense and foreign affairs, a Glenn administration would likely surprise everyone, conservative and liberal alike. Judging from the past, it would be a personal, idiosyncratic mix of dove and hawk, defense spender and Pentagon skeptic, with a still unclear approach to the challenge of a growing Soviet empire.

It is his wide-ranging social vision that would probably spark the most controversy in a Glenn administration. Unless Glenn the president differed radically from Glenn the senator, his social programs would particularly gall those who see him as a former military hero with vaguely conservative leanings. Glenn's social vision, in which the federal government takes an active role to be sure that "nobody in this country really starves or does not have some kind of health care," is a natural outgrowth of his decidedly liberal voting record in the Senate, one that opposes prayer in school and tuition tax credits for families with children in private schools.

It reflects his identification with Bobby Kennedy, as well as a political philosophy reaching back to the New Deal in its postulates that the federal government has the responsibility to take an active role in the welfare of the people. It is not a view Glenn grew up with in the insular, self-reliant confines of New Concord, Ohio. But it explains why many people who remember him as a young man feel that Glenn has changed, and not for the better.

"I think sometimes the worst place to go for an opinion of somebody is their hometown," Glenn responds. "The people there don't want to think you have broadened your views. I don't know anybody who doesn't wish that we lived in simpler days, but that's not the way things are going to work. I think having compassion for those who have less than we have was something I grew up with. The only difference was that in a small town like New Concord, people were far more prone to help each other out. They did for each other the way people in a big city should do, but don't. You end up with a great number of people who are just ignored by society. They don't have a neighbor they've known for 20 years, nor do they have somebody who comes in to take care of them when they're sick. If they're down on their luck, or between jobs or unemployed, they don't have someone to bring them a side of beef.

"There are different visions of liberalism," Glenn maintains. "I think the people of New Concord are every bit as liberal as anybody else. They will do anything to help out a neighbor, to help out somebody in trouble in the community. That's their form of liberalism. That's basically what things like Medicaid and food stamps are all about—trying to have compassion for those who really are having difficulty."

Although he normally votes on the side of the big spenders in the Senate, Glenn claims there is a pragmatic edge to his liberalism, an aspect of accountability. Nor does he believe that the federal government must always be the employer of last resort. He criticizes the size and massive growth of federal entitlement programs, but, perhaps mindful of the controversy he generated when he barely hinted at a voluntary form of Social Security, he speaks only in generalities about where he would try to cut the budget if he were president.

Glenn would like to see himself as a small-town liberal, retaining some of the "old values" such as self-reliance and mixing them in with the largess of big government.

He has, for example, proposed a "national volunteers program" to help young people finance their college education through public service. Under the proposal, a high school senior could volunteer for public service in his community and be paid a subsistence grant by the federal government. Once the public service was completed, he or she would be eligible for tuition grants toward college or vocational school.

Glenn has also proposed an education and training trust fund that would provide subsistence and retraining loans of up to $10,000 for unemployed or underemployed men and women, to be repaid over a period of 20 years. The money would be used to seek training for better jobs. "It's not a giveaway or a grant," Glenn notes. "All money lent out would be repaid through payroll deductions once the recipient starts making a living wage." Notes one Glenn aide about the program: "The great thing about it is that, for many people, there'd be no way they would be able to get this assistance. No bank would loan them the money."

A president is often remembered as much by the style of his years in the Oval Office as by the substance of his politics. Dwight Eisenhower spent a great amount of time on the golf links, relying heavily on the military tradition of "chain of command," the civilian equivalent of "delegation of authority." Reagan is considered a delegator, who makes firm decisions after all the preliminary work has been done by others.

Carter, on the other hand, was a master of detail, husbanding almost all important chores for himself, and delegating as little as possible. As a Georgia gubernatorial candidate, Carter pledged to read every bill that came before him. His relations with Congress were equally flawed. A Democrat who opposed Carter for the presidential nomination correctly predicted that Carter would never be able to work with Congress. "This is going to be a 'Jimmy knows best' administration," he warned.

The temptation is strong to consider Glenn a Democratic Eisenhower. Eisenhower, notes presidential scholar Stephen Hess, "was a genial, shrewd, optimistic, confident, successful small-town American of sixty-two years" when he took office in 1952. (Glenn would be 63 if he took office in January 1985.) "He had devoted his life to government service in the military. A newcomer to partisan politics, he was not unfamiliar with bureaucratic politics. He had spent much time abroad, which gave a somewhat anomalous internationalist cast to his otherwise conventional beliefs. He was also the best-liked man of his era. Like many professional military men," Hess adds, "he had a high regard for Congress, though not for congressmen."

Because of striking similarities, some have already made the "Ike in a spacesuit" connection between Glenn and Eisenhower. But in some ways Glenn resembles Carter as well. Both share an unshakable belief in themselves and their religious values. In one important way Glenn is more like Jimmy Carter than Ike. Both Glenn and Carter love detail and are determined to absorb every minute aspect of a problem rather than delegate authority. Glenn the presidential candidate, for example, involved himself in the planning of his announcement, including the placement of the traveling press corps.

Much of the ultimate success of a Glenn presidency would be determined by Glenn's style of management from the White House. How capable would he be of formulating a legislative program, then shepherding it through Congress? To accomplish his legislative program Glenn would have to gather first class people around him and delegate authority. But in nearly a decade on Capitol Hill, Glenn has not built a really outstanding staff, the equal of either Walter Mondale's when he was a senator, or of Ted Kennedy's today. It suggests that the problems Glenn might face on taking office would be much closer to home than Tel Aviv, Managua or Moscow.

"He is not a networker or a coalition builder," notes political scientist and former White House staffer Tom Cronin. Glenn's reputation as a loner has dogged him from his earliest days in the military, through his time as an astronaut and all through his career as a senator. It has been cited as the reason for Glenn's mediocre Senate and campaign staffs, which are only now improving.

For all of his congeniality and sincerity, some believe that Glenn is uncomfortable with the idea of having to rely on anyone other than himself. "The kind of people who are really good airplane pilots are not really good politicians," maintains veteran Democratic Congressman Morris K. Udall of Arizona, himself a former World War II pilot. But Udall concedes that the notion of "Glenn the loner" can easily be overblown. "The fact is that this place is populated heavily by loners," Udall declares. "I've been on a House committee for ten years and have never been in the homes of any members. I've probably bounced into their wives at some social function, but I couldn't tell you very much about their kids or their problems. Yet the process around here is always to talk about 'my dear friend,' 'my ancient ally,' and so on."

This impression of Glenn as a solitary figure is reinforced by the feeling that he lacks any close circle of advisors or "wise men" to turn to for counsel. But Glenn's circle of confidants, though smaller than some others', has grown in the years since he has thought seriously about the presidency. Morton Kondracke of the *New Republic*, for example, notes that on defense matters "Glenn's position papers get drafted by a team including former Navy undersecretary James Woolsey, a member of the Scowcroft Commission [on disarmament and nuclear nonproliferation]; John Kester, former executive assistant to the Secretary of Defense [Harold] Brown; and Charles Moskow, a military sociologist." Kondracke added one of Glenn's oldest and closest friends—some say his alter ego—retired Marine Corps Lieutenant General Thomas H. Miller.

As for "wise men," Glenn's stable is impressive. It is a liberal group of solons: former Senator Abraham D. Ribicoff, former Undersecretary of State Joseph Sisco, former Defense Secretary Harold Brown, former Secretary of State and Senator Edmund S. Muskie and former Ambassador Sol Linowitz, all of whom have served as advisors to Democratic presidents.

As a decision-maker, Glenn is deliberate, even slow. But once his mind is made up, he follows his course with an obsessive stubbornness, one trait he shares with Reagan. As president, Glenn would undoubtedly surround himself with numerous advisors, if only for political cosmetic reasons. His decisions would not be made on-the-spot, but in lonely, cautious deliberations in which he would be conscious that he was involved in history-in-the-making. Once made, the decisions—unless quickly shown to be wrong—usually would be cast in concrete.

Glenn's relations with Congress could assume several shapes, but he would try to avoid the pitfalls of the Carter administrations. Carter was hobbled by a weakness in give-and-take, the one mechanism that can keep the Oval Office and the Hill synchronous. If Glenn were to follow Carter's disastrous route in alienating Congress, he would prove to be an inept president. But the parallel need not hold in "President" Glenn's relations with Congress. Glenn is basically a more affable person than Carter. And as a senator with years of experience, he has acquaintances (if not friends) to call upon for help, plus an intimate knowledge of the pressure points and power centers of the American legislature.

Some believe that it is in the arena of foreign affairs Glenn would clearly come into his own as president. They implicitly believe that Glenn the Marine hero in two wars and explorer in space is a cool-headed but fierce opponent of the Soviet empire, a president who would arm the nation to the teeth in defense of freedom. In the Oval Office, he would be the ultimate nemesis for an expanding Communist world.

Perhaps. But more realistically, the crystal ball is clouded and unsure. In the Senate Glenn is considered an expert on military affairs by many on both sides of the aisle. He did support the B-1 bomber and nerve gas, but he has also been an opponentof the MX and some other weapons appropriation bills. Most important, as a candidate for the Democratic nomination, Glenn has been following his party's increasingly dovish line in opposing Reagan's policies. This is particularly true in Central America, where Glenn is against Reagan's aid to the "contras" in Nicaragua, and opposed to increased military aid to El Salvador.

"While Central America is vital to our national security interests," Glenn says today, "the existing situation isn't as threatening right now as the administration indicates it is." In late July 1983, Glenn criticized Reagan's show of force in the region, including the dispatch of the aircraft carrier USS *Ranger,* as well as a cruiser, three destroyers and a frigate to international waters off Nicaragua. "I think the American people are misled when Reagan talks about this just being a routine training exercise."

Glenn decries statements by the American ambassador to Nicaragua about the possibility of a blockade. "I get concerned about the bluff of this whole thing," Glenn says. "If we're seriously talking about a blockade, we're talking about a different situation than when the Cuban missile crisis was under way and we sent the Soviets scurrying back to their own land with the missiles aboard that ship. In the ensuing 20 years the Soviet Navy has become a very major force. If they try and send a freighter through to Nicaragua to test our will—along with a modern Soviet cruiser with surface-to-surface and surface-to-air missiles on it—we have to have made our decision in advance. Are we going to stop them? Are we going to sink them if necessary? What are we going to do?"

When Glenn is asked if he can foresee "any conditions in Central America right now" in which he as president "would authorize the dispatch of American troops," he is noncommital. "Well, your 'right now' is a big qualifier," Glenn replies. "Let's say that all Latin America was going Communist. Let's say that we saw the ships coming in that were unloading missiles, analogous to the Cuban missile crisis. Would we take action? Why, of course we would. We'd be crazy not to." Glenn plainly asserts that any American president, faced with a situation where "all

Latin America was going Communist," would have to meet such a challenge by sending in American troops.

But Glenn does not believe the El Salvador situation is threatening. "In the present situation, a good part of the guerrilla force in the hills are not even dedicated Marxist-Leninist Communists," he says. "Many of them are there because the right-wing death squads operating with impunity out of the government itself have killed their relatives. There are about 5,000 to 7,000 guerrillas up in the hills of El Salvador. That's hardly a major invasion force that can sweep across Mexico to the United States. Nor is it likely to be a force large enough to really take over Central America. Nicaragua's help for the guerrillas in El Salvador is obviously of concern to us, and of great concern to me. But I think when we start violating our pledge, our agreement to the Organization of American States, in trying to dump another government by covert action, meanwhile calling it something else, I think that in the long term it doesn't bode well for us as far as setting precedents for how we will deal with other nations."

Glenn says that he wants to be "very careful" in describing the conditions under which he as president would be willing to commit American combat forces in Central America. "You have to be very careful as to whether you are talking about some Communist activity or a real threat to the United States," Glenn maintains. "That's an assessment you can't make in a hypothetical case."

It is clear Glenn's criteria for military action are different from Reagan's. Glenn insists that the only excuse for U.S. military involvement in Central America would be if "we really feel that there are sufficient forces built up down there that they would be able to take over Mexico. That is one of their stated aims and that is when their move would threaten this country." But Glenn notes: "That's an extreme situation. It's not one in which we find ourselves right now."

Glenn's position on Central America has gained him support among the doves, a group that was once little attracted to him, but whose allegiance he now believes he needs to win the Democratic party nomination. But simultaneously, Glenn has started to alienate others who are his natural allies. When, in late July

1983, Glenn appeared on the David Brinkley television show *This Week* to discuss his opinions on Central American policy, it raised a furor among conservatives.

"My phone rang off the hook after that show," says Tom Miller. "The calls were from some of our military friends telling me 'if that's his position, we're going to Reagan.'" Miller attributes at least part of Glenn's dovish attitude to simple party politics, the need to ingratiate himself with the liberal powers that be in order to win the nomination. Glenn's views on Central America are "not like him," says Miller, who adds: "He has a long road yet before him to get the nomination, and he's trying to walk the fence."

Despite Glenn's pronouncements on Central America, Miller is not worried that former Colonel John Glenn will be lacking in military determination should the need arise. "I don't think Glenn is the least bit hesitant to use military force," Miller says, "but he would be conservative in determining when to use it. I really think you could draw a parallel between him and Jack Kennedy in the Cuban missile crisis. Glenn would be a strong enough leader to take the bull by the horns if he had to."

Miller's portrait of Glenn as a Cold War Warrior may be a misguided evaluation, one that reflects the Colonel John Glenn that was. Or, as someone truly close to Glenn, it may be that Miller is drawing aside the curtain of presidential politics to reveal the true man.

There is a second area of foreign affairs in which Glenn will face presidential dilemmas. That is the Middle East, and the question of Glenn's genuine—or half-hearted—support of Israel. Glenn has been a strong and frequent critic of Israeli foreign policy. When combined with his express desire to include the Palestine Liberation Organization in Middle East peace negotiations, it could signal a tougher line taken toward Israel in a Glenn administration than in those of recent American presidents.

But Glenn insists that his support of the Jewish state is unwavering. His differences with Israel, he maintains, are similar to those the United States often has with its closest allies. "We share with Israel an indissoluble bond of democratic and Judeo-Christian values unique in its region of the world," he says. Even though he is against Jewish West Bank settlements, Glenn declines to call for sanctions against Israel.

But there remains an unease about Glenn among some American Jews that could hurt his political campaign and, if he became president, color our relations with Israel. Milton Wolf, Glenn's finance chairman, noted once that Glenn's problem with American Jews is that he is not a "hundred percenter" in his support of Israel. One prominent Democratic lawmaker claims that "American Jews are unforgiving. They not only want you voting right, they want to hear that you really feel it." But Glenn will not do what his advisors think is needed, at least not now.

Former Senator Abraham D. Ribicoff, who, like Milt Wolf, is Jewish, and who was Glenn's chairman on the Senate Government Operations Committee, calls charges that Glenn is "no friend" of Israel "completely without basis." Ribicoff says they are spread by his political opponents. But it is true that Glenn has hurt himself with pro-Israeli Americans by his sometimes belligerent criticism of the Begin government, an impatience that Glenn displayed at a private dinner party at Averell Harriman's house on September 14, 1982. Columnist William Safire reported that in the course of the evening Glenn denounced Begin for using U.S. equipment for "nondefensive" purposes. "One of the guests then suggested to the senator that he might not understand the psychologyof Menachem Begin, who learned about the need for security during the Holocaust. The man said that as a Jew, he could relate to Begin's fears, a point not easy to get across.

"At that point," Safire wrote, "Senator Glenn bristled and said he resented the question. Does he have to be Jewish to understand the problems of the Middle East? When the man tried to explain that was not what he meant, Glenn pursued the point until the man, embarrassed and frustrated, gave up." Nearly a year after the incident, Glenn tries to play it down, conceding that he did not handle it well as he should have. He insists that his longtime support of the state of Israel should far outweigh one night's indiscretion.

The Glenn policy on Israel could not differ in extreme form from that consistently followed by American presidents since Harry Truman. But John Glenn, who believes a lasting peace in the area requires some legitimate Palestinian presence, would undoubtedly try to make history in that tumultuous region.

The human qualities of a president have always been important to the American electorate, and here Glenn shines in the eyes of observers. Republican Senator Jake Garn of Utah, elected to the Senate the same year as Glenn, notes: "In the Senate, you quickly get to know which ones are sincere, and which ones are out for publicity." Garn recalls that in 1976, after the death of his wife, Hazel, John and Annie Glenn were among only a handful of people who seemed to care how Garn and his four children were bearing up under the loss. "Everyone was kind and considerate at the beginning," Garn recalls, "but John and Annie, for many, many months after, and even now, ask about the kids and about how I am doing."

Garn, who has remarried and now has a family of seven, respects and admires Glenn, even if he disagrees with him on most social issues. He especially respects Glenn's expertise on defense matters, noting that "too many people on both sides of a military question haven't the faintest idea what they're talking about." But Garn's overall reaction to Glenn combines admiration for his human qualities with respect for his grasp of important issues, notably defense and foreign policy. These, of course, are the two qualities that make Glenn the Democrat who is most feared by the Reagan White House.

"The presidency is not merely an administrative office," FDR declared in 1932. "That's the least of it. It is more than an engineering job. It is pre-eminently a place of moral leadership." Roosevelt's cousin Theodore put it more succinctly, calling the presidency "a bully pulpit" from which to inspire and to lead.

Today, political scientists like former White House fellow Tom Cronin contend that "we do not elect intellectuals to the

White House; we elect brokers—but you want a broker who gets along with people. And John Glenn gets along with people because he likes them and enjoys them. What's more, people know that. And to a politician, that's powerful stuff."

One of Glenn's aides calls him "a charismatic moderate, a person of stability with a healthy dose of pragmatism." In his view Glenn has the potential to unite the people, to take elements from the political right and left and mold them into a public policy acceptable to the broadest cross-section of the electorate. In endorsing Glenn's candidacy this summer, liberal Massachusetts Senator Paul Tsongas put it this way: "Of all the Democrats in the race, he is the one most likely to be elected with a mandate—the only one who would come into office with enough popular acclaim to bring about serious change."

What serious change would "President" Glenn try to enact? Most likely, it would include tax increases to pay for social programs slashed by the Reagan administration, large increases in outlays for scientific and industrial research, tax breaks for business, help for ailing smokestack industries, protectionist measures against foreign imports, as well as a reasonably large Pentagon budget.

His former aide Len Bickwit says a Glenn administration would be "a creative presidency." Speaking to fellow Democrats last summer, Glenn said that he would consider instituting an informal question period in the House of Representatives. As president, he would field questions from lawmakers, much as the British prime minister is interrogated in the House of Commons. Glenn believes it might be one way to "soften" the hard edge of confrontation between the legislative and executive branch.

In reporting on Glenn's remarks, Washington columnist David Broder noted that some of Glenn's fellow Democrats found his proposal "as naive as the promises Jimmy Carter made during his campaign: to conduct cabinet meetings in public or make the Justice Department independent of presidential control...proposals promptly forgotten when he became President."

But Broder could not help but wonder: Was Glenn's idea "the naive question of a man who does not really understand the presidency? Or the simple, direct expression of a man who can bring openness and trust to the White House?"

Broder's dilemma is the nation's. No one can be sure how a presidential candidate will perform once confronted with what Thomas Jefferson aptly called the "splendid misery" of the presidency.

John Glenn has two opportunities to reach the White House: the election of 1984 or that of 1988, when he will be 67, still several years younger than Reagan when he first took office.

Should John Glenn reach the White House, he will almost certainly make his an active administration. Not as rapid or frenetic as Kennedy's, or as tranquil as Eisenhower's, or as egoistic as Johnson's, or as ideological as Reagan's. But in his own, sometimes plodding, persistent manner, John Herschel Glenn, Jr., Marine pilot, war hero, astronaut, millionaire businessman, U.S. senator, would undoubtedly place an indelible stamp on the Oval Office, one likely to be as well remembered as his historic flight into space.

Notes

CHAPTER ONE

Selection of keynote speaker and other material: interview with Robert Strauss.

Library of Congress speech research: interview with John Glenn.

Loudon Wainwright recollections: interview with Loudon Wainwright.

Jimmy Breslin column: *New York Daily News,* July 13, 1976.

"I made only one early decision..." Jimmy Carter, *Keeping Faith,* (New York: Bantam Books, 1982), p. 35.

Jody Powell recollections: interview with Jody Powell.

Annie Glenn on planned disruptions: interview with Annie Glenn.

1980 election night in Ohio: interview with Steve Avakian.

Glenn as friend in need: interviews with Rene Carpenter, Martin Sammon.

Atmosphere in Glenn home: interview with Annie Glenn.

"I've had the ticker tape parades: interview with John Glenn.

CHAPTER TWO

Air Force One arriving Cape Canaveral 2/23/62: John Glenn oral history, John F. Kennedy Memorial Library, Boston, 1964.

Glenn recollection of first JFK visit: oral history.

Ben Bradlee recollections: Ben Bradlee, *Conversations with Kennedy* (New York: W. W. Norton, 1975), p. 191.

Sailing with Jack and Bobby: oral history.

Kennedy's attraction to Glenn: Theodore H. White, *The Making of the President, 1960* (New York: Atheneum, 1961).

"All of us salute the brave cosmonauts...": Presidential Papers, John Fitzgerald Kennedy, 1961.

"Do we have a chance of beating the Soviets...": Lyndon Baines Johnson, *The Vantage Point* (New York: Holt, Rinehart & Winston, 1971), p. 28.

"...landing a man on the moon...": JFK Presidential Papers, 1961.

"If Glenn were only a Negro": Merle Miller, *Lyndon, an Oral Biography* (New York: Random House, 1980), p. 34.

"He came down the ramp": oral history.

Annie Glenn on Jackie Kennedy: interview with Annie Glenn.

Lyn's airsickness on Air Force One: interview with Lyn Glenn Freedman.

"There were jumpers too...": *Washington Post,* February 27, 1962.

DEATH, TRIUMPH AND A BUS STRIKE: *New York Daily News,* March 2, 1962.

Glenn's speech and introduction by John McCormack: *Congressional Record,* February 26, 1962.

Caroline and "Where's the monkey?" remark: oral history.

Glenn recollection of speech: interview with John Glenn.

Glenn family life: interview with Lyn Glenn Freedman.

Voas on astronaut selection: interview with Robert Voas.

Glenn encounter with rowdy teenagers and aftermath: *Washington Star, Washington Post, New York Times,* March 14, 15, & 18, 1962.

Glenn grounding by JFK: oral history, interviews with John Glenn, Rene Carpenter.

"Either a liberal Republican or a conservative Democrat...": *Saturday Evening Post,* February 22, 1964.

Glenn denies voting for Nixon: interview with John Glenn.

RFK broaches subject of running for Senate: interview with John Glenn.

Glenn relations with RFK children: interview with Father Richard McSorley.

JFK personally lobbies for Glenn: interview with John A. Wiethe.

Glenn at Lincoln Memorial and U.S. Capitol: interviews with John Glenn and Robert Voas.

Glenn's letters to friends: *Saturday Evening Post,* February 22, 1964.

CHAPTER THREE

Description of New Concord on day Glenn born: *Cambridge Daily Jeffersonian,* July 18, 1921.

Description of early history of New Concord: William L. Fisk, *A History of Muskingum College* (New Concord, Ohio: Muskingum College, 1977) and *New Concord, A Sesquicentennial History, 1828-1978* (New Concord, Ohio: Muskingum College Archives)

Crossburnings: interviews with Jerry Wolfrom, Carl Anker.

Histories of Glenn's parents: *Zanesville Times Recorder,* March 3, 1962.

Description of Glenn, Sr.: interview with Lyn Glenn Freedman.

"There was no contradiction..." Tom Wolfe, *The Right Stuff* (New York: Bantam Books, 1980), p. 112.

New Concord during prohibition: interview with Mary Steele; files of *Cambridge Daily Jeffersonian, Zanesville Times Recorder.*

Description of Glenn childhood: interview with John and Annie Glenn, Walter Chess, Mary Steele.

Recollections of Clara Glenn: interview with and written recollections of Wilbur Frame.

Annie's history as a stutterer: interviews with Annie Glenn, John Glenn, Lyn Glenn Freedman.

John's role in helping Annie: interviews with John Glenn, Annie Glenn.

KKK activities in USA: Alistair Cooke, *America,* 1974.

Depression memories: interviews with John and Annie Glenn.

Glenn friendship with Harford Steele: interviews with John Glenn, Mary Steele.

Glenn visiting young Annie while she was ill: interview with Mary Jane Veno.

Problems with sister Jean: interviews with Lyn Glenn Freedman, Mary Steele, Jim Bryen, Robert Amos, Carl Anker.

Glenn at Muskingum College: interviews with John and Annie Glenn, Carl Anker, Walter Chess, Jim Bryen.

Glenn, Sr.'s fear over son's flight training: *Zanesville Times Recorder.*

Rumblings of war, air training: interview with John Glenn; Carl Anker, Tom Miller.

CHAPTER FOUR

Letter to mother of Anderson Stock: Glenn papers, Library of Congress.

Deadstick landing in Korea: interviews with John Glenn, John Giraudo, Tom Miller.

"How the bullets sparkle": Glenn letter to Annie, reprinted in *Zanesville Times Recorder.*

No remorse at having killed in wartime: interview with John Glenn.

Description of Corpus Christi, early flight training and World War II action: interviews with John Glenn, Annie Glenn, Tom Miller; also Shirley Thomas, *Men of Space* (New York: Chilton, 1962).

Definition of, and views on, "sniveling": interviews with John Glenn, Tom Miller; also Michael Kramer profile of Glenn, *New York,* January, 1983.

Glenn meets Charles Lindbergh: interviews with John Glenn.

Glenn first mission, loss of Monte Goodman: interviews with John Glenn, Tom Miller.

Pete Haines on Glenn's reliability: Shirley Thomas, *Men of Space.*

Donald L. May recollections: Thomas, *Men of Space.*

Glenn's near-fatal bombing runs: interview with John Glenn, Tom Miller, Woody Woodbury.

"Today, I finally got a MiG...": Glenn in letter to Annie, reprinted in *Zanesville Times Recorder,* 1952.

CHAPTER FIVE

F. K. Coss on Glenn's determination: Thomas, *Men of Space,* p. 16.

Glenn lobbies superiors: interviews with John Glenn, Tom Miller.

Difficulties with higher math: interviews with John Glenn, Tom Miller.

Glenn preps for transatlantic speed run: interviews with John Glenn, Tom Miller.

Sonic booms: interviews with John Glenn.

Glenn reception in New York: *New York Times,* July 17, 1957.

First U.S. satellite: Thomas, *Men of Space,* pp. 73-75.

Eisenhower and initial plans for astronaut selection: interviews with Robert Voas, Rene Carpenter.

Glenn nearly passed over: interviews with John Glenn, Robert Voas, Tom Miller, Jake Dill.

CHAPTER SIX

Thoroughness of Lovelace testing: interview with John Glenn.

Description of Lovelace Clinic: interviews with John Glenn, Rene Carpenter, Robert Voas; Tom Wolfe, *The Right Stuff.*

Carpenter recollection of Glenn: interview with Scott Carpenter.

Need to find candidate immune to space stress: NASA scientific paper, 1960 (in Glenn papers, Library of Congress).

Humoring psychiatrists: interviews with Rene Carpenter, John Glenn.

"Danger is admitted...": NASA scientific paper (in Glenn papers, Library of Congress).

Interest in first born and eldest: interview with John Glenn.

NASA press conference: interview with Ralph Morse.

Questioning of astronauts: NASA transcript.

May Craig question: interview with Ralph Morse.

"I wound up staying three days": interview with Ralph Morse.

"This is a pretty cynical town": James Reston, *New York Times,* April 10, 1959.

Life contract: interview with Loudon Wainwright.

DeOrsey letter to Glenn complaining of press leaks: Glenn papers, Library of Congress.

Glenn gets Hoppe column killed: Glenn personal papers, Library of Congress.

Background of Henri Landwirth: interview with Henri Landwirth.

"There was a lot of socializing...greatest swordsman in Navy": confidential interview with former astronaut.

Glenn concern over potential scandal: interviews with John Glenn, Scott Carpenter.

Confrontation with other astronauts over sexual excesses: interviews with John Glenn, Scott Carpenter, Rene Carpenter, Tom Miller.

Peer votes: interviews with John Glenn, Robert Voas, Scott Carpenter, Tom Miller.

CHAPTER SEVEN

Glenn's initial rage at not being chosen: interviews with John Glenn, Tom Miller, Robert Voas.

"Marine Stands Out as Astronaut Choice": Marvin Miles, *Space-Aviation Magazine,* March 21, 1961.

"They originally scheduled four, five suborbital flights": interview with John Glenn.

Astronaut training before Glenn's flight: interviews with John Glenn, David Glenn, Robert Voas.

Survival training: Glenn papers, Library of Congress.

David Glenn joins father at training: interview with David Glenn.

Glenn's thoughts on death: interview with Lyn Glenn Freedman.

Glenn's relationship with children during their childhood and period of teenage rebellion: interviews with John Glenn, Annie Glenn, Lyn Glenn Freedman and David Glenn; also Rene Carpenter, Tom Miller.

Annie Glenn's "confrontation" with Lyndon Johnson: interviews with John Glenn, Annie Glenn, Lyn Glenn Freedman, David Glenn, Loudon Wainwright, Ralph Morse; also Wolfe, *The Right Stuff,* p. 260.

"The Mercury space capsule umbilical is out...": NASA transcript, February 20, 1962.

"The sunlight was very brilliant": Glenn formal written report on space flight, NASA, 1962.

Anti-nausea precautions: interview with John Glenn.

Mechanics of heat shield: interview with William Hines.

"We have a message from Mercury control": NASA transcript.

$100,000 "insurance policy" from DeOrsey: interview with John Glenn.

Glenn's apprehension on re-entry: interview with John Glenn.

Kennedy remarks on successful flight: *New York Times,* February 21, 1962.

"You old son of a bitch, you made it!": interview with John Glenn.

CHAPTER EIGHT

"I talked to Bobby about it": interview with John Glenn.

"Ohio needs new blood...": Wayne Hays quoted in *Time,* January, 1964.

"The Kennedys wanted Young out..." interview with Wayne Hays.

Glenn in smoke-filled room: interview with John Wiethe.

Steve Young campaign jibes at Glenn: *Cleveland Plain Dealer,* January, 1964.

"Some people worked their way up...": interview with John Glenn.

1964 state party convention: interviews with John Glenn, Robert Voas; also Loudon Wainwright, *Life,* January 1964.

Steve Young campaign attacks: *Cleveland Plain Dealer,* January-February, 1964.

Description of Glenn's bathroom fall and aftermath: interviews with John Glenn, Annie Glenn, Don Oberdorfer, Warren Baltimore, Robert Voas, Lyn Glenn Freedman, David Glenn; also Rev. Frank Erwin comments on Glenn's agility, in *Parade,* April 1, 1962.

Attempt to have Glenn remain in race: interviews with John Glenn, Annie Glenn, Wayne Hays, John Wiethe, Warren Baltimore, Don Oberdorfer.

"I'm in a hide-and-seek campaign": Steve Young, *Time,* March 27, 1964.

Glenn withdrawal statement, comments to reporters, medical statement and Steve Young reaction: *New York Times,* March 31, 1964.

Glenn looking for excuse to quit: interviews with Don Oberdorfer and Wayne Hays.

"After Dad's fall...": interview with Lyn Glenn Freedman.

CHAPTER NINE

"We had saved a little money...": interview with John Glenn.

Leo DeOrsey and role as astronauts' financial advisor, including endorsement accounts, and "Houston Deal": interviews with John Glenn, Rene Carpenter; also Glenn oral history.

JFK questioning of *Life* deal: interviews with John Glenn, Robert Voas, Rene Carpenter; also Glenn oral history.

Glenn's tenure at Royal Crown Cola: interviews with John Glenn, Nolan Murrah.

Glenn's visit to aborigine village: interview with John Glenn.

Landwirth as hotel manager: interviews with John Glenn, Henri Landwirth, Scott Carpenter, Rene Carpenter.

Negotiations for Holiday Inn franchise: interviews with John Glenn, Henri Landwirth.

Description of Glenn real estate holdings: interviews with John Glenn, Henri Landwirth, Bill White.

CHAPTER TEN

"I went with him on first campaign swing...": interview with John Glenn.

RFK haunted by failure: Richard Goodwin, "A Day," *McCall's,* June 1970.

"The John Glenns, Jim Whitakers...": Pierre Salinger, *American Journey: The Times of Robert Kennedy* (New York: Harcourt Brace Jovanovich, 1970), p. 167.

"I don't recall him taking foolish risks": John Glenn oral history, JFK Library, 1969.

RFK physical strength: interview with John A. Wiethe.

"The middle fork of Salmon River...": interview with Annie Glenn.

Similarities and differences between Glenn and RFK: interview with Tom Miller.

Glenn's change since leaving New Concord: interviews with Walter Chess, Tom Miller.

"It has now become part of Myth of Camelot...": Merle Miller, *Lyndon, an Oral Biography* (New York: Ballantine Books, 1980), p. 463.

JFK Vietnam legacy contradictory: Arthur M. Schlesinger, Jr., *Robert F. Kennedy and His Times* (Boston: Houghton Mifflin, 1978), p. 725.

RFK hesitation to challenge LBJ and subsequent press criticism when he did: Schlesinger, *RFK and His Times.*

RFK compassion: interview with John Glenn.

Glenn not involved with issues during RFK campaign: interview with Arthur M. Schlesinger, Jr.

"John Glenn has been a friend of my family...": Sen. Edward M. Kennedy during Democratic fundraising dinner, March 3, 1983.

Election night scene in California, June 5, 1968, Jerry Greene and Paul Healy, *New York Daily News,* June 6, 1968.

RFK meeting with black militants: Schlesinger, *RFK and His Times,* p. 908.

Pete Hamill recollections of scene before shooting: *American Journey,* p. 335.

"And then I had to tell each kid he was dead": interview with John Glenn.

"Each of the children has to face this situation": interview with Father Richard McSorley.

Glenn role in planning funeral mass and later at Arlington: Leonard Bernstein, Ann Buchwald, quoted in *American Journey,* pp. 24-28.

CHAPTER ELEVEN

Antagonism toward Glenn from RFK liberals: interview with Peter O'Grady.

Early strategy for 1970: interviews with Peter O'Grady, Monica Nolan.

Howard Metzenbaum's talent for moneymaking and early history: *Current Biography,* July 1980.

Glenn's naivete as a campaigner: Abe Zaidan, *Akron Beacon Journal Sunday Magazine,* February 12, 1978.

Glenn lulled into thinking election assured: interviews with Warren Baltimore, Steve Kovacik, Steve Avakian, Tom Brazaitis.

Possible vote fraud in 21st District: denial by Kovacik: interviews with Steve Avakian, Steve Kovacik.

CHAPTER TWELVE

America turns its back on its heroes: John Glenn quotation after 1970 primary loss; cited in William Himes interview on 15th anniversary of Glenn's space flight, *Chicago Sun-Times,* 1977.

"One of biggest disappointments of my life": interview with John Glenn.

"The loss made him determined": interview with Monica Nolan.

Glenn's anger after 1970 loss: interviews with John A. Wiethe, Peter O'Grady.

Glenn pays political dues: interviews with Steve Avakian; also, Mark Goodman, "John Glenn Takes an Earth Walk—Again": *New Times*, January 11, 1974.

Glenn as chairman of environmental hearings: interview with John Glenn.

Indy 500 crash recollections: interviews with John Glenn, Annie Glenn, Warren Baltimore.

Saxbe an enigma: *Almanac of American Politics*, 1974.

Watergate history: Frank Van Riper, James Wieghart; Watergate scandal coverage, *New York Daily News*, June 18, 1972-August 9, 1974.

Glenn relations with Gilligan: interviews with Steve Avakian, Steve Kovacik.

Metzenbaum "a mixture of good and bad traits": confidential interview with member of Congress.

Metzenbaum's legislative history in Ohio: *Current Biography*, 1980.

Gilligan's plans for national prominence: interviews with Steve Avakian, Steve Kovacik, Peter O'Grady; also Mark Goodman, *New Times*.

Gilligan and "messy" primary: Myra McPherson, *Washington Post Magazine*, January 12, 1975.

Labor support of Metzenbaum: interview with Peter O'Grady.

Glenn on defiance of Gilligan: interviews with John Glenn, Steve Avakian; also Myra McPherson, *Washington Post Magazine;* Mark Goodman, *New Times.*

CHAPTER THIRTEEN

Description of opening of Glenn '74 primary campaign: interviews with Steve Avakian, Steve Kovacik; also *New York Times* reports, December, 1973.

Glenn and anti-Semitism: interviews with John Glenn, Morris Udall, Abraham Ribicoff, Roy Meyers, Steve Avakian, Steve Kovacik.

Metzenbaum-Glenn feud: interviews with John Glenn, Roy Meyers, Len Bickwit, Warren Baltimore, Tom Brazaitis, Bill White, Burt Hoffman, Steve Avakian, Steve Kovacik, Monica Nolan, Peter O'Grady, John A. Wiethe; also Metzenbaum interviews, *Cleveland Plain Dealer*, 1970-74.

"John Glenn, my main astronaut!"; other reactions and descriptions: Mark Goodman, *New Times.*

Failings of road show campaign: interview with Steve Kovacik.

Recruitment of Kovacik: interviews with Steve Kovacik, Roy Meyers.

Kovacik's marriage: Myra McPherson, *Washington Post Magazine;* Robert Walters, "Senator John Glenn: From Astronaut to Keynote Speaker," *Parade*, July 11, 1976.

Flat Iron Cafe: Robert McGruder, *Cleveland Plain Dealer*, April 19, 1974.

Glenn-Metzenbaum tax controversy: James M. Perry, "Why Glenn Orbits in Ohio," *National Observer*, April, 1974.

"My accountant thinks I'm crazy": interview with John Glenn.

"This year, everybody ought to release tax returns": John Glenn 1974 campaign press release.

Metzenbaum agitation on campaign's collapse: Abe Zaidan, *Akron Beacon Journal*, February 12, 1978.

Organized labor efforts against Glenn: interviews with Monica Nolan, Steve Kovacik.

Ethel Kennedy reneging on campaign commitment and endorsement by Jacqueline Onassis: interviews with John Glenn, Steve Kovacik, Monica Nolan.

Glenn "never held a job": interviews with Steve Kovacik, Steve Avakian; also Abe Zaidan, *Akron Beacon Journal.*

Description of City Club incident: interview with Roy Meyers.

"That's a damn lie!": *Cleveland Plain Dealer,* May 4, 1974.

"I served 23 years in the United States Marine Corps…": John Glenn quoted in Mark Shields column, "Will Glenn Woo Nashua?" *Boston Globe,* January 1, 1983.

CHAPTER FOURTEEN

"He was not raised as a politician": confidential interview with congressional aide.

Glenn support of abandoned Carter proposals: interview with Len Bickwit.

Interest group ratings: *ADA World,* 1974-82; American Conservative Union *Battle Line,* 1974-82.

"On many issues John is liberal": interview with Senator Jake Garn.

Glenn a center left politician: Morton Kondracke, "John Glenn's Right Stuff," *New Republic,* May 26, 1982.

Glenn an "important senator": *Almanac of American Politics,* 1980, p. 49.

Glenn's votes and views on Israel-related issues: interviews with John Glenn, Abraham Ribicoff, Len Bickwit, Ed Furtek, Greg Schneiders.

Fight over black U.S. attorney: interview with Representative Louis Stokes; also report on controversy in *Willoughby News Herald,* November 17, 1977.

Glenn's civil rights record compared with others: interviews with Louis Stokes, Maxine Isaacs.

Glenn on abortion, squeal rules: interview with John Glenn.

Glenn success on floor amendments: interview with Len Bickwit.

Glenn confrontation with Robert Byrd: Robert Walters, *Parade.*

Glenn's attempts to keep low profile: Tom Brazaitis, *Cleveland Plain Dealer,* Winter, Spring, 1975.

Glenn "out of touch": interview with Amos Kermisch; also *Cleveland Plain Dealer,* August 28, 1977.

Bill White's protectiveness: interviews with Bill White, Tom Brazaitis; also David Osborne, "Lost in Space with John Glenn," *Mother Jones,* May 1983.

Glenn at Springfield convention: interview with Peggy Simpson.

Glenn assessment of Carter presidency: interview with John Glenn.

Start of bad relations with Carter: confidential interview with former Glenn aide; interview with Steve Kovacik.

Glenn's disavowal of national political ambition so soon after coming to Senate: interview with John Glenn.

Kirbo as Glenn's strongest advocate: interview with Jody Powell.

Questions over Glenn's tax status: Bill Boyarsky, *Los Angeles Times,* July 13, 1976.

David Brinkley reaction: *Cleveland Plain Dealer,* July 13, 1976.

Glenn's gloom at post-keynote party: Richard Reeves, *Convention* (New York: Harcourt Brace Jovanovich, 1977), p. 77.

Carter's attempt to reach Glenn with turndown: interviews with Greg Schneiders, Steve Avakian; also Richard Reeves, p. 189.

Effect of loss of Iran radars: interviews with John Glenn, Carl Ford, Jody Powell.

"Rosalynn read an advance text": Jimmy Carter, *Keeping Faith*, p. 238.
"I've never had a President talk to me that way...": interview with John Glenn.
Description of dedication ceremonies in Groton: Tom Brazaitis, *Cleveland Plain Dealer*, April 8-11, 1979.

CHAPTER FIFTEEN

Campaign surplus: interview with Bill White.
Description of Ohio's diversity: interview with John Glenn; also *Almanac of American Politics*, 1980, p. 847-50.
Glenn's dislike of Ted Kennedy: interviews with Steve Avakian, Steve Kovacik.
"Somebody putting on the light": interview with Bill White.
"Height of naivete": confidential interview with Mondale supporter.
"Quick kill" theory: Bill White, Glenn Campaign Manual.
Direct mail effort: interview with Vann Snyder.
Glenn's money men: interview with Bill White; also Osborne, *Mother Jones*.
Campaign primary strategy: Bill White, Campaign Manual.
Glenn's attempt to improve speaking: interviews with Dale Butland, Dennis Fitzgibbons, Art Buchwald.
First post-Kennedy survey: Gallup Poll, January 13, 1983.
"At this early stage of the race": interview with John Glenn.
Glenn's preparations for Gridiron speech: interviews with John Glenn, Art Buchwald, Dale Butland, Greg Schneiders.
"First let me say I'm not dull": transcript of Glenn Gridiron speech, March 26, 1983.
"A new *Los Angeles Times* poll": Robert Shogan, *Los Angeles Times*, May 15, 1983.
Description of Glenn "summit" with campaign aides and discussion of "focus groups": interview with Greg Schneiders.
Description of Glenn, Mondale appearances at DNC meeting in Detroit: David Broder, *Washington Post*, July 15, 1983; Adam Clymer, *New York Times*, July 27, 1983.

CHAPTER SIXTEEN

Glenn's social vision: interview with John Glenn.
Parallels with Eisenhower: Stephen Hess, *Organizing the Presidency*, Brookings Institution, Washington, 1976, p. 59.
"He's not a networker...": interview with Tom Cronin.
Good pilots make bad politicians: interview with Rep. Morris K. Udall.
Glenn's advisory team: Morton Kondracke, *New Republic*, August 8, 1983.
Glenn's views on Central America: interview with John Glenn.
"I think it's an overshow of force": Glenn on "This Week with David Brinkley," ABC-TV, July 31, 1983.
Glenn's Jewish problem: confidential interview with Democratic member of Congress.
"Completely without basis": interview with former Senator Abraham Ribicoff.

Confrontation at Harriman house: William Safire column, "Glenn on Israel," *New York Times*, February 3, 1983.
"Place of moral leadership": Anne O'Hare McCormick, "Roosevelt's View of the Big New Job," *New York Times Magazine*, September 11, 1932.
"We do not elect intellectuals": interview with Tom Cronin.
"It would be a creative presidency": interview with Len Bickwit.

Photo Credits

Glenn at age four: Glenn collection
John and Annie in "The Cruiser": Glenn collection
Glenn as a naval air cadet: Glenn collection
Wedding picture: Glenn collection
Glenn with his parents: *Cambridge Jeffersonian*
The "MiG Mad Marine": Glenn collection
Glenn with Lyn and Dave: *Cambridge Jeffersonian*
"Project Bullet": Wide World Photos
Project Mercury press conference: Ralph Morse, *Life* magazine, © 1959, Time, Inc.
Mercury astronauts in spacesuits: NASA
Glenn in training: Wide World Photos
Glenn in Friendship 7: NASA
Glenn gives "thumbs up": NASA
Glenn inspects capsule: NASA
Glenn with John Kennedy at Canaveral: NASA
New Concord sign: *Cambridge Jeffersonian*
New York ticker tape parade; Wide World Photos
Joint session of Congress: Wide World Photos
Glenn receives degree: Glenn collection
Glenn in hospital bed: Wide World Photos
With Robert Kennedy: Wide World Photos
Glenn, Barrett and Metzenbaum: Wide World Photos
Glenn with Jimmy Carter: Wide World Photos
Glenn on convention floor: Glenn collection
Glenn giving keynote address: Glenn collection
Glenn sworn in by Mondale: Glenn collection
Glenn family picture: Judith Goodman
Glenn announces candidacy: *Cambridge Jeffersonian*
The Glenns at home: Judith Goodman
Back cover photo: Michael Rougier, *Life* magazine, © 1962, Time, Inc.

Index